Person–Environment Psychology

New Directions and Perspectives
Second Edition

Person–Environment Psychology

New Directions and Perspectives
Second Edition

Edited by

W. Bruce Walsh
The Ohio State University
Kenneth H. Craik
University of California, Berkeley
Richard H. Price
University of Michigan

LEA LAWRENCE ERLBAUM ASSOCIATES, PUBLISHERS
2000   Mahwah, New Jersey   London

Lawrence Erlbaum Associates, Inc., Publishers
10 Industrial Avenue
Mahwah, NJ 07430

Cover design by Kathryn Houghtaling Lacey

Library of Congress Cataloging-in-Publication Data
Person–environment psychology : new directions and per-
spectives / edited by W. Bruce Walsh, Kenneth H. Craik,
Richard H. Price. — 2nd ed.
    p. cm.
Includes bibliographical references and index.
ISBN 0-8058-2470-7 (cloth : alk. paper) — ISBN
0-8058-2471-5 (pbk. : alk. paper)
Environmental psychology. I. Walsh, W. Bruce, 1937-   . II.
Craik, Kenneth H. III. Price, Richard H.
    1999
    —dc21

                                          99-30603
                                             CIP

Books published by Lawrence Erlbaum Associates are printed
on acid-free paper, and their bindings are chosen for strength
and durability.

Printed in the United States of America
10 9 8 7 6 5 4 3 2 1

Contents

New Directions in Person–Environment Psychology
An Introduction

W. Bruce Walsh
The Ohio State University

Richard H. Price
University of Michigan

Kenneth H. Craik
University of California, Berkeley

A variety of theoretical approaches to person–environment psychology have been developed over the years that represent a rich range of intellectual perspectives. It is the purpose of this second edition to again link the past and the present and to look toward the future in reviewing new directions in person–environment psychology. Stated differently, the main thrust of this volume is to present contemporary models and perspectives that make some sensible predictions concerning the individual and the environment using the person–environment relationship. Within a person–environment framework, these models and perspectives are concerned with how people tend to influence environments and how environments tend to reciprocally influence people. Thus, this edition presents new directions in person–environment psychology and the implications for theory, research, and application.

The first edition presented seven contemporary approaches to person–environment psychology: a life domains approach; a theory of personality types and work environments; interactional models and the concept of goals; the individual as an interactive agent in the environment; a model for making sense of environments; interpersonal relationships as links between person and environment; and a transactional approach to close relationships.

This volume presents eight new directions in person–environment psychology: a socioanalytic perspective on person–environment interaction; a holistic, developmental, systems-oriented perspective; a person–environment psychology of organizations; a social ecological model of well-being; an evaluative image of places; models of matching for patients and treatment programs; working lives in context; and the lived day of an individual from a person–environment perspective. Chapter 9 focuses on modeling and managing change in people and environment transactions. Chapter 10 summarizes, and to some extent, integrates these different approaches to person–environment psychology.

Chapter 1 by Hogan and Roberts provides a perspective on person–environment interaction based on socioanalytic theory. In this context, the authors argue that behavior is a function of a person's personality, the role he or she plays during an interaction, and the agenda for the interaction. They define the word *personality* in terms of a person's identity, and the word *situation* in terms of roles and agendas operating in interaction sequences that have well defined beginnings and endings. Roles and agendas create social expectations, and people may or may not comply with them depending on whether their compliance is consistent with their identity. In summary, these authors believe people enter situations because they expect to attain certain goals.

Chapter 2 by Wapner and Demick presents a holistic, developmental, systems-oriented perspective of person-in-environment psychology. Goals of chapter 2 are first, to provide a brief overview of a holistic, developmental, and systems oriented perspective; second to compare and contrast this perspective with representative models of person–environment psychology illustrated by previous work of contributors to volumes I and II; and third to delineate problems for future empirical inquiry that will continue to elaborate the holistic functioning of person-in-environment systems across the life span. By elaborating these goals the authors hope to advance not only their person-in-environment perspective, but other theoretical perspectives of person–environment psychology.

Chapter 3 by Schneider, Smith, and Goldstein focuses on person–environment fit from the perspective of work organizations. The environments of interest are formal work organizations and their components (jobs, functions, teams) rather than societal cultures, schools or psychiatric wards. The authors first review the contemporary organizational literature on person–environment fit and propose some emerging themes. They present an alternative view of organizational behavior based on the principles of person–environment fit, the attraction–selection–attrition (ASA) model. The ASA model assumes an extreme person-based position on the nature of organizational behavior, a position that emphasizes the attributes of people as the defining characteristics of an organization and the foundation determinants of organizational behavior. A summary of recent research relevant to critical propositions of ASA theory is presented, namely, the hypothesis that over time organizations tend toward homogeneity of personality. These studies offer partial support for the ASA concept of the modal personality of members of an organization, although the course of that homogeneity is open to debate.

Chapter 4 by Little suggests that at one level, individuals are characterized by relatively fixed traits, suggesting that human behavior may be ordered and measured along defined dimensions of traits and factors. At another level, people act on the basis of *free traits*. Free traits are culturally scripted patterns of conduct carried out as part of a person's goals, projects, and commitments independent of that person's inclinations (fixed traits). Little suggests that free traits defined by the Big Five Factors, and personal contexts defined by narrative sketches and videotapes, facilitate the pursuit of personal projects and a sense of adaption and well-being. To the extent that people are engaged in personal projects that are meaningful, well-structured, supported by others, efficacious, and not too stressful, their well-being is enhanced, and the person–environment process is rewarding.

Chapter 5 by Nasar suggests the perceived visual quality of our surroundings has important impacts on human experience and behavior. Perceived visual quality of our surroundings may evoke strong emotions like delight or fear. It can act as a stressor. It can lead us to make inferences about places and people and influence our behavior, leading us to avoid, or go to, certain places. Thus, Nasar suggests our perceptions of physical environments tend to influence our behavior. He notes that perceived visual quality arises from the person, the environment, and ongoing interaction between the two. It may vary with biology, personality, social and cultural experience, goals, expectations, and internal and external factors.

Chapter 6 by Timko, Moos, and Finney presents a general model of person–environment congruence for clients in residential treatment facilities. The model matches the client's level of functioning (in the cognitive, psychological, and social domains) with the treatment programs' level of support, performance demands, and structure. Moos predicts that as clients' cognitive and psychosocial skills improve they should be able to cope with a more demanding, less structured setting. Moos further predicts that supportive relationships may moderate potentially problematic consequences of interpersonally stimulating and performance-oriented environments. That is, high levels of interpersonal stimulation and performance expectations, offered in the context of high support, may be beneficial for impaired clients.

Chapter 7 by Wicker and August illustrates the viability of naturalistic inquiry as a means of theorizing about person–environment relationships. This approach, substantive theorizing, presumes close scrutiny of a limited domain of human activity may yield important insights that broader surveys might miss. Human work, as revealed in the stories of Ghanaians, ex-patriots in Ghana, and late career American women, has been the author's substantive domain. They represent people as sense-makers of objectives, conditions, and events in their lives. They further suggested that people attend to, interpret, and respond to happenings in different ways, depending on their cognitive schemas or cognitive maps, including those representing major life pursuits. In this context, Wicker and August also suggest seven normative social systems they believe are significant environments in people's working lives.

Chapter 8 by Craik suggests that understanding person–environment transactions involves the interplay among traits, goals, and behavior settings. On the individual side, we have *goals* (the inside perspective) and *personality traits* (the outside perspective). The environment is defined in terms of *behavior settings*; it seems that behavior settings are implicated in the actions of people as they pursue major life goals. Behavior settings link people and environments according to behavioral rules and individual pursuits. Personality traits may be viewed as facilitating or thwarting the pursuit of life goals in a behavior setting context. Operationally, this person–environment behavioral process is video recorded during the lived day of an individual. Traits, goals, and behavior settings can then be analyzed in terms of the ongoing person–environment process.

Chapter 9 by Stokols, Clitheroe, and Zmuidzinas focuses on a particular facet of human environment transactions, namely, the circumstances surrounding fundamental changes in the structure and subjective qualities of peoples' relationships with their surroundings. The authors note that the issue of change is central to the study of people environment transactions, since transactional relationships involve dynamic and reciprocal influences between individuals and groups, on the one hand, and their social physical environments on the other. Thus, the transactional perspective assumes that continual changes are inherent in the nature of peoples' relationships with their environments, and that these changes vary considerably in their scope, magnitude, behavioral, and health consequences.

Finally, chapter 10 by Walsh, Craik, and Price summarizes and integrates the person–environment approaches (chaps. 1 through 8). Chapter 10's aim is to address two comparative issues: Are the models of person–environment relationships different, and if so, what are their distinctive elements? Also, what are the implications of system concepts for person–environment psychology? It is within these contexts that we summarize and integrate these new directions in person–environment psychology.

The first edition of *Person–Environment Psychology* (1992) is still available from Lawrence Erlbaum Associates, ISBN 0-8058-0344-0.

1

A Socioanalytic Perspective on Person–Environment Interaction

Robert Hogan
Brent W. Roberts
University of Tulsa

Mischel's (1968) behaviorist critique of personality psychology challenged the intellectual legitimacy of the field and set off the so-called *person–situation debate*. This debate concerned the locus of causation for social behavior—are our actions a function of factors inside us or factors in "situations"?—and the controversy was one of the most intense of the post-World War II era. What is the status of that once heated argument 25 years later? Some (Kenrick & Funder, 1988) suggest it is over. Others (Jones, 1990; Ross & Nisbett, 1991) maintain that personality is largely irrelevant as an explanation of social behavior. Still others (Ickes et al., 1997) conceptualize the problem in a way that synthesizes the valid points of both sides of the controversy. Although the person–situation debate may seem like a minor squabble between factions of an academic subdiscipline, it has major implications for environmental psychology in general, because when we summarize situations, we get the environment. Situations are specific environments, and the causal significance of environments is part of this discussion.

This chapter has three goals. First, we argue that the person–situation debate was a red herring that did little to improve our understanding of the links between personality and environment, primarily because it left the meaning of situations unspecified. Second, we provide a perspective on per-

1

son-environment interaction based on socioanalytic theory (Hogan, 1996). Earlier discussions of the person-situation debate were largely empirical and atheoretical; socioanalytic theory provides a framework for defining and classifying persons and situations and specifying the important components of both. Third, we argue that the most important situations many people face are found at work; that bosses' personalities are the primary determinants of occupational situations, and this is a major source of stress and unhappiness for many people.

Another View of the Person–Situation Debate

Mischel (1968) framed the terms of the person-situation debate as follows: If there is such a thing as personality (as the term has traditionally been understood), then people's behavior should be consistent across situations—no other personality psychologist, other than Mischel and his students, has ever made this claim. Mischel reviewed the empirical literature on this issue and decided there was no evidence to show behavior is consistent across situations. He then concluded that: personality as traditionally defined does not exist; and people's actions are primarily explained by factors in *situations* (the environment).

We believe the debate stimulated by these conclusions was futile from the outset, and we say this for four reasons. First, why should we use consistency of behavior as criteria to determine whether stable personal dispositions organize social conduct? Why not use consistency of personal *intentions* that are reflected indirectly only by behavior and that are demonstrably stable (Hogan & Hogan, 1996), or use the consistency of individual behavior over time, which is also well-established—cf. Hogan, Hogan, & Roberts (1996)? Second, at no point has there been any effort to define how much consistency in behavior would be sufficient to permit the inference that *personality* exists. Third, the problem of defining consistency, one of the oldest in philosophy, may be unsolvable in principle. And finally, the term *situation*, as in "person-situation debate," is still undefined; there is no agreement about what the word means or how many different kinds of situations there are (Pettigrew, 1997).

Since the 1930s, many writers have suggested that the personality research agenda involves a systematic evaluation of how situational effects influence dispositional promptings. The more astute writers (e.g., Murray, 1938) noted that this research agenda depends on having a taxonomy of personal characteristics and of situations; the ability to classify situations is essential. Sells

(1963) noted that "the most obvious need in evaluating the manifold encounter of organism and environment is a more satisfactory and systematic conceptualization of the environment" (p. 700). Frederiksen (1972) remarked that " ... we lack a satisfactory classification of situations. We need a systematic way of conceptualizing the domain of situations and situational variables before we can make rapid progress in studying the role of situations in determining behavior" (p. 115). Pervin (1976) observed that " ... we know little about the dimensions people use to perceive and organize situations" (p. 465). Pervin (1978) later concluded that: "what is of interest in relation to both these approaches [i.e., situationism and interactionism] is that often the concept of situation is left undefined and frequently it is used interchangeably with the concepts of stimulus and environment" (p. 75). Currently, very little has changed.

The Five-Factor model (Goldberg, 1990) is a generally accepted taxonomy of personality characteristics based originally on factor analytic studies of observer ratings (cf. Tupes & Christal, 1992/1961), the model states that all personality descriptors can be adequately classified in terms of five broad dimensions: *Extraversion, Adjustment, Agreeableness, Conscientiousness,* and *Intellect/Openness.* There is substantial empirical support for this taxonomy, and general agreement regarding its utility, but there is no comparable classification of situations. What are we to make of the astonishing fact that at the end of the 20th century a taxonomy of situations still doesn't exist? The answer, we believe, is that situations have yet to be adequately conceptualized.

Reversing Shweder's (1982) argument regarding the mythical nature of personality, we would like to suggest that there is no referent for the term *situation* as it is normally understood. Because psychologists can use the word reliably, they think it has a referent; but, like witch, tooth fairy, or "true score", there is nothing in the world that corresponds to the word. We do think that it is possible to conceptualize the term *situation* to make it sensible, but this requires thinking in a way that is quite different from a behaviorist's understanding of situational factors.

Our view is that behavior is a function of a person's personality, the role he or she plays during an interaction, and the agenda for the interaction. We define the word *personality* in terms of a person's reputation and identity, and we define the word *situation* in terms of the roles and agendas operating in interaction sequences, which have well-defined beginnings and endings. Roles and agendas create social expectations, and people may or may not comply with them depending on the degree to which their compliance is consistent with their reputation and identity. Our perspective closely parallels Argyle's (1976) analysis; Argyle assumes that people enter situations because they expect to attain certain goals; Argyle defines *situations* in terms of the basic features of interactions, which he believes are analogous to games; these include goals, rules, roles, environmental settings, and the required skills.

Our basic insight comes from some earlier research on personality and team performance (cf. Hogan, Raza, & Driskell, 1988). We designed a 3-person team task and we thought all three roles had equal status. We soon realized the participants perceived one role as having more status than the other two. If a nondominant person was assigned the high status role, then the team performed poorly; if, at the same time, a dominant person was assigned a low status role, then the two would compete over who was in charge, and team performance suffered accordingly. Therein may lie a key to the question of how and in what ways aspects of the environment influence dispositional tendencies. Yet before proceeding, we need briefly to outline our overall perspective.

SOCIOANALYTIC THEORY

Socioanalytic theory attempts to combine the best insights of Freud and psychoanalysis (Bowlby, 1980) with the best insights of Mead and role theory (Goffman, 1958; Sarbin, 1954). The essential features of the model can be summarized in terms of five propositions.

1. Human nature and personality are best understood in the context of human evolution.
2. Evidence from a variety of sources shows that people evolved as group-living, culture-using animals. People always live in groups, every group has a status hierarchy, and status is defined in terms of the values of the culture.
3. People are primarily motivated by a small number of unconscious biological needs. Our evolutionary history suggests that these include needs for social acceptance, status, and predictability and meaning—because having them enhances a person's chances for survival and reproductive success.
4. People are, in a sense, compelled to interact and most of our time and energy each day is spent in planning, conducting, and evaluating our interactions. Interaction largely concerns efforts to preserve or enhance status and acceptance, is an exchange process, and what is exchanged is status and acceptance (Wiggins & Broughton 1985).

5. There is an inherent tension underlying social interaction because efforts to enhance status tend to diminish acceptance, and efforts to enhance acceptance tend to reduce status. This is so because an individual's success usually comes at the expense of someone else–which creates rivalries; whereas being accepted usually comes at the price of conforming to another's wishes–which reduces opportunities for success.

Personality

Socioanalytic theory distinguishes between personality from both the observer's, and the *actor's* perspective. From the observer's perspective, personality is the distinctive features of another person's social behavior, these unique features are summarized in terms of a person's reputation, as reported by those who know them. Allport (1937) defined reputation as an insignificant and superficial phenomena of no consequence for understanding personality. Generations of personality psychologists believed this definition. The fundamental insight underlying a role-theoretical perspective (e.g., Goffman, 1958; Ichheiser, 1970) is that most people are intensely motivated to keep their reputations in good shape. People are willing to die for the sake of their reputations–always a useful test of a construct's significance. Moreover, because the best predictor of future behavior can be past behavior, and reputations reflect a person's past behavior, reputations are a rough, yet useful, way to estimate how a person will behave in the future. Furthermore, there is a well-defined structure to reputations, and that is the subject of the Five-Factor model (Goldberg, 1990). Reputations are described in terms of trait words and they reflect the degree of status and social acceptance a person enjoys in his or her community. Finally, people seem preprogrammed to perceive one another in terms of the dimensions of the Five-Factor model, i.e., in terms of their relative degrees of *self-confidence, social impact, charm, trustworthiness*, and *intellectual talent*. Thus, the Five-Factor model seems to be the implicit personality theory of observers. Personality from the observers' perspective can be assessed with reasonable reliability, and these assessments can be used to forecast future behavior–a person who has a reputation as a wit will often be witty.

Personality from the actor's perspective concerns the structures within people that cause, create, or explain why they behave as they do, and why they have their particular reputation. Our understanding of personality from the actor's perspective is not very extensive because it can be studied only indirectly–usually through the introspective accounts of actors. Nonetheless, two aspects of personality from the actor's perspective seem relatively well established: genetically based temperaments (Buss & Plomin, 1975), and the story that an actor typically tells about him or herself (McAdams, 1993). We refer to these self-stories as *idealized self-images* or *identities*; they are unique to each person, and as a result, are hard to measure.

The concept of *identity* refers to how we think about and define ourselves and how we want others to think about us. The content of our self-definitions—identity—can be sorted into three domains, or categories. The first domain of identity—*the interpersonal domain*—concerns how we see ourselves in our various roles and relationships; e.g., "I am a friend of Bill." The second—*the ideal domain*—concerns our goals, hopes, and aspirations; e.g., "I intend to be famous someday." The third—*the values domain*—concerns our values, the aspects of our identity that help us make decisions throughout the day; e.g., "I am someone who values money, friendship, social service, fun, etc." (cf. Baumesiter, 1997).

Identities are rooted in the history of each person's development. Identities begin with temperament—being shy will constrain a person's interactional style in certain ways. But identities are subsequently shaped by a person's efforts to negotiate acceptance and status during interactions from childhood to early adulthood. Adults generally are less self-conscious about their identities than adolescents unless they are having problems in their lives and they want to change.

All interactions require roles, regardless of whether they are *self-* or *other-defined*. Regarding self-defined roles or identities, being homeless, a thug, or an addict is often as much of an identity choice as being an academic. There are vast individual differences in the respectability and strategic value of the identities that people choose. Why do people chose self-defeating identities? Laziness, bad judgment, bad luck, and self-deception all influence these choices. Why do people persist in self-defeating identities? Three reasons come to mind. First, people strenuously resist change, and to change your identity is to change the very core of your psychological being. When this happens, such changes are usually in the nature of a conversion experience—Patty Hearst the socialite became an operative in the Simbianese Liberation Army. Second, people may not change their identities because they lack the resources—money, education, self-control, social support—to do so. And third, what may seem to be a self-defeating identity to others may nicely serve the individual's selfish purposes and fit well with the ecology of his or her lifestyle.

Identity—personality from the actor's perspective—translates into reputation—personality from the observer's perspective—because each identity dictates a certain self-presentational style and lifestyle. Helping the poor supports an altruistic identity; driving an exotic car supports a sporty identity; publishing scholarly articles supports an intellectual identity. Moreover, no matter what a person's intentions may be during an interaction, others will assume that he or she is intentionally telling them how he or she would like to be regarded, and will evaluate his or her performance accordingly. Even those who claim only "to be themselves" may put on a careful act in order to let others know they are"being themselves" (Schlenker & Weigold, 1990). Finally, these self-presentational processes operate in every interaction, including psychological experiments and assessment center exercises (cf. Baumeister, 1982).

Drawing on the distinction between prediction and explanation, we use reputation to predict others' behavior and identity to explain it; these two aspects of personality serve different analytical purposes. Within each individual the two aspects of personality are connected; people use their identities to decide whether and how they will interact with others; how they interact with others creates their reputations; feedback from their reputations may modify their identities.

Interaction

As noted here, people are, by nature, compelled to interact because *interaction* is where the action is (Goffman, 1958). People need attention, acceptance, and opportunities for success, in structured, predictable, or meaningful format—that is what interaction provides. During interaction, attention and acceptance are exchanged in amounts proportional to status. Le Carre (1993) captures this insight nicely in the following scene, which describes a villainous arms dealer:

> "As his boat now mastered the harbor, so ... Mr. Richard Onslow Roper mastered the round table, the terrace and the restaurant. Unlike his boat he was not dressed for spectacle ... Nevertheless, he commanded. By the stillness of his patrician head. By the speed of his smile and the intelligence of his expression. By the attention lavished on him by his audience, whether he spoke or listened. By the way everything around the table, from the dishes to the bottles ... to the faces of the children, seemed to be ranged toward him or away from him"(p.165).

What do we need in order to have an interaction? Every interaction has the same underlying structure. There must be an agenda—a project, pretext, or theme, in terms of which the interaction is organized—and there must be roles or parts to play during the interaction, because people cannot and do not simply get together and "groove". The roles and the agenda provide the context or psychological vehicle for an interaction, during which time individuals also pursue status and acceptance. With no agenda and no roles to play, interaction becomes very difficult. In everyday life, we move from one interaction to the next, and each interaction sequence has its own roles and corresponding agenda. People need to interact, yet outside their roles, they often have little to say to one another.

Roles

Roles are the parts we play during interaction, and every interaction requires that they be available. *Formal interactions*—wedding ceremonies, presidential inaugurations—are tightly scripted, with well-defined roles, and there is often little variation in how they are played, regardless of who is in them. *Informal interactions*—casual conversations in a restaurant—are loosely scripted, and the part we play is the one we have made up for ourselves—our *identities* are generic roles we carry with us from one interaction to the next. Interactions at work, where many of us spend the largest part of our waking hours, are largely governed by organizational roles and our identities. Thus, a normal adult spends a substantial amount of time each day interacting in roles defined by others. One of the luxuries of high status, or of having nothing left to lose, is the ability to define one's own roles.

In order systematically to cross persons with situations, we need taxonomies of both. The Five-Factor Model is a provisional taxonomy of person characteristics. Situations can be defined by interactions, and interactions are composed of roles and agendas. There are no agreed on taxonomies of roles, but we would like to propose a Big Three taxonomy. The first category of roles is defined in terms of status; typically unequal status. The following terms express roles organized by status: Parent–child; teacher–student; supervisor–subordinate; guru–disciple; young–old. In every interaction the roles can be classified along this dimension.

The second category of roles concerns the in group/out group distinction—is the other person a friend or an enemy? This distinction sharply modifies the manner where we relate to others and is reflected in the question, "Is the other person a coeval, a member of my tribe, team, organization, race, nationality, religion, social class, family, or club?" People have a perverse, almost infinite, capacity to make ingroup or outgroup distinctions; the prototype for this capacity may be stranger anxiety that develops around 9 months of age.

The third category of roles concerns the degree to which one is willing to be intimate with the another person. Relevant roles presented here include boyfriend–girlfriend; husband–wife; male–female; gigolo–mistress.

Many roles can be classified in terms of these categories, but this is an area for future investigation.

Agendas

Group dynamics research tells us that the behavior of the members of a team is primarily determined by their roles and the team task (Hackman, 1968). In the same way, during social interaction people's behavior will be determined by their roles and by the agenda of each interaction. Moreover, just as people can play more than one role simultaneously, more than one agenda can operate during an interaction. For example, no matter what the public agenda may be, each person will be trying privately not to lose status or acceptance. Nonetheless, it would be useful to have a taxonomy of public agendas.

Here is where Holland's (1985) model of people and occupations is helpful. Hogan et al. (1988) show that every team task in the United States Navy can be reliably classified in terms of Holland's types—most U.S. Navy tasks are combinations of realistic and conventional activities. So, we believe there are possibly only six public agendas, individually or in combination, for general interactions. We can get together and fix something (realistic), analyze something (investigative), decorate something or entertain someone (artistic), help someone (social), manipulate or persuade someone (enterprising), or regulate something (conventional).

Moreover, Holland and his colleagues provide overwhelming evidence for our belief that people choose activities and interactions that are consistent with their identities and avoid activities and interactions discordant with their identities. Thus, artistic people prefer and enjoy artistic tasks and interactions and often dislike conventional tasks and interactions.

Person–situation literature has generally overlooked the fact that interest inventories explicitly ask about peoples' preferences for situations, and an analysis of interest items leads directly to a taxonomy of situations. Consider the following items from the MVPI (Hogan & Hogan, 1997): "I am often invited to parties with important and influential people;";"I enjoy group projects and working with others;" "I like to spend time discussing scientific problems with my friends;" "I don't like people who are all business;" "I go to a lot of parties with my friends." Respondents use these items to tell us about the kinds of interactions they prefer and the kinds of interactions they avoid.

It is a straightforward task to determine the structure of these items, and the structure is a provisional taxonomy of situations. The taxonomy—Holland's model—is well understood, different from the Five-Factor model but systematically related to it (cf. Hogan & Blake, 1996). Moreover, the links between identity, as reflected in a person's preferences for specific activities and interactions, and reputation, as reflected in observer descriptions of that person, are straightforward. Hogan and Hogan (1996), for example, show that people with specific activity preferences—e.g., helping others, making money, solving problems, having fun—are described in characteristic ways by peer informants. Finally, peoples' past choices of situations predict their future involvement in them—preferences for situations, as assessed with interest measures, predict occupational membership, tenure, and change. These preferences are extraordinarily stable over time; the reason is because people choose, define, and specialize in particular types of situations depending on their identities, and identities are quite stable over time.

RECASTING THE PERSON/SITUATION DEBATE

This suggests a way to disambiguate the person–situation debate by allowing us to define the terms. First, persons can be defined in terms of their identities and reputations—we do not have a good taxonomy of identities, but identities are related to reputations, and reputations can be profiled in terms of the Five-Factor model. Identities tell us how people want to be perceived; reputations tell us how they are perceived and are likely to behave.

Second, situations can be defined in terms of the agendas and roles available for an interaction; agendas and roles translate into expectations. If people know the agenda for an interaction and the roles that they and others will be playing, they can formulate expectations about others' behavior, and about others' expectations regarding their own behavior. People generally comply with expectations when they are aware of them because they realize compliance and noncompliance have implications for their reputations. As a person's ability to forecast behavior of others goes up, his or her energy to complete the interaction goes up and the level of stress goes down. Conversely, to the degree that a person is unclear about the roles, agendas, and expectations that operate in an interaction, he or she will be stressed. The point is that situations are defined in terms of what people believe others will expect when they get together, e.g., "When I meet with my boss tomorrow, I think she will want answers to the following questions, and if I am to maintain my reputation for competence, I should have some reasonable answers ready." If two people enter an interaction with differing expectations—different views of the relevant roles and agenda—they will then be in different situations, although they are in the same physical setting, and they may find the interaction stressful, unless they come to an agreement about what they can expect from each another.

We suggest that situations be defined in terms of peoples' theories about the expectations of the other participants in an interaction (cf. Schneider, 1975; Weick, 1979). This definition has at least three implications that should be explained. First, our evolutionary history as a group-living animal has endowed us the capacity to perceive others' expectations and a willingness to respond to them—this is Mead's (1934) central assumption. Second, there are individual differences in peoples' sensitivity and responsiveness to other peoples' expectations. These individual differences can be measured by, for example, the Empathy Scale of the California Psychological Inventory (cf. Hogan, 1969). Persons who are insensitive to others' expectations may, at least in the short term, get their way, especially if the other partners to the interaction are sensitive and have less power. However, insensitive people also tend to be socially obtuse, delinquent, or neurotic and are described by others as "self-centered," "socially inept," and "unkind," (cf. Hogan & Hogan, 1997, p. 19) which means that they are not liked or trusted. Finally, if one person has more status or power than another participant in an interaction, then that person will set the agenda for the interaction, and may ignore the expectations of less powerful participants. In these asymmetric interactions, the expectations of the powerful but insensitive person define the situation where others find themselves. This may become a particular kind of 'hell' for the less powerful.

Here is the most important point of this chapter. The authors have, in principle, specified the elements needed to complete the personality research agenda. Personality can be defined in terms of the Five-Factor Model. Situations can be defined in terms of interactions. Interactions can be defined in terms of their agendas—which can be classified in terms of Holland types; and their *constituent* roles—which can be classified in terms of the "Big Three"—status, affiliation, and intimacy. Finally, we can say that *behavior*—what we do at a given time—is a function of our identities, the part or role we are playing in an interaction, and the agenda for the interaction. Behavior is a function of what we do to support our identities; what we do to honor our role obligations; and what we are required to do in terms of the agenda of the interaction—if we want the interaction to continue. All of this explains why the relationship between personality and behavior must be evaluated by aggregating over a large number of interactions (not situations). It also explains why that relationship will always be less than r = 1.0.

The interaction in a person–situation interaction is between a person's identity, the role he or she must play in an interaction, the agenda for the interaction, and the implications of the interaction for a person's reputation. If either the scripted role or the agenda contradict a person's identity—i.e., if the behaviors they entail send the wrong self-presentational message and potentially damage the person's reputation, e.g., a dominant person is required to play a subordinate role—then the person will experience conflict, which may or may not get resolved. Ambitious, competitive, blue collar workers, if denied a chance to move into management, may try to become union officials as a way of resolving the tension between their identities and the roles they are required to play in the workplace.

SUMMARY OF THE SOCIOANALYTIC PERSPECTIVE ON PERSON–ENVIRONMENT INTERACTIONS

The foregoing is fairly—perhaps even needlessly—abstract. In this section we try to make the analysis more concrete. Figure One summarizes our argument in its most general form. It depicts the influences on one "individual" in an "interaction." The situation—the interaction—is defined by the expectations both parties bring to it. These expectations reflect each participant's agenda for the interaction. Agendas can be divided into public and private components. The public components can be classified in terms of Holland's types. The private components of agendas involve seeking three basic goals: status, acceptance, and predictability.

Figure 1.1 further specifies that expectations are also determined by the role each individual plays in an interaction. The roles we play depend on their availability in our group or in society. For example, work roles can be placed in three categories: boss, peer, or subordinate. Identity and reputation determine what roles you are willing to enter, what roles you are willing to play, and how you will play them. The relationships among identity, reputation, and role are bidirectional—the relationships among these units of our model are reciprocally related (Roberts, 1994; 1996). Our identities inform, and are informed by, the roles that we play. Likewise, feedback regarding our reputations influence our self-perceptions (identity), and our self-perceptions (identity) cause us to behave in ways that affect our reputations.

The evaluation of a person's performance during an interaction forms two feedback loops. As actors, we evaluate our success or failure in the inter-

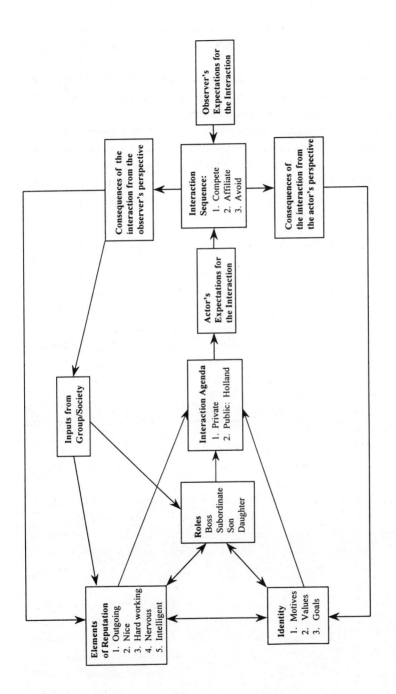

The Individual   The Interaction

FIG. 1.1. A General Model for Person/Situation Interaction.

action and our evaluation will tend to validate or change our identity. The other person's evaluation of the interaction will tend to shape our reputation.

Note once again that the situation is defined entirely in terms of an actor's perceptions of him- or herself, of the other's expectations, and of the reputational consequences of the expected behavior.

Putting all these considerations together results in three broad classes of behavior during the interaction: (a) you can accommodate to the other person and try to get along with him/her; (b) you can compete with the person and try to outperform him/her; or (c) you can withdraw from the interaction. Once again, whatever you do will be evaluated by others and their evaluations will shape your reputation.

LEADERSHIP FROM A SOCIOANALYTIC PERSPECTIVE

Although other people are the most pervasive and important "situations" we face day to day, few psychologists other than Holland (1985) and Schneider (1975) incorporate people as situations into their conceptual models, perhaps because of the pervasive individualistic bias of American psychology and its focus on decontextualized individual thoughts, feelings, and behaviors (Hogan, 1976). Nonetheless, other people are our situations; moreover, higher status people are disproportionately more powerful situations for lower status people who must deal with them.

Our evolutionary history mandates that we live in groups, and that each group has a status hierarchy, defined in terms of the values of the culture. In the long run, then, leadership—possessing high status in a group—must be a resource for a group's survival and success. Leadership serves several adaptive purposes for a group. It simplifies decision making and permits more decisive group action; quick responses are imperative when a group is faced with imminent danger. Leadership also focuses action by coordinating group behavior as opposed to fostering competing individual agendas. Group level actions such as organizing mutual defense or regulating the gathering and distribution of food should increase the probability of survival for most members of a group.

Although an evolutionary perspective on leadership might seem to suggest that leaders are born and not made, the suggestion is wrong because having the right disposition does not mean that one will become a leader. Leadership is a role that is conferred on a person by certain others as part of the larger process of social exchange, and a person then brings that role with him or her to subsequent interactions. Leadership is often conferred through what Holloman (1986) describes as "headship"; for example, governing boards usually select University presidents without significant input from faculty, staff, or students. Such leadership is *appointed*. Group members can also sometimes select their leader, as when the electorate votes politicians into office, or when players select a team captain. Such leadership is *emergent*. In either case, having a leadership role means the person has a higher status and more power than his or her constituency, at least in principle.

From a Socioanalytic perspective then, leadership is a role that is conferred on a person as part of the social exchange process (Hollander & Julian, 1969). The commodity that is exchanged is status, and this status is displayed by means of cultural symbols. In return, leaders are expected to represent, validate, or define the group's values and goals. They are able to do this because being in a leadership role provides access to power, which is manifested in the control of such resources as others' compliance, and access to people, money, and knowledge.

The characteristic style with which a person handles the symbols of leadership represents the group's values and goals, and uses power, will shape that person's reputation as a leader. A leader's reputation also largely defines the climate for his or her constituency, and that climate becomes the situation when people interact with their managers, supervisors, department chairs, union bosses, CEOs, and bowling league presidents. Thus, a leaders' personality will define his or her leadership style or reputation, and that style will in turn define the situation his or her subordinates typically face when dealing with that person.

The Role of Leadership in Defining Situations

Two characteristics typify emergent and appointed leaders. First, they usually have the technical skills and knowledge necessary to do the job. And second, they consciously and actively want to be in charge; they will be *ambitious* (the topic of ambition seems to make psychologists uneasy) nonetheless, high status people—including Freud, Ghandi, and Einstein—are usually ambitious, despite any transparent protestations of modesty.

Emergent and appointed leaders differ in terms of how they direct their attention. Successful emergent leaders will pay close attention to the expectations of the group when they are the leader, and will use those expectations when doing their jobs. Successful appointed leaders will pay more attention to the expectations of the people who appointed them—i.e., to "board relations"—and may ignore the lower status people in their organizations. Thus, seeds of alienation between appointed leaders and their subordinates are structural. Great appointed leaders such as Nelson and Grant were popular with their subordinates, but this lesson is lost on many CEOs, managers, and supervisors.

Emergent leaders attend to their colleagues' expectations; the subordinates are part of the situation for emergent leaders—because they take their expectations into account. Conversely, appointed leaders primarily attend to the expectations of the people who appointed them; consequently, they tend to ignore the expectations of their subordinates who then perceive them as poor leaders. This may explain the finding (cf. Hogan, Curphy, & Hogan, 1994) that about 60% of people in managerial positions in corporate America are described by their subordinates as incompetent. It also points out what those people could do to improve the performance ratings they receive from their subordinates—i.e., pay attention to the valid expectations of the subordinates.

PERSONALITY AND LEADERSHIP STYLE

Many writers have linked aspects of leadership to personality. For example, Bernard (1926) noted that "any person who is more than ordinarily efficient in carrying psychosocial stimuli to others and is thus effective in conditioning collective responses may be called a leader." (quoted by Bass, 1990, p. 12) Bass (1990) reviewed hundreds of studies concerning the link between such personality traits as *extraversion, interpersonal competence,* or *power motivation,* and effective leadership. This effort is probably futile; a person's personality, his or her status in a group, and his or her effectiveness as a leader are separate issues—i.e., pushy, arrogant people often attain leadership positions, but tend to be ineffective.

It might be more useful to consider how personality affects leadership style. Leadership style reflects the manner in which leaders handle the demands and expectations of the leadership role. Thus, leadership research should investigate the links between a person's personality, leadership style, and the kind of situations they create for others.

We can illustrate how personality influences leadership style and how it affects a constituency using two personality configurations: the narcissistic and avoidant personality disorders. Hogan, Curphy, and Hogan (1992) suggest that the standard DSM IV, Axis 2 personality disorders provide a preliminary taxonomy of factors leading to managerial derailment, and our discussion elaborates their point. Our research of these two types of leaders comes from subordinate's descriptions (cf. Hogan & Hogan, 1997), as well as our cumulative experience in management development. The following describes two midlevel managers whom we know well. The discussion is anecdotal, but interested readers may view it as proposing hypotheses to be tested in future research.

Narcissism has a high base rate in managers (see Hogan, Raskin, & Fazzini, 1992). Narcissists are characterized by a grandiose sense of self-importance, an obsession with success and power, and a belief that they are unique or special people to whom others naturally owe respect and obedience. Narcissists tend to gravitate toward leadership positions and their excessive self-confidence makes them feel entitled to these roles. To say with sincerity "I can get this [country, state, city, organization, team] moving again" entails a healthy dose of positive self-regard that narcissists have in ample supply.

Unfortunately, other characteristics of narcissists undermine their ability to lead. For example, they need constant admiration, they have an unreasonable sense of entitlement, they are exploitative, they ignore the needs and feelings of others, and they are easily threatened by, or become envious of, others, including their subordinates. Narcissistic leaders are, therefore, unable to develop 'normal' relationships with their constituency—and the first task of leadership is to build a team.

Narcissists expect others to comply with their requests, and they do not expect to be required to defend or justify their decisions. They expect others to admire them, respect them, and comment promptly and favorably on their accomplishments. When things go right, they expect others to give them credit for success; when things go wrong, they expect others to take the blame. They expect loyalty and support as a matter of course rather than as something that they must earn, and they expect others will sense their power and see them as natural leaders.

The leadership style of narcissists creates a strong environment for their constituencies. To maintain positive relationships with narcissists, subordinates must constantly feed their grandiosity because narcissists distrust persons who do not flatter them. Furthermore, subordinates must be perpetually vigilant to please them, and this creates a climate of insecurity. Because of their insensitivity, insecurity, and preoccupation with their own success, narcissistic leaders are unable to acknowledge their subordinate's achievements, and may even take credit for them. Thus, subordinates will be confronted with a leader who not only demands respect and obedience but is also a potential rival and competitor, all of which threaten and demoralize them.

Figure 1.2 combines our description of the narcissistic leader with our previous analysis of person–environment interaction. The narcissistic leader
brings to the role an identity emphasizing uniqueness and natural superior-
ity. He or she also brings a relatively negative reputation marked by
grandiosity and selfishness. Because narcissistic leaders are obsessed with
power relationships, they will expect others to pay attention to them, follow
their orders, take the blame for their failures, and praise them for any successes. These expectations will feed back to the narcissistic leader, simultaneously reinforcing the inflated self-image and undesirable reputation. A
consistent set of expectations, some rather perverse, creates the climate of
tension and hostility described here.

A second syndrome common among incompetent managers is the avoidant
personality disorder. Such people seem overtly self-confident but cautious, detached, somewhat introverted, and tending to avoid interactions with new people in new places. They are also rule-abiding, and carefully support
organizational rules, values, and procedures. Others describe them as steady,
unassuming, cautious, and moderate. At their best, avoidant leaders seem "vir-
tuous"; at their worst they are seen as indecisive, irrational, conforming, and
somewhat authoritarian. They go about their duties in a low profile fashion,
preferring to implement—but never challenge—policies set by their seniors;
they are extremely reluctant to define new goals for the group or change existing systems and values. Despite their seeming self-confidence, they are deeply
concerned about not making mistakes and not being criticized—they are primarily motivated by a fear of failure.

How will this personality configuration influence leadership style and the
climate of a group? Avoidant leaders will be reluctant to use the symbols of
leadership; some will see this as modesty, others will see it as weakness. In
contrast to the narcissist, the avoidant leader's sensitivity to the group's
norms and strong cathexis to proper social behavior should create confidence that they will attend to the group's expectations. On the other hand,
because they fear being criticized, they will tend toward over control and will
lack creativity in solving problems. They will also have difficulty creating or
acting on change—a core requirement of leadership (Gardner, 1989). In using power, they will be cautious and reward good organizational citizenship
and rule-following behavior. In contrast to the narcissist, the avoidant person will not rend the fabric of civility needed for group performance, but
neither will they pressure subordinates for improved performance.

Such people's expectations primarily concern what they do not want to
happen. They do not want to change, try new techniques, methods, or tech-

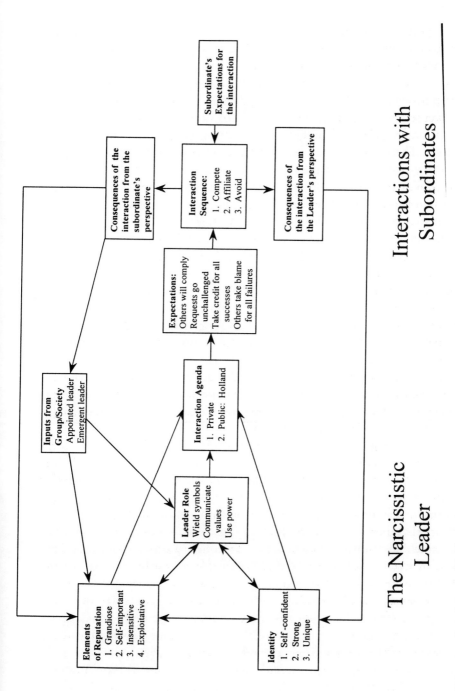

The Narcissistic
Leader

Interactions with
Subordinates

FIG. 1.2. A Specific Example of Person/Situation Interaction.

19

nology, take chances, rock the boat, have problems with their superiors, and do not want their subordinates to cause them any problems. Although their conservatism will allow their subordinates to know what to expect in the future, their lack of forcefulness may invite more dominant members of the group to challenge their authority, leading to confusion when the group must make decisions. Thus, the avoidant personality will create a climate of unassertive conformity that maintains the status quo, but may handicap the group's ability to handle change or develop a new vision for the future. Finally, avoidant leaders will not be effective advocates for their teams when dealing with senior people in the organization. Rather, they will pass on unchallenged, absurd, and ridiculous requests from more senior people, not understanding that loyalty must go both ways.

Such leaders create a clear, but spongy, environment for their subordinates. Subordinates primarily must be careful not to threaten them. They are most readily threatened when they must do something unusual, out of the ordinary, or not covered by existing rules and procedures. They will not readily change procedures or innovate, they strongly prefer to maintain the status quo, and they are extremely reluctant to challenge senior people on behalf of their subordinates. The bad news is that if subordinates want procedures to change, they will have to implement the change themselves; the good news is that their leader will rarely challenge them or question their failure to follow the chain of command. Subordinataes can, however, expect that their efforts at innovation may be met with passive resistance and no follow through.

CONCLUSIONS

To the degree that the personality research agenda depends on systematically crossing person variables with situation variables, we need taxonomies of both. Although we have a reasonably well-defined taxonomy of people—the Five-Factor model (Wiggins, 1996)—there is no such taxonomy of situations. On the one hand, this makes the entire person–situation debate moot. On the other hand, this is, or should be, a major embarrassment for people interested in the effects of environments on individuals. In our view, the concept of a situation has been inadequately conceptualized from the outset; as Wittgenstein (1953) noted, in psychology there are empirical methods and conceptual confusions.

Socioanalytic theory provides a basis for thinking about situations; from a socioanalytic perspective, there are clear structural requirements for interactions—in order for an interaction to occur, there must be an agenda and roles for the participants to play. Agendas can be taxonomized using the Holland RIASEC model. Roles can be classified in terms of the Big Three—in terms of their relative status, intimacy, and ingroup or outgroup membership.

Knowing the agenda for an interaction and what roles others will play, one can predict the others' performance, and perhaps, the others' expectations about one's own performance. People are innately sensitive to social expectations and naturally disposed to respond to them—if they perceive them and if they care about the other person's favorable regard. Theories about what others expect during an interaction are the "situation" for individual actors.

For an interaction to proceed, only one person need care about the others expectations. The person who does not care will tend to control the interaction according to the principle of least interest—i.e., he or she who has the least interest in continuing an interaction will control it. When high status people deal with lower status people, they often control the interaction; the same is true when leaders interact with subordinates. In such interactions, leaders define, or in a sense become, the situation for the subordinates—because they are the focus of the subordinates' theory of the interaction.

Thus, leaders, managers, and supervisors largely define the situation for those who must report to them or depend on their good wishes. But subordinates have clear expectations about the performance of leaders worthy of respect. To the degree that leaders or managers ignore the expectations of their subordinates, they alienate them, stress them, and make their lives miserable. Bad leadership, not drink, is the curse of the working class.

REFERENCES

Allport, G. W. (1937). *Personality: A psychological interpretation*. New York: Holt.

Argyle, M. (1976). Personality and social behavior. In R. Harré (Ed.), *Personality*. Oxford, England: Blackwell.

Bass, B. M. (1990). *Bass and Stogdill's Handbook of Leadership*. New York: The Free Press.

Baumeister, R. F. (1982). A self-presentational view of social phenomena. *Psychological Bulletin, 91*, 3–26.

Baumeister, R. F. (1997). Identity, self-concept, and self-esteem: The self lost and found. In R. Hogan, J. A. Johnson, & S. R. Briggs (Eds.), *Handbook of Personality Psychology*, pp. 681–711. San Diego: Academic Press.

Bernard, L. L. (1926). *An introduction to social psychology*. New York: Holt.

Bowlby, J. (1980). *Attachment and loss*. New York: Basic Books.

Burns, J. M. (1978). *Leadership*. New York: Harper & Row.

Buss, A., & Plomin, R. (1975). *A temperament theory of personality*. New York: Wiley.

Etzioni, A. (1961). *A comparative analysis of complex organizations*. New York: The Free Press.

Frederiksen, N. (1972). Toward a taxonomy of situations. *American Psychologist, (2)*, 114–123.

French, J. R., & Raven, B. (1959). The bases of social power. In D. Cartwright (Ed.), *Studies in social power*. Ann Arbor: University of Michigan Institute for Social Research.

Freud, S. (1913). *Totem and taboo*. New York: Vintage Books.

Gardner, J. W. (1989). *On leadership*. New York: The Free Press.

Goffman, E. (1958). *The presentation of self in everyday life*. New York: Doubleday.

Goldberg, L. R. (1990). An alternative "description of personality": The Big Five factor structure. *Journal of Personality and Social Psychology, 59*, 1216-1229.

Hackman, J. R. (1968). Effects of task characteristics on group products. *Journal of Experimental Social Psychology, 4*, 162-187.

Hogan, R. (1969). Development of an empathy scale. *Journal of Consulting and Clinical Psychology, 33*, 307-316.

Hogan, R. (1975). Theoretical egocentrism and the problem of compliance. *American Psychologist, 30*, 533-540.

Hogan, R. (1996). A socioanalytic perspective on the Five Factor model. In J. Wiggins (Ed.), *Theories of the five factor model* (pp. 163-179). New York: Guilford.

Hogan, J., & Hogan, R. (1996). *Motives, Values, Preferences Inventory Manual*. Tulsa: HAS.

Hogan, R., & Blake, R. J. (1996). Vocational interests: Matching self-concept and the work environment. In K. R. Murphy (Ed.), *Individual differences in behavior in organizations* (pp. 89-144). San Francisco: Jossey-Bass.

Hogan, R., Curphy, G., & Hogan, J. (1994). What we know about leadership. *American Psychologist, 49*, 493-504.

Hogan, R., & Hogan, J. (1997). *Hogan Development Survey Manual*. Tulsa: HAS.

Hogan, R., Raskin, R., & Fazzini, D. (1990). The darkside of charisma. In K. E. Clark & M. B. Clark (Eds.) *Measures of leadership* (pp. 343-354). Greensboro: Center for Creative Leadership.

Hogan, R., Raza, S., & Driskell, J. E. (1988). Personality, team performance, and organizational context. In P. Whitney & R. B. Ocsman (Eds.) *Psychology and Productivity*. New York: Plenum.

Hogan, R., Hogan, J., & Roberts, B. W. (1996). Personality measurement and employment decisions. *American Psychologist, 51*, 469-477.

Holland, J. L. (1985). *Making vocational choices: A theory of personalities and work environments* (2nd ed.). Englewood Cliffs, NJ: Prentice-Hall.

Hollander, E. P., & Julian, J. W. (1969). Contemporary trends in the analysis of leadership processes. *Psychological Bulletin, 71*, 387-397.

Holloman, C. R. (1986). Leadership and headship: There is a difference. *Personnel Administration, 31*, 38-44.

Ichheiser, G. (1970). *Appearances and realities*. San Francisco: Jossey-Bass.

Ickes, W., Snyder, M., & Garcia, S. (1997). Personality influences on the choice of situation. In R. Hogan, J. A. Johnson, & S. R. Briggs (Eds.) *Handbook of Personality Psychology* (166-198). New York: Academic.

Jones, E. E. (1990). *Interpersonal perception*. New York: Freeman.

Kenrick, D. T., & Funder, D. C. (1988). Profiting from controversy: Lessons of the person-situation debate. *American Psychologist, 43*, 23-34.

Le Carre, J. (1993). *The night manager*. New York: Knopf.

McAdams, D. P. (1993). *Stories we live by*. New York: Morrow.

Mead, G. H. (1934). *Mind, self, and society*. Chicago: University of Chicago Press.

Mischel, W. (1968). *Personality and assessment*. New York: Wiley.

Murray, H. S. (1938). *Explorations in personality*. New York: Oxford.

Pervin, L. A. (1976). A free-response description approach to the analysis of person-situation interaction. *Journal of Personality and Social Psychology, 34*, 465-474.

Pervin, L. A. (1978). Definitions, measurements, and classifications of stimuli, situations, and environments. *Human Ecology, 6*, 71-105.

Pettigrew, T. (1997). Personality and social structure. In R. Hogan, J. A. Johnson, & S. R. Briggs (Eds.), *Handbook of personality psychology* (pp. 417-439). New York: Academic Press.

Roberts, B. W. (1994). *A longitudinal study of the reciprocal relations between women's personality and occupational experience.* Unpublished doctoral dissertation, University of California, Berkeley.

Roberts, B. W. (1996, August). An *alternative perspective on the relation between work and psychological functioning: The reciprocal model of person–environment interaction.* Paper presented at the 104th Annual Convention of the American Psychological Association, Toronto, Canada.

Ross, L., & Nisbett, R. E. (1991). *The person and the situation.* New York: McGraw-Hill.

Sarbin, T. R. (1954). Role Theory. In G. Lindzey (Ed.)"""""" *Handbook of Social Psychology.* Reading, MA: Addison-Wesley.

Schlenker, B. R., & Weigold, M. F. (1990). Self-consciousness and self-presentation: Being autonomous versus appearing autonomous. *Journal of Personality and Social Psychology, 59,* 820–828.

Schneider, B. (1975). Organizational climates: An essay. *Personnel Psychology, 28,* 447–479.

Sells, S. B. (1963). An interactionist looks at the environment. *American Psychologist, 18,* 696–702.

Shweder, R. A. (1982). How relevant is an individual difference theory of personality? *Journal of Personality, 43,* 455–485.

Tupes, E. C., & Christal, R. E. (1992/1961). Recurrent personality factors based on trait ratings. *Journal of Personality, 60,* 225–251.

Weick, K. E. (1979) *The social psychology of organizing* (2nd ed.). Reading, MA: Addison-Wesley.

Wiggins, J. S. (Ed.), (1996). *The Five-Factor Model of personality: Theoretical perspectives.* New York: Guilford.

Wiggins, J. S., & Broughton, R. (1985). The interpersonal circle: A structural model for the integration of personality research. In R. Hogan & W. H. Jones (Eds.), *Perspectives on personality.* Greenwich, CT: JAI.

Wittgenstein, L. (1953). *Philosophical investigations.* Oxford: Blackwell.

2

Person-in-Environment Psychology: A Holistic, Developmental, Systems-Oriented Perspective

Seymour Wapner
Clark University

Jack Demick
Suffolk University
and
University of Massachusetts Medical School

For some time, psychologists have introduced the role of *the context* in psychology most generally (e.g., Bronfenbrenner, 1977; Sameroff, 1975, in developmental psychology; Minuchin, 1974; Wandersman, 1990, in clinical psychology; Proshansky, Ittelson, & Rivlin, 1970; Wapner, Kaplan, & Cohen, 1973, in environmental psychology; Altman, 1975; Asch, 1955, in social psychology) and in personality theory more specifically (e.g., Endler & Magnusson, 1976; Mischel, 1973). This has led to a new field of inquiry, person–environment psychology (e.g., Walsh, Craik, & Price, 1992). Although our approach to human experience and action falls under this general rubric, we prefer the term *person-in-environment psychology* to stress the transactional nature of our perspective. That is, our approach focuses on a holistic analysis of the entities—*person and environment*—comprised of mutually defining as-

25

pects that constitute the whole (person-in-environment system), that is, people embedded in their physical, interpersonal, and sociocultural environments. One must treat the totality rather than deal with one aspect of the whole (person or environment) without treating the other. This transactional idea, along with other aspects of our approach, distinguishes our work from many other approaches presented in this volume.

Thus, given the rapid growth of research in what has been described as person–environment psychology and its potential for future development, the goals of this chapter are (a) to provide a brief overview of our perspective—characterized as holistic, developmental, and systems-oriented; (b) elaborate our perspective by comparing and contrasting it with representative models of person–environment psychology (illustrated by previous works of contributors to this volume and by contributions already published in the previous volume of this series); and (c) delineate open problems for future empirical inquiry that will continue to elaborate what we consider a critical problem for the new subfield of person–environment psychology, namely, the holistic functioning of person-in-environment systems across the life span. Elaboration of these goals will help advance not only our perspective but also the other theoretical perspectives and models of person–environment psychology more generally.

Our discussion is predicated on the related notions of *perspectivism* and of *interrelations among problem, theory, and method*. Stated most simply, perspectivism assumes that any object, event, or phenomenon is always mentally viewed from a particular standpoint, or world view that is capable of definition (cf. Lavine, 1950a, 1950b, on interpretationism; cf. *constructivism* here). This leads us to assert that inquiry and knowledge are always biased and there is no process that is neutral observation. In line with this (cf. Altman, 1997), we maintain that there is also considerable value in uncovering the ways where one's theoretical orientation determines what one studies (problem) and how one studies it (method). Accordingly, following a brief overview of our perspective, an attempt will be made to demonstrate how individual assumptions inherent within our approach penetrate aspects of both our own and others' empirical research. This strategy will hopefully make explicit the heuristic potential of our approach. Open research problems from our own and related approaches will then be delineated.

BRIEF OVERVIEW OF PERSPECTIVE

Our perspective, based on an elaboration and extension of Werner's (1926; 1948/1957) organismic-developmental theory, is:

1. *holistic*, as it assumes that all part-processes—biological and physical, psychological (*action* and the experiential processes of *cognition*, *affect*, and *valuation*), and sociocultural—are interrelated, and must be considered in relationship to the total context of human activity, and that the person-in-environment system is the unit of analysis (where the person and the environment mutually define one another, and together, constitute the whole);

2. *developmental*, as it assumes, in keeping with the formal, organizational *orthogenetic principle* (Werner & Kaplan, 1956, 1963) that person-in-environment system development proceeds from a relative lack of differentiation toward the goal of differentiation and hierarchic integration of organismic functioning; and

3. *systems-oriented*, as the unit of analysis is the person-in-environment system where the *biological and physical* (e.g., health), *psychological* (e.g., self-esteem), and *sociocultural* (e.g., role) levels of organization of the person are operative, and are interrelated with the *physical* (e.g., natural and built environment), *interpersonal* (e.g., friends and relatives), and *sociocultural* (e.g., rules and regulations of society) levels of organization of the *environment*.

An ongoing research program from our perspective (e.g., Wapner, 1977, 1981, 1987; Wapner & Demick, 1992, 1998) focuses on changes (progressive development and regressive change) in individuals' action and experience (cognitive—sensori-motor, perceptual, conceptual; affective; and valuative) following a *critical life transition*. A critical transition has been conceptualized here as a potent perturbation to any part of the person-in-environment system, at any level of organization. Thus, perturbations may be initiated at the biological or physical (e.g., onset of diabetes), psychological or intrapersonal (e.g., having a failure experience), or sociocultural (e.g., taking on a new job or role) level of the person or at the physical (e.g., natural disaster), psychological or interpersonal (e.g., falling in love), or sociocultural (e.g., governmental introduction of mandatory automobile safety belt usage) level of the environment. For example, we have systematically studied a variety of such life transitions ranging from a child's transition into nursery school (e.g., Ciottone, Demick, Pacheco, Quirk, & Wapner, 1980) through an older adult's transition to a nursing home (e.g., Wapner, Demick, & Redondo, 1990).

While traditional personality psychologists might be most interested in the problem of individual differences in life transitions, our approach alternatively advocates a differential psychology in the context of a more general developmental psychology. Thus, the general developmental orthogenetic principle has been used in our transition research as a basis for conceptualizing individual differences in human action and experience. Specifically, individual differences in the person's transactions with the environment are characterized in these developmental terms. Least developmentally advanced are: (a) *dedifferentiated* person-in-environment system states (the person's transactions are characterized as going along with the immediate situational context). Somewhat more advanced are: (b) *differentiated and isolated* person-in-environment system states (e.g., the person isolates himself or herself from the physical, interpersonal, or sociocultural environmental contexts); and (c) *differentiated and in conflict* person-in-environment system states (e.g., the person is in conflict with the physical, interpersonal, or sociocultural contexts). Most advanced developmentally are *differentiated and hierarchically integrated* person-in-environment system states (e.g., the person is able to separate and subordinate short term for long term goals). Characteristic modes of coping related to each of these individual differences are discussed here in the section on individual differences.

These holistic, developmental, and systems ideas have strong implications for methodology. Our research has been concerned both with describing the relations among and within the parts (person, environment) that make up the integrated whole (person-in-environment system) and with specifying the conditions that make for changes in the organization of these relations. Thus, our approach is wedded to the assessment of both the "what"—explication (description)—and the "how"—causal explanation (nature of underlying processes)—rather than being restricted to one or the other.

Relevant here is Maslow's (1946) distinction between *means-oriented* and *problem-oriented* research. Whereas the former method dictates the range of problems that can be studied, the latter gives priority to the phenomenon being studied. From our perspective, problem-oriented research calls for different methodologies depending on the nature of the problem. That is, some methods, like experimental methods, are appropriate for the study of certain aspects of a phenomenon (e.g., cognitive style and conditions, like planning vs. not planning that affect adaptation to critical transitions), whereas other methods (e.g., phenomenological methods) yield access to different aspects of a phenomenon (e.g., experiential changes following critical transitions). This distinction is intricately involved in the ongoing debate of whether psychology should remain restricted to the methods of the natural science tradition, or whether it should augment these with, or substitute for them, alternative methods (e.g., phenomenological and narrative methods) that are more appropriate to the uniqueness of psychology's subject matter. Moreover, a qualitative *human science* methodology may serve as an appropriate first step for conducting a quantitative analysis using *natural science* methodologies.

THEORETICAL ASSUMPTIONS AND CATEGORIES
OF COMPARISON

Our elaborated perspective is currently comprised of a set of interrelated assumptions about human action and experience in the complex, everyday life environment. In Table 2.1, these assumptions are delineated, and where relevant, compared across contributing authors to volumes I and II of *Person–Environment Psychology*. Furthermore, the major of these assumptions are described in more detail here and used as categories for comparing our approach and those represented in these volumes. Where relevant, several categories employed by Walsh et al. (1992) in their commentary on volume I will also be used as dimensions of comparison.

World View

There is a major difference between the underlying *world view* (Altman & Rogoff, 1987) or *world hypothesis* (Pepper, 1942, 1967) of our approach and many others'. Specifically, *our approach adopts elements of both organismic (organicist) and transactional (contextual) world views*. The organismic world view is embodied by an attempt to understand the world through the use of synthesis, that is, by putting its parts together into a unified whole. It highlights the relationships among parts, but the relationships are viewed as part of an integrated process rather than as unidirectional chains of cause–effect relationships. The central feature of a transactional world view is that the person and the environment are conceptualized as parts of a whole; one cannot deal with one aspect of the whole without treating the other (cf. Cantril, 1950; Ittelson, 1973; Lewin, 1935; Sameroff, 1983; Wapner, 1987). Specifically, the transactional view treats the " ... person's behaving, including his most advanced knowings as activities not of himself alone, nor even primarily his, but as processes of the full situation of organism-environment." (Dewey & Bentley, 1949, p. 104)

These world views have figured within our approach in the following ways. First, they have impacted our choice of paradigmatic problems (e.g., critical person-in-environment transitions across the life span) as well as of methods (i.e., methodological flexibility depending on the nature of the problem and multiple methods toward a complete characterization of action and experience). Second, they have suggested that holistic, ecologically oriented research is a necessary complement to more traditional laboratory work, and that it might be conducted through reducing the number of focal individuals

TABLE 2.1

Assumptions of Holistic, Developmental, Systems-Oriented Perspective and Comparison With Other Perspectives

Category of Comparison	Holistic, Developmental, Systems-Oriented Approach (Wapner & Demick)	Altman et al. (1992)	Buss (1995)	Heyman & Dueck (1992)	Hogan (1982)	Little (1987)	Magnusson & Torestad (1992)	Nasar & Fisher (1993)	Ozer (1986)	Pervin (1992)	Peterson (1992)	Schneider (1987)	Stokols (1992)	Swindle & Moos (1992)	Walsh & Holland (1992)	Wicker (1992)
World View	Organismic/Transactional (Organicist/Contextual)	X	X			X					X		X			X
Philosophical Underpinnings	Constructivism (Interpretationism)	X	X	X			X	X					X	X		X
Levels of Integration	Functioning at different, although related, levels of integration (biological, psychological, sociocultural)	X	X			X		X			X					
Unit of Analysis	Person-in-environment as system state	X					X	X					X	X		
Holism	Person-in-environment system operates as a unified whole in dynamic equilibrium			X			X	X								
Aspects of Experience/Equilibration Tendencies										X						

(Table 2.1 Continued)

(Table 2.1 Continued)

Category of Comparison	Holistic, Developmental, Systems-Oriented Approach (Wapner & Demick)	Altman et al. (1992)	Buss (1995)	Heyman & Dweck (1992)	Hogan (1982)	Little (1987)	Magnusson & Torestad (1992)	Nasar & Fisher (1993)	Ozer (1986)	Pervin (1992)	Peterson (1992)	Schneider (1987)	Stokols (1992)	Swindle & Moos (1992)	Walsh & Holland (1992)	Wicker (1992)
Concept of Person	Defined with respect to levels of integration: Physical/biological, psychological (cognition, affect, values) and sociocultural (e.g., roles) and mutually defining aspects of person; multiple intentionality	X	X			X	X							X		
Concept of Environment	Defined with respect to levels of integration: Physical (things), interpersonal (people) and sociocultural (rules, mores, customs) as mutually defining aspects of environment	X	X			X	X	X					X	X		
Concept of Personality and Psychopathology	Holistic, dynamic definition of personality as related to environmental context (here, reflecting degree of self-world differentiation)	X					X			X	X				X	

31

Category of Comparison	Holistic, Developmental, Systems-Oriented Approach (Wapner & Demick)	Altman et al. (1992)	Buss (1995)	Heyman & Dweck (1992)	Hogan (1982)	Little (1987)	Magnusson & Torestad (1992)	Nasar & Fisher (1993)	Ozer (1986)	Pervin (1992)	Peterson (1992)	Schneider (1987)	Stokols (1992)	Swindle & Moos (1992)	Walsh & Holland (1992)	Wicker (1992)
Structural and Dynamic Analysis	Focus on structural (part-whole) and/or dynamic (means-ends) analyses		X							X			X		X	
Concepts, Principles and End points of Development	Mode of analysis of person-in-environment, contextual functioning across the life span; in addition to ontogenesis concerned with micro-genesis, phylo-genesis, etc.; homeostasis works in accordance with orthogenetic principle toward optimal self-world relationship (e.g., microgenetic, mobility, freedom, self-mastery)	X					X						X	X	X	

(Table 2.1 Continued)

Category of Comparison	Holistic, Developmental, Systems-Oriented Approach (Wapner & Demick)	Altman et al. (1992)	Buss (1995)	Heyman & Dweck (1992)	Hogan (1982)	Little (1987)	Magnusson & Torestad (1992)	Nasar & Fisher (1993)	Ozer (1986)	Pervin (1992)	Peterson (1992)	Schneider (1987)	Stokols (1992)	Swindle & Moos (1992)	Walsh & Holland (1992)	Wicker (1992)
Adaptation	Congruent person-in-environment system state: Optimal relationship between person and environment	X					X			X				X	X	
Individual Differences	Differential developmental psychology complementary to general developmental psychology		X				X				X				X	
Multiple Worlds	Different experiential worlds or spheres of activity													X		X
Theory of Action	Relationship of experience (intention) and action					X										
Reinforcement and Other Underlying Processes	Process underlying change in equilibrial state of person-in-environment system										X					X

33

studied rather than the number and kind of interrelationships among aspects of the person, environment, and the systems to which they belong. This will help us conceptualize problems that are more in line with the complex character of everyday life, and that cut across various aspects of persons and their environments (cf. Demick & Wapner, 1988b).

With respect to the other theories represented in these volumes that differ from ours, those that treat the biological and/or psychological levels (e.g., Peterson, 1992; Walsh & Holland, 1992) would predominantly be termed *interactional* or *mechanistic*, emphasizing a sensorial analysis of the effects of isolated independent variables within the person (e.g., personality types) or the environment (e.g., patterns of reinforcement) on dependent variables (e.g., psychological functioning of the person). In contrast, our underlying transactional world view appears to be most shared by Altman, Brown, Staples, and Werner (1992). Assuming that individuals and their psychological processes are embedded in, and inseparable from, their physical and social contexts, these researchers have attempted to examine close relationships with respect to social and cultural contexts (linkages between the cultural importance of family and kin and close relationships over time) as well as physical contexts (environmental aspects of close relationships).

Most compatible with our organismic underpinning is the recent work of Magnusson and Torestad (1992), who speak to the interaction of biological and psychological factors. Specifically, they regard:

> ... biological factors as constantly involved in a process of reciprocal interaction with mental factors, a process that in turn influences and is influenced by the individual's interaction with the environment, via the mediating cognitive-emotional system of the individual ... the interaction process in which an individual is involved with the environment can be described in terms of an active adaptation process. (p. 104)

They also note that "the way an individual functions in the process of interaction with his or her environment changes across time." (p. 107) However, differences between Magnusson and Torestad's approach and our's include developmental differences (i.e., our use of the orthogenetic principle systematically specifies the nature of progression and regression in all developmental processes, whereas they speak only to ontogenetic change); and differences in the unit of analysis (e.g., whereas they talk of reciprocal causality whereby a person can change the environment and vice versa, our transactional view requires treatment of both parts—person and environment—as the appropriate whole).

Philosophical Underpinnings

Our perspective assumes a *constructivist* view of knowledge. Specifically, we assume that *cognitive processes involve a person's active construction of objects of perception and thought.* Such an approach rejects all "copy" theories of perception and asserts that reality is relative to a person's interpretation or construction (cf. Lavine, 1950a, 1950b). In line with this, human beings are regarded as striving agents capable of creating, constructing, construing, and structuring their environments in various ways, and of acting in terms of their own experience. Wapner, Kaplan, and Cohen (1973) have characterized such striving in terms of Kuntz's (1968) notion that the individual, functioning at the sociocultural level, exhibits a "rage for order." These ideas lead to consideration of the distinction between the *physical* versus *experienced* environment, which has also been referred to as the *behavioral environment* (Koffka, 1935); *umwelt, phenomenal world, self-world* (von Uexkull, 1957); and *psychological environment* (Lewin, 1935).

This constructivist assumption is readily apparent in a study by Dandonoli, Demick, and Wapner (1990) that demonstrated that the cognitive–developmental status of the individual penetrates and plays a relatively powerful role in the way that he or she organizes a new environment to which he or she is exposed.

> Age differences (comparing children ages 5 to 7, 8 to 10, and 11 to 13, and adults) in experience and representation of a large-scale spatial arrangement (University Common Room) biased in an "integrated" versus a "part-quality" manner were assessed. Through verbal recall, drawings, classification, and memory reconstruction, it was found that ... adults' representations were characterized by an integration of parts into socially relevant, meaningful wholes, whereas children produced representations consisting of groupings of isolated, fragmented parts ... even when exposed to a part-quality room arrangement, adults experienced and represented the spatial arrangement in terms of socially relevant, meaningful wholes. (p. 26)

The constructivist assumption is readily shared by many contributors to these volumes. For example, drawing on Barker's (1968) ecological perspective, Wicker (1992) concluded that:

> Person–environment transactions are viewed in terms of people's continuing attempts to make sense of events that occur in behavior settings. This sense-making process occurs at both the individual and group levels, and in response to continually changing events that emanate from both within and be-

yond the settings that people currently occupy. Sense-making is a dynamic, cyclical process linking the ecological environment with the psychological process of attending, acting, interpreting, and remembering. (p. 189)

In a related manner, Swindle and Moos (1992) have focused on "life stressors and social resources in various life domains and their association with health outcomes." (p. 1) In their multiple risk factor stress and coping model, they have broadened their conceptualization to include coping responses and cognitive coping strategies, noting that such processes generally involve " ... coherent patterns of appraisal, planning, retrospection, and effort that translate an individual's goals and beliefs about himself or herself into effective action ... " (p. 19) What distinguishes our work from the others, however, is that for us, the constructivist assumption reinforces the belief that there is the need to complement assessments of, for example, the geographic environment with those of the experienced environment.

Levels of Integration

This assumption states that *organism-in-environment processes may be categorized in terms of levels of integration* (Feibelman, 1954; Herrick, 1949; Novikoff, 1945a, 1945b; Schneirla, 1949), *that is, biological (e.g., breathing), psychological (e.g., thinking), and sociocultural (e.g., living by a moral code)*. Thus, there is a contingency relationship: Functioning at the sociocultural level requires functioning at the psychological and biological levels, and functioning at the psychological level requires functioning at the biological level. The levels differ qualitatively and functioning at one level is not reducible to functioning on the prior, less complex level, because we assume that higher level functioning does not substitute for, but rather integrates and transforms, lower level functioning (Wapner & Demick, 1990; Werner, 1948/1957).

This assumption has played a very important role in our research, and highlights a significant driving notion, namely, *rejection of reductionism*. Although most theoretical perspectives recognize that various relationships obtain between biological and psychological functioning and psychological and sociocultural functioning, the contingency relationship for defining various levels of integration is interpreted for use in different ways. One alternative that we strongly reject is *biological reductionism* that assumes functioning is determined completely by the biological structure and state of functioning of the organism.

Such a reductionist approach usually means an attempt to understand psychological functioning by translating its principles into those involving only biological terms (e.g., genetic bases of personality). In contrast, our approach has taken the position that levels of integration must be considered in any analysis of psychological functioning. Focus on a particular level depends on the specific question or issue posed, or confronted together with the recognition that impact on one level affects all other levels of functioning, that is, the functioning of the whole. In general, there is no single way of analyzing or explaining action and experience independent of the goals of the analysis. This position permits exploration of the same phenomena that concern biological and sociocultural determinists without excluding either biology or culture (cf. Wapner & Demick, 1998).

Thus, from our perspective, those formulations that ascribe individual functioning *either to heredity or to the environment* (see Walsh, Craik, & Price, 1992) as well as those that attempt to describe the role of each in percentage terms represent a fundamental error because both these formulations logically permit the possibility of genetic or environmental factors playing no role at all (cf. Magnusson & Torestad, 1992). The assumption that the individual functions at multiple levels of integration means that both genetic and environmental factors must always be taken into account. Our position fits most closely with that recently expressed by Lewontin (1994). His model of development includes genetic differences, environmental differences, and developmental noise, an unknown source of developmental variation, "thermal noise at the molecular level that determines when cell division occurs and how long it takes." (Lewontin, 1994, p. 26) A given structure may provide different phenotypic characteristics depending on the nature of the environment. Hence, from our perspective, both factors must always be operative and interactive.

Unit of Analysis

This basic assumption holds that the person-in-environment system is the *unit of analysis with transactional (experience and action) and mutually defining aspects of person and environment.* Treating the person-in-environment as the unit of analysis has the advantages that it corresponds to, and represents the complexity of, the real life situation; that it suggests analysis of the individual's behavior and experience in a variety of contexts (thus, environmental context is built into and an essential part of the unit of analysis); and that it is both comprehensive and flexible in uncovering sources of variation underlying behavior. This assumption has figured prominently in our research for some time. Specifically, it has led to an unwavering commitment to conceptualizing *the individual* (as a system at the various levels of integration), *individual-in-group*, *individual-in-organization*, and *organization-in-environment* systems (see Mayo, Pastor, & Wapner, 1995).

Relevant to this conceptualization, for example, is Peterson's (1992) work on interpersonal relationships as a link between person and environment. In contrast to theories that posit unidirectional conceptions of causality, Peterson's focus is on a more general framework of reciprocal causality, or interdependence. Acknowledging the need to look equally at both partners in a relationship as well as at their interdependence, Peterson views interaction episodes as the basic materials that make up relationships. In our terminology, interpersonal relationships (the whole) are comprised of mutually defining aspects of the (focal) person and the environment (the other), and the transactions between them.

HOLISM, ASPECTS OF EXPERIENCE, AND EQUILIBRATION TENDENCIES

We also assume that *the person-in-environment system operates as a unified whole so that a disturbance in one part affects other parts and the totality.* This holistic assumption holds not only for functioning among levels of integration (biological, psychological, sociocultural), but also for functioning within a given level. For example, on the psychological level, such part-processes as the *cognitive* aspects of experience (including sensory motor functioning, perceiving, thinking, imagining, and symbolizing) as well as the *affective* and *valuative* aspects of experience and *action*, operate contemporaneously and in an integrated fashion in the normal functioning adult (cf. Wapner & Demick, 1990). Finally, related to this notion, we also assume that the tendency toward equilibration is a basic end that operates at all levels of organization (e.g., homeostatic mechanisms at the biological level, perceptual adaptation at the psychological level, and sociocultural adaptation to a new environment following relocation). Thus, *person-in-environment systems are assumed to operate in a dynamic equilibrium.*

These holistic assumptions are consistent with the work of several other contributors to these volumes. For example, Pervin (1992) united the concepts of person and environment in his discussion of goals and their implementation through plans with their cognitive, affective, and behavioral components (psychological levels of integration). In a similar manner, Magnusson and Torestad (1992) highlight cognitive and emotional factors in the person as essential determinants of behavior and Heyman and Dweck

(1992) are interested in how children respond cognitively, affectively, and behaviorally to failure situations. Although these researchers have clearly acknowledged the important role of psychological part-processes (and their interrelations) in human functioning, their approach differs from ours insofar as we also acknowledge *valuative processes*—an area sorely underexplored in both general and developmental psychology—as functioning in an interdependent manner with cognition, affect, and action (as an exception among the contributors to these volumes, see Nasar & Fisher, 1993, and their related work).

Concept of Person

We define the person aspect of the person-in-environment system with respect to levels of integration, and so assume that *the person is comprised of mutually defining physical/biological (e.g., health), intrapersonal/psychological (e.g., self-esteem), and sociocultural (e.g., role as worker, family member) aspects.* Furthermore, in line with our constructivist assumption, we regard individuals as active, striving, purposeful, goal-oriented agents capable of spontaneously structuring, shaping, and construing their environments in various ways, and acting in terms of their own experience.

We also assume that human beings are characterized by *a rage for order* (Kuntz, 1968) and by *multiple intentionality*. That is, the person transacting with his or her environment has the capacity to focus on different objects of experience such as the self, an object, and the relation between both. Moreover, the person has the capacity to *plan*, which involves plotting future courses of action that move the person-in-environment system from some initial state of functioning to some end state (Wapner & Cirillo, 1973).

Little's (1987) work implies a similar concept of person. That is, through his focus on personal projects (extended sets of personally relevant action) as the unit of analysis, he has detailed concrete ways that individuals act on environments. These ways, or projects, may typically involve (among other things) physical (e.g., going on a diet), intrapersonal (e.g., doing well at school), and sociocultural (e.g., being a good mother) aspects of self. However, relationships among personal projects at the differing levels of integration remain an open empirical problem.

Concept of Environment

Analogous to our conceptualization of person, we assume that *the environment aspect of the person-in-environment system is comprised of mutually defining*

*physical (e.g., natural and built objects), interpersonal (e.g., spouse, friend, co-worker),
and sociocultural (e.g., rules and mores of the home, community, and other cultural
contexts) aspects* (cf. Demick & Wapner, 1988a). Again, we do not focus on
the person or on the environment per se, but rather, consider the person and
the environment relationally as parts of one whole.

Although several contributors (e.g., Little, 1987, Stokols, 1992) share our
multifaceted view of the environment, the work of Buss (1995) is especially
noteworthy. That is, in his discussion of evolutionary psychology as a new
paradigm for psychological science, he notes that current contextual evolutionary analysis takes place at several levels; namely, the historical selective
context, the ontogenetic context, and immediate situational inputs (the experiential context). Both our elaboration of Wernerian theory, and his of
evolutionary approaches, attempt to explicate all forms of contextual input
within a unifying framework.

Concepts of Personality and Psychopathology

In line with what has been presented here, we assume *holistic, dynamic definitions of personality and of psychopathology as related to environmental context.* Specifically, our conceptualizations revolve around a major dimension of
person-in-environment system functioning, namely, the *degree of
self-object(world) differentiation* (Werner, 1948/1957).

This critical dimension of self–object (things and people) differentiation
in personality and in psychopathology was developed in the contexts of
Werner and Kaplan's (1963) work on symbolic formation and Wapner and
Werner's (1957) work on perceptual development. In the context of the former, E. Kaplan (1952), for example, found that relative to speech directed toward others (*outer* speech), speech directed toward self (*inner* speech) is more
abbreviated, holophrastic, personal, and differentiated with articulated subject matter (see Werner & Kaplan's, 1963, classic volume, *Symbol Formation,*
for numerous examples from personality and abnormal psychology). In the
context of the latter, Carini (1965), for example, found that, in adjusting a lu-
minous rod in a dark room to verticality, catatonic schizophrenics exhibited
the most extreme dedifferentiation between self and object (evidenced by
closeness of the adjusted rod with tilted body), less for paranoid schizophrenics, and least for normal adults (see Wapner & Werner's, 1957, *Perceptual Development,* for additional examples from personality and abnormal
psychology).

More recently, in the context of Wapner's (1987) research program on critical person-in-environment transitions, Demick and Wapner (1980) studied

the effects of environmental relocation on members of a psychiatric thera-peutic community and found that: (a) regarding self experience, schizo-phrenics exhibited increased diffuseness, and antisocial personalities' heightened awareness of body boundaries, on two test occasions closest to the move (2 to 3 days before and after, relative to 3 to 4 weeks before and af-ter), whereas staff showed no such differential changes; (b) in regard to envi-ronmental experience, schizophrenics' descriptions of various locations became less accurate and detailed closer to the relocation; and (c) regarding the experience of self-environment relations, schizophrenics' rated their rela-tionships with others as less intense and permanent, and antisocial personal-ities rated their relationships as more intense, on the occasions closest to the move, whereas staff showed no such changes.

These data led to the following developmental conceptualization of some aspects of psychopathology and hospitalization outcome. Whereas schizo-phrenics typically exhibit a lack of differentiation between self and world with an egocentric focusing on self (e.g., increased diffuseness of body boundaries, decreased focus on the physical environment, lesser significance placed on interpersonal relationships); antisocial personalities reveal rigid, differentiated boundaries between self and environment with an overfocusing on environment at the expense of on self (e.g., heightened awareness of body boundaries, increased focus on both the physical and in-terpersonal aspects of the environment). Furthermore, the stress of reloca-tion exacerbates the symptomatology and fosters developmental regression by creating greater rigidity of the figure–ground relationship typical of the particular pathology.

The concept of the degree of self-world differentiation has also suggested the use of multiple means to foster optimal self-world relationships in nor-mal, psychopathological, and neuropathological individuals, namely, flexi-bility, stability, and integration of the person-in-environment system(s). This conceptualization is also applicable not only to individual personality and psychopathology but also to family systems theory. For example, see Demick and Wapner (1988b) on family patterns generated by the differential prac-tices of open versus closed adoption (communication vs. no communication between adoptive and biological parents).

Although some authors (e.g., Altman et al., 1992; Magnusson & Torestad, 1992; Peterson, 1992) have attempted to integrate developmental consider-ations (e.g., time, continuity, and change) into their conceptualizations of person–environment psychology, ours is the only perspective that draws largely on a formal developmental theory (Werner, 1948/1957) attempting to integrate the person, the environment, and the relationships between them. Our conceptualization also has methodological implications for the measurement of personality (see Walsh, Craik, & Price, 1992).

That is, trait and other conceptualizations attempt to describe the individual in general terms, somewhat independent of the particular context, and assume consistency of behavior independent of context. We all know people who are *very* aggressive when interacting with some others and who are *not at all* aggressive when interacting with different others. This suggests that, instead of seeking characterizations of people independent of context, it would be quite effective, albeit complicated, to characterize people as operating with respect to some variable, for example aggression, in terms of a range score: some individuals, for example, might be characterized as more or less aggressive *independent* of interpersonal or sociocultural context (small range score); and others might be characterized as more or less aggressive *depending* on the nature of the context (broad range score).

Finally, most other contributions have focused primarily on normal personality rather than on psychopathology. A notable exception to this is the work of Pervin (1992). That is, sharing our assumption of the continuity between normal and abnormal behavior, he first highlights goals and their implementation as a general process inherent in person–environment psychology; he goes on to acknowledge that in a similar manner:

> Psychopathology can be understood in terms of the absence of goals, goals conflict (e.g., conflicts between wishes and fears), or problems in goal implementation; that is, disturbances can appear in the cognitive, affective, or behavioral components of goal systems or in the relations among the parts of the system. (pp. 79–80)

Analogously for us, both normal and abnormal functioning revolve around the crucial dimension of the degree of self–other differentiation. For example, individuals who operate on a formally less mature developmental level (e.g., children, schizophrenics) have less clearly differentiated boundaries between themselves and outer objects than do normal adults (e.g., Des Lauriers, 1962; Liebert, Werner, & Wapner, 1958).

STRUCTURAL AND DYNAMIC ANALYSES

We view the person and the environment as structural components of the person-in-environment system. Again, drawing on the theme of self-world differentiation, our *structural*, or *part–whole, analyses* focus on the characteristic structure of person-in-environment systems with an eye toward discerning whether the parts of subsystems (e.g., focal child and mother) are more or less differentiated or integrated with one another in specifiable ways (cf. Ainsworth, Blehar, Waters, & Wall, 1978, on attachment patterns). We also view *dynamic*, or, *means–ends*, *analyses* as complementary aspects of a formal description of a person-in-environment system. Focusing on the dynamics of a system entails a determination of the means (e.g., rational vs. irrational discussion) where a characteristic structure or goal (e.g., a later curfew) is achieved or maintained. For some time, we have, for example, focused on the cognitive process of planning, that is, the verbalized plotting of a future course of action, as one of a number of the means by which the person-in-environment system moves from some initial state of functioning to some end state.

Although some of the contributors have capitalized on either structural (e.g., Walsh & Holland, 1992) or dynamic (e.g., Heyman & Dweck, 1992; Pervin, 1992) analyses, no other theory of person–environment functioning except our own attempts to integrate structural and dynamic analyses as complementary aspects of a formal description of person-in-environment system states. Furthermore, the relations between structural and dynamic aspects of systems is an area that appears worthy of additional empirical investigation. For example, our paradigmatic research on the transition to retirement (Hanson & Wapner, 1994; Hornstein & Wapner, 1984, 1985; Wapner, Demick, & Damrad, 1988) has complemented structural analyses (the retiree's organization of their experiential worlds of home and work) with dynamic analyses (the relationship between the retiree's planning for and actuality of retirement) toward a more complete picture of the retiree's experience. Yet to be done are studies that examine the ways the dynamics of means–ends relationships (e.g., planning) impact the structural status of the person-in-environment system (e.g., reorganization of experiential worlds). See the next section on multiple worlds.

CONCEPTS, PRINCIPLES, AND ENDPOINTS OF DEVELOPMENT

Our view of development transcends the boundaries within which the concept of development is ordinarily applied. For most psychologists, development is restricted to child growth, to ontogenesis. We, in contrast, *view development more broadly as a mode of analysis of diverse aspects of person-in-environment functioning*. This mode of analysis encompasses not only ontogenesis, but also microgenesis (e.g., development of an idea or percept), pathogenesis (e.g., development of neuro- and psycho-pathology), phylogenesis (development of a species), and ethnogenesis (e.g., development of a culture).

Components (person, environment), relations among components (e.g., means–ends), and part-processes (e.g., cognition) of person-in-environment systems are assumed to be developmentally orderable in terms of the orthogenetic principle (Kaplan, 1959, 1967; Werner, 1948/1957, 1967). The orthogenetic principle defines development in terms of the degree of organization attained by a system. *The more differentiated and hierarchically integrated a system is, in terms of its parts and of its means and ends, the more highly developed it is said to be.* Optimal development entails a differentiated and hierarchically integrated person-in-environment system with flexibility, freedom, self-mastery, and the capacity to shift from one mode of person-in-environment relationship to another as required by goals, demands of the situation, and by the instrumentalities available (e.g., Kaplan, 1959, 1967; Wapner, 1987; Wapner & Demick, 1990).

The orthogenetic principle has also been specified with respect to a number of polarities that at one extreme (left) represent developmentally less advanced, and at the other (right) more advanced functioning (cf. Kaplan, 1959, 1967; Werner, 1948/1957; Werner & Kaplan, 1956). These polarities, using relevant examples from the traditional subfield of personality psychology, are as follows:

>   1. *Interfused to subordinated.* In the former, ends or goals are not sharply differentiated, and in the latter, functions are differentiated and hierarchized with drives and momentary states subordinated to more long-term goals. For example, for the impulse-ridden child, watching television is not differentiated from the need to complete a homework assignment (i.e., each is viewed as a short term goal); in contrast, the more developmentally advanced child differentiates and subordinates the short term goal (television watching) to the long term goal (doing well in school).
>
>   2. *Syncretic to discrete.* Syncretic refers to the merging of several mental phenomena, whereas discrete refers to functions, acts, and meanings that represent something specific and unambiguous. Syncretic thinking is represented, for example, by the schizophrenic's lack of differentiation between inner and outer experience (i.e., lack of separation of one's feelings from that of others); in contrast, discrete is exemplified by the normal adult's capacity for accurately distinguishing between one's own feelings and those of others.

3. *Diffuse to articulate.* Diffuse represents a relatively uniform, homogeneous structure with little differentiation of parts, whereas articulate refers to a structure where differentiated parts make up the whole. For example, diffuse is represented by the law of *pars pro toto* as is the case in the autistic individual's displeasure at variation from some routine set of behaviors; articulate is represented by the experience where distinguishable parts make up the whole, each contributing to, yet being distinguishable from, the whole.

4. *Rigid to flexible.* Rigid refers to behavior that is fixed and not readily changeable, whereas flexible refers to behavior that is readily changeable, or plastic. Rigid is exemplified by the obsessive compulsive's perseveration, ceremoniousness, changeability, and routine behavior; flexible implies the capacity to change depending on the context and particular arrangements of a given situation.

5. *Labile to stable.* Finally, labile refers to the fluidity and inconsistency that go along with changeability, whereas stable refers to the consistency or unambiguity that occurs with fixed properties. For example, lability is evident in the behavior of the histrionic personality, who characteristically displays rapidly shifting and shallow expression of emotions.

As noted earlier, although several contributors have attempted to introduce developmental theories within their conceptualizations, few have done so utilizing systematic developmental principles. As an exception, Walsh and Holland (1992) evoked the developmental notion of differentiation when they note that an individual who resembles many types of environments is undifferentiated, or in their usage, poorly defined with respect to the self. Furthermore, we argue that significant advances in theory and method may obtain were investigators to incorporate developmental beliefs into their theorizing. For example, Swindle and Moos (1992) attempted to integrate a stress and coping framework with an ecologically life domains perspective. Although they acknowledged numerous life domains (e.g., work, friends, marriage, children, extended family) and raised important questions as to possible relationships among them, there is no systematic organization of these life domains vis-a-vis, for example, the orthogenetic principle.

Adaptation

We conceptualize *adaptation as a congruent person-in-environment system state consisting of optimal relationships between the person and his or her environment.* This stands in marked contrast to those approaches that conceptualize adaptation as either the general adaptation level of the person (Helson, 1948) or adaptation of the individual to a particular sociocultural context, such as the family (e.g., Minuchin, 1974) or society at large (e.g., Vygotsky, 1978).

Conceptions of adaptation somewhat similar to our own have been echoed by several authors in volume I of *Person–Environment Psychology*. For example, Walsh and Holland's (1992) theory of personality types and work environments " ... assumes that behavior is a function of the *match* or *congruence* between an individual's personality and psychological environment." (p. 35) Pervin's (1992) research in person–environment psychology also focused on the match, or fit, between undergraduate student characteristics and college characteristics. Specifically, his hypothesis was:

> the size of the discrepancy between the individual's AI (needs) and the CCI (press) would be associated with the size of the discrepancy between the student's predicted and actual performance, increases in health difficulties, and dissatisfaction with college. (p. 73)

However, what distinguishes our concept of adaptation from that of the others' lies in our underlying world view and corresponding analytic strategy. That is, whereas other authors have attempted, literally, to match characteristics of the individual (e.g., personality types, needs) with characteristics of the environment (e.g., environmental types, press), our transactional approach—that advocates that the parts, the person and the environment, must be treated relationally as parts of one whole—has alternatively led to the assessment of adaptation through examination of the structural characteristics of the person-in-environment system as a whole.

Individual Differences

There is a major difference in the concept of individual differences between our approach and all of the others. That is, several approaches either interpret individual differences as a source of error or as manifest in different personality dimensions (e.g., Walsh & Holland, 1992) or psychopathological states (e.g., Pervin, 1992). In contrast, we see individual differences as contributing to a differential developmental psychology that is complementary to a general developmental psychology.

Our developmental analysis of self-world relationships utilizing the orthogenetic principle may be applied to describe individual differences in a broad variety of content areas and modes of coping. One approach to formulating individual differences according to this developmental scheme was presented by Apter (1976). Specifically, she studied some relations between an individual's formulation of plans for leaving an environment and his or her coping with discrepancies between the expectation and the actuality of environmental transactions. Planning groups included college seniors with clearly articulated plans as to what they would do after graduation; and others with no such plans.

In terms that are developmentally orderable with respect to the orthogenetic principle, status of plans was related to modes of coping as follows:

1. *Dedifferentiated P-in-E state.* The senior without plans coped with transactional conflict by *accommodation*; where a student who expected the facilities to work properly took no action, conforming outwardly to "fit in" with the environmental conflict between expectation and actuality;

2. *Differentiated and isolated P-in-E state.* The senior in process of making plans, somewhat less invested in and more differentiated from the environment, coped by *disengagement*; distancing himself or herself from the environment by mocking it;

3. *Differentiated and in conflict P-in-E state.* The senior, again without completely articulated plans, kicks a washing machine that is the source of the conflict and copes with frustration, anger, and disappointment through general usage of the strategy of *nonconstructive ventilation*; and

4. *Differentiated and hierarchically integrated P-in-E state.* The senior with securely established and highly articulated plans handles transactional conflict by *constructive assertion*; that is, with coping by planned action where he or she is less dominated by emotions, and engaged in a hierarchically integrated self-world relationship.

Among the contributors included in this volume, Heyman and Dweck's (1992) concept of individual differences is most consistent with our own. That is, within the framework of a general developmental psychology (e.g., focusing on the general problem of adaptive motivation), these researchers have identified individual differences between those who view failure in terms of learning goals (emphasizing the development of competencies) versus performance goals (emphasizing the evaluation of competence). Whereas the former maintain a mastery-oriented response following failure (obstacles viewed as an occasion for learning), the latter often exhibit a helpless motivational reaction that leads to debilitation.

Multiple Worlds

Another approach to individual differences concerns our assumption of multiple worlds. In our culture, different yet related experiential worlds

(Schutz, 1971), or spheres of activity, consist of the *multiple worlds of family, work, school, recreation, community, etc.* Each of these worlds usually occupies distinct spatio-temporal regions, involves different sets of people, and operates according to different sets of rules. For us, empirical issues concern the relative centrality of these worlds in the individual's life, the relationship of these worlds to each other, and the manner of movement from one world to another. In line with the orthogenetic principle, we ask whether the worlds are relatively fused, relatively isolated, in conflict, or integrated with one another. For example, critical person-in-environment transitions are often initiated when there is acquisition of a new world (e.g., beginning a new job), replacement of one world by another (e.g., migration to a new country), or excision or deletion of one world (e.g., retirement).

Relevant here are two methods that have been used to explore the nature of these worlds and the relations among them. One method was used by Hornstein and Wapner (1985) in a study on retirement. It utilized a questionnaire consisting of various parts designed to assess the structural relationship between the participant's work world and other social worlds. The first part asked participants to identify the experiential worlds they saw as central to their lives, and to choose from schematic diagrams (e.g., showing separation, overlap, etc. of worlds). The second part involved asking a series of questions designed to assess the importance for the participant of five experiential worlds (work, family, friends, community, and recreation), and the structural relationship among them as experienced by the respondent. Each participant was categorized as belonging to one of three structural categories, namely, isolated, moderate, or close degree of integration between work and other worlds. According to Hornstein and Wapner (1985), the findings of these procedures, together with extensive interviews using phenomenological methods, provided "four distinct ways of conceptualizing and experiencing retirement—as a transition to old age, as a new beginning, as a continuation of preretirement life structure, and as an imposed disruption" (p. 291).

A second method utilized what has been called a Psychological Distance Map for people (PDM, Wapner, 1977). It consists of putting names of persons in small circles on a piece of paper at varying distances from another circle labeled "me." Instructions are given to place the circles so that the closer to the "me" circle, the greater the relative importance of the person in the added circle to the participant, and also to number the sequence of entry of the added circles. After this is completed, the participant is interviewed concerning the entries on his or her PDM with respect to factors such as range, direction, content, location, and connections among persons represented.

One analysis focused on the person's environmental origin over the course of a six-month exposure to a new university environment (Wapner, 1978). Among other findings, it was evident that the number of entries from the home "world" decreased significantly with time, whereas the number of entries from the university "world" increased markedly. Moreover, the number of participants reporting at least some home to university connections increased significantly over time, which points to the integration of the home and school worlds from the perspective of the student undergoing the transition to college. (See Minami, 1985 for an elaboration of the use of the PDM for studying social networks.)

We also distinguish *mytho-poetic*, *ordinary-pragmatic*, and *scientific-conceptual* attitudes as well as the experienced worlds corresponding to these attitudes. Consider the experience of thunder. As an aspect of the mytho-poetic world, thunder has expressive qualities: it is personally threatening, bodes ill, and is ominous. As part of the ordinary pragmatically viewed world, thunder may signal impending rain and remind the individual to take a course of action to avoid being struck by lightning. As a phenomenon in the scientific world, thunder is viewed as occurring in specifiable, objective circumstances, and has general features such as its intensity that may be defined, measured, and investigated. These worlds may be analyzed similarly to multiple worlds. For example, we might examine: the *patterns* of an individual's experienced worlds (e.g., dedifferentiated, differentiated and isolated or in conflict, differentiated and hierarchically integrated); the *centrality* of a particular reality in his or her total experience (e.g., a scientifically oriented person with an artistic side); individual differences in the *dominant*, overall character of the experienced world at a particular time and the relative *salience* of each mytho-poetic, practical, and scientific aspect; and the individual's relative *control* over shifts between these general attitudes.

Our assumption of multiple worlds is most compatible with the work of Swindle and Moos (1992). That is, these researchers focus on life stressors and social resources in various *life domains* and their association with health outcomes. In this regard (cf. also Wicker, 1992, on the related concept of the behavior setting), Swindle and Moos (1992) noted that:

> Daily life is a mosaic of potentially interdependent life settings and relationships. As an individual moves from work to home to play, the "personal community" (Fischer, 1982) is composed of a variety of people in different settings, and different goals and rewards are salient in each setting. Modern life offers a wealth of potential life domains within which a person can realize a variety of personal agendas. (p. 4)

Although our concept of multiple worlds and Swindle and Moos' concept of life domains appear almost identical, there is a major difference in terms of the ways they are analyzed. That is, Swindle and Moos have assessed life domains with respect to content categories; namely, relationship dimensions, goal orientation or personal growth dimensions, and system maintenance and change dimensions. Alternatively, as noted earlier, our approach has characteristically advocated structural analyses aimed at assessing the relations among worlds.

THEORY OF ACTION

In line with Walsh, Craik, and Price (1992), we believe an important problem related to the transactions of the person with the environment concerns the relations between experience and action. This problem has entered into our paradigmatic studies of critical person-in-environment transitions where we have attempted to study the change from wanting to do something (i.e., intentionality) to doing it (i.e., carrying out the action). Here, based on the musical instrument metaphor (tuning vs. activating inputs) that Turvey (1977) employed in analyzing neurophysiological processes, we have examined: usage of automobile safety belts prior to and following mandatory legislation (e.g., Demick, Inoue, Wapner, Ishii, Minami, Nishiyama, & Yamamoto, 1992); initiating a diet regime (Raeff, 1990); abstention from the use of alcohol (Agli, 1992); and abstention from the use of tobacco (Tirelli, 1992). For example, tuning corresponds to the category we have described as *general factors*, which may be necessary but not sufficient for action (e.g., in the case of automobile safety belt usage, a basic belief in the need for safety belts; in the case of dieting, sociocultural pressure to be thin). Activating corresponds to our second category of *precipitating events* (*specific precursors* or *triggers*), which serve as the initiators of action (e.g., in the case of seat belt usage, wanting to serve as a role model for children in the car; in the case of dieting, seeing oneself in a videotape of a social occasion). Thus, the translation of experience to action requires both general factors and specific precipitating events.

Furthermore, because the goals and instrumentalities governing action differ at the various levels of integration (biological, psychological, sociocultural), we have attempted to develop systematic, holistic constructs accounting for relations between and among levels. Utilizing Wapner's (1969) earlier application of these categories to relations among cognitive processes, we have documented that the relations between any two levels (e.g., the individual and society) may be: *supportive* (e.g., personal opinion about safety belt usage and public policy coincide); *antagonistic* (e.g., personal opinion and public policy are antithetical); or *substitutive/vicarious* (e.g., substituting the good of society for one's own desires). Such conceptualization has the potential to shed light on important questions concerning experience and action such as: What are the mechanisms that underlie the ways rules and regulations at the sociocultural level (e.g., environmental conservation) become translated into individual functioning at the psychological level (e.g., energy usage, recycling)? Conversely, how does the need for the quality of human functioning at the biological (e.g., physical health) and psychological (e.g., life satisfaction) levels become actualized at the sociocultural level (cf. Demick & Wapner, 1990)?

Little's (1987) work on personal projects represents one body of research that is concerned with the relationship between experience and action. However, in contradistinction to our approach that attempts to assess the ways in which intentionality and experience become translated into action, Little emphasized the assessment of "intentional action in context" and in so doing, was concerned with the end product of the translation in and of itself.

Reinforcement and Other Underlying Processes

Although reinforcement (Walsh, Craik, & Price, 1992) neither enters as a central feature of the perspective nor is directly handled, it may clearly operate as one of the many processes underlying change in the equilibrial status of the person-in-environment system. Because our focus on change is characterized developmentally (e.g., a developmentally advanced person-in-environment system state is described as differentiated and hierarchically integrated), we are concerned with processes that underlie the achievement of that state, and reinforcement may be one of a variety of processes that operate toward achieving that end. This is consistent with Werner's (1957) distinction between process and achievement: For example, although two children may obtain the same IQ scores on a standardized intelligence test, the underlying processes that they have utilized toward obtaining their final answers most probably reflect different patterns of cognitive assets and liabilities.

Problem Formulation and Methodology

We see Walsh, Craik, and Price's (1992) issue of prediction in person–environment psychology as follows. Prediction is linked to the general perspective of *natural science* that focuses on: observable behavior and explanation in

terms of cause–effect relationships; an analytic analysis that begins with parts
and assumes that the whole can be understood through addition of those elements; the adoption of scientific experimentation as the appropriate methodology. In contrast, the *human science* perspective (e.g., Giorgi, 1970),
Wapner (1987) believed:

> specifies as its goal the understanding of experience or the explication of struc-
> tural relationships, pattern, or organization that specifies meaning ... adopts
> the descriptive method ... seeks detailed analysis of limited numbers of cases
> that are presumably prototypic of larger classes of events ... carries out qualita-
> tive analysis through naturalistic observation, empirical, and
> phenomenological methods. (p. 1434)

As we see it, because explication makes focal the meaning of a phenomenon or what is explained and causal explanation focuses on underlying process (e.g., the question of "how" and under what conditions developmental
transformation is reversed, arrested, or advanced), both approaches have advantages and limitations. While the "natural science" approach may be characterized by precision and reliability, it may also suffer from lack of validity; in
contrast, while the "human science" approach may be characterized by validity, it may suffer from lack of precision and reliability. Accordingly, both of
these approaches to understanding complement each other and should be
fostered.

For us, a central issue concerns when these methods should be used. This
depends on the level of complexity of the phenomenon under investigation.
Phenomena on the level of complex features of human experience—where
manipulation and control of conditions is not possible—may more appropriately be analyzed by human science methods; in contrast, less complex and
more simplified phenomena where conditions can be manipulated and controlled may be appropriately addressed by the methods of natural science.
Moreover, the integration of both qualitative and quantitative aspects of
methodology, such as rating scales, followed by open-ended questions as to
the basis for the ratings, and drawings of the development of a cognitive spatial organization followed by an inquiry concerning starting point, sequence,
and mode of sketch map construction (see Schouela, Steinberg, Leveton, &
Wapner, 1980), provides a more complete picture of experience and behavior
than either of the approaches independently.

Furthermore, as Wapner and Demick (1998) described, we too strongly
believe that:

holistic, ecologically oriented research is a necessary complement to more traditional laboratory work and that it should be conducted through reducing the number of focal individuals ... studied rather than the number and kind of interrelationships among aspects of the person, of the environment, and of the systems to which they belong. In addition to helping us conceptualize problems that are more in line with the complex character of everyday life, such reframing may also help psychology both to see itself and to be seen by others as a unified science, that is, one concerned not only with the study of isolated aspects of human functioning, but also with the study of problems that cut across various aspects of persons and various aspects of environments. (cf. Demick & Wapner, 1988a; Wapner, 1977)

Several contributors to these volumes share our methodological eclecticism. In this regard, most notable is the work of Wicker (1992), who attempts to integrate traditional research paradigms with naturalistic alternatives (e.g., humanistic, existential, phenomenological theories and methods) within his elaborated ecological perspective; and Peterson (1992) who, in his study of interpersonal relationships, advocates the use of multiple methodologies (e.g., descriptive research, true experiments, natural experiments, single subject designs, interviews, interaction records). It is noteworthy that Peterson's position grew out of his work as a clinical psychologist; here, we share his sentiment that, in all research, theory and praxis should be "flip sides of the same coin" and that the clinical method has the potential to complement significantly more traditional methods of research (cf. also Ozer, 1986; Stokols, 1992).

FUTURE DIRECTIONS

While the perspective described herein is embedded in a long history, there remains the potential for its further development, as well as the manifestation of its heuristic implications for uncovering and shaping significant research problems that have both theoretical and practical value for the burgeoning subfield of person–environment psychology. Some directions for future research are presented synoptically here (for more complete discussions, see Wapner & Demick, 1998, 1999).

> 1. *Levels of integration.* Any theory that attempts to integrate person and environment may benefit from a holistic conceptualization of both. Thus, the person is comprised of biological–physical, psychological–intrapersonal, and sociocultural aspects; analogously, the environment may be seen as having physical, interpersonal, and sociocultural

aspects. In light of more recent research in the field of personality, advances in a holistic conception of the person may be made through further delineation and subsequent integration of such concepts as the self, representation of the past, and social representation of person–environment episodes. Analogously, the multidimensional concept of environment might be further delineated in light of burgeoning research in the field of environmental psychology. More research is needed not only on the relationship between levels at any given point in time, but on how the relationships between and among levels change developmentally; for example, ontogenetically, microgenetically, and pathogenetically.

2. *Critical person-in-environment transitions*. Our category system used in identifying sites where perturbations may initiate critical person-in-environment transitions (i.e., at the biological, psychological, sociocultural levels of the person or the physical, interpersonal, sociocultural levels of the environment). Such research has the potential to augment our understanding of the holistic functioning of person-in-environment systems across the life span, as we see it a critical problem for the subfield of person–environment psychology.

3. *Planning*. Our approach has also suggested that the systematic study of the cognitive process of planning (defined by Wapner & Cirillo, 1973, as "a symbolic preparatory action in that the planner conceives of, imagines a method independently of carrying out the concrete actions embodying that method"), has the potential to advance our understanding of the goal-directed nature of person-in-environment functioning.

4. *Valuative processes*. Although researchers have typically assessed cognitive, affective, and behavioral processes within the person aspect of the person-in-environment system, we advocate that inclusion of the psychological part-process of valuation (prioritizing) may shed light on the holistic aspect of person-in-environment functioning.

5. *Experience and action*. More attempts are needed to demonstrate how individual experience becomes translated into concrete action; for example, using our conceptualization of the relationship between experience (intentionality) and action provides a treasury of open problems for research. Related to this problem is the general notion of relationships within and among levels of integration.

6. *Conditions facilitating developmental change*. It seems relevant for person–environment psychology to ask what conditions and processes suggest directions for fostering developmental progression. From our own work, a number of these (although not exclusive) may include: self-world distancing (e.g., embedding emotional material in the distant past); anchor point (e.g., physical or interpersonal home base from

which to explore new environments); reculer pour mieux sauter (literally, 'draw back to leap'; implies the spiral nature of development); triggers to action (e.g., specific precursors to action activated by the immediate environmental context); and individual differences (toward a differential psychology in the context of a general developmental psychology). See Wapner and Demick (1998) for a more complete discussion of these.

7. *Robust personality factors.* To what extent are our categories of self–world relationships, (namely, *dedifferentiated, differentiated and isolated, differentiated and in conflict, differentiated and hierarchically integrated* person-in-environment systems) related to the Five-Factor model of personality (McCrae & Costa, 1987) that considers *extraversion, agreeableness, conscientiousness, emotional stability,* and *openness* (cf. Walsh, Craik, & Price, 1992)?

8. *Reconceptualization of personality and of psychopathology.* What are the implications of transactional models of person–environment psychology for reconceptualizing individual personality and psychopathology? Do these models imply continuity or discontinuity between normal and abnormal person-in-environment functioning? What are the implications of these models not only for individual functioning, but also, for example, for familial and/or organizational personality and psychopathology?

9. *Integration of psychology as a whole.* In what ways does the development of the subfield of person–environment psychology aid in integrating the rather disparate field of psychology as a whole? What are the implications of person–environment psychology for clinical, developmental, experimental, personality, and social psychology? Can we generate integrative or grand theories of person–environment functioning that demonstrate the powerful roles of both context and development? As we see it, the answers to these and related questions have the potential to occupy researchers in the field of person–environment psychology for some time to come and ultimately to shed light on the holistic functioning of person-in-environment systems across the life span.

REFERENCES

Agli, S. (1992). *General factors and precipitating events involved in the cessation of alcohol consumption among college women.* Honor's thesis, Worcester, MA: Clark University.
Ainsworth, M. D., Blehar, M., Waters, E., & Wall, S. (1978). *Patterns of attachment.* Hillsdale, NJ: Lawrence Erlbaum Associates.
Altman, I. (1975). *The environment and social behavior.* Pacific Grove, CA: Brooks/Cole.
Altman, I. (1997). Environment and behavior studies: A discipline? Not a discipline? Becoming a discipline? In S. Wapner, J. Demick, T. Yamamoto, & T. Takahashi (Eds.), *Handbook*

of Japan–U.S. environment behavior research: Toward a transactional approach (pp. 423–434). New York: Plenum.

Altman, I., Brown, B. B., Staples, B., & Werner, C. M. (1992). A transactional approach to close relationships: Courtship, weddings, and placemaking. In W. B. Walsh, K. H. Craik, & R. H. Price (Eds.), *Person–environment psychology: Models and perspectives* (pp. 193–241). Hillsdale, NJ: Lawrence Erlbaum Associates.

Altman, I., & Rogoff, B. (1987). World views in psychology: Trait, interactional, organismic, and transactional perspectives. In D. Stokols & I. Altman (Eds.), *Handbook of environmental psychology* (Vol. 1, pp. 1–40). New York: Wiley.

Apter, D. (1976). *Modes of coping with conflict in the presently inhabited environment as a function of variation in plans to move to a new environment.* Unpublished master's thesis, Worcester, MA: Clark University.

Asch, S. E. (1955). Opinions and social pressure. *Scientific American, 193,* 31–35.

Barker, R. G. (1968). *Ecological psychology: Concepts and methods for studying the environment of human behavior.* Stanford, CA: Stanford University Press.

Bronfenbrenner, U. (1977). Toward an experimental ecology of human development. *American Psychologist, 32,* 513–531.

Buss, D. (1995). Evolutionary psychology: A new paradigm for psychological science. *Psychological Inquiry, 6*(1), 1–30.

Cantril, H. (1950). *The why of man's experience.* New York: Macmillan.

Carini, L. P. (1965). *An experimental investigation of perceptual behavior in schizophrenics.* Doctoral dissertation, Clark University, Microfilm No. 13009.

Ciottone, R., Demick, J., Pacheco, A., Quirk, M., & Wapner, S. (1980, November). *Children's transition from home to nursery school: The integration of two cultures.* Paper presented at the annual meeting of the American Association of Psychiatric Services for Children, New Orleans, LA.

Dandonoli, P., Demick, J., & Wapner, S. (1990). Physical arrangement and age as determinants of environmental representation. *Children's Environments Quarterly, 7*(1), 26–36.

Demick, J., & Wapner, S. (1980). Effects of environmental relocation upon members of a psychiatric therapeutic community. *Journal of Abnormal Psychology, 89,* 444–452.

Demick, J., & Wapner, S. (1988a). Children-in-environments: Physical, interpersonal, and sociocultural aspects. *Children's Environments Quarterly, 5*(3), 54–62.

Demick, J., & Wapner, S. (1988b). Open and closed adoption: A developmental conceptualization. *Family Process, 27*(2), 229–249.

Demick, J., & Wapner, S. (1990). Role of psychological science in promoting environmental quality: Introduction. *American Psychologist, 45*(5), 631–632.

Demick, J., Inoue, W., Wapner, S., Ishii, S., Minami, H., Nishiyama, S., & Yamamoto, T. (1992). Cultural differences in impact of governmental legislation: Automobile safety belt usage. *Journal of Cross-Cultural Psychology, 23*(4), 468–487.

Des Lauriers, A. (1962). *The experience of reality in childhood schizophrenia.* New York: International Universities Press.

Dewey, J., & Bentley, A. F. (1949). *Knowing and the known.* Boston: Beacon.

Endler, N. S., & Magnusson, D. (1976). Toward an interactional psychology of personality. *Psychological Bulletin, 83,* 956–979.

Feibelman J. K. (1954). Theory of integrative levels. *British Journal of Philosophy of Science, 5,* 59–66.

Fischer, C. S. (1982). *To dwell among friends: Personal networks in town and city.* Chicago: University of Chicago Press.

Giorgi, A. (1970). Towards a phenomenologically based research in psychology. *Journal of Phenomenological Psychology, 1,* 75–98.

Hanson, K., & Wapner, S. (1994). Transition to retirement: Gender differences. *International Journal on Aging and Human Development, 39*(3), 189–208.

Helson, H. (1948). Adaptation level as basis for a quantitative theory frame of reference. *Psychological Review, 55,* 297–313.

Herrick, C. J. (1949). A biological survey of integrative levels. In R. W. Sellars, V. J. McGill, & M. Farber (Eds.), *Philosophy for the future* (pp. 222–242). New York: Macmillan.

Heyman, G. D., & Dweck, C. (1992). Achievement goals and intrinsic motivation: Their relation and their role in adaptive motivation. *Motivation and Emotion, 16*(3), 231–247.

Hogan, R. (1982). A socioanalytic theory of personality. In M. Page (Ed.), *Nebraska symposium on motivation, Vol. 30.* Lincoln: University of Nebraska Press.

Hornstein, G., & Wapner, S. (1984). The experience of the retiree's social network during the transition to retirement. In C. M. Aanstoos (Ed.), *Exploring the lived world: Readings in phenomenogical psychology* (pp. 119–136). Atlanta: Georgia College Press.

Hornstein, G., & Wapner, S. (1985). Modes of experiencing and adapting to retirement. *International Journal on Aging and Human Development, 21*(4), 291–315.

Ittelson, W. H. (1973). Environmental perception and contemporary perceptual theory. In W. H. Ittelson (Ed.), *Environment and cognition* (pp. 1–19). New York: Seminar Press.

Kaplan, B. (1959). The study of language in psychiatry. In S. Arieti (Ed.), *American handbook of psychiatry* (Vol. 3, pp. 659–668). New York: Basic Books.

Kaplan, B. (1967). Meditations on genesis. *Human Development, 10,* 65–87.

Kaplan, E. (1952). *An experimental study on inner speech as contrasted with external speech.* Unpublished master's thesis, Clark University, Worcester, MA.

Koffka, K. (1935). *Principles of gestalt psychology.* New York: Harcourt Brace.

Kuntz, P. G. (1968). *The concept of order.* Seattle: University of Washington Press.

Lavine, T. (1950a). Knowledge as interpretation: An historical survey. *Philosophy and Phenomenological Research, 10,* 526–540.

Lavine, T. (1950b). Knowledge as interpretation: An historical survey. *Philosophy and Phenomenological Research, 11,* 80–103.

Lewin, K. (1935). *A dynamic theory of personality.* New York: McGraw Hill.

Lewontin, R. C. (1994). *Inside and outside: Gene, environment and organism.* Heinz Werner Lecture Series (Vol. XX). Worcester, MA: Clark University Press.

Liebert, R., Werner, H., & Wapner, S. (1958). Studies in the effect of lysergic acid diethylamide. *Archives of Neurology and Psychiatry, 79,* 580–584.

Little, R. B. (1987). Personality and the environment. In D. Stokols & I. Altman (Eds.), *Handbook of Environmental Psychology* (Vol. 1, pp. 206–244). New York: Wiley.

Magnusson, D., & Torestad, B. (1992). The individual as an interactive agent in the environment. In W. B. Walsh, K. H. Craik, & R. H. Price (Eds.), *Person–environment psychology: Models and perspectives* (pp. 89–126). Hillsdale, NJ: Lawrence Erlbaum Associates.

Maslow, A. H. (1946). Problem-centering versus means-centering in science. *Philosophy of Science, 13,* 326–331.

Mayo, M., Pastor, J. C., & Wapner, S. (1995). Linking organizational behavior and environmental psychology. *Environment and Behavior, 27*(1), 73–89.

McCrae, R. R., & Costa, P. T. (1987). Validation of the five-factor model of personality across instruments and observers. *Journal of Personality and Social Psychology, 52,* 81–89.

Minami, H. (1985). *Establishment and transformation of personal networks during the first year of college: A developmental analysis.* Unpublished PhD dissertation, Clark University, Worcester, MA.

Minuchin, S. (1974). *Families and family therapy.* Cambridge, MA: Harvard University Press.

Mischel, W. (1973). Toward a cognitive social learning reconceptualization of personality. *American Psychologist, 80,* 252–283.

Nasar, J. L., & Fisher, B. (1993). "Hot spots" of fear and crime: A multi-method investigation. *Journal of Environmental Psychology, 13*, 187–206.

Novikoff, A. (1945a). The concept of integrative levels and biology. *Science, 101*, 209–215.

Novikoff, A. (1945b). Continuity and discontinuity in evolution. *Science, 102*, 405–406.

Ozer, D. J. (1986). *Consistency in personality: A methodological framework.* New York: Springer-Verlag.

Pepper, S. C. (1942). *World hypotheses.* Berkeley: University of California Press.

Pepper, S. C. (1967). *Concept and quality: A world hypothesis.* LaSalle, IL: Open Court.

Pervin, L. A. (1992). Transversing the individual-environment landscape: A personal odyssey. In W. B. Walsh, K. H. Craik, & R. H. Price (Eds.), *Person–environment psychology: Models and perspectives* (pp. 71–87). Hillsdale, NJ: Lawrence Erlbaum Associates.

Peterson, D. R. (1992). Interpersonal relationships as a link between person and environment. In W. B. Walsh, K. H. Price, & R. H. Price (Eds.), *Person–environment psychology: Models and perspectives* (pp. 127–155). Hillsdale, NJ: Lawrence Erlbaum Associates.

Proshansky, H. M., Ittelson, W. H., & Rivlin, L. G. (Eds.). (1970). *Environmental psychology: Man and his physical setting.* New York: Holt, Rinehart & Winston.

Raeff, C. (1990). *General factors and precipitating events influencing action: Initiation of a weight loss regimen.* Unpublished master's thesis, Clark University, Worcester, MA.

Sameroff, A. (1975). Transactional models in early social relations. *Human Development, 18*, 65–79.

Sameroff, D. J. (1983). Developmental systems: Contexts and evolution. In P. H. Mussen (Ed.), *Handbook of child psychology* (Vol. 1, pp. 237–294). New York: Wiley.

Schneider, B. (1987). The people make the place. *Personnel Psychology, 40*, 437–453.

Schneirla, T. C. (1949). Levels in the psychological capacity of animals. In R. W. Sellars, V. J. McGill, & M. Farber (Eds.), *Philosophy for the future* (pp. 243–286). New York: MacMillan.

Schouela, D. A., Steinberg, L. M., Leveton, L. B., & Wapner, S. (1980). Development of the cognitive organization of an environment. *Canadian Journal of Behavioural Science, 12*, 1–16.

Schutz, A. (1971). *Collected papers, Vols. I–III.* (M. Natanson, Ed.). The Hague, Netherlands: Nijhoff.

Stokols, D. (1992). Environmental quality, human development, and health: An ecological view. *Journal of Applied Developmental Psychology, 13*, 121–124.

Swindle, R. W., & Moos, R. H. (1992). Life domains in stressors, coping, and adjustment. In W, B. Walsh, K. H. Craik, & R. H. Price (Eds.), *Person–environment psychology: Models and perspectives* (pp. 1–33). Hillsdale, NJ: Lawrence Erlbaum Associates.

Tirelli, L. (1992). *Resistance from and attempts to stop smoking.* Unpublished manuscript, Clark University, Worcester, MA.

Turvey, M. T. (1977). Preliminaries to a theory of action with reference to vision. In R. Shaw & J. Bransford (Eds.), *Perceiving, acting, and knowing* (pp. 211–265). Hillsdale, NJ: Lawrence Erlbaum Associates.

von Uexkull, J. (1957). A stroll through the world of animals and men. In C. H. Schiller (Ed.), *Instinctive behavior.* New York: International Universities Press.

Vygotsky, L. S. (1978). *Mind in society: The development of higher psychological processes.* Cambridge, MA: Harvard University Press.

Walsh, W. B., & Holland, J. L. (1992). A theory of personality types and work environments. In W. B. Walsh, K. H. Craik, & R. H. Price (Eds.), *Person–environment psychology: Models and perspectives* (pp. 35–69). Hillsdale, NJ: Lawrence Erlbaum Associates.

Walsh, W. B., Craik, K. H., & Price, R. H. (1992). Person-environment psychology: A summary and commentary. In W. B. Walsh, K. H. Craik, & R. H. Price (Eds.), *Person–environment psychology: Models and perspectives* (pp. 243–269). Hillsdale, NJ: Lawrence Erlbaum Associates.

Wandersman, A. (1990). Dissemination. In P. Tolan, C. Keys, F. Cherntak, & L. Jason (Eds.), *Researching community psychology: Issues of theory and methods*. Washington, DC: American Psychological Association.

Wapner, S. (1969). Organismic–developmental theory: Some applications to cognition. In J. Langer, P. Mussen, & N. Covington (Eds.), *Trends and issues in developmental theory* (pp. 35–67). New York: Holt, Reinhart, & Winston.

Wapner, S. (1977). Environmental transition: A research paradigm deriving from the organismic–developmental systems approach. In L. van Ryzin (Ed.), *Proceedings of the Wisconsin Conference on Research Methods in Behavior–Environment Studies* (pp. 1–9). Madison: University of Wisconsin Press.

Wapner, S. (1978). Some critical person–environment transitions. *Hiroshima Forum for Psychology, 5*, 3–20.

Wapner, S. (1981). Transactions of person-in-environments: Some critical transactions. *Journal of Environmental Psychology, 1*, 233–239.

Wapner, S. (1987). A holistic, developmental, systems-oriented environmental psychology: Some beginnings. In D. Stokols & I. Altman (Eds.), *Handbook of environmental psychology* (pp. 1433–1465). New York: Wiley.

Wapner, S., & Cirillo, L. (1973). *Development of planning*. Public Health Service Grant Application, Clark University, Worcester, MA.

Wapner, S., & Demick, J. (1990). Development of experience and action; Levels of integration in human functioning. In G. Greenberg & E. Tobach (Eds.), *Theories of the evolution of knowing: The T. C. Schneirla conference series, Vol. 4* (pp. 47–68). Hillsdale, NJ: Lawrence Erlbaum Associates.

Wapner, S., & Demick, J. (1992). The organismic-developmental, systems approach to the study of critical person-in-environment transitions through the life span. In T. Yamamoto & S. Wapner (Eds.), *Developmental psychology of life transitions* (pp. 243–265). Tokyo, Japan: Kyodo Shuppan.

Wapner, S., & Demick, J. (1998). Developmental analysis: A holistic, developmental, systems-oriented perspective. In W. Damon (Series Ed.) & R. M. Lerner (Vol. Ed.), *Handbook of child psychology: Vol. 1. Theoretical models of human development* (5th ed., pp. 761–805). New York: Wiley.

Wapner, S., & Demick, J. (1999). Developmental theory and clinical psychology: A holistic, developmental, systems-oriented approach. In W. K. Silverman & T. H. Ollendick (Eds.), *Developmental issues in the clinical treatment of children and adolescents* (pp. 3–30). Needham Heights, MA: Allyn & Bacon.

Wapner, S., Demick, J., & Damrad, R. (1988, April). *Transition to retirement: Eight years after*. Paper presented at the annual meetings of the Eastern Psychological Association, Buffalo, NY.

Wapner, S., & Werner, H. (1957). *Perceptual development*. Worcester, MA: Clark University Press.

Wapner, S., Demick, J., & Redondo, J. P. (1990). Cherished possessions and adaptation of older people to nursing homes. *International Journal on Aging and Human Development, 31*(3), 299–315.

Wapner, S., Kaplan, B., & Cohen, S. (1973). An organismic-developmental perspective for understanding transactions of men in environments. *Environment and Behavior, 5*, 255–289.

Werner, H. (1926). *Einführung in die Entwicklungpsychologie*. Leipzig: Barth (2nd ed., 1933; 3rd ed., 1953; 4th ed., 1959).

Werner, H. (1948/1957). *Comparative psychology of mental development*. New York: International Universities Press. (Originally published in German, 1926, in English, 1940)

Werner, H. (1957). The concept of development from a comparative, organismic point of view. In D. B. Harris (Ed.), *The concept of development: An issue in the study of human behavior.* Minneapolis: University of Minnesota Press.

Werner, H., & Kaplan, B. (1956). The developmental approach to cognition: Its relevance to the psychological interpretation of anthropological and ethnolinguistic data. *American Anthropologist, 58,* 866–880.

Werner, H., & Kaplan, B. (1963). *Symbol formation.* New York: Wiley.

Wicker, A. W. (1992). Making sense of environments. In W. B. Walsh, K. H. Craik, & R. H. Price (Eds.), *Person–environment psychology: Models and perspectives* (pp. 157–192). Hillsdale, NJ: Lawrence Erlbaum Associates.

3

Attraction–Selection–Attrition: Toward A Person–Environment Psychology of Organizations[1]

Benjamin Schneider
University of Maryland

D. Brent Smith
Cornell University

Harold W. Goldstein
Baruch College, CUNY

This chapter first presents a brief overview of four themes emerging from per-son- environment (P–E) fit research and theory that focus on: *the individual, affective outcomes of fit, positive consequences of good fit,* and the *"E" in "P–E"* comprised of nonperson attributes. Attraction–Selection–Attrition (ASA, Schneider, 1987) theory is introduced as an alternative perspective on P–E fit, one that focuses on organizations, effectiveness, emphasizes the potential negative consequences of good fit, and treats "E" as an outcome of the persons in the environment. A summary of recent research relevant to the critical propo-

[1]Work on this paper was facilitated by a Contract from the U. S. Army Research Institute for the Behavioral and Social Sciences (A. R. I.) to the first author. The paper represents the authors' approach to understanding organizations from a personality perspective; it should not be read to represent the opinions of A. R. I., the U. S. Army, or the Department of Defense.

sitions of ASA theory is provided, as are examinations of two recent studies directly testing the homogeneity proposition of ASA theory. Implications of ASA theory for continued research on individual differences in the context of organizational effectiveness are noted in the chapter's conclusion.

INTRODUCTION

Few concepts in the history of psychology transcend time, topic, and scholars. Topics such as the role of rewards in behavior, the nature of intellectual competencies, and the formation of personality do just that. The progenitors of psychology, as well as those claiming to make a significant contribution to the general field of psychology, have focused on these sorts of issues. These central topics have stirred considerable debate, and subsequently, stimulated a great deal of research yielding impressive (and voluminous) conceptual and empirical results.

One topic receiving perhaps more debate than all others, while remaining contentious, concerns the relative contribution of personal and situational attributes in understanding causes of behavior. Especially during the late 1960s (e.g., Mischel, 1968) and the 1970s (e.g., Bowers, 1973; Endler & Magnusson, 1976; Magnusson & Endler, 1977; Pervin & Lewis, 1978), this debate raged with most scholars in psychology eventually adopting some version of the interactional (person X situation) framework.

The interactional framework proposes that the behavior of people is a joint function of their personal characteristics, and the characteristics of the environment in which they function, in interaction. The interactional framework is the generic model where the more specific concept of person–environment (P–E) *fit* resides. The P–E fit framework goes beyond the interactional framework in its prediction by suggesting that behavior is understood based on the "fit" of person to an environment.

P–E fit theory and research has a long history in psychology. Murray (1938) is one of the first key figures in P–E fit theory and research. Murray's theory proposed a list of needs that required fulfillment, and also that environments could serve to facilitate or obstruct attainment of the needs of individuals. Murray spoke about environments in terms of positive and negative press; meaning that some environments had *positive press* (fit) or facilitated the attainment of needs (yielding satisfaction) whereas other environments had *negative press* and frustrated need fulfillment (yielding dissatisfaction). Another early theorist with a similar focus was Goldstein (1939) whose organismic theory emphasized the relationship between a person's qualities and the nature of the tasks they confront in the environment.

Interestingly, the concept of fit is quite evident in disciplines other than psychology. Consider, for example, Durkheim (1947), the father of modern sociology, on the concept of mechanical solidarity in his 1853 treatise, *The Division of Labor*:

> When a certain number of individuals ... are found to have ideas, interests, sentiments, and occupations not shared by the rest of the population, it is inevitable that they will be attracted toward each other under the influence of these likenesses. They will seek each other out, enter into relations, associate, and thus, little by little, a restricted group, having its special characteristics will be formed in the midst of the general society. (p. 14)

For Durkheim, the concept of fit was central to solidarity and essential for the emergence of culture.

In this chapter, we write about P–E fit from the perspective of work organizations; the environments of interest are formal work organizations and their components (jobs, functions, teams) rather than societal cultures (as in Durkheim), schools, or psychiatric wards (as in Moos, 1976). We first review contemporary organizational literature on person–environment fit and propose some emerging themes. Then, we present an alternative view of organization behavior based on the principles of P–E fit, the *Attraction–Selection–Attrition* (ASA) model (Schneider, 1987). The ASA model assumes an extreme, personological position (Schneider, 1989) on the nature of organizational behavior, a position that emphasizes attributes of people as defining characteristics of an organization and the foundation determinants of organizational behavior. Next, we present summaries of two recent studies carried out by Schneider and his colleagues (Simco & Schneider, 1997; Schneider, Smith, Taylor, & Fleenor, 1998) to test a central proposition of ASA theory—the hypothesis that over time, organizations tend toward homogeneity of personality. These studies offer partial support for the ASA concept that the modal personality of members of an organization, although the course of that homogeneity is still open to debate (Schneider et al., 1998).

PERSON–ENVIRONMENT FIT THEORY AND RESEARCH

Generally, P–E fit theorists propose that not only do both person and environment function to influence behavior, but it is the fit between these two concepts that is critical for understanding behavior. These theorists operationalize fit as some index of the degree of similarity, overlap, or convergence between a particular set of person-related attributes and a set of environment-related attributes. There are two broad approaches to theory and research concerning the person-environment fit nexus. One approach views aspects of the environment (or the person) as moderating relationships between the person (or environment) and some individual level criterion of interest. Hackman and Oldham's (1980) theory of work motivation is one example of a person variable moderating the relation between an environmental variable and a criterion. Hackman and Oldham proposed that jobs with high motivating potential yield increased levels of motivation, especially for people with strong higher order need strength. That is, the relation between job attributes and motivation is enhanced for people with strong higher order needs. Fiedler's (1967) leadership contingency theory is another prominent person-environment fit theory where individual level variables moderate environment-criterion relationships. Fiedler proposed that leaders will be effective to the degree that their own personality is conducive to the degree of *situation favorableness* they encounter in their environment.

The other approach to P-E fit theory views *fit* as a predictor of outcomes, such as an individual's vocational choice, adjustment, and long term satisfaction. Research typical of this approach examines multiple dimensions of person and environment simultaneously, indexes the degree that they fit, and uses that index as a predictor of various individual outcomes. Holland's (1985) theory of vocational choice is perhaps the most widely studied example of this approach. Holland proposed that people choose careers based on the perceived fit of their interests to different career environments. For Holland, the career environment is a function of the interests of the people in the career, making the career environment a direct function of the career interests of the people employed there. Holland (1985) described an interactive relationship between people and environments such that " ... the character of an environment reflects the nature of its members and the dominant features of an environment reflect the typical characteristics of its members" (p. 35).

Artistic careers, for example, are characterized by people who are complicated, disorderly, emotional, expressive, idealistic, imaginative, impractical, impulsive, and so forth (Holland, 1985, p. 21). Thus, environments peopled by artistic types stimulate people to engage in artistic activities, foster artistic competencies and achievements, encourage people to see themselves as they are (complicated, disorderly, emotional, expressive), and reward people for the display of artistic values (p. 38). There is a mutually reinforcing reciprocity between the nature of the environment and the people who choose particular careers—thus, a particular career environment emerges. Since the 1960s, research on Holland's theory (1985) has revealed that people seek and choose careers where their interests fit their career environment, and when they fit, they are more satisfied and better adjusted to their career; when they do not fit, they leave, and join career environments that are a better fit for them.

Holland's (1985) conceptualization of fit is but one of many contemporary P–E fit models. For example, the person–environment fit model that has received most recent attention in organizational science is the one proposed by Chatman (1989, 1991) and her colleagues (O'Reilly, Chatman, & Caldwell, 1991). In this research, the values of individuals (assessed prior to the time they join an organization) are compared to the culture of the organization they join. Organizational culture is operationalized in terms of the values incumbents ascribe to the organization (these values are the same ones that newcomers respond to; however, in this case, incumbents make attributions concerning organizational values and not their own, individual values). Research indicates that the stronger the fit between an individual's values and the organization's culture, the more satisfied, committed, and productive they are likely to be.

It is beyond the scope of this chapter to summarize all theories and literature with regard to P–E fit; others have focused on that task (c.f., Kristof, 1996). What we do want to consider are some of the key issues that have materialized with regard to P–E fit, and then to position ASA theory as one that addresses some of these concerns.

EMERGENT THEMES IN PERSON–ENVIRONMENT FIT THEORY AND RESEARCH

The briefly reviewed conceptualizations of person–environment fit theories, although clearly not exhaustive (see Kristof, 1996), reveal some common themes. First, there exists ambiguity in how fit may be operationalized. Recent articles by Edwards (1991) have encouraged alternatives to the ubiquitous *difference scores*. Difference scores are used to contrast a profile of the attributes of individuals with a profile of attributes of the environment, and (in its most common form), for each point in the respective profiles, the difference is calculated and squared. These squared differences are then summed (Cronbach & Gleser, 1953); larger sums represent poorer fit. Edwards (1991) recommended the use of a polynomial regression procedure, rather than Euclidean distance difference scores, because it simultaneously considers the main effects of the individual and the environmental variables and their interaction as potential correlates of a criterion of interest. Such a procedure, Edwards appropriately argued, permits researchers to apportion variance to main effects and interactions, thus, more fully understanding the importance of fit. However, the calculation of fit is, itself, but one of many important methodological issues in conducting P-E fit research.

A second issue concerns the fact that there is a clear bias in the P-E fit literature for an individual level of analysis in criteria of interest—job satisfaction, adjustment, commitment, turnover, and performance (Schneider, 1996). To our knowledge, there is no research on the relationship between P-E fit and organizational performance and effectiveness. This may be a result of the tendency of P-E fit researchers to focus on individual affective outcomes. The question of interest in research on organizational consequences of P-E fit would be the degree to which an organization is more effective when fit is high for the people who join the organization than when fit is low. For example, in the work of O'Reilly et al. (1991) are the accounting firms more effective when the members who join are a better fit?

A third issue is the fact that most fit research employs various indices of individual affect (e.g., adjustment, satisfaction) or the behavioral consequences of such affect (e.g., absenteeism, turnover) as the criterion of interest, rather than on other potential criteria of interest, such as individual performance or effectiveness. Perhaps this is because a great deal of the studies on P-E fit have been tests explicitly of Holland's (1985) *theory of vocational choice*, or, Dawis and Lofquist's (1984) *Theory of Work Adjustment* (TWA). Holland's theory proposes that individuals whose vocational interests fit the career environments they enter will experience greater career satisfaction. The TWA theory makes a similar proposal, this time regarding the fit of individual desires (e.g., for autonomy, variety, or considerate supervision) to organizational rewards (on these same dimensions) with an outcome of individual satisfaction and adjustment. Research on P-E fit has rarely been concerned with individual performance or productivity (exceptions include Day & Bedeian, 1995; O'Reilly et al., 1991) and the relationship between P-E fit and indicators of individual, let alone organizational, effectiveness, has not received much attention.

Fourth, with the exception of Holland's theory, the *environment* in the P-E fit equation is conceptualized in terms of nonperson attributes. With the exception of Holland (1985), theories of P-E fit make the implicit assumption that the attributes of people are neither relevant nor important with regard to what the environment is or contains. Thus, for Hackman and Oldham, the job is something "out there," as is culture for Chatman and her colleagues (Schneider, Goldstein, & Smith, 1995).

Lastly, all fit theories implicitly propose only positive consequences to arise from fit despite considerable evidence for the advantages of heterogeneity or diversity in solving at least some classes of problems (cf., Herriot & Pemberton, 1995). In contrast, the ASA model presented next suggests that the consequences of fit may not be all positive. In fact, good fit may result in diminished effectiveness for organizations. However, to invoke these potential negative consequences of good fit requires moving beyond the individual to the group or organization level of analysis that, as noted earlier, would be inconsistent with the focus on individual outcomes dominating existing research on person–environment fit.

ASA THEORY: AN OVERVIEW

Schneider (1983a, 1983b, 1987, 1989; Schneider et al., 1995) outlined a theoretical framework of organizational behavior based on the mechanism of person–environment fit that integrates both *micro* (individually focused) and *macro* (organizationally focused) theories. This view proposes that the goals of the organization as articulated by the founder make up the core or essence of the organization. The organizational goals, and the culture that emerges to attain these goals are thus believed to be a reflection of the personal attributes (e.g., personality) of the founder. It is the outcome of three interrelated dynamic processes, *attraction, selection,* and *attrition* (ASA), that determines the kinds of people in an organization. That is, certain types of people are attracted to, and prefer, particular types of organizations; organizations formally and informally select certain types of people to join the organization; and attrition occurs when people who do not fit a particular organization leave. Those people who become part of the organization and stay based on these processes, in turn, define the nature of the organization and its structure, processes, and culture. As Schneider (1987) stated, "the people make the place."

A number of interesting contrasts can be made between ASA and the P–E fit theories presented here (see Table 3.1). To begin, ASA as a person-based framework, like Holland's (1985), proposes that environments are defined by the characteristics of the people in them. In addition, as a *meso* (House, Rousseau, & Thomas-Hunt, 1995), *cross-level* (Klein, Dansereau, & Hall, 1994), or *person–environment* model, ASA theory focuses on organizational level outcomes with the criteria of interest including the resultant structure, culture, and effectiveness of organizations; not individual affect and behavior. The ASA model also acknowledges the potential negative consequences

TABLE 3.1

Contrasting P–E Fit Theory and ASA Theories

Level of Analysis	Traditional P–E Fit Theory Individual Level	ASA Theory Organizational Levels
Issue	Affective Outcomes	Effectiveness/Performance Outcomes
Consequences of "Good" Fit	Positive	Negative*
	Positive affect	Inability to adapt to changes
	Job satisfaction	Less innovation; rigidity
	Proper socialization	Less challenging of norms
	Harmony/Cooperation	"Group think"
"E" in the "P–E" equation	Comprised of nonperson attributes	Comprised of person attributes

*Note. ASA allows for the positive consequences predicted by P–E fit theory for "good" fit and also highlights potential negative outcomes of good fit.

of good P–E fit. Although certain positive consequences, such as harmony, positive affect, and effective socialization, and adjustment, are likely associated with good fit, ASA theory suggests that good fit and homogeneity may lead to an organization's inability to adapt and change as the environment where the organization functions changes. That is, an organization that becomes homogeneous in its members, especially members of management, may be unable to adjust when the strategic environment demands change, may lack needed innovation or fail to challenge existing norms, and, in general, reflect "group think" at an organizational level (Schneider, 1983b).

ASA theory suggests several empirically testable propositions in these domains. All of the propositions concern the etiology of organizational processes, structure, and culture as a function of the ASA cycle. The key propositions are: (a) the starting point for the ASA cycle is said to be the founder of the organization; (b) the consequence of the ASA cycle is said to be homogeneity of personality in an organization; and (c) the consequence of homogeneity of personality is said to be rigidity in adaptation when the need for change emerges.

We explore these key propositions next. First, we review thinking and qualitative research on the effects of the founder on the long term ASA cycle believed to eventuate in homogeneity. Then, a summary of quantitative research on various facets of the ASA cycle, and the inclination of that cycle to yield homogeneity, is described. An in-depth description of two recently completed pieces of research that provide additional evidence regarding the tendency for organizations to be defined by relative homogeneity of personality follows. Lastly, we expand the conceptualization of potential negative consequences of homogeneity of personality as a result of the ASA cycle, and some contingencies, or boundary conditions, on the prediction of negative consequences from homogeneity are presented.

THE ROLE OF THE FOUNDER IN THE ASA FRAMEWORK

The logic of the ASA framework begins with the personality of an organization's founder. Like Schein's (1992) writings on organizational culture, Schneider (1987) views the founder as the central determinant of organizational behavior. Founders' decisions and actions early in the life of the organization are said to be driven by, and are reflections of, his or her personality. The founder's actions reduce the inherent ambiguity associated with the formative period in an organization's life. In addition, it is through the founder's actions that the organization articulates its goals and basic managerial philosophy (McGregor, 1960) and begins to evolve a particular strategy, structure, and culture. ASA theory views goals as operationalizations of the personality of the founder, and it is the process of attempting to achieve these goals that results in the enactment of practices and policies that define structure and culture (Schein, 1992; Schneider, 1987). Therefore, ASA theory proposes that the so-called environmental attributes of organizations (practices, policies, and structure) are enacted by the founder in pursuit of goals, and are reflections of the founder's personality.

Based on founders' early decisions, organizations may grow and prosper requiring increasingly large numbers of employees. ASA proposes that potential employees are initially attracted to the founder and the organization he or she has created. This is followed by hiring decisions that tend to reproduce the way the founder thinks and behaves. As Schein (1992) remarked:

> Founders not only choose the basic mission and the environmental context in which the new group will operate, but they choose the group members and bias the original responses that the group makes in its effort to succeed in its environment and to integrate itself. Organizations do not form accidentally or spontaneously ... Founders not only have a high level of self-confidence and determination, but they typically have strong assumptions about the nature of

the world, the role that organizations play in that world, the nature of human nature and relationships, how truth is arrived at, and how to manage time and space. They will, therefore be quite comfortable in imposing those views on their partners and employees as the fledgling organization copes. (pp. 211–213)

Schein (1992) presented several case studies demonstrating the inclination of founders to choose managers and executives similar to themselves as they strive to achieve early successes in their newly formed organizations.

These selection strategies and procedures driven by the founder are utilized by the organization in future recruitment and hiring. Thus, organizations appear to have a proclivity to choose individuals who match the collective characteristics of current members, or who fit the basic competencies, interests, personality, and culture of the organization. We focus now on additional research that demonstrates this proclivity, regardless of consideration of the founder and his or her influence.

FACETS OF THE ASA CYCLE AND THE INCLINATION TOWARD HOMOGENEITY

Schneider (1987), Schneider et al. (1995), and Schneider, Kristof, Goldstein, and Smith (1997) have reviewed literature relevant to the ASA framework. Current research suggests support for the major propositions of ASA, although at this writing only two previously published studies present a direct test of the homogeneity of personality proposition. For example, some research reveals that people are attracted to organizations with characteristics that match their own personalities (Tom, 1971) or that they think will be instrumental to them in attaining valued outcomes (Vroom, 1966). There is also research that reveals people are likely to leave organizations they do not fit (Jackson, Brett, Sessa, Cooper, Julin, & Peyronnin, 1991; O'Reilly et al., 1991) and that people choose organizations that fit their need structures (e.g., high need for achievement people choose to work in organizations with individual incentive systems; Bretz, Ash, & Dreher, 1989; Turban & Keon, 1993). There is also research suggesting that organizations consciously make selection and promotion decisions that serve to clone the personality attributes of the dominant coalition (Argyris, 1958; Pinfield, 1995) or fit the personality of the founder of the organization (Schein, 1992). Pinfield (1995) not only noted the use of political, historical, and social issues in making selection and promotion decisions; he also documented how those making such decisions attempt to later guarantee that their decisions were appropriate! In summary, research provides indirect support for the kinds of actions on the part of individuals and organizations that ASA theory argues promotes homogeneity in organizations; all focusing on achieving an individual-organization fit.

Research by Turban and Keon (1993) and O'Reilly et al. (1991) perhaps best capture the kinds of research that has been done relevant to the ASA model. O'Reilly et al.'s field research was described previously in this chapter. Their research in accounting firms reveals that new accountants, who join firms where the fit of their own values to the accounting firms' culture is high, are more likely to be satisfied, productive, committed, and remain with the accounting firms two years later. We interpret these findings to mean the accounting firms become more homogeneous over time regarding the values of their members because those who fit best remain.

Turban and Keon (1993) conducted a laboratory study to assess the inclination of people to be attracted to organizations that fit their own personality. They assessed student personality for *self esteem* (SE) and *need for achievement* (nAch), then had the students read descriptions of organizations that constituted the manipulation of reward structure, centralization, organizational size, and geographical dispersion of plants. Results revealed main effects for decentralization and pay for performance, and several interactions as hypothesized emerged. Specifically, participants in the research who were low on SE were more attracted to decentralized and larger firms; participants who were high on nAch were more attracted to organizations that rewarded performance rather than seniority. We interpret this laboratory study to be a test of the inclination of people to be attracted to organizational processes and structures that fit their personalities, and infer that the long term consequence of this attraction process is homogeneity of personality in organizations.

To our knowledge, there are but two published studies that directly test the extent to which there is actually homogeneity of personality in organizations. Research of this kind is sparse because it requires significant numbers of people from multiple organizations (Schneider et al., 1995). The first published study was conducted in England by Jordan, Herriot, and Chalmers (1991) who sampled 4 organizations containing 344 managers. Jordan et al. (1991) demonstrated that the factors of the *16PF* (a factor analytically derived personality measure, authored by Cattell) significantly discriminated among both incumbents' occupations and organizations. In other words, they found that different personalities characterized various occupations as a function of the organization where that occupation exists. Therefore, Jordan et al. (1991) provide evidence supporting the idea that personality is related to the occupations where people work and the specific personality attributes related to an occupation vary across organizations.

As far as ASA theory is concerned, this suggests that the well-known relationship between personality and occupation is, once again, substantiated (e.g., Hogan & Blake, 1996), but organizational differences in personality within occupations is also true—as ASA theory would predict. Indeed, in Schneider's (1987) original paper he presented the hypothesis that accountants who work for the YMCA would likely share some attributes with accountants who work for a stock brokerage house, but that in other attributes, the two sets of accountants would differ. In the next study to be described, this idea of personality similarity within occupations, with differences across organizations, is pursued in greater detail, using biodata as the individual differences variable of interest. Then a large-scale study across 132 organizations is summarized, directly assessing the extent that there is homogeneity of personality in organizations.

THE BIODATA STUDY OF HOMOGENEITY

Simco and Schneider (1997) proposed that, because life history experiences contribute to personality and interests, such experiences should prove useful in segmenting people into careers, and further, into the organizations where they carry out their careers (Schneider & Schneider, 1994). The two careers they studied were accountants and attorneys. The accountants (N = 309) worked in four different accounting firms, and the attorneys (N = 378) in two different law organizations (one in the private sector and one in the public). A series of stepwise multiple discriminant analyses, using biodata items as predictors, revealed the following:

1. Biodata is a significant discriminator of accountants from attorneys, not an unusual finding in the career literature (Holland, 1985). The squared canonical correlation for this discrimination was .60 (p < .01), based on 26 biodata items.
2. Biodata significantly discriminates between attorneys working in private sector vs. public sector law organizations. The squared canonical correlation for this analysis was .55 (p < .01), based on 27 biodata items.
3. Biodata significantly discriminates among the four accounting firms where the accountants work. The squared canonical correlation for this analysis was .29, based on 15 biodata items.

Sample life history experience items that make each of these discriminations are shown in Table 3.2.

Additional information about the study is significant. It was difficult differentiating *accountants* (who are conventional) from *attorneys* (who are enterprising) when choosing two adjacent careers from Holland's (1985) hexagonal model. In that model, adjacent careers are hypothesized to be more similar to each than others. In other words, first separating accountants from attorneys was, hypothetically, difficult; then, separating members of each career further into their membership organization, should have proven even more difficult. Second, the biodata items that differentiated attorneys from accountants were different from those items useful for distinguishing between members of the two law organizations, on the one hand, and mem-

TABLE 3.2

Sample Life History Experience Items That Differentiate Occupational and Organizational Membership

Items Differentiating Accountants from Attorneys

Accountants Higher

• Performance in high school math courses

• Participating in a professional fraternity or sorority while in high school

Attorneys Higher

• Participating in high school debating or dramatics groups or clubs

• Volunteering to help political candidates while in college

Items Differentiating Membership in Public From Private Law Organizations

Public Higher

• Voting in elections

• Attending social events while in high school

Private Higher

• Rank of law school attended

• Employment in current law organization prior to present employment there

Items Differentiating Membership in Four Accounting Organizations

• Participation in a college professional fraternity/sorority

• Population of town/city live in while in high school

bers of the four accounting firms, on the other. Finally, there was some preliminary evidence gathered by Simco and Schneider that suggested the cultures of the organizations also differed: Accounting differed from law, and the two law organizations differed from each other (the results for the accounting firms were weak).

The results of the Simco and Schneider (1997) study extend the work of Jordan et al. (1991) and provide more evidence supporting the homogeneity of persons within organizations, this time, based on life history experiences.

THE PERSONALITY STUDY OF HOMOGENEITY

The central proposition of ASA theory is the prediction that organizations tend toward homogeneity of personality. As noted here, only one earlier study that of Jordan et al. (1991), has directly tested this idea, and some support for the proposition was found. In addition, the recent study reported by Simco and Schneider (1997), using biodata, provides support for the general idea of homogeneity in regard to individual attributes.

In a second published study, supported by the Center For Creative Leadership (CCL) and the United States Army Research Institute for the Behavioral and Social Sciences (A. R. I.), the personality data for 12,379 individuals in 132 public and private U.S. businesses were analyzed (Schneider et al., 1998). Personality was measured using the Myers-Briggs Type Indicator (MBTI), a measure administered to participants in various leadership and management development programs at CCL. The sample of 132 organizations represents all organizations where at least 25 participants completed the MBTI; thus, the minimum sample of respondents for any one of the organizations was 25 managers.

The analysis of the data employed stepwise multiple discriminant analysis with the four MBTI continuous scale scores used to predict organizational membership. In fact, four significant discriminant functions were extracted, indicating that a significant proportion of the variance in organizational membership across the 132 organizations was accounted for by the four continuous scales of the MBTI.

In fact, the MBTI is most frequently used by consultants and vocational counselors in the form of profiles or types, not based on discriminant function weights, but on dichotomies of each of the four continuous scales used in the discriminant analysis. In combination, this produces the 16 MBTI types that have become so familiar to managers and executives in the public and private sectors.

Treating the MBTI as categorical data, a nonparametric chi-square likelihood ratio test of the relationship between the 16 MBTI types and the 132 organizations produced a chi-square of 4308.64 (p < .0001), again suggesting a significant relationship between personality and organizational membership. For the chi-square analysis, each of the 12,379 individual managers was "typed" and placed in one of the 16 (types) by 142 (organizations) cells of the resultant matrix. The chi-square analysis tests for the degree that these placements are different from the chance expectations of people in the cells of the matrix—the significant effect indicates that, as predicted by ASA, people are *not* randomly distributed in the matrix!

ON HOMOGENEITY AND ITS CONSEQUENCES: THE DARK SIDE OF GOOD P–E FIT

Argyris (1958) proposed that organizations indeed attract and select what he termed *right types*. For Argyris, right types are managers who conform in background and personality to the existing power elite in an organization. Argyris further proposed that a consequence of having right types in management was "dry rot." He proposed that over time organizations would stultify—that they would be unable to deal with changes the environment demanded for continued existence and success.

Most person–environment theories propose that desirable, beneficial outcomes are consequences of the good fit between individuals and organizations. Like Argyris, Schneider (1987) and his colleagues (Schneider et al., 1995; Schneider et al., 1997) do not ascribe to the universal good that accrues as a function of good fit. Good fit may yield primarily positive outcomes for individuals over the short term, mainly in having adjustment, satisfaction, and commitment. However, in contrast, research indicates that over the long term, this cycle can yield homogeneity in thinking, decision making and action (Denison, 1990; Miller, 1990). Thus, ASA theory proposes that for *organizational* and *longitudinal* outcomes, good fit may be detrimental to organizational health. Good fit may produce a shared perspective on the part of an organization's principle decision makers that leads to strategic myopia; ultimately hindering their ability to both perceive, and consequently adapt to, environmental changes. By implication of the ASA cycle, the organization's strategy and its environment will become misaligned over time. In practice, ASA suggests that homogeneity may be useful in the early stages of an organization's life cycle to promote growth through harmony, collegiality, and a unified focus on the organization's initial goals. But, through time, a shift toward heterogeneity (at least, in the perspectives, backgrounds, and personalities of the principle decision-makers), will increase the likelihood of an accurate assessment of an organization's strategic environment.

Schneider hypothesizes that some negative consequences of good P–E fit are homogeneity in thinking, decision-making, and action resulting in an organization's inability to adapt to changing demands of the environment (or the inability to recognize the significance of changes in the environment). It can be inferred from this hypothesis that outcomes of the ASA cycle may include a lack of innovation, increased groupthink, low risk taking, limited boundary spanning, strategic and competitive predictability (or adherence to an entrenched, ineffective set of strategic goals), as well as an inability to absorb the diversity of persons, places, or processes. This negative aspect of good fit has received little direct research.

Indirectly, evidence for the negative consequences of good fit emerges from Miller (1990; 1992) who presented compelling evidence for the demise of successful organizations over time due to a kind of arrogance on the part of organizational decision-makers to pursue what made them successful *in extremis*. He presents evidence, for example, to support the idea that companies successful at innovation in the design and development of new electronic products pursue the design and development of increasingly arcane and useless products by carrying to extreme the very processes and procedures that yielded their initial success.

It is a relatively short inferential leap to suggest that over time, successful organizations increasingly attract people who more narrowly fit the culture of the organization, and through this fit, succeed in inadvertently narrowing the niche in the marketplace where the organization's products are appropriate. In essence, good fit and subsequent homogeneity carries to extreme the same processes and procedures that produced initial success, yielding exquisite minutiae and improved sameness, rather than adapting to the changing environment necessary to continue to be competitive.

In a unique and interesting study, Miller (1992) provided evidence from 97 firms regarding the fit of the organization to the uncertainty of the environment. His data revealed that the organizations that were best adapted to an uncertain environment had the least internal homogeneity in structures and processes; those least well adapted to an uncertain environment had the best internal homogeneity across structures and processes. Again, it is a short inferential leap to argue that the organizations with the most diversity of personality were the ones with the least internal fit, but the best fit to the external environment, and vice versa. Research like the Miller (1992) study, with addition of personality measurement, is mandatory to directly test the negative consequences of good fit for organizational effectiveness.

Although such research, to our knowledge, does not yet exist, research similar to Miller's does exist. Denison (1990, pp. 79–80), for example, in his exploration of culture as a correlate of organizational performance, makes the observation that his results suggest that "A strong, consistent culture is an asset to an organization in the short term, but over the longer term, particularly when an organization's environment changes rapidly, that consistency can compromise an organization's ability to adapt effectively."

Perhaps most interestingly, research on P–E fit by proponents of the positive consequences of good fit also yields data suggesting that all may not be positive. Thus, in a recent review of research on the Holland career–career environment fit literature, Walsh and Holland (1992) find that the consequences of fit are not always positive. For example, their review supports the conclusion that fit yields personal and vocational adjustment, integration, vocational maturity, and planfullness. However, some of the research they review reveals that fit is negatively related to measures of decision making, sociability, and problem solving ability. The latter are the kinds of issues most likely, in our opinion, to be reflected in performance effectiveness.

Although we have somewhat brought in question the assumption of all-positive consequences of good fit, it is important to remember that nothing is black and white, or is as simple as whether good fit is bad. We need to look more closely at the issue, exploring potential boundary conditions of these effects, to gain a better understanding of the bad side of good fit. In an attempt to begin this process, we examine the following issues: good fit for whom? good fit of what? and good fit when?

Good Fit for Whom

In Schneider's (1987) original hypothesis regarding the negative consequences of homogeneity, he made no distinction between groups (or levels) in an organization where homogeneity may be detrimental. On further reflection, a lesson could be learned from social psychology. Since the 1950s, social psychologists have known that homogeneity in the members of a group hinders that group's ability to perform problem solving and decision making tasks (Hoffman, 1959). Janis (1972) in his exposition of the groupthink phenomenon, posits as one antecedent of groupthink, ideological homogeneity among the members of the group. This suggests that Schneider's proposition may be most applicable for groups in organizations for whom it is the primary responsibility to perform problem solving, and strategic decision making tasks. Most notably, these groups have been labeled top management (executive) teams (TMTs) or, as Hambrick and Mason (1984) call them, the "upper echelons."

With research focus now on top management teams, strategic management literature (Priem, 1990) provides evidence in support of Schneider's hypothesis. Bourgeois (1985) investigated the relationship between goal consensus within a TMT and organizational performance. Considering goal diversity to be one indicator of heterogeneity in the TMT, Bourgeois found a significant positive correlation between diversity and organizational performance. Similarly, Grinyer and Norburn (1975) found that for a subset of financially successful firms, there was a negative correlation between TMT consensus and organizational performance.

Thus, there appears to be some support for the dark side of good fit regarding upper management teams. However, perhaps there is no dark side of good fit when discussing other members of an organization (i.e., general subordinates, line workers, or laborers). The point is, the *who* of good fit is an interesting issue for further research.

Good Fit of What

Another interesting issue, not specified in the original Schneider work, is good fit in regard to what characteristics? That is, on what characteristics, or attributes, are we focusing when we think of fit? Members of an organization can have good fit on a number of different aspects; goals, dispositions, values, and attitudes to name a few—and we have treated these generically in this chapter under the rubric "personality." Perhaps fit on certain characteristics may lead to negative consequences, and fit on other characteristics may lead to positive consequences.

This issue can be further explored in the framework of Muchinsky and Monahan's (1987) dual models of congruence—*supplementary congruence* and *complimentary congruence*. Supplementary congruence (or fit) regards the idea of congruence between the individual and the group of people who comprise the environment. That is, congruence occurs when the individual has characteristics similar to characteristics of persons in the organization. Complimentary congruence (or fit) refers to the match between an individual's talents and the corresponding needs of the environment. That is, complimentary congruence occurs when the characteristics of the individual match the needs of the organization.

Which fit are we referring to, supplementary fit or complimentary? Perhaps supplementary fit is needed on some characteristics whereas complimentary fit is needed on others. For example, organizational effectiveness may increase when there is supplementary congruence on the goals, or vision, of the organization. That is, organizational effectiveness may be increased when the individual has the same goals and vision as all members of the organization; fit on this characteristic may increase organizational effectiveness because everyone is focused on attaining the same objective. However, complimentary congruence may be desired on other characteristics, such as problem solving perspectives. That is, organizational effectiveness may increase if different members have different perspectives or talents regarding problem solving and decision making. Such differences would be an example of complimentary congruence—each has attributes that fit organizational needs, but they do not share attributes.

Further research is needed to address the issue of *what* characteristics fit research might focus on and the subsequent positive or negative outcomes of fit. George (1992) noted some interesting avenues of such potential study. For example, she asks: Are complimentary fit and supplementary fit compatible, or are they always incompatible. Additional theoretical and empirical work is needed in this area.

Good Fit When

A final issue regarding some contingencies on the positive and negative consequences of good fit concerns the issue of the timing of good fit—to question when good fit may be positive or negative. This is an interesting issue that has not yet been explored, yet the works of Miller (1990; 1992) and Denison (1990), summarized earlier, provide some clues.

Following their logic, early in the life of an organization good fit may be positive for organizational effectiveness, but later in the life cycle of the organization, relatively poor fit may be required among members. This poor fit would produce some conflict, turmoil, and stress for the members involved but, simultaneously, could permit the differences in perspective that can yield effectiveness in identifying new strategies and the tactics required for effectiveness in a changed environment. Thus, it is later in an organization's life cycle that good fit may have negative consequences; earlier, good fit may yield the harmony and cooperation required for early effectiveness.

Another issue regarding the *when* of good fit might be related to the level of crisis people in the organization experience. In times of crisis, good fit may be a major problem for an organization because the evidence from the crisis literature reveals that, in times of crisis, homogeneity increases (perhaps as a function of the desire for directive leadership; Goldstein, 1993). Thus, the crisis appears to overwhelm the situation yielding homogeneity of needs, stress reactions, and so forth (Hamblin, 1958).

To counteract the potential homogenizing effects of crisis, with the accompanying uniformity in the likely reactions to the crisis, organizations might best strive for heterogeneity as their norm—in times of crisis perhaps there would be less homogeneity as a result. That is, by increasing the diversity of people in an organization, one expands the chances of gaining the different reactions and perspectives needed to overcome the crisis. This diversity in perspective is crucial because crises are characterized as incidents important to the functioning and continued survival of an organization.

Another important reason to increase the diversity of persons when faced with a crisis is that a crisis is a perception (Billings, Milburn, & Schaalman, 1980). Therefore, it can be perceived in many different ways and from many different perspectives. What one person may see as an invigorating challenge and opportunity, another may perceive as a threatening, stress-laden event (Bass, 1990; Billings et al., 1980; McCauley, 1987). Having heterogenous persons may increase the ways that a situation is framed or perceived (Bolman & Deal, 1991), and perhaps expand the pool of possible reactions and solutions to the crisis.

SUMMARY AND CONCLUSION

We have summarized a substantial amount of information in this chapter. In its original formulation ASA theory (Schneider, 1987) contained 7 propositions in regard to attraction, selection, attrition, homogeneity, and a proposition concerning the hypothesized, long-term, negative consequences of homogeneity for organizational effectiveness. In this chapter, the focus has been on P–E fit, especially as it emerges, over time, through the ASA cycle, and the consequences of that fit for homogeneity of personality and accompanying organizational consequences.

We, and Schneider in his earlier work (e.g., Schneider 1983a, 1983b, 1987), wrote as if homogeneity of personality in organizations is caused totally by the ASA cycle. In the ASA model, little credence is given to the role of *the environment* in creating personalities. That is, the environment is frequently considered to affect an individual's personality through the process of organizational socialization (e.g., Louis, 1990). In socialization literature, however, the environment to which people are socialized is separated conceptually from the socialization practices used. Schneider (1983a) noted that research on socialization is dominated by the study of what happens in *total institutions* (e.g., police, soldiers, or priests) that are characterized by people oriented toward structure to begin with—and who create structured environments for newcomers—because this structure fits both those who do the socialization and those who become socialized. Indeed, Schneider (1983a) argued that socialization proceeds well in most organizations because those attracted to, and selected by, the organization begin, in some sense, presocialized. In any case, we would argue that it would be difficult, indeed, for an organization to reprogram people's reports of their early life history experiences so, at a later point in life, they report they had common experiences when growing up, and that these common reports now reveal homogeneity of biodata in organizations as in Simco and Schneider's (1997) research.

It is hard to break away from the situationist perspective in the interpretation of why organizations may be characterized by people with similar life history experiences or personalities (Staw, 1991). Even in the research literature on P-E fit, the "E" is conceptualized as somehow separate from the "P." Thus, with the exception of Holland's theory of the career environments, other perspectives on, and approaches to, the measurement of environments place the environment "out there," and separate from, the attributes of people in the environment. In this chapter, the focus has been on the organizational consequences of P-E fit, especially the consequences that accrue as a result of the personality of the members of the organization. In our view, it is the people there who make an environment (or organization) what it is.

As yet, we have no direct evidence on the implications of such homogeneity for the ways recruitment, selection, and socialization are actually practiced in organizations; the strategies, structures, and cultures that evolve in organizations characterized by different modal personalities, much less the implications of homogeneity for eventual organizational effectiveness. The ASA conceptualization reviewed here, however, does contribute to the evidence accumulating in regard to potential roles individual differences might play in understanding organizational phenomena. There has been a clear tendency in psychology and the organizational sciences to deny the potential importance of the individuals in a situation to be an influence on, if not the major one on that situation; people are interesting, the literature seems to say, but not when it comes time to understanding important *organizational* phenomena.

Schneider (1996) suggested that a failure of academics and practitioners to explore the linkages between individuals' attributes and organizational phenomena could marginalize those who study individual differences regarding the study of larger aggregates. When we know that stock brokerage houses attract, select, and retain different kinds of people than do YMCAs; clearly the nature of those organizations cannot be understood without explicating the attributes of the people there. Yet, organizational scholars appeal to issues like strategy, structure, and culture as the key differences between organizations that ignore the underlying etiology of those, seemingly, more tangible facets of organizations. This results, for example, in organizational change strategies that focus on strategy, structure, and culture while denying the importance of changing the psychology of the people already there, or attracting, selecting, and retaining new people, who can attempt to align strategy, structure, and culture to the demands of the environment. We hypothesize the documented failure of many attempts at organizational change is a result of a failure to pay attention to the attributes of the people, especially management, in the organization.

The ASA framework provides interesting and useful person-based perspectives on the etiology of organizational strategy, structure, and culture. Evidence is beginning to accumulate to show that facets of the framework have validity. Future research must explore the longitudinal evolution of the ASA framework, consequences of the predicted homogeneity for organizational effectiveness, and boundary conditions under which homogeneity is a positive or negative force for organizational effectiveness.

REFERENCES

Argyris, C. (1958). Some problems in conceptualizing organizational climate: A case study of a bank. *Administrative Science Quarterly, 2*, 501–520.
Bass, B. M. (1990). *Bass and Stogdill's handbook of leadership,*(3rd. ed.) New York: Free Press.
Billings, R. S., Milburn, T. W., & Schaalman, M. L. (1980). Crisis perception: A theoretical and empirical analysis. *Administrative Science Quarterly, 25*, 300–315.
Bolman, L. G., & Deal, T. E. (1991). *Reframing organizations.* San Francisco: Jossey- Bass.
Bowers, K. S. (1973). Situationism in psychology: Analysis and critique. *Psychological Review, 80*, 307–336.
Bourgeois, L. J., III. (1985). Strategic goals, perceived uncertainty and economic performance in volatile environments. *Academy of Management Journal, 28*(3), 548–573.
Bretz, R. D., Jr., Ash, R. A., & Dreher, G. F. (1989). Do people make the place? An examination of the attraction–selection–attrition hypothesis. *Personnel Psychology, 42*, 561–581.
Chatman, J. (1989). Improving interactional organizational research: A model of person-organization fit. *Academy of Management Review, 14*, 333–349.
Chatman, J. (1991). Matching people and organizations: Selection and socialization in public accounting firms. *Administrative Science Quarterly, 36*, 459–484.

Cronbach L. J., & Gleser, G. (1953). Assessing similarity between profiles. *Psychological Bulletin, 50*, 456-473.

Dawis, R. V. & Lofquist, L. H. (1984). *A psychological theory of work adjustment: An individual differences model and its application.* Minneapolis: University of Minnesota Press.

Day, D. D., & Bedeian, A. G. (1991). Work climate and Type A status as predictors of job satisfaction: A test of the interactional perspective. *Journal of Vocational Behavior, 38,* 39- 52.

Denison, D. R. (1990). *Corporate culture and organizational effectiveness.* New York: Wiley.

Durkheim, E. (1853/1947). *Division of labor in society, 2nd ed.* Glencoe, IL: Free Press.

Edwards, J. R. (1991). Person-job fit: A conceptual integration, literature review, and methodological critique. *International Review of Industrial/Organizational Psychology, 6,* 283- 357. New York: Wiley.

Endler, N. S., & Magnusson, D. (Eds.). (1976). *Interactional psychology and personality.* New York: Hemisphere.

Fiedler, F. E. (1967). *A theory of leadership effectiveness.* New York: McGraw-Hill.

George, J. M. (1992). The role of personality in organizational life: Issues and evidence. *Journal of Management, 18,* 185-213.

Goldstein, H. W. (1993). *Crisis leadership: Followers in crisis.* Unpublished PhD dissertation, Department of Psychology, University of Maryland, College Park.

Goldstein, K. (1939). *The organism.* New York: American Book.

Grinyer, P., & Norburn, D. (1975). Planning for existing markets: An empirical study. *International Studies in Management and Organization, 7,* 99-122.

Hackman, J. R., & Oldham, G. R. (1980). *Work redesign.* Reading, MA: Addison-Wesley.

Hamblin, R. L. (1958). Leadership and crisis. *Sociometry, 21,* 322-335.

Hambrick, D., & Mason, P. (1984). Upper echelons: The organization as a reflection of its top managers. *Academy of Management Review, 2,* 193-206.

Herriot, P., & Pemberton, C. (1995). *Competitive advantage through diversity: Organizational learning from differences.* London, UK: Sage.

Hoffman, L. R. (1959). Homogeneity of member personality and its effect on group problem solving. *Journal of Abnormal and Social Psychology, 58,* 27-32.

Hogan, R. T., & Blake, R. J. (1996). Vocational interests: Matching self-concept to the work environment. In K. R. Murphy, (Ed.), *Individual differences and behavior in organizations.* San Francisco: Jossey-Bass.

Holland, J. L. (1985). *Making vocational choices: A theory of careers.* Englewood Cliffs, New Jersey: Prentice-Hall.

House, R. J., Rousseau, D. M., & Thomas-Hunt, M. (1995). The meso paradigm: A framework for the integration of micro and macro organizational behavior. In L. L. Cummings & B. M. Staw (Eds.), *Research in organizational behavior* (vol. 17, pp. 71-114). Greenwich, CT: JAI.

Jackson, S. E., Brett, J. F., Sessa, V. I., Cooper, D. M. , Julin, J. A., & Peyronnin, K. (1991). Some differences make a difference: Individual dissimilarity and group heterogeneity as correlates of recruitment, promotion, and turnover. *Journal of Applied Psychology, 76,* 675-689.

Janis, I. L. (1972). *Victims of groupthink.* Boston: Houghton Mifflin.

Jordan, M., Herriot, P., & Chalmers, C. (1991). Testing Schneider's ASA theory. *Applied Psychology: An International Review, 40,* 47-54.

Klein, K. J., Dansereau, F., & Hall, R. J. (1994). Levels issues in theory development, data collection, and analysis. *Academy of Management Review, 19,* 195-229.

Kristof, A. L. (1996). Person-organization fit: An integrative review of its conceptualizations, measurement, and implications. *Personnel Psychology, 49,* 1-49.

Louis, M. (1990). Acculturation in the work place: Newcomers as lay ethnographers. In B. Schneider (Ed.), *Organizational climate and culture*. San Francisco: Jossey-Bass.

Magnusson, D., & Endler, N. S. (Eds.). (1977). *Personality at the crossroads: Current issues in interactional psychology*. Hillsdale, NJ: Lawrence Erlbaum Associates.

McCauley, C. D. (1987). Stress and the eye of the beholder. *Issues and Observations, 7,* 1-16.

McGregor, D. M. (1960). *The human side of enterprise*. New York: McGraw-Hill.

Miller, D. (1990). *The Icarus paradox: How exceptional companies bring about their own downfall*. New York: HarperCollins.

Miller, D. (1992). Environmental fit versus internal fit. *Organization Science, 3,* 159-179.

Mischel, W. (1968). *Personality and assessment*. New York: Wiley.

Moos, R. H. (1976). *The human context*. New York: Wiley-Interscience.

Muchinsky, P. M., & Monahan, C. J. (1987). What is person–environment congruence?: Supplementary vs. complementary models of fit. *Journal of Vocational Behavior, 31,* 268-277.

Murray, H. (1938). *Explorations in personality*. New York: Oxford University Press.

O'Reilly, C. A., Chatman, J., & Caldwell, D. F. (1991). People and organizational culture: A profile comparison approach to assessing person–organization fit. *Academy of Management Journal, 34,* 487-516.

Pervin, L. A., & Lewis, M. (Eds.). (1978). *Perspectives in interactional psychology*. New York: Plenum.

Pinfield, (1995). *The operation of internal labor markets: Staffing practices and vacancy chains*. New York: Plenum.

Priem, R. (1990). Top management team group factors, consensus, and firm performance. *Strategic Management Journal, 11,* 697-478.

Schein, E. H. (1992). *Organizational culture and leadership*, 2nd ed. San Francisco: Jossey-Bass.

Schneider, B. (1983a). Interactional psychology and organizational behavior. In B. M. Staw & L. L. Cummings (Eds.), *Research in organizational behavior*, Vol. 5 (pp. 1-31). Greenwich, CT: JAI.

Schneider, B. (1983b). An interactionist perspective on organizational effectiveness. In K. S. Cameron & D. S. Whetten (Eds.), *Organizational effectiveness: A comparison of multiple models* (pp. 27-54). New York: Academic Press.

Schneider, B. (1987). The people make the place. *Personnel Psychology, 40,* 437-454.

Schneider, B. (1989). E = f(P, B): The road to a radical approach to person–environment fit. *Journal of Vocational Behavior, 31,* 353-361.

Schneider, B. (1996). When individual differences aren't. In K. R. Murphy (Ed.), *Individual differences and behavior in organizations*. San Francisco: Jossey-Bass.

Schneider, B., Goldstein, H. W., & Smith, D. B. (1995). The ASA framework: An update. *Personnel Psychology, 48,* 747-773.

Schneider, B., Kristof, A. L., Goldstein, H. W., & Smith, D. B. (in press). What is this thing called fit? In N. R. Anderson & P. Herriot (Eds.), *Handbook of selection and appraisal*, 2nd ed. (pp. 393-412). London: Wiley.

Schneider, B. & Schneider, J. L. (1994). Biodata: An organizational focus. In G. S. Stokes, M. D. Mumford, & W. A. Owens (Eds.), *Biodata handbook* (pp. 423-450). Palo Alto: CPP Books.

Schneider, B., Smith, D. B., Taylor S., & Fleenor, J. (1998). Personality: A test of the homogeneity of personality hypothesis in organizations. *Journal of Applied Psychology, 83,* 462-470.

Simco, J. L., & Schneider, B. (1997). Life history experiences as correlates of organizational membership. Unpublished manuscript: University of Maryland, College Park.

Staw, B. M. (1991). Dressing up like an organization: When psychological theories can explain organizational action. *Journal of Management, 17,* 805-819.

Tom, V. R. (1971). the role of personality and organizational images in the recruiting process. *Organizational Behavior and Human Performance, 6,* 573–592.

Turban, D. R., & Keon, T. L. (1993). Organizational attractiveness: An interactionist perspective. *Journal of Applied Psychology, 78,* 184–193.

Vroom, V. R. (1966). Organizational choice: A study of pre- and post-decision processes. *Organizational Behavior and Human Performance, 1,* 212–226.

Walsh, W. B., & Holland, J. L. (1992). A theory of personality types and work environments. In W. B. Walsh, K. H. Craik, & R. H. Price (Eds.), (1992). *Person–environment psychology: Models and perspectives* (pp. 35–70). Hillsdale, NJ: Lawrence Erlbaum Associates.

4

Free Traits and Personal Contexts: Expanding a Social Ecological Model of Well-Being[1]

Brian R. Little
Carleton University[2]

INTRODUCTION

Peter is hiding in the washroom, escaping from the nonstop stimulation of his teaching day. His students see him as a classic extravert—outgoing, provocative, and a bit outrageous. But, they are missing something fundamental about their teacher's behavior.

Paula is on the way to a meeting at her new job where the *formal* project, as written in her Daytimer®, is "brief the marketing department about the Excelsior account." Her *personal* project is actually "getting that jerk, Barry, off my back." On the way to the meeting, she runs into an old colleague who asks, "Hey Paula, how's the new job?." "Terrible," she replies.

---

[1]Based on a paper, "Personal Contexts: A Rationale and Methods for Investigation," presented to the symposium on Person–Environment Psychology: Contemporary Models and Perspectives, American Psychological Association Annual Meeting, New York City, August 13, 1995. I am very grateful to Rick Price and Ken Craik for challenging and thoughtful comments on the initial draft of this chapter.

[2]Part of the research reported in this chapter was undertaken during my tenure as the Royal Bank Faculty Fellow in University Teaching at McGill University. I wish to thank colleagues at McGill and my students in the Social Ecology Laboratory at Carleton University for stimulation and support. Grants from the Social Sciences and Humanities Research Council of Canada and the Canadian Center for Management Development to the author and Dr. Susan D. Phillips are gratefully acknowledged.

A videotape of Maria's apartment shows a squalid, sparsely furnished room in a high crime area of an inner city. When her parents announce that they have arranged for her to move to a safer, larger apartment uptown, she says, "No way, I'm staying right where I am."

In this chapter, we explain how each of these imaginary vignettes captures an important, and relatively common, feature of everyday life and provide an explanation for what is going on in each case. We explain how each vignette has implications for the subjective well-being of the person involved and how a compelling account of the behavior of the three protagonists requires concepts and assessment methods that go beyond those conventionally used in person–environment psychology. Beginning with an overview of our own social–ecological perspective (Little & Ryan, 1979; Little, 1989), we describe the centrality of personal projects in explaining and predicting human well-being and adaptation. Two missing links in the model will be identified. One will augment conceptions of fixed traits with propositions for the study of what we term *free traits*; the other will expand on conceptions of environments by exploring *personal contexts*. We will then report on three research programs stimulated by these theoretical extensions, and conclude with an overview of an expanded perspective on the social–ecology of well-being. In the course of doing this, we will make clear why Peter, Paula, and Maria's conduct makes more sense to us now than it did before we began to explore free traits and personal contexts.

A SOCIAL ECOLOGICAL MODEL OF WELL-BEING

Since the 1970s, personality researchers have explored diverse aspects of person–environment interaction and their impact on human well-being and adaptation (e.g., Walsh, Craik, & Price, 1992). Our contribution to this research has been the development of a social–ecological perspective, displayed in schematic form in Fig. 4.1 (Little, 1972, 1976, 1983; Little & Ryan, 1979). Human well-being, broadly conceived (Block F) is postulated as being influenced by stable aspects of the person, such as trait and temperamental variables (Block A), and stable aspects of the environmental context (Block B). As in related approaches to person–environment psychology (e.g., Altman & Rogoff, 1987; Bronfenbrenner, 1979; Moos, 1973, 1979), these influences are postulated as having direct, indirect, bidirectional, and interactive effects on well-being.[3]

---

[3]Figure 4.1 is simplified in that only the main paths relevant to the theoretical argument of the chapter are illustrated. Interactive effects are not explicitly graphed.

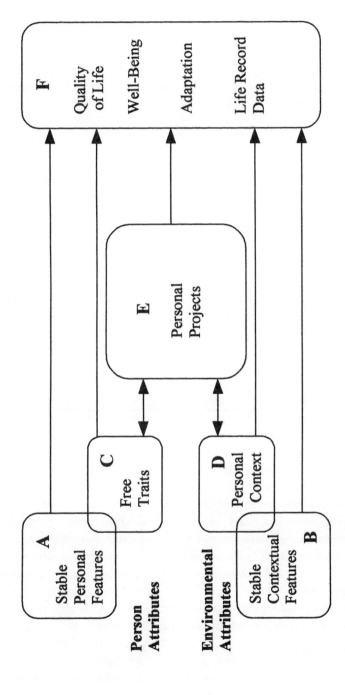

FIG. 4.1 A social–ecological framework for the study of person–interaction.

89

There is considerable evidence for the direct effect of relatively fixed features of individuals on their well-being. For example, well-being is influenced directly by *extraversion* (positively) and *neuroticism* (negatively), in part, because these stable traits are strongly associated with the experience of positive and negative affect (Argyle & Lu, 1990; Emmons & Diener, 1986; Heady & Wearing, 1989). The operation of indirect paths is exemplified by the finding that extraverts characteristically seek out situations that are stimulating, and congruent with, their needs, leading to enhanced well-being (e.g., Emmons & Diener, 1986).

The direct effect of environmental or contextual variables on well-being is also well established. The general stressfulness of environmental influence, in particular, has been shown to influence levels of well-being and exact psychological costs, even in the face of apparent physiological adaptation (see Evans, 1982).

The interaction between blocks of person and environmental variables and the ways that such interactions should be conceptualized and measured has been a major preoccupation of researchers in person–environment psychology (Altman & Rogoff, 1987; Endler, 1983; Krahé, 1992; Little, 1987c). Our approach to this issue has been the development of a unit of analysis termed *personal projects* (Little, 1983). Personal projects are extended sets of personally salient action that are influenced both by personal and contextual variables in dynamic interaction. Personal projects can range from banal routines to ventures of surpassing importance. They may be solitary or communal, onerous or easy. Projects may be forsaken or obsessed over. They may be the very essence of a flourishing life or the sign that things are going tragically awry. Research on personal projects has been extensively reported elsewhere (Little, 1987a, 1989, 1993, 1998), we sketch only the major trends of the research program here.

The methodological tool we use is Personal Projects Analysis (PPA) that provides several modular components to: (a) elicit personal projects from respondents, (b) gather appraisals from respondents for 10 of these projects on dimensions (typically 15–20) that tap theoretically and clinically important issues related to adaptation and well-being, rating (from 0–10) how much enjoyment, stress, control, etc., they experience in their personal projects; and (c) provide methods for examining the hierarchical structure of a person's projects, their linkages with other elements of the self, and their impact on each other and the surrounding ecology (see Little, 1983, 1989, 1998).

We conceive of personal projects as *carrier units* for person–environment transactions, because it is through them that personality propensities and environmental affordances are brought in direct contact. There is clear evidence that the Big Five traits of personality (neuroticism, extraversion, openness to experience, agreeableness, and conscientiousness (Costa & McCrae, 1985; John, 1990) are closely associated with individuals' appraisals of their projects (Little, Lecci, & Watkinson, 1992). Conscientiousness, for example, is strongly related to the efficacious pursuit of projects, but perhaps more surprisingly, with project enjoyment. Extraversion, similarly, is linked with perceived project success, but as expected, especially with projects in the interpersonal domain.

Since the inception of our research program, we have been concerned with showing how personal projects are intimately linked with the environmental affordances where they are conceived and enacted. Indeed, one of our formal theoretical propositions is that human adaptation is enhanced to the extent that individuals have a perception of control based on an accurate reading of the ecosystem resources and constraints where they are embedded (Little & Ryan, 1979).[4] Recent research, for example, has examined well-being as a function of the extent to which individuals' projects are impacted by the economic climate of the region where they live (Yetim, 1993) and by the extent that the organizational climate of work environments promotes or hinders personal project pursuit (Phillips, Little, & Goodine, 1996).

Although the theoretical framework where personal projects has been developed is a social–ecological one, the PPA methodology has been used to operationalize concepts drawn from diverse theoretical perspectives, including *Murrayan need theory* (Omodei & Wearing, 1990), *humanistic–organismic theory* (Sheldon & Kasser, 1997) *control theory* (Brunstein, 1993) and *classical learning theory* (Ogilvie & Rose, 1996). Indeed, a major goal of the methodology is to render commensurable constructs drawn from contrasting explanatory systems (Little, 1987c).

The appraisals of personal projects can be aligned into five theoretical factors: *project meaning, structure, community* (or support), *efficacy*, and *stress* (Little, 1989). To the extent that people are engaged in projects that are meaningful, well structured, supported by others, efficacious, and not too stressful, their well-being is enhanced. More importantly from an applied perspective, we can help change, modify, and enhance the effectiveness of a person's project system (Christianson, Backman, Little, & Nguyen, 1997; Krahé, 1992; Little, 1987a, 1989).

---

[4]This proposition contrasts, in some respects, with those emphasizing the adaptive wisdom of positive illusions (Taylor & Brown, 1988). We see veridical ecological perception as a necessary, if not sufficient, condition for adaptation (see Colvin & Block, 1994; Baumeister (1989).

In this respect, personal projects differ from fixed traits and the more intractable aspects of our slow changing environments (such as the prevailing economic or unemployment conditions). Whether through self-initiated activity, the nudges of others, or professional intervention, personal projects can be reconstrued and reconfigured. This tractability of personal projects facilitates the two aspirations of a social-ecological perspective—it provides both a method for exploring the roots of human well-being and some possible routes for its enhancement (Little, 1989; Little, Lecci, & Watkinson, 1992).

It has become increasingly clear, however that the linkages between persons, projects, and environments, as depicted in Blocks A, B, and E in Figure 4.1, are unable to handle some of the subtleties and potentially important nuances of person-environment interactions captured in the chapter opening vignettes. Conventional trait accounts might offer plausible accounts of why Peter is a dynamic teacher. Yet, why is he hiding, feet up, in the washroom? Paula has problems with her personal projects relating to Barry, who may indeed be a jerk. But, why does she dismiss the whole job situation as "terrible"? The economic and environmental realities of Maria's environment might predict rough times. But that is not the way she sees her situation at all, and is resolute in staying. Does she see something her parents do not? In all three cases, it appears that our understanding of the person's well-being requires further understanding of the transactions they engage in with their contexts. We must expand the blocks of variables in our social-ecological model.

MISSING LINKS: AN OVERVIEW OF FREE TRAITS AND PERSONAL CONTEXTS

Many contemporary perspectives on personality assume that, by age 30, traits are relatively fixed, or to use James' terms, *set like plaster* (Costa & McCrae, 1994). As we explain here, we are more inclined to see traits as only half plastered. Other perspectives see trait behavior as scripted activity in the service of goal pursuit (Read, Jones, & Miller, 1990) and as essentially cultural constructions (Shweder, 1975; Semin & Fiedler, 1991).

Although it is possible to see these as explanatory adversaries, each perspective has a core validity worth preserving (cf. Craik, 1986) and each may effectively explain aspects of an individual's behavior at different levels of analysis (Wakefield, 1989). We agree that, at one level, individuals are characterized by relatively fixed traits. Yet at another level, people act on the basis of what we call *free traits* (Little, 1996). Free traits are culturally scripted patterns of conduct that are carried out as part of a person's goals, projects, and commitments, independent of that person's "natural" inclinations. By natural, I refer to behavior strongly rooted in temperamental characteristics or traits with a genetically linked, biological (e.g., neurophysiological) base (Kagan, 1995). An instructive case would be a classic Eysenckian introvert (e.g., Eysenck, 1987, 1990), characterized by chronically high resting levels of neocortical arousal, but who acts in a way that appears extraverted. We will term this person a "pseudo-extravert". Such conduct could be construed as disingenuous or misleading. Yet, it might also be deeply principled, and enacted in the service of a valued commitment or project. By expanding the person side of the person–environment model to include free traits alongside the more durable fixed traits of classic personology, we discover new, and potentially important, questions about human well-being are opened up for exploration.[5]

A second needed augmentation to our social–ecological model is represented by what we have called *personal contexts* (Block D, Fig. 4.1). Personal contexts are the idiosyncratically construed objects, situations, settings, and circumstances of our daily lives. They are comprised of focal elements that can range from "my dog, Bob," to "the prevailing atmosphere of misery in our country." Conventional environmental assessment aims at minimizing the 'noise' of individual differences to get a clearer valid signal of real environmental features (Craik, 1976). The concept of a personal context, is explicitly idiosyncratic at the outset. As the study of personal projects and free traits are intended to *contextualize person assessment*, the study of personal contexts is designed to *personalize contextual assessment*.

To my knowledge, the term *personal context* has not been explicitly used to designate *a unit of analysis* for interactional or personality psychology, but given the pervasiveness of both of its constituent terms, it is highly likely that the term has been used, perhaps even in a formalized sense (although initial keyword searches have not yielded any relevant hits). However, the concept is scarcely a novel one. In many respects the idea that our conduct is influenced by the subjective construal of our circumstances and contexts is a conceptual

---

[5]One of this volume's editors, Rick Price, has raised the important issue of whether "free traits" may be essentially what might be called "personal roles." Certainly, the invoking of role constructs in explaining disingenuous behavior is important. I believe that acting on the basis of personal projects (some of which may be role enactments) offers a more fine grained and potentially wider array of analytic possibilities. For example, if a highly agreeable person is constrained to act in a forceful, dominant, even aggressive fashion when trying to complete the project "get a refund for my inoperative snowblower", it is not clear that role constructs are as salient as are project characteristics such as importance, time urgency, impact on other projects, etc. Clearly, the links between projects and roles deserve scrutiny as valuable topics in their own right.

commonplace of personality, environmental, and interactional psychology. It is all the more notable, therefore that there has been little research that actually elicits samples of people's personal contexts and explores both their content and idiosyncratic effects on human conduct.

The reason for this, I believe, is the same reason that goal and action constructs, pervasive as theoretical constructs for decades, attracted only sporadic research attention in personality psychology until the development of methodological frameworks where they could be sampled and appraised (Little, 1983, 1987c). In turn, these units derived from the personal construct methodology of Kelly (1955) the first to provide ways of actually sampling and appraising the personal constructs used by individuals to anticipate events in their lives. A central concern of this chapter is that personal contexts, suffused as they are throughout the assumptive frameworks of our research in person–environment psychology, also need to be captured by methodological probes before their explanatory potential can be adequately gauged. These probes should allow us to measure theoretically important variables, but more centrally, from a personological perspective, they should enable us to sample, enumerate, and explore the idiosyncratic contextual elements of a person's life (cf. Carlson, 1971). Thus, we need assessment devices that allow us to say: "*here* are the personal constructs she uses to see the world," "*these* are the personal projects he is currently pursuing," or "*those* are the key elements of Jean's personal context." The common element, literally, in such methodologies is that they are all strictly *personal.*

Although explicit methodologically focused research on personal contexts has been sparse, there has been extensive research, spanning many decades, on several closely related intellectual tasks. First, the conceptual development of ideas of subjectively construed environments has a long and respected history in personality psychology. At the most inclusive level, Lewin postulated the importance of the "life space" as the necessary and proper focus for psychological research (Lewin, 1935). Murray (1938), in differentiating beta press from alpha press, emphasized the importance of distinguishing between subjectively perceived environments and the objective environments that, in part, gave rise to them. Given the current ascendancy of goal units in personality psychology and the topicality of models of human well-being, it is interesting to recall Murray's (1938) definition of press: "The press of an object is what it can do to the subject or for the subject—the power that it has to affect the well-being of the subject one way or another" (p. 121).

This statement summarizes the rationale for expanding our social–ecological model of well-being to include concerns about free traits and personal contexts, and acknowledges the historical provenance of these concepts.[6] We turn now to a more detailed examination of these new analytic units for person–environment psychology.

FREE TRAITS AND WELL-BEING: HUMAN NATURES, NEEDS, AND NICHES

As described earlier, there are strong links between personality traits and well-being. Extraversion, for example, is a good predictor of the extent that individuals are likely to experience high levels of life-satisfaction and happiness (Argyle & Lu, 1990). Yet, I suspect that the prediction, understanding, and promotion of well-being might be enhanced if we consider extraversion, and possibly other Big Five traits, not only as the fixed dispositions assumed in traditional trait theory but as free traits (Little, 1996) influenced by contextual factors and the core pursuits individuals commit themselves to (Little, 1996). Recall that we view free traits as culturally scripted patterns of conduct that are carried out in the service of projects being pursued by the individual, even if such patterns are not "natural" to that person. We propose that such seemingly disingenuous action serves adaptive purposes including helping to improve one's quality of life and that of others. But it can also exact costs.

My students and I recently initiated a program of empirical research on free traits based on the following 6 propositions:

> 1. Individuals differ in the biological disposition to extraversion, for example, in their need for neocortical stimulation (Eysenck, 1987). This is their *genotypic extraversion* and can be regarded as a constituent aspect of their "first natures" (Little, 1996).
> 2. Individuals differ in the extent that they are seen by others as being extraverted. This is their *phenotypic extraversion*, and may derive directly from genotypic propensities or may be learned sufficiently well to have become "second nature" to them.[7]
> 3. Genotypic and phenotypic extraversion are partially independent, therefore in a given population there will be some individuals who are *pseudo-extraverts*, *real extraverts*, *pseudo-introverts*, and *real introverts*

---

[6]For a more detailed treatment of the historical background of concepts linking personality and environmental psychology see Little (1987c).

[7]The distinction between genotypic and phenotypic traits, and the complexities of their interaction with the environment, is of long standing interest in behavioral genetics (e.g., Scarr & McCartney, 1983). Although the argument for free traits does not require demonstration of a strong genetic component of a given trait, some of the more interesting aspects of the model arise when genetic influences are operative.

based on the concordance or discordance between their genotypic and phenotypic extraversion.

4. Protractedly acting "out of character" (i.e., as a pseudo-extravert or pseudo-introvert) induces strain that can exact costs in well-being. The greater the discordance with first natures, the greater will be the strain. At first, costs will involve psychological discomfort; eventually they may result in declines in health and physical well-being.

5. The costs of acting out of character can be mitigated by the availability of "restorative niches" where individuals have a chance to express their first natures.[8]

6. Environments differ in the extent that they afford niches where first natures can be enacted and restored.

I will briefly elaborate on each of these 6 propositions.

First, individual differences in the biological bases of extraversion and its genetic origin are increasingly recognized among personality researchers (Eysenck, 1990). One of the most extensively researched hypotheses is that variation in extraversion arises from differences in chronic levels of stimulation in the neocortex, with extraverts chronically under, and introverts over, an optimal level of arousal (Eysenck, 1987). Thus, extraverts will be more likely to seek stimulation by acting on the environment or directly arousing the neocortex through ingestion of Central Nervous System (CNS) stimulants. Contrastingly, true introverts will be more likely to avoid stimulating situations and will have their performance temporarily enhanced by ingestion of CNS depressants. Seeking stimulation, by extraverts, and solace, by introverts, has a plausible neurophysiological base, sufficient to allow us to characterize these propensities as "first natures."

The second proposition is concerned with precisely the types of observations that gave rise to the great trait debate in personality in the late 1960s and early 1970s. Largely stimulated by Mischel's (1968, 1990) multipronged analysis of the predictive and explanatory insufficiency of orthodox trait models, the belief that fixed traits could yield high probability predictions about human conduct in particular settings became discredited. Both contextual and cognitive guides to behavior were invoked as part of the situationist critique of trait psychology (Argyle & Little, 1972; Krahé, 1992; Little, 1987; Mischel, 1968).

There was, to be sure, a vigorous response by trait psychologists in personality psychology (Block, 1977; Craik, 1986), and subsequent developments

---

[8]The idea of restorative environments was introduced by Kaplan (1983) and there is a growing research interest in the topic (Hartig, Book, Garvill, Olsson, & Garling, 1996).

enhanced both the explanatory sophistication and predictive precision of trait concepts (Buss & Craik, 1983, 1984; Krahé, 1992; Wiggins, 1974). Nonetheless, a case can be made that there is individual variability in the extent to which people display extraverted behavior in different contexts, discrepancies in how individuals and others appraise their extraversion, and occasions when extraversion is prescribed by the behavior setting or demands of the valued projects being pursued.

Proposition three suggests simply that the relationship between genotypic and phenotypic extraversion is not invariably high. The extent of disjunction will be determined by the operation of situational, social and cultural norms. The concepts of pseudo-extraversion and pseudo-introversion are invoked in order to highlight the fact that as a result of the partial independence of genotypic and phenotypic extraversion, some individuals can be regarded as acting disingenuously.

The fourth proposition advances the idea that strain is induced in individuals who act out of character for intense or protracted periods. In the case of pseudo-extraversion, there are several reasons why there are likely to be costs for this discrepant conduct. Acting in a manner that requires suppression of natural tendencies, in itself, has an impact on the autonomic nervous system and may influence immune system functioning (Pennebaker, 1989; Wegner, 1989). Also, there is a distinctive feature of pseudo-extraverted behavior.[9] Acting "extravertedly" involves entering into stimulating behavior settings, engaging in sociable exchanges with others, or being the center of attention in a group—all of which may cause an increase in neocortical arousal. Because pseudo-extraverts are, by definition, true introverts, they are already chronically over an optimal level of neocortical arousal. They are, thus, likely to find that periods of extraverted conduct extract a toll in terms of effectiveness of problem solving and ability to process information effectively. This is likely to lead to strain, perhaps exacerbated by increased autonomic arousal at very high levels of neocortical arousal.[10]

---

[9]The extraversion dimension is distinctive in that acting out of character generates the neocortical state least conductive to effective performance. In the case of neuroticism, to the extent that it is mediated by differences in thresholds for autonomic arousal, it may show similar costs for individuals who are acting in a pseudo-stable manner. Disingenuous conduct, in the case of the other Big Five dimensions, would not seem to introduce costs that directly reflect the operation of antagonistic states of arousal.

[10]Note, also that pseudo-introverts may likely experience a lowering of neocortical arousal when engaged in introverted, slow-paced tasks and would, consequently, be below optimal arousal level and require an exciting restorative niche. It is less likely that they will experience the additional exacerbation of autonomic arousal when bored, however, and in this respect are likely to cope somewhat better than pseudo-extraverts, who are faced with both debilitating levels of autonomic and neocortical arousal.

These propositions focus on the individual's first nature needs; propositions 5 and 6 deal with environmental *niches*. The concept of niches is a mainstay of evolutionary theory and has been readily incorporated into the fields of developmental and personality psychology (e.g., Buss, 1987; Tooby & Cosmides, 1990). Next, we describe two types of niches—*restorative niches* and *specialization niches*.

In our model, a restorative niche is a place or setting, often at a very microscale, where individuals who are acting out of character may escape in order to restore their first natures. Our model predicts that the perceived availability of a restorative niche in itself will be a key factor in mitigating the strain of free-traited behavior. Clearly, a niche that is restorative for one individual may not be for another. A pseudo-introvert, who is naturally extraverted but has been pursuing an introverted project or role, may need to restore herself at a blast-your-socks-off rock concert. It is at precisely the same concert that her pseudo-extraverted friend is likely to seek respite by going outside for a moment of quiet (perhaps, under the pretext of needing fresh air).

The final proposition underscores the fact that environments vary in the extent that they provide for the expression of different traits. *Specialization niches* are settings where individuals with specialized orientations are given full opportunity to have those propensities expressed and valued (Little, 1972, 1976). A mainstay of research in person–environment psychology has been the study of person–environment fit, the extent that individuals are able to find niches to express their interests, orientations, and competencies (Pervin, 1968; Price, 1974). Two examples of environments that can channelize, or constrain, the expression of natural traits are *families* and work *settings*.

One of the most provocative findings in behavioral genetics has been that the effect on children raised in the same family environment makes them *more different* from one another (Plomin & Daniels, 1987), underscoring the fact that siblings are frequently highly dissimilar in personality. A recently published, decades-long exploration of the birth order effect by Sulloway (1996) argues that earlier-born children, relative to later-born, have a greater choice of niches through which to express their personalities and also attract parental investment. Later-born children, rather than competing for niches with older, more competent siblings, adopt the more adaptive Darwinian strategy of *niche diversification*. Sulloway (1996) documents the far-reaching implications that such familial niche-picking strategies have for first-born conservativism and later-born receptivity to revolution and creative change. From our free trait perspective, the first claim to specialization niches by earlier-born children and the potential exclusion of later-born children suggests that it may be particularly the latter group who are most apt to act disingenuously. An introverted first-born can nestle into the niche of being reflective, quiet, and studious, whereas the later-born sibling, equally introverted, may need to seek out or create a niche of pseudo-extraverted gregariousness. If this assumption is correct, we would predict that later-born siblings would be particularly in need of restorative niches, and in the absence of such niches, are likely to have lower levels of well-being.

More speculatively, we suggest a similar process occurs within organizations, when early-comers (those who have already filled the most desirable, or normatively mandated, niches) may preclude late-comers, or less powerful organizational members, from occupying niches that would be congruent with their first natures. The late-comers will then be particularly attuned to discovering or creating special niches in which to be themselves. To the extent that such niches are not forthcoming, and they are forced to act out of character, we would expect these individuals, like younger siblings, to feel both an acute sense of unfairness with the work environment and a heightened need for restorative niches. We shall revisit this issue when we discuss personal contexts in the work environment later in this chapter.

A central assumption of the free trait model is that free-traited behavior is motivated by factors that go well beyond acting out of one's natural temperament. Such protracted acts of "disingenuous" conduct may arise out of commitments to enduring concerns, core projects, or vital roles that give meaning to a person's life (Little, 1999; McGregor & Little, 1998). Thus the reasons for the quotation marks around the word "disingenuous." Although pseudo-extraversion may be unnatural, it may be entirely ingenuous in that it reflects the person's core projects. That the price of such integrity may be a compromise with one's well-being and health is a source of perplexity in many lives. Note that here we have deliberately chosen the ambiguous phrase "acting out of character" as a description of such behavior. The phrase can mean, in one sense of "out," that you are acting away from, or against, your true character or nature. Yet it can also mean acting "on behalf of" or "as expressive of" one's true character. Both senses of the word are implicated in our model of free traits. One may act unnaturally (sense 1) in order to act on principle (sense 2).[11]

---

[11]It is possible (indeed likely) that individuals will engage in projects that are entirely consistent with their natural traits. Do we wish to refer to this as free-traited action? Logically, it would make sense to do so; but we have invoked the concept of free traits to highlight the problematic domain of people acting out of character. I would suggest, then that we might differentiate such trait-project consistent action from inconsistent action by referring to it as "natural action" (see Little, 1987c) and view it as a relatively nonproblematic aspect of free traits. I am much indebted to Ken Craik for helping me see the need to make these and other distinctions clear as we begin to elaborate the construct of free traits.

Not all disingenuous conduct is free-traited behavior in the sense that we have proposed here. A pseudo-extravert can act extravertedly if forced or coerced into it. We suspect that such behavior will increase strain and impose greater costs. Here, the motivational theory of Deci and Ryan (1991) is particularly relevant. They argue that behavior undertaken for autonomous reasons (our acting out of character sense 2) is more strongly motivated and likely to persist than action undertaken for coercive reasons.

We have begun testing some of the components of the free trait model in our laboratory.[12] Students were asked to rate their own extraversion as well as how they felt they were regarded by others. They also completed a set of well-being measures, and after being told what a restorative niche was, were asked to rate the extent to which they had access to a such a niche where they could truly be themselves. Based on proposition 4, we hypothesized that the greater the discrepancy between self and others ratings of extraversion, the lower would be their scores on measures of well-being. Based on proposition 5, we hypothesized that having access to restorative niches would be related to well-being, and further that such behavior would mitigate the costs of acting out of character.

The results were encouraging. First, discrepancies in self versus others'perceptions of extraversion were inversely related to well-being measures. Second, there was a strong relationship between perceived access to a restorative niche and well-being. Finally, as hypothesized, those with access to a restorative niche were less likely to pay the cost of acting discrepantly. For low niche available participants there was a significant negative correlation between discrepancy and well-being, whereas for high niche available subjects there was no correlation.[13]

We return now to the first vignette that began this chapter—the image of Peter hiding in the school washroom. It will now be apparent that we see Peter as a classic Eysenckian introvert who has found his restorative niche in the washroom, where the overload of excited and exciting students can be at least temporarily reduced. That the students' excitement may have been stimulated, in part, by Peter's own pseudo-extraverted classroom antics is likely something he is well aware of. Indeed, Peter's core project this term at school may have been precisely "to make my History class more exciting." His extraverted behavior in the classroom may be taken at face value by his students

---

[12]I am very grateful to Neil Chambers and Hugh Hotson, who are assisting in these exploratory studies in our social ecology laboratory.

[13]It should be emphasized that these are preliminary findings and suggestive only. The prediction regarding perceived physical well-being was not supported in this pilot study (indeed it was in the opposite direction to what we had anticipated). We are still puzzling over this.

and they may be genuinely surprised that he needs to escape from what appears to be so natural. His pseudo-extraversion may also not be fully appreciated by his partner, who wonders why her spouse "peters out" after a particularly stimulating evening of socializing. Peter may or may not realize that by acting out of character he may be running the risk of burning out. From our theoretical perspective, the fact that he has discovered a restorative niche is a propitious sign.

PERSONAL PROJECTS AND PERSONAL CONTEXTS AT WORK: A DIFFERENTIAL LINKAGE EFFECT?

As described in the chapter's overview, personal contexts are the idiosyncratically construed objects, situations, settings, and circumstances of daily life. We suggested that in some respects personal contexts are a conceptual commonplace in person–environment psychology, yet in other respect, they are virtually unstudied. I will now clarify this claim.

A frequently adopted methodological tool in environmental psychology is the use of *environmental attribute checklists* (see Craik & Feimer, 1987, for a comprehensive review of such measures). Typically, such attribute checklists are used to search for stable, objective features of the environment or organizational climate of the sort we would use in Block B of the social–ecological model. Richards (1990), however, has raised some important questions about ambiguities in the level of analysis where this kind of research is formulated. He suggested that, although the aspiration of much climate scale work has been valid descriptions of the objective environment, in fact, the psychometric models adopted in such research have typically been based on individual level measurement.[14] Ironically, much of the research in environmental psychology concerned with objective contextual features has been research on personal context appraisal. Obviously, from a personological perspective, assessment of the stability with which individuals appraise aspects of their environments, and the correlates and consequences of such contextual construal, are not idiosyncratic noise, but precisely the kind of signal we attempt to detect and explore.

The specific checklist we have used over the years contains a list of environmental features designed to assess the major dimensions of variation in organizational climates of different settings. It has been augmented with

---

[14]For example, test–retest reliabilities are frequently calculated by indices measuring the consistency of individual level responses, rather than the stability of mean level scores of settings across occasions.

descriptors relevant to the search for gender differences (see Phillips, Little, & Goodine, 1996, for details on its use in applied research).

We have recently presented the findings of a study based on the social–ecological framework (Fig. 4.1) that illustrates the importance of personal contexts as appraised through measures of perceived organizational climate. In a study of Canadian senior managers in both the public and private sectors, we obtained appraisals of personal projects, personal contexts, and various indicators of well-being. One finding from the initial study was sufficiently striking that we were, at first, rather skeptical about its nature and generality.

In essence, the finding was this: when we look at the appraisals individuals give of their personal projects (e.g., in terms of how enjoyable they are, how under their control, how stressful) and the appraisals they give of their own particular work environment, marked differences occur when these attributes are intercorrelated. Women managers in our sample showed a striking project–context linkage effect, with high, pervasive patterns of intercorrelation between project and contexts appraisals. For men, such linkages were largely absent, in fact, not substantially different from what would be expected by chance alone. For women there is virtually a three-fold greater linkage between contexts and projects than there is for men. After checking various potential artifacts that might explain the results we proceeded to carry out an independent replication, expecting to find some shrinkage in the magnitude of the effect. In fact, the replication study showed an even higher linkage differential between men and women (Phillips, Little, & Goodine, 1996).

The search for an explanation of these differential linkage findings has proven intriguing. In presenting the study to various colleagues, we have found the results serve as a type of projective test for various explanatory preferences. Some colleagues suggested the findings represent the operation of gender differences in field dependence, with men more likely to differentiate projects from their surrounding contexts than women. Others invoked the same construct, but labeled it as field sensitivity, with women being more attuned to, and observant of, surrounding contextual features. From a more evolutionary perspective, it has been suggested that the results may reflect proximal versus distal scanning of the ecosystem, associated in primates with male and female scanning patterns, respectively. Under this hypothesis, women are more likely to monitor the immediate work environment, whereas males are more likely to monitor the distal environment (of company predators, perhaps?) beyond the immediate milieu.

Our own tentative explanation now draws on the work of Berry (e.g., Berry & Sam, in press) and Stewart (1990) and invokes what we term an *adaptive scanning perspective*. We assume that successful adaptation to any eco-setting requires appropriate scanning of the environment, particularly, the scanning of cues relevant to successful management of one's personal projects. We anticipate that individuals who are newcomers, latecomers or minority members in a given environment are particularly sensitive to information flow within the environment. Such is the case with women managers in our initial studies. As relative strangers in a prestructured land, they need to learn the nature of that structure in the context of their own ongoing projects and they need to orient to the linkages between ongoing projects and the surrounding context (see Korabik, 1993). Note that this does not mean that women managers are necessarily sensitive to the context alone, nor to their own projects, but to the relationships between those two domains.[15] Nor does the differential linkage finding entail that there was high agreement among the women in their attributions about either their projects or environments. Indeed, to obtain the effect we have described, it is necessary for there to be fairly substantial variation in appraisals of both projects and contexts. That the results are more likely to reflect differences in being fully assimilated into the work environment than gender per se is supported by our recent findings with men and women who are working in local government, in contrast with large federal departments. Here, the proportion of women in senior management is much closer to that of men and here we find there is a substantial reduction of the differential linkage effect (Phillips, Little, & Goodine, 1996).[16]

One practical implication of this type of research on personal context appraisals is that it suggests there may be some individuals in an organization, particularly those who may be relatively new, marginalized, or under-represented, who may serve an early warning function by being sensitive to underlying patterns in the workplace. Like the canaries used by miners to detect gases underground, such individuals may get the first whiff of potential discord in an environment. Less ominously, they may also be able to sniff

---

[15]In a sense female participants in these studies were construing via implicit canonical correlations, extracting optimal degrees of covariation between their projects and contexts.

[16]It is important to emphasize that the linkage effect we are describing was assessed at the *group* level in this research. For both theoretical and applied reasons it will be important to see if it can be recovered at an *individual* level of analysis. We are currently working on this and are dealing with technical issues that arise (such as finding an individual level analog to climate scale measures and having enough projects to yield sufficient power to detect linkages).

out centers of support or unoccupied niches that could yield benefits both to themselves and their organizations.

Consider again the vignette of Paula's not-so-propitious transition to her new job. If we assume that the project of "getting Barry off my back" is a core project for her, the results of our studies on project–context linkage would suggest that the difficulties she is experiencing there will be tightly connected with her general appraisal of the work climate, hence, her general dismissal of the whole job environment as "terrible". We would predict that later in the process of acculturation into the work setting she will begin to differentiate the attributes of the projects she is pursuing from the personal context where they are embedded. Whether contextual appraisals that are filtered through the lenses of one's personal projects are *veridical* is, of course, a key question, and one not yet addressed in our research on gender and management. As mentioned earlier, this question is a central one in the social–ecological perspective guiding our research (Little & Ryan, 1979). For now, we leave the question of the accuracy of environmental scanning in work settings an open empirical question. In the interim, however, it may be suggested that individuals who are newcomers to organizations, or remain minorities in them, may have insights to the subtle organizational nuances, niches, frustrations, and facilitators that are less readily detected by their more fully assimilated colleagues. As a relative stranger in the office, Paula may appear at odds with the rest. Yet, her tightly linked construals may be less a sign of strangeness than of estrangement, and there may be some redeemable wisdom in her first impressions.

Personal Contexts and Idio-Tapes:
Directly Sampling the Images of Daily Life

In the project–context linkage research our appraisal of personal contexts was based on individuals' attributions of characteristics to a global environment—the organizational climate of their workplace. In this section, we introduce an approach that *directly solicits* depictions of individual's personal contexts. To explain the logic behind this new method it will be helpful to discuss two other approaches to the study of people's environmental experience, the narrative perspective of McAdams, Sarbin, and others (e.g., McAdams, 1996; Sarbin, 1983, 1986) and Craik's (this volume) explorations of videotaping daily life.

McAdams recently made a convincing case for the importance of narrative theory in personality psychology and the need to solicit and study the life stories that construct individuals' identities (McAdams, 1996). McAdams proposed that contemporary personality psychology has a 3-tiered structure. *Trait concepts* reside at level one. Level two comprises constructs that he calls *personal concerns*, such as personal strivings (Emmons, 1986), personal projects, and life tasks (Cantor, 1990). McAdams argued that the second tier units are more dynamic and contextually sensitive than level one constructs. Level three is devoted to personal life stories and the ways individuals create identities (the process of *selfing* as McAdams terms it).

I find this three-tier structure compelling, although I have suggested several renovations that would provide for more effective use of the conceptual space in our field (Little, 1996). Indeed, taking up more or less permanent residence on the second floor of McAdam's model with our work on personal projects, we occasionally go down to the ground floor and join forces with the "trait-ers" (Little, Lecci, & Watkinson, 1992). And there is no denying that we have been found up in the loft listening to the narrative theorists, particularly the voice of Sarbin (1983, 1986), an early, innovative and influential protagonist of narrative theory in both personality and environmental psychology.

This third floor exposure was a major impetus to the development of an exercise that I assign to students in personality and assessment psychology courses. I ask them to type a two-page, single-spaced personal sketch about their life. The paper can take any form they feel is instructive for understanding of them. I ask them to write from the perspective of a sympathetic, but objective, third party: someone who knows them very well, "perhaps better than they know themselves," to invoke a splendid phrase of Kelly's (1955) that he used in similar exercises with his therapeutic clients. These sketches, together with a self-chosen pseudonym, are passed in on the second day of lectures and are distributed to all students in the class. They then form the focus of a research journal that the students keep throughout the course. In it, they write mini essays, critiques, and reviews of the material in the text and lectures; often clarifying, explaining, and expanding on aspects of the personal sketch.

Something quite extraordinary happens when individuals receive the sketches of fellow students on the second day of class. The sharing of these often very poignant portrayals of their peers seems to generate an immediate mutual respect. The fact that we take great efforts to maintain the anonymity of the sketches added a rather strange twist to the exercise: the students became intimate strangers.[17]

---

[17]The term "familiar stranger" has been used by Milgram (1970) to describe individuals one has extended passive contact with, but with whom there is no mutual acknowledgment (such as the recognizable people waiting at the bus stop each day). In our case, there is another level of intimacy and complexity in that the students can have fairly superficial relationships with the real "David" in their class during the year, without knowing that he is also the "speedball" character about whom they have been reading intimate material in the class sketches.

A common feature of these sketches has been the centrality of place, set-ting, and context descriptions in the life stories. The invoking of atmosphere and the setting of stage are standard conventions in narrative and dramatic discourse and there are a notable number of sketches that begin with varia-tions on the theme, "it was a cold and windy night in Ottawa when a scrawny kid called Rupert came into the world." For a broad based picture of the more dominant contextual themes in a person's life, the narrative sketch is a useful methodological tool.

An alternative approach to personal context assessment has recently been advanced that shifts the analytic focus from life as a whole to the lived day. Our expert guide here is Craik (chap. 8, this volume). Craik and his students have pioneered in having participants use small video recorders to capture the events of their day. Drawing both on Barkerian (1968) environmental psychology and literary theory, Craik's invoking of the quotidian as a focus for our exploration of the contexts of lives is richly evocative: "Lives are lived day by day, one day at a time, from day to day, day after day, day in and day out. Lives as we experience them are inherently quotidian" (Craik, 1991, p.1). The actual videotaping of a lived day advances Barker's early plea for hemerographic studies of people's lives and the need for objective recordings of the proceedings and occurrences of daily experience as a necessary step *prior* to systematic theorizing about person–environment relationships (Barker & Wright, 1951; Barker, Shoggen, & Barker, 1955).

Craik showed how episodes in a videorecord can be viewed through the theoretical lenses of alternative perspectives, including behavior setting the-ory, personal goals analysis, and trait psychology (Craik, 1998). Thus, a given sequence of actions may be construed as the claim of the particular campus behavior setting, as part of her personal project of "helping out my friend," or as a prototypical instance of the trait of "nurturance" (Craik, 1998).

One of the most intriguing aspects of Craik's research is what he reported as a FASTFORWARD impulse that judges feel when viewing the videorecordings where they wish to speed up the tape to get to something noteworthy. This raises the provocative question of whether psychologists may be "inadvertently engaged in a conspiracy to make persons and social life much more interesting and intriguing than they really are?" (Craik, 1998, p. x)

Narrative sketches and videotapes provide effective and complementary methods for assessing the personal contexts of people's lives. The latter pro-vides a record of what actually goes on in a daily life; the former provides a person's construal of the significance of context in their life story. Reflecting on the complementary strengths of these two approaches and on the practical and conceptual complexities entailed in compiling a videorecording, another possible way of approaching personal context assessment became apparent to us. Why not merge the goals of videotaping and life stories by having individuals take us through an *imaginary videotaping* of their personal contexts? The FASTFORWARD impulse could be circumvented because individuals would only shoot the salient images and scenes that were central to their unfolding story. Out of these musings a technique we term *idio-tape analysis* has emerged.

The essential idea in idio-tape analysis is that individuals are asked to write down the images, scenes, or objects that they feel are important to understanding their lives. By giving them freedom to envisage scenes and create images of their personal contexts they can bring into focus what might be technically difficult or impossible with a real videocamera. Hidden objects, past memories, future selves, imaginary settings, feared intrusions, shades of significance, and atmospheric subtleties can come into view. These are idiosyncratic imaginal "videotapes," or simply, idio-tapes.[18] Although we are just at the early stages of development of this technique we are encouraged by what we have seen so far in the protocols of our respondents. Next, I briefly explain the technique.

The first component of idio-tape analysis is the elicitation of a sampling of the images that are salient and important in the lives of the respondents. Although it is possible to ask directly for such elements, we found it helpful to provide a set of examples as guidelines and to explain the goal of idio-taping in detail to our respondents. In our initial explorations we provided the following explanation:[19]

> We are interested in studying the ways in which people are influenced by their daily circumstances, surroundings and conditions under which they live—the everyday things (including objects, other people, roles, relationships, etc.) with which we must cope and which may be the source of both pain and delight. We call these aspects of our surroundings our personal contexts. The elements of our personal contexts often take the form of highly personal images and can range from "my cat, Mits," to the image of oneself as "currently unemployed in a faltering economy".

---

[18]Note we could just as appropriately talk about *ideo*-tapes, emphasizing the imaginal, ideational aspects of the exercise. I prefer the *idio* root because of its emphasis on the singular, idiosyncratic, and idiographic nature of the probes. The only admonition I would offer regarding this new term is to ensure that a hyphen is not placed between the "t" and the "a," or we may find that the topic attracts the misguided interests of primate psychopathologists.

[19]These instructions are intended for fairly advanced undergraduate students and need to be modified for different groups.

We would like you to identify some of the elements of your own personal context by imagining that you were videotaping significant aspects of your life. Clearly there are an almost limitless array of things that you could record, but some would stand out as particularly important to you and significant for understanding your life. So what we would like you to do is imagine that you are in possession of a very special kind of videorecorder—one that allows you to record anything that is distinctively important for you. We call these idio-tapes (because they encourage you to display your idiosyncratic images and view of the world). The special features of an idio-tape are as follows: It can zoom back into past memories to reveal possible past sources of your current circumstances. It can penetrate beneath the surface of things so that you are able to "record" not only surface details but also deeper aspects of the context (e.g., a video-tape might just show a picture of your roommate Lisa; an idio-tape might describe her as "that bitch Lisa who won't let me sublet this summer").[20]

Another feature of an idio-tape is that it allows you to zoom in to very close, minute details of your personal context or to pan as wide as you feel it important to go. For example, you might feel that it is impossible to truly understand your life without taking into account that you are currently living in a country that is in the throes of political upheaval, or that you are pregnant and a key aspect of your current context is the absence of a place where you would feel comfortable raising your baby.

We do not want to restrict the concept of your personal context to the "outside environment". A key aspect of your personal context might be the circumstances provided by your current health, or the things about which you are worried and fretting. Or the feelings of love that you are experiencing for the first time in years.

The first step in completing the idio-tape method is to simply list the elements of your personal context in short phrases. Usually these are images that can be captured in a phrase. List these down the left hand column of the idio-tape record under the heading "Image". Write down as few or as many images as you feel comfortable generating. If you would like some examples to help get started, please turn to page three, otherwise please list them in column 1 of page 2. If you do take this option, please indicate in the space provided that you preferred to look at some examples.[21]

---

[20]It should be noted that in Craik's videorecording he also has explored the individual's own narrative commentary the videorecording. The distinctive feature of idio-tapes is not in their affording narrative accounts, but that they provide a broader array of images for exploration.

[21]Note. For those choosing to look at an example we provided this one: Here are the images for Karen, a 21-year-old part time student living in Toronto. Her idio-camera reveals: my boyfriend, looking mean; my strange but adored cat, Mits; mom, worried all the time and pressuring me to leave David; and me, out of work again, pregnant and terrified.

After respondents have generated a set of focal images they are asked to com-ment on the significance of this image with respect to the quality of their lives and general well-being. Finally, they are asked to rate each image on a set of appraisal dimensions that we anticipate will serve as predictors of well-being. These include ratings (from 0–10) on how positive or negative the image is in terms of the affect it generates. As in personal projects analysis, idio-tape ap-praisals can be analyzed *ipsatively*, using the single case, or *normatively*, by look-ing at mean scores on rating scales. We are also exploring dimensions relating to the vividness of the image and whether it is subjectively close or distant. Just as with units drawn from life stories, idio-tape images can be coded for the presence of thematic features. For example, we have found it possible to code the images in terms of the extent that they facilitate or block the expres-sion of agency and communion (cf. McAdams, Hoffman, Mansfield, & Day, 1996; Wiggins, 1992).

The initial results of studies with idio-taping of personal contexts suggest it is an enjoyable and revealing exercise for the "idiographers."[22] Students generated focal images that were striking. One woman's image, for example, was of a drawer in her bedroom that contained her high school academic medals. For her, the significance of this image was as a reminder that she *was* bright and competent, notwithstanding her current academic disappoint-ments. Another respondent listed an image of her grandmother's identifica-tion number on her arm—a poignant symbol of her family's history and of her ethnic identity.

When ratings on the dimensions were used to predict aspects of well-being, an interesting pattern emerged. It was primarily ratings of the neg-ative affect associated with the images that predicted (inversely) well-being. Negative affect of images was most strongly correlated with a measure of global efficacy—the extent that the students saw their personal projects as a whole, progressing effectively, and likely to be successfully completed. The more negative the idio-tape images the less efficaciously did respondents ap-praise their current set of personal projects (Reid, 1996).

Further examination of the thematic content of the idio-tape images re-vealed a significant relationship between life satisfaction and the extent the idio-tapes were rated by judges as involving *agency impeding* images. This find-ing is reminiscent of several of our personal project studies, where perceived

[22]I wish to thank Tim Pychyl and Imelda Mulvihill for allowing me to use the first version of idio-taping in their ongoing study of student transitions at Carleton, and Pamela Reid, who used these ex-ploratory data in her honour's thesis (Reid, 1996).

impedance plays an important role in lowering well-being (Phillips, Little, & Goodine, 1996; see also Stokols & Shumaker, 1982).

These very preliminary analyses of the images that students have of their personal contexts suggest that those images most associated with lowered enjoyment of life are those where the self is frozen in inaction, or otherwise impeded, in the pursuit of valued goals. Given our premise that life meaning is deeply influenced by the extent that individuals are able to pursue their core projects (Little, 1999), this convergence between research on personal projects and personal contexts is encouraging.

We now return to Maria's apartment, and suggest that she may, indeed, be seeing something very different than her parents do, both in her current context and her projected one "uptown." Her idio-tape might reveal the looming figure of her boyfriend, who has been sharing the apartment with her for several weeks (without her parents' knowledge), and who has told her that a move uptown would strain their relationship. Her tape might also zoom in on a closeup of her dog, sustaining her through some rough times, and a juxtaposed image of a newspaper clipping containing the ominous phrase "No Pets" in the ads for the new apartment uptown.[23]

HABITATS OF THE HEART:
SUMMARIZING AN EXPANDED MODEL OF WELL-BEING

We have proposed three expansions to a social–ecological model of well-being. First, free traits were advanced as a needed complement to our conventional views of fixed traits on the person side of person–environment psychology. Free traits were defined as patterns of conduct in the service of one's personal projects that run counter to one's natural temperamental or trait dispositions. Pseudo-extraversion was given as an example of this strategy. We also proposed that there is a corresponding environmental feature that comes into view when discussing free-traited behavior, and that is the availability of restorative niches that one's first nature can be indulged as a respite from acting out of character.

The second proposed expansion of the model involved personal context assessment on the environment side of the field. It was proposed that idio-

---

[23]There are numerous priming instructions and "frames" that we could use with idio-tapes that could serve an important winnowing function, allowing us to sharpen various research questions. For example we could use affect filters ("give us your most horrible (or joyous) images"), split screens ("show us what you think your Mom's view of your personal context would be and how it links up with yours") audiotracks ("what conversations might be going on here") and juxtaposition with the images from real videotapes.

syncratic patterns of environmental appraisal are of substantive interest in their own right, above and beyond their function in allowing us to aggregate responses to form consensual appraisals of environments. The possibility of a differential linkage effect was discussed, where certain groups are likely to have strong associations between appraisals of their personal projects and their work climates, in particular, those who are relative strangers or latecomers to the environment.

Third, a new methodology was introduced for the direct elicitation and appraisal of the personal contexts where individuals act out their days. Idio-tape analysis uses a metaphorical, highly personalized videotape to capture the salient symbols, objects, and environmental attributes that an individual is embedded in.

Each of these expansions of the social–ecological model exposes a strong affective component linking persons and environments. Each in its way seems to expose "habitats of the heart"[24]–those special places and niches where we can be ourselves, pursue our core projects, and communicate through the medium of deeply personal images.

We can conclude by examining what light our revised model can cast on the personal contexts Peter, Paula, and Maria found themselves in at the beginning of the chapter, and in particular, reflect on the implications for their well-being.

Peter's behavior we would now describe as involving the operation of free traits. He is a pseudo-extravert, one who is seen by his students and colleagues as an outgoing, extraverted fellow, but who is neurophysiologically introverted, and hence, in need of lowered levels of stimulation. The washroom is Peter's restorative niche. Even there, his colleagues may wish to converse during his "lowering his arousal" project, and hence, he may find he needs to hide even further by lifting his feet and ensuring that he remains undetectable. Peter's well-being is contingent on his being able to pursue his core project of teaching well, but also on the need to seek respite from the overload created by his pseudo-extraverted conduct. Access to a place where he can nurture his first nature, a restorative niche, will be critical for him.

Paula's well-being will depend on whether she is able to pursue her core projects in her new job by finding nurturing niches and avoiding the frustrative traps that dot her adaptive landscape. Her well-being will reflect the beneficence and supportiveness of her work environment, particularly as

---

[24]Although the term is a play on "Habits of the Heart" (Bellah, Madsen, Sullivan, Swidler, & Tipton, 1985), it is not gratuitous. Indeed, the intimate association of a sense of scale and place in the development of a sense of social identity and public participation is a key Tocquevillian (1969) theme.

they play out in terms of her valued projects and pursuits. It will also be enhanced by the way that her initial impressions and concerns are taken seriously by others as offering potentially important insights into the nature of the organization. Perhaps even Barry might come around. In granting her personal constructions some credence, he might get off her back and on to her side.

Maria's needs will remain opaque to those wishing to understand her unless they can see her environment through her own perspective. For her, an uptown apartment, where no dogs are allowed and problems with her boyfriend are exacerbated, provides no perks and many impediments. In Maria's heart, her current habitat will do just fine, and if she is able to communicate the images that sustain her motivation to her parents the resistance she has to moving will appear a little less perplexing to them.

In the final analysis, human well-being, from the view of our expanded social-ecological model, amounts to striking a workable balance between the natures we are endowed with and the niches we inhabit, as we pursue our personal projects and support others in their own core pursuits.

REFERENCES

Altman, I., & Rogoff, B. (1987). World views in psychology: Trait, interactional, organismic and transactional perspectives. In D. Stokols & I. Altman (Eds.), Handbook of environmental psychology (pp. 7–40). New York: Wiley.

Argyle, M., & Little, B. R. (1972). Do personality traits apply to social behavior? Journal for the Theory of Social Behavior, 2, 1–35.

Argyle, M., & Lu, L. (1990). The happiness of extraverts. Personality and Individual Differences, 11, 1011–1017.

Barker, R. G. (1968). Ecological psychology: Concepts and methods for studying the environment of human behavior. Stanford, CA: Stanford University Press.

Barker, R. G., Schoggen, M., & Barker, L. S. (1955). Hemerography of Mary Ennis. In A. Burton (Ed.), Case histories in clinical and abnormal psychology, Volume II: Clinical studies of personality (pp. 768–808). New York: Harper & Row.

Barker, R. G., & Wright, H. F. (1951). One boy's day: A specimen record of behavior. New York: Harper & Row.

Baumeister, R. (1989) The optimal margin of illusion. Journal of Social and Clinical Psychology, 8, 176–189.

Bellah, R. N., Madsen, R., Sullivan, W. M., Swidler, A., & Tipton, S. M. (1985). Habits of the heart: Individualism and commitment in American life. Berkeley: University of California Press.

Berry, J. W., & Sam, D. L. (in press). Acculturation and adaptation. In J. W. Berry, M. H. Segall, & C. Kagitcibasi (Eds.), Handbook of cross-cultural psychology. Volume 3, social behavior and applications.

Block, J. (1977). Advancing the science of personality: Paradigmatic shift or improving the quality of research? In D. Magnusson & N. Endler (Eds.), Psychology at the crossroads: Current issues in interactional psychology (pp. 37–63). Hillsdale, NJ: Lawrence Erlbaum Associates.

Bronfenbrenner, U. (1979). The ecology of human development. Cambridge, MA: Harvard University Press.

Brunstein, J. C. (1993). Personal goals and subjective well-being: A longitudinal study. Journal of Personality and Social Psychology, 65(5), 1061–1070.

Buss, D. M. (1987). Selection, evocation, and manipulation. Journal of Personality and Social Psychology, 53, 1214–1221.

Buss, D. M., & Craik, K. H. (1983) The act frequency approach to personality. Psychological Review, 90, 105–125.

Buss, D. M., & Craik, K. H. (1984). Acts, dispositions and personality. In B. A. Maher, & W. B. Maher (Eds.), Progress in experimental personality research: Normal processes, Volume II (pp. 241–301). New York: Academic Press.

Cantor, N. (1990). From thought to behavior. "Having" and "doing" in the study of in personality and cognition. American Psychologist, 45, 735–750.

Carlson, R. (1971) Where is the person in personality research? Psychological Bulletin, 75, 203–219.

Christiansen, C, Backman, C, Little, B. R., & Nguyen, A. (1997). Personal projects: An approach to studying occupation and well-being. (Manuscript submitted for publication.)

Colvin, C. R., & Block, J. (1994). Do positive illusions foster mental health? Psychological Bulletin, 116, 3–20.

Costa, P. T., & McCrae, R. R. (1985). The NEO Personality Inventory. Odessa, FL: Psychological Assessment Resources.

Costa, P. T., & McCrae, R. R. (1994). Set like plaster? Evidence for the stability of adult personality. In T. Heatherton & J. L. Weinberger (Eds.), Can personality change? (pp. 21–40). Washington, DC: American Psychological Association.

Craik, K. H. (1976). The personality research paradigm in environmental psychology. In S. Wapner, S. Cohen, & B. Kaplan (Eds.), Experiencing environments (pp. 55–80). New York: Plenum.

Craik, K. H. (1986). Personality research methods: An historical perspective. Journal of Personality, 54, 18–51.

Craik, K. H. (1990). Environmental and personality psychology: Two collective narratives and four individual story lines (pp. 141–168). In I. Altman & K. Christensen (Eds.), Environment and behavior studies: Emergence of intellectual traditions. New York: Plenum.

Craik, K. H. (1998). The lived day of an individual: A person–environment perspective. In. W. B. Walsh, R. K. H. Craik, & R. H. Price (Eds.), New directions in person–environment psychology (2nd edition). Mahwah, NJ: Lawrence Erlbaum Associates.

Craik, K. H., & Feimer, N. (1987). In D. Stokols & I. Altman (Eds.), Handbook of environmental psychology (Vol. 2). New York: Wiley (pp. 891–918).

Emmons, R. A. (1986). Personal strivings: An approach to personality and subjective well-being. Journal of Personality and Social Psychology, 51, 1058–1068.

Deci, E., & Ryan, R. M. (1991). A motivational approach to self: Integration in personality. In R. Dienstbier (Ed.), Nebraska symposium on motivation: Vol. 38. Perspectives on motivation (pp. 237–288). Lincoln: University of Nebraska Press.

Emmons, R. A., & Diener, E. (1986). An interactional approach to the study of personality and emotion. Journal of Personality, 54, 371–384.

Emmons, R. A. (1986). Personal strivings: An approach to personality and subjective well-being. Journal of Personality and Social Psychology, 51, 1058–1068

Endler, N. S. (1983). Interactionism: A personality model, but not yet a theory. In M. M. Page (Ed.), Personality: Current theory and research (pp. 155–200). Nebraska Symposium on Motivation (1982). Lincoln, NB: University of Nebraska Press.

Evans, G. W. (1982). *Environmental stress*. New York: Cambridge University Press.

Eysenck, H. J. (1987). Arousal and personality: The origins of a theory. In J. Stelau & H. J. Eysenck (Eds.), Personality dimensions and arousal (pp. 1–13). New York: Plenum.

Eysenck, H. J. (1990). Biological dimensions of personality. In L. Pervin (Ed.), *Handbook of personality theory and research* (pp. 244–276). New York: Guilford.

Heady, B., & Wearing, A. (1989). Personality, life events and subjective well-being: Toward a dynamic equilibrium model. *Journal of Personality and Social Psychology, 57*, 731–739.

John, O. P. (1990). The "Big Five" factor taxonomy: Dimensions of personality in the natural language and in questionnaires. In L. Pervin (Ed.), *Handbook of personality theory and research* (pp. 66–100). New York: Guilford.

Kagan, J. (1995) Galen–s prophecy: *Temperament in human nature*. New York: Basic Books.

Kaplan, S. (1983). A model of person–environment compatibility. *Environment and Behavior, 15*, 311–323.

Kelly, G. A. (1955). The psychology of personal constructs. New York: Norton.

Korabik, K. (1990). Androgyny and leadership style. *Journal of Business Ethics, 9*, 283–292.

Korabik, K. (1993). *Strangers in a strange land: Women managers and the legitimization of authority*. Paper presented at the annual meeting of the Canadian Psychological Association, Montreal, Quebec.

Krahé, B. (1992). *Personality and social psychology: Toward a synthesis*. London: Sage.

Lecci, L., Okun, M., & Karoly, P. (1994). Life regrets and current goals as predictors of psychological adjustment. *Journal of Personality and Social Psychology, 66*(4), 731–741.

Lecci, L., Karoly, P., Briggs, C., & Kuhn, K. (1994). Specificity and generality of motivational components in depression: A personal projects analysis. *Journal of Abnormal Psychology, 103*(2), 404–408.

Lewin, K. (1935) *A dynamic theory of personality*. New York: McGraw-Hill.

Little, B. R. (1972). Psychological man as scientist, humanist and specialist. *Journal of Experimental Research in Personality, 6*, 95–118.

Little, B. R. (1976). Specialization and the varieties of environmental experience: Empirical studies within the personality paradigm. In S. Wapner, S. B. Cohen, & B. Kaplan (Eds.), *Experiencing the environment* (pp. 81–116). New York: Plenum.

Little, B. R. (1983). Personal projects: A rationale and method for investigation. *Environment and Behaviour, 15*(3), 273–309.

Little, B. R. (1987a). Personal projects analysis: A new methodology for counseling psychology, *Natcom, 13*, 591–614.

Little, B. R. (1987b). Personal projects and fuzzy selves: Aspects of self-identity in adolescence. In T. Honess & K. Yardley (Eds.), *Self and Identity: Perspectives Across the Life Span*. London: Routledge & Kegan Paul.

Little, B. R. (1987c). Personality and the environment. In D. Stokols & I. Altman (Eds.), *Handbook of Environmental Psychology* (pp. 205–244), –. New York: Wiley.

Little, B. R. (1989). Personal projects analysis: Trivial pursuits, magnificent obsessions, and the search for coherence. In D. Buss & N. Cantor (Eds.), *Personality psychology: Recent trends and emerging directions* (pp. 15–31). New York: Springer-Verlag.

Little, B. R. (1993). Personal projects and the distributed self: Aspects of a conative psychology. In J. Suls (Ed.), *Psychological perspectives on the self*. (Vol. 4, pp. 157–181). Hillsdale, NJ: Lawrence Erlbaum Associates.

Little, B. R. (1996). Free traits, personal projects and idio-tapes: Three tiers for personality research. *Psychological Inquiry, 8*, 340–344.

Little, B. R. (1998). Personal project pursuit: Dimensions and dynamics of personal meaning. In P. T. P. Wong & P. S. Fry (Eds.), *The human quest for meaning: A handbook of psychological research and clinical applications*. (pp. 193–212). Mahwah, NJ: Lawrence Erlbaum Associates.

Little, B. R. (1999). Personality and motivation: Person action and conative evolution. In L. A. Pervin & O. P. John (Eds.),. *Handbook of personality theory and research* (2nd ed., pp. 501–524). New York: Guilford.

Little, B. R., Lecci, L., & Watkinson, B. (1992). Personality and personal projects: Linking Big Five and PAC units of analysis. *Journal of Personality, 60,* 501–525.

Little, B. R, & Ryan, T. J. (1979). A social ecological model of development. In K. Ishwaran (Ed.), *Childhood and Adolescence in Canada* (pp. 273–301). Toronto: McGraw-Hill Ryerson.

Makinen, J., & Little, B. R. (1997). Economic dimensions of personal projects and the prediction of well-being. Manuscript submitted for publication.

McAdams, D. P., Hoffman, B. J., Mansfield, E. D., & Day, R. (1996). Themes of agency and communion in significant autobiographical scenes. *Journal of Personality, 64,* 339–377.

McGregor, I., & Little, B. R. (1998). Personal projects, happiness and meaning: On doing well and being yourself. *Journal of Personality and Social Psychology, 74,* 494–512.

Milgram, S. (1970). The experience of living in cities. *Science, 167,* 1461–1468.

Mischel, W. (1968). *Personality and assessment.* New York: Wiley.

Mischel, W. (1990) Personality dispositions revisited and revised: A view after three decades. In L. A. Pervin (Ed.), *Handbook of Personality: Theory and Research* (pp. 111–134). New York: Guilford.

Moos, R. H. (1973). Conceptualizations of human environments. *American Psychologist, 28,* 652–665.

Moos, R. H. (1979). A social–ecological perspective on health. In G. Stone, F. Cohen, & N. E. Adler (Eds.), *Health psychology.* San Francisco: Jossey-Bass.

Murray, H. A. (1938). *Explorations in personality.* New York: Oxford University Press.

Ogilvie, M. D., & Rose, K. M. (1996). Self-with-other representations and a taxonomy of motives: Two approaches to studying persons. *Journal of Personality, 63*(3), 633–679.

Omodei, M. M., & Wearing, A. J. (1990). Need satisfaction and involvement in personal projects: Toward an integrative model of subjective well-being. *Journal of Personality and Social Psychology, 59*(4), 762–769.

Palys, T. S., & Little, B. R. (1983). Perceived life satisfaction and the organization of personal project systems. *Journal of Personality and Social Psychology, 44*(6), 1221–1230.

Pennebaker, J. W. (1989). Confession, inhibition, and disease. In L. Berkowitz (Ed.), *Advances in experimental social psychology* (Vol. 22, pp. 211–244). New York: Academic Press.

Phillips, S. D., Little, B. R., & Goodine, L. (1996). *Organizational climate and personal projects: Gender differences in the public service.* Ottawa: Canadian Centre for Management Development.

Read, S. J., Jones, D. K., & Miller, J. C. (1990). Traits as goals-based categories: The importance of goals in the coherence of dispositional categories. *Journal of Personality and Social Psychology, 58,* 1048–1061.

Reid, P. (1996). *Personal context analysis and perceived life satisfaction: Lights, camera, action!* Unpublished BA honors thesis, Carleton University, Ottawa, Ontario.

Richards, J. M. (1990). Units of analysis and the individual difference fallacy in environmental assessment. *Environment and Behavior, 22,* 307–319.

Ruehlman, L. S., & Wolchik, S. A. (1988). Personal goals and interpersonal support and hindrance as factors in psychological distress and well-being. *Journal of Personality and Social Psychology, 55*(2), 293–301.

Salmela-Aro, K. (1992). Struggling with self: The personal projects of students seeking psychological counselling. *Scandinavian Journal of Psychology, 33,* 330–338.

Salmela-Aro, K., & Nurmi, J. (1996). Depressive symptoms and personal project appraisals: A cross-lagged longitudinal study. *Personality and Individual Differences, 21,* 373–381.

Sarbin, T. R. (1983). Place identity as a component of self: An addendum. *Journal of Environmental Psychology, 3,* 337–342.

Sarbin, T. R. (Ed.). (1986). *Narrative psychology: The storied nature of human conduct.* New York: Praeger.

Scarr, S., & McCarney, K. (1983). How people make their own environments: A theory of genotype-environment effects. *Child Development, 54,* 424–435.

Semin, G. R., & Fiedler, K. (1991). The linguistic category model, its bases, applications and range. In W. Stroebe & M. Hewstone (Eds.), *European Review of Social Psychology,* Vol. 2, (pp. 1–30). Chichester, England: Wiley.

Sheldon, K. M., & Kasser, T. (1997). Not all personal goals are personal. Comparing autonomous and controlled reasons for goals as predictors of effort and attainment. (Manuscript submitted for publication.)

Shweder, R. A. (1975). How relevant is an individual difference theory of personality? *Journal of Personality, 43,* 455–484.

Stewart, A. J. (1990). Discovering the meaning of work. In H. Y. Grossman & N. L. Chester (Eds.), *The experience and meaning of work in women's lives* (pp. 261–271). Hillsdale, NJ: Lawrence Erlbaum Associates.

Stokols, D., & Shumaker, S. (1982). The psychological context of residential mobility and well-being. *Journal of Social Issues, 38,* 149–171.

Sulloway, F. (1996). *Born to rebel.* Cambridge, MA: MIT Press.

Taylor, S. E., & Brown, J. D.. (1988). Illusion and well-being: A social psychological perspective on mental health. *Psychological Bulletin, 103,* 193–210.

Tocqueville, Alexis de. [1835–1840]. (1969). *Democracy in America.* Edited by J.P. Mayer and Translated by George Lawrence. Garden City: Doubleday, Anchor Books.

Tooby, J., & Cosmides, L. (1990). On the universality of human nature and the uniqueness of the individual: The role of genetics and adaptation. *Journal of Personality, 58,* 17–68.

Wakefield, J. C. (1989). Levels of explanation in personality theory. In D. M. Buss & N. Cantor (Eds.), *Personality psychology: Recent trends and emerging directions* (pp. 333–346). New York: Springer-Verlag.

Walsh, W. B., Craik, K. H., & Price, R. H. (Eds.). (1992). *Person environment psychology: Models and perspectives.* Hillsdale, NJ: Lawrence Erlbaum Associates.

Wegner, D. M. (1989). *White bears and other unwanted thoughts.* New York: Viking/Penguin.

Wiggins, J. S. (1974 February). *In defense of traits.* Invited address to the ninth annual Symposium on Recent Developments in the use of the MMPI, Los Angeles, CA.

Wiggins, J. S. (1992). Agency and communion as conceptual coordinates for the understanding and measurement of interpersonal behavior. In W. M. Grove & D. Cicchetti (Eds.), *Thinking clearly about psychology* (pp. 89–113). Minneapolis: University of Minnesota Press.

Yetim, U. (1993). Life satisfaction: A study based on the organization of personal projects. *Social Indicators Research, 29,* 277–289.

5

The Evaluative Image of Places

Jack L. Nasar
The Ohio State University

I recall walking through an unfamiliar city. It was a pleasant morning, I was enjoying the new scenery and I felt good. At some point, however, the character of the environment changed, and I believed I might be entering an unsafe area. I cannot tell you what features led to my inference or whether my inference was accurate, but it led me to change directions to avoid this area.

The visual character of our surroundings has important impacts on human experience. It can evoke strong emotions such as delight or fear. It can act as a stressor or as a restorative. It can lead us to make inferences about places and people. It can also influence our behavior, leading us to avoid or go to certain places. Perhaps you can think of areas in your city or neighborhood that you tend to visit or avoid due in part to their visual quality. We all respond not only to what appears before us, but to inferences derived from visual cues; we also respond to nonvisual properties of places. The visual quality of an individual's surroundings has powerful effects on that person's experience. For the city environment, multiply this individual experience by the millions of people who experience our cities daily. For these people, the city landscape typically lacks a consistent agreeable quality. American cities such as Boston or San Francisco may have some pleasant spots, but dullness, ugliness, and disorder prevail (Tunnard & Pushkarev, 1981).

City form represents an aggregated person–environment phenomenon. Through many acts by individuals, organizations, and governments, we continue to shape and reshape our cities. Unfortunately, too often we get a visual tragedy of the commons (Hardin, 1968). Alone, each act may appear harmless, but the aggregate looks disordered, monotonous, and ugly. City form

117

continually changes as a result of the multitude of actions, and because of this, shaping city form differs from the other visual arts, such as painting or sculpture. It also differs in that it affects many people in their day-to-day activities. As Lynch (1960) suggested, the shaping and reshaping of the city "should be guided by a 'visual' plan: a set of recommendations and controls which would be concerned with visual form on the urban scale." We need to know how the public evaluates their surroundings: Their evaluative image. What visual features produce the effects? How can we measure them?

This chapter examines the evaluative quality of our visual surroundings. It reviews empirical research on preferred and feared features. It discusses some new directions in research and application, including historiometric inquiry, evaluative mapping, visual quality programming, computer visual simulation, and psychophysiological responses. It concludes with a discussion of questions for the future of theory, research and application.

THE VISUAL ENVIRONMENT

From a public policy standpoint, governments have the power to control the visual quality of places that impact public life. They can not control the appearance of your living room, but they can regulate the appearance of public areas, from the exterior of buildings outward or the realm of urban design (Shirvani, 1985, p. 6). This is where issues of public policy meet issues of aesthetics (Goldberger, 1983). Whether a development occupies private or public land, or involves private or public resources, the exterior is a public object. American laws make it subject to public controls such as building codes, sign ordinances, and design review (Pearlman, 1988). The present chapter centers on the visual quality of public places. More specifically, it centers on perceived visual quality, for visual quality or form alone is not enough. It is the human perception and evaluation of the form that gives it meaning.

This stress on appearance does not imply a disregard for other factors that make for successful places. Rather, it suggests that decisions on appearance also have important impacts, and that we should use scientific knowledge to inform such decisions.

EVALUATIVE EXPERIENCE

Public places can evoke extreme and intense feelings, but also typically evoke smaller changes in feelings. This chapter considers the entire range of affective or emotional responses to the environment, including the more extreme positive reactions sometimes referred to as *aesthetic* response (cf. Wohlwill,

1974). I will avoid using the term *aesthetic* because of its connection to artistic endeavors, where some kind of aesthetic statement may have more importance than pleasure, and because of some individuals' view that we cannot quantify aesthetics. Psychological research can quantify human emotional experiences of the physical environment as *affective appraisals* (Russell & Snodgrass, 1989). An *affective appraisal* implies an attribution to the built environment, such as individuals' judgments that they like a particular place or that a certain type of person lives there.

Clearly, judgments of pleasantness represent an important aspect, if not the most important aspect, of the evaluative image, but the evaluative image has other dimensions. Using a variety of research strategies and measures, research has found four salient aspects of human emotional appraisals of places—*pleasantness, arousing, exciting*, and *relaxing* (Russell & Snodgrass, 1989; Ward & Russell, 1981). A potency dimension, although possibly relevant to environmental response, did not emerge as critical. *Pleasantness* (pleasant–unpleasant), a purely evaluative dimension, and *arousing* (arousing–sleepy), a dimension independent of evaluation, represent orthogonal axes. Mixes of pleasantness and arousal produce excitement and relaxation. We experience exciting places as more pleasant and arousing than boring ones. We experience a mixture of pleasantness and sleepiness as *relaxing*, and a mixture of unpleasantness and arousal as fearful or distressing. Although others have examined dimensions of meaning (Watson, Clark, & Tellegen, 1988), the Ward and Russell studies have most relevance to environmental assessment (cf. Russell & Snodgrass, 1989). Other research has either overlooked the physical environment (Heise, 1970; Osgood, Suci, & Tannenbaum, 1957) or has confounded judgments of environmental features (perceptual/cognitive responses) and emotional responses to them (Canter, 1969; Hershberger, 1969; Kuller, 1972). In contrast, Ward and Russell (1981) studied dimensions of emotional meaning for the *physical* environment. Additional work confirmed the relevance of similar emotional meaning for urban scenes (Nasar, 1988a). This chapter stresses the aspects of evaluative response having the most importance for theory, research and human experience—pleasantness, excitement (interest), restoration (relaxingness), and fear.

WHY STUDY THE EVALUATIVE IMAGE OF PUBLIC PLACES?

For theory, understanding the evaluative quality of places has a central role in psychology, due to the influence of emotion on thoughts and behavior.

For application, the effects on spatial behavior have importance to geography and city planning: two fields interested in understanding patterns of human movement through space. For establishing guidelines to make places enjoyable, the evaluative image also has direct application to design professions. Unfortunately, designers often disregard or misjudge popular values, thereby producing uninviting places (Blake, 1974; Devlin & Nasar, 1989; Gans, 1974; Groat, 1982; Nasar, 1989b; Nasar & Kang, 1989a). The differences go beyond differences in intensity of preference. What architects like, the public dislikes, and what the public likes, architects dislike. For example, we asked architects and other professionals to evaluate *high* style and *popular* style homes. Not only did the groups differ in their pattern of preferences, but also the architects liked best the homes the public liked least, and vise versa. Figures 5.1 and 5.2 are examples of the kinds of homes receiving these opposite ratings. Such expert–lay differences can result in designs incompatible with the preferences of the inhabitants and passersby.

Appearance is important. Anecdotal evidence points to the importance of appearances. Realtors talk about the way curbside appearance sells a home.

FIG. 5.1. Example of the type of style most liked by architects and least liked by non-architects (based on Devlin & Nasar, 1987).

FIG. 5.2. Example of the type of style least liked by architects and most liked by non-architects (based on Devlin & Nasar, 1987).

Retail districts throughout the United States try to change their visual image to attract extra business. We travel thousands of miles to visit places of beauty. We spend extra money for a room with a view. We complain about not having access to a window in our office or if we have a window, we complain about the view from it. Scientific studies confirm what this anecdotal evidence suggests: Visual quality is important. Research consistently shows perceived appearance and its evaluative quality as a central aspect of human response to *architecture* (Hershberger, 1969), *community satisfaction* (Lansing, Marans, & Zehner, 1970), *quality of residential environment* (Carp, Zawadski, & Shokron, 1976), and *residential scenes* (Horayangkura, 1978). Consider the behavior of squatter settlers in new, industrialized housing (cf. Nasar & Di Nivia, 1987). We observed the changes they made to their housing unit. These units lacked heat or insulation, and they lacked security for windows or doors. The area had cold weather, and it had problems with crime and burglary. Did the residents add insulation, heaters, or security equipment? No. Many residents spent money first on painting the house exterior to make it look better.

Unites States policy acknowledges the need and possibility of *quantifying* visual quality in the environment. Aesthetics and related terms such as beauty, compatibility, and harmony appear in federal, state, and local planning guidelines. The National Environmental Policy Act (1969) and the Coastal Zone Management Act (1972) mandate consideration of aesthetic variables. Federal and state courts grant aesthetics alone as an adequate basis for design controls (Pearlman, 1988). Communities use various financial, administrative, and regulatory techniques to control appearance (cf. Shirvani, 1985). Sign ordinances and guides are widespread (Ewald & Mandelker, 1977). A survey found that 93% of United States cities with populations over 100,000, and 83% of cities and towns with populations over 10,000 use design review to control appearance (Lightner, 1993). Only 3% of the communities limited design review to historic areas.

In controlling the visual environment, we must consider the effects on the many individuals who experience it (Lynch, 1960). Any given form will vary in the probability of its evoking a strong image among various observers. Acknowledging possible individual differences in response, Lynch also stressed the areas of substantial agreement. He argued that the group image, representing a consensus among many people, has value to the design and planning professionals, who shape places for use by many people. Following the scientific direction and Lynch, this chapter emphasizes the "public" *evaluative images*—responses shared by large numbers of people.

A THEORETICAL FRAMEWORK

The evaluative image arises from the person, the environment, and the ongoing interaction between the two. It may vary with biology, personality, socio-cultural experience, goals, expectations, internal, and external factors. The environment has many attributes. Observers, depending on both internal and environmental factors, overlook some attributes, attend to others, and evaluate what they see. This evaluation may involve varying amounts of mental activity. On one hand, it may involve feelings relating directly to the structure of the form. This would require little to no cognition or mental activity. On the other hand, it may arise from the content (meaning) of the form. The latter would require mental activity to recognize the content, place it into a mental framework, and then evaluate it.

Because of each human's uniqueness and unique experiences, the evaluative image of a given place or city will certainly vary across observers. Although true, this assumption leads us to no analysis useful for urban design. Science attempts to bring order to experiences that appear varied by finding agreement or universal principles. We can imagine the possible levels of agreement as varying from absolutely no agreement to perfect agreement. Although we do not share the same evaluative images with one another (perfect agreement), this does not mean we have absolutely nothing in common. The shared physical reality, physiology, and culture would produce areas of agreement in the evaluative image. Early research (Fechner, 1876) and newer studies (Canter, 1969; Hershberger, 1969; Hesselgren, 1975; Kasmar, Griffin, & Mauritzen, 1968; Kaplan & Kaplan, 1989; Nasar, 1988) confirm a strong consensus on evaluations and environmental evaluations, including similarities in response across cultures (Hull & Revell, 1989; Ulrich, 1993).

An evolutionary perspective may help explain the importance of visual quality. According to one theory, to survive, humans would have had to notice, recognize, *evaluate*, and act on events that might benefit or threaten their well-being (cf. Kaplan & Kaplan, 1982). Failure to do so would have threatened their survival. Thus, over thousands of generations, those who survived would pass on a genetic predisposition to place some priority on the evaluative image.

A broader evolutionary argument states that for thousands of years the humans species lived in the savannas of East Africa, and as a result, some contemporary human nature (and person–environment relationships) relates to our species' solutions to adaptive problems of that ancestral environment (Orians, 1986; Hogan, 1982; Appleton, 1975; Tooby & Cosmides, 1990). However, as we can only extrapolate from models of life in that era, some experts have difficulty developing and testing inferential models of living conditions then (Tooby & DeVore, 1987). Research also suggests the possibility of rapid evolutionary change (Weiner, 1995), suggesting that some adaptations to earlier conditions may have been replaced with adaptations to more recent conditions. Furthermore, humans lived an agricultural life ten thousand years ago. Still, modern evolutionary theory has made some advances for differential reproductivity, resource acquisition, and social exchange (Buss, 1995; Tooby & Cosmides, 1989). With the present knowledge, assertions that present day psychological phenomenon must have persisted via adaptive advantage appear circular, unless we have a more detailed explanation regarding reproductive advantage, resource value, gender roles, and social exchange.

PROBABILISTIC RELATION BETWEEN ENVIRONMENT AND BEHAVIOR

Research on environmental evaluation often takes a stimulus–response form, suggesting an environmental determinism, but evaluative responses conform to the interactional perspective (cf. Moore, 1989). This means that the physical environment does not determine behavior, but that behavior is not independent of the physical environment. Cognitive processes represent important mediating factors in human evaluative response. Evaluative responses have probabilistic relations to physical attributes of the environments.

Following Brunswik's probabilistic model (cf. Craik, 1983), humans may have a variety of evaluative responses to any environment. Given a set of circumstances, a particular evaluative response has probabilistic relationships to environmental perception and cognition. Perception and cognition, in turn, have probabilistic relationships to one another and the physical character of the built environment. The probabilities result from the ongoing interaction between individuals and the environment. This means that individuals and groups may have certain idiosyncratic patterns of evaluation. Because of shared biology, culture, and environment, humans will exhibit some agreement in their evaluative response to certain physical features. This model suggests two components of evaluative response.

On one hand, we can experience emotion independent of, and prior to, cognition (cf. Zajonc, 1984). This kind of evaluative response represents a rapid, initial response to gross environmental characteristics that Zajonc called *preferenda*. It precedes and occurs independently of recognition, comprehension, or cognition. It is a direct response to *formal variables*. These variables involve the structure of form, including physical properties and relationships. These might include shape, proportion, rhythm, scale, color, illumination, shadowing, geometry, hierarchy, systems of spatial relations, complexity, incongruity, ambiguity, surprise, novelty, and order (Groat & Despres, 1990; Lang, 1987; Weber, 1995; Wohlwill, 1976). One responds to them "for their own sake" (Lang, 1987, p. 187).

On the other hand, we can experience emotions resulting from cognition (Lazarus, 1984; Zajonc, 1984). Such cognition need not involve rational calculation, but can include categorization and inference without conscious thought (Kaplan & Kaplan, 1989). In relation to the environment, such cognitive influences may well take on greater importance than cognition-free affect. As we inhabit the environment and have to navigate through it, we need to make sense of it (Kaplan & Kaplan, 1989). *Symbolic* (or *content*) variables take on importance. *Symbolic* or *content* variables have to do with the meanings of the forms. The word *symbolic* refers to "a sign by which one knows or infers a thing," or "to throw or put together" (Neilson, Knott, & Carhart, 1960). It throws together the object and the observer's experience and associations. Beyond the experience of pure form, humans experience the environment through mediating variables, properties that relate to the environment but reflect the individual's internal representation of and associations with it (Moore, 1989). The meanings may take a *denotative* or *connotative* form. *Denotative* meanings refer to judgments of what the place is; *connotative* meanings refer to inferences about the quality and character of the environment and its users. Evaluative responses to the content of formal organization involve both kinds of meanings. They relate to an individual's recognition of types, categorization of objects with the same formal structure, or a composite of physical elements and relations (Groat & Despres, 1990; Norberg-Schulz, 1965). Although people may appreciate formal features for their own sake, evaluation of content depends on a cognitive process. The individual recognizes the denotative meaning (or the content of a formal structure), and infers connotative meanings to it. For example, a *visual* feature (such as grilles on windows) may serve as a useful probabilistic cue for a *nonvisual* attribute of an urban place, such as residents' concern about crime (Craik & Appleyard, 1980). This process may have helped humans survive (Kaplan & Kaplan, 1989). Confronted with something that could threaten or enhance survival, we have to be able to recognize what it is, evaluate it, and act on that evaluation. In summary, evaluative response has probabilistic relationships to physical attributes of the built environment. The probabilities stem from the ongoing interactional experience of persons with their surroundings.

Because the evaluative image results from a two-way process between the observer and the environment, we can improve the evaluative image by either shaping the observer or the physical environment. We can educate observers to notice and evaluate things differently, as do museums when they provide text or tape recorded material to explain the art. To some extent, signs and information may change people's evaluations of their surroundings (Gifford, 1980; Leff, 1978; Leff et al., 1974; Nasar & Julian, 1985; Purcell, 1995; Purcell & Nasar, 1992, Wilson & Canter, 1990). Changes in the physical form of the environment can have more direct, widespread, and lasting effects. By shaping the physical and spatial form of our cities (Shirvani, 1985), urban design can influence the experience of many people. We must learn how to shape the future of our cities so that humans enjoy the result.

NEGATIVE EVALUATION: FEAR OF CRIME

People experience fear of crime as a major background stressor. It involves a perceived threat to a person's existence or well-being (cf. Baum et al., 1985, p.

185). Americans view crime as a main problem threatening quality of life in the United States (Gallup Poll, 1989). Fear is widespread with many people afraid to walk in their neighborhoods and feeling unsafe in their neighborhoods, shopping areas, work, and school (Bureau of Justice Statistics, 1984; New York Times, 1994). Fear of crime is a repetitive event. Most U.S. residents have experienced fear, and many experience it daily (National Opinion Research Center, 1987). Fear often elicits a stress reaction to avoid, reduce, or cope with the threatening situation (Riger, 1985). It limits activities, makes people feel like prisoners in their homes and neighborhoods, disrupts neighborhood cohesion, and worsens health (Taylor, 1989; Ross, 1993). As a stressor, it may well lead to intense physical symptoms and disease (Calhoun & Calhoun, 1983).

Hot Spots of Fear

Fear has an uneven distribution over space, time and populations. Some areas and times of day evoke higher levels of fear than others and some populations (vulnerable groups such as the poor elderly, and females) experience higher level of fear than others. Following the use of the term *hot spot* that refers to a high crime area (Maltz, Gordon, & Friedman, 1990), I refer to *hot spots of fear*. Hot spots of fear evoke higher levels of fear than other situations. Although hot spots of fear may be inaccurate, they may result from evolutionary forces. According to Ornstein (1991), over the thousands of years from Neanderthal to the present, fear had a lopsided payoff.

> Fail to respond to a real danger, even if that danger would kill you only 1/10,000 as often, and you will be dead. A few years later, you will be deader in evolutionary terms, for fewer of your genes will be around. However, an overreaction to danger produces only a little hysteria ... little or no loss of reproductive ability ... If panic in response to a threat in all case improved survival by even 1/10,000, those who panicked would be 484 million times more populous than those who did not. (p. 262)

This suggests a genetic predisposition to respond with fear to potential dangers, such as an attack.

Levels of Fear

We can look at hot spots of fear at two levels. At one level, you may experience an intangible worry about the chance of victimization. You may feel that a neighborhood or park is unsafe at a particular time. As a result of this generalized fear, you may avoid the area, or if passing through it, walk with others, carry protection or monitor your immediate surroundings for cues to potential danger (Goffman, 1971). At another level, you may experience a direct fear of danger of attack in your immediate surroundings.

Climate of Fear. Many factors may affect a generalized feeling of fear. One of these factors refers to the physical environment, the *broken window hypothesis* (Wilson & Kelling, 1982). According to this theory, certain cues may convey a breakdown in social order, and thus, suggest the possibility of crime in the area (Skogan & Maxfield, 1981; Wilson & Kelling, 1982). These cues, called *incivilities*, can take a social or physical form. *Social incivilities* include public drunkenness, gangs, or prostitution; *physical incivilities* include vandalism, boarded up buildings, or litter (Perkins, Meeks, & Taylor, 1992). Research shows that incivilities arouse general anxiety about potential victimization, creating a climate of fear (Nasar, 1983; Perkins et al., 1992; Taylor, 1989; Warr, 1990). For example, Schroeder and Anderson (1984) found graffiti, signs of abuse, vacant buildings, and litter associated with judgments of low security. I describe later how people give negative evaluations to incivilities and visual nuisances.

Fear of Immediate Danger. Another set of cues relating directly to anticipation of attack may evoke a fear of immediate danger. Of course, some incivilities, such as gangs may also suggest an immediate threat, but incivilities do not necessarily cue immediate danger. They convey a more general message about the possibility that an area is unsafe. For example, a boarded up building may not lead you to anticipate an immediate attack, but it may lead you to judge an area as less safe. As with incivilities, the cues to immediate danger result from both social and physical conditions. In a climate of fear (perhaps a dangerous area after dark), an approaching stranger may evoke an immediate fear. The stranger has become a social cue to fear. You do not need to perceive the stranger to experience fear. You may infer the possibility of the social condition (possible attacker) from physical cues. For fear in public places, two *interrelated* physical cues may produce inferences evoking fear: *concealment* (or blocked prospect) and *entrapment* (barriers to escape).

Concealment (blocked prospect), in the physical sense, refers to a visual occlusion of space big enough to hide a potential offender, and from where the offender could watch and emerge to attack. Concealment refers to the affordance of the feature from a potential offender's point of view. *Blocked prospect* refers to the affordance from the potential victim's point of view. (A long wall may hide someone, but only the corner offers a place of conceal-ment where an offender could hide and surprise a victim.) Other objects, such as trees, shrubs, or alcoves large enough to hide someone, could afford an attacker concealment. Dark spots caused by shadows or glare can also limit what you can see, and thus afford offenders opportunities for conceal-ment.

The potential fear related to concealment has theoretical and practical im-portance because it seems to contradict one prominent evolutionary theory of environmental preference. According to this theory, humans should like places offering open vistas (prospect) and enclosure (refuge), and they should like views to places that look as if they would afford prospect and refuge when they arrived there (Appleton, 1975). Appleton referred to the views toward prospect and refuge as secondary, or anticipated, prospect and refuge. Ac-cording to the evolutionary argument, contemporary humans like these fea-tures because the features had an evolutionary advantage (Appleton, 1975). For our Pleistocene hunter-gatherer ancestors, prospect and refuge allowed them to see without being seen, and this would have helped them hunt and capture food, and afford them protection from animate threats to survival (Lorenz, 1964, p. 181). Those humans who noticed and favored these fea-tures would have more likely survived, and passed on their genes to contem-porary humans.

The earlier discussion of openness conforms with Appleton's (1975) views on prospect: Contemporary humans prefer prospect. Views toward places of cover or enclosure, however, may elicit a different reaction. We may prefer a view toward secondary refuge or a place of enclosure when we feel safe, but in a climate of wariness, a view to a place of enclosure should evoke fear. In ur-ban settings (surely unknown in the Pleistocene era), such views (secondary refuge) could hide a potential attacker looking out. Just as seeing without be-ing seen offered an evolutionary advantage to early hunters (Lorenz, 1964, p. 181), it offers an advantage to the predatory criminal, a hunter of other hu-mans. Offenders tend to select targets and behave to enhance their ability to see without being seen (Archea, 1985; Brown & Altman, 1983; Stoks, 1983; Taylor & Nee, 1988; Tiffany & Ketchel, 1979; Wise & Wise, 1985). Thus, secondary refuge, as defined by Appleton (1975), may have different functionalities. In some situations, it may represent a positive affordance, of-fering the observer perceived protection or refuge; but in others, it may repre-sent a negative affordance, affording concealment for a potential attacker. Perhaps, we should refer to secondary refuge as *cover* in recognition of these dual affordances, and characterize it as either *refuge* or *concealment* depending on the desirability of the cover to the passerby.

Features that impede escape or connection to potential observers or helpers should also increase risk for a victim and decrease it for an offender. Facing possible entrapment, individuals would want to avoid or escape physically bounded areas. When confronted with someone perceived as a potential offender, individuals would feel less safe if the immediate surroundings impede their escape (Appleton, 1975). Even in the absence of a visible stranger, they might fear such places, because of the anticipated entrapment should an offender appear. *Entrapment* refers to the difficulty a person would have escaping if confronted by a potential offender. When motivated to escape, how much energy must the person expend?

Other researchers have referred to surveillance as a variable related to entrapment (barriers to escape) and concealment (blocked prospect). By reducing concealment and entrapment, surveillance permits people to observe strangers or criminal activity, and increases the risk to the offender of being identified and apprehended (U. S. Department of Justice, 1980; Murray, Motoyama, & Rouse, 1980; Newman, 1972).

In summary, the theory suggests that in a climate of fear, concealment (hiding places and darkness) and entrapment (barriers to escape) would evoke site-specific fears. Research confirms the relationship of these features to fear. One set of studies examined various measures of fear of areas with extreme variation in prospect, concealment (then called refuge), and escape by use of responses to a map, onsite responses, and observations of behavior (Nasar & Fisher, 1993). Although confirming the expected higher levels of fear for females over males and for nighttime over daytime, the results also revealed higher levels of fear associated with blocked prospect, concealment, and blocked escape. The observations of spatial behavior confirmed avoidance of areas with these features after dark. Another study on the same site found difficulties in police surveillance associated with the feared areas (Nasar & Fisher, 1993). In addition, a higher rate of vandalism suggested that criminals took advantage of the affordance to commit the crime.

A follow-up study used physical measures and moved from these extreme conditions to a more typical outdoor place (Nasar, Fisher, & Grannis, 1993). It measured concealment as the size of the potential hiding place (such as a tree trunk), and the prospect as the distance from the observer to the hiding place. The analysis merged these two measures. As the distance to a hiding place decreases, the occluding edge of the hiding place blocks more of the view. This improves concealment for a potential offender, and hinders a passerby from observing or escaping someone hiding. The combination of size and distance to hiding places provided a measure of the potential danger of the hiding place to a passerby. For escape, it measured the size and distance to barriers around the path. Respondents marked a site plan with the routes they used and the areas they feared after dark. Overlay maps revealed frequently used paths and 16 areas varying in fear level. The study confirmed fear as associated with concealment and prospect, and blocked escape.

A third study requested females to take a walk after dark and describe their feelings into a tape recorder as they proceeded (Nasar & Jones, 1997). Analysis of their comments in relation to the environment confirmed increases in fear associated with the presence of concealment (hiding places and dark spots), and to a lesser extent, entrapment. The social cues seemed related to an attack situation. When alone, the presence of a stranger (entrapment) evoked fear. The presence of groups of people (surveillance, potential helpers from entrapment) reduced fear.

The variable termed *mystery* (Kaplan, 1989) has been advanced primarily as a predictor of preference for our surroundings. However, some findings for mystery appear to parallel those for the dual affordances for cover (concealment and refuge). Similar to cover, *mystery* (the promise of new information ahead) leaves the observer uncertain about what lies ahead. People often prefer scenes with mystery (cf. Kaplan, 1989), but some research suggests that people can also experience feelings of fear associated with it. In a study of urban parks, Schroeder and Anderson (1984) found judgments of safety associated with two variables related to concealment and mystery. The average distance into the scene (amount of grass, water, or openness) increased rated safety and the prominence of shrubs (hiding places) decreased it. Herzog (1987) found respondents disliking narrow, shadowy canyons high in mystery. In unthreatening situations, such as a pleasant hike through familiar surroundings, individuals may enjoy the uncertainty of views entailing mystery or cover. That enjoyment would probably change rapidly, however, if they heard sound of a possible predator ahead. In a climate of fear or danger, views toward mystery and cover would probably evoke fear. The difference in response to the same feature may relate to its compatibility to the humans "purposes and inclinations" (Kaplan, 1995, p. 173) or to its uncertainty and arousal (Wohlwill, 1976). In familiar safe conditions, the uncertainty would be compatible with the purpose of exploring. In a climate of fear, the uncertainty would be incompatible with the need to avoid a danger that may lurk ahead. If the proximate environment appears to afford potential attackers, the ability to see without being seen, passersby might infer the possibility of an attacker in hiding. They need not see the attacker. The affordance (a dark spot or hiding place) always affords hiding even when unoccupied. The anticipation of a possible concealed offender would evoke fear.

In summary, at one level, pervasive cues of incivilities, such as poor maintenance and graffiti, may cue the stranger, resident, and potential offender alike of a breakdown in the social order and the potential for crime, creating a climate of fear and crime. At another level, when passersby feel vulnerable, they may see uncertainty or the promise of new information as a direct potential danger. The hidden information would reduce preference and evoke fear. In familiar conditions, the passerby may view the same uncertainty as desirable. For the potential offender, the same features might appear as an attractive hiding place. Thus, the same place may look pleasant in daylight and fearful after dark to the passerby, and although it may look fearful to the passerby, it may look safe to a potential offender.

POSITIVE EVALUATION:
TWO MODELS FOR VISUAL PREFERENCE

I have described an unfavorable side of emotional response: fear. Now, consider *preference* and *interest*. Researchers have proposed two kinds of theories to explain visual preferences. One theory views preference as dependent on arousal (Berlyne, 1971, Mandler, 1984; Wohlwill, 1976). Several kinds of variables may affect arousal, but collative variables, and in particular, complexity and novelty, have garnered the most research attention (Berlyne, 1971). Figure 5.3 shows the expected relationship between these variables, arousal (interest) and preference. As you can see, interest should increase with arousal generated by complexity. Preference should have an inverted U-shaped relationship to complexity, arousal, and interest. Low complexity would evoke low preference. Increases in complexity would produce increases in preference up to a point, called the *optimum level of arousal*. Further increases in complexity would produce a downturn in preference. The model has two processes. In one, individuals low in arousal (i.e., to the left of the peak) seek an arousal boost through reduced structure and increased uncertainty from the collative variables. They would seek diverse exploration to increase their uncertainty and arousal. In the other, individuals high in arousal (i.e., to the right of the peak) seek a reduction in uncertainty through increased structure and decreased uncertainty from the collative variables (Wohlwill,

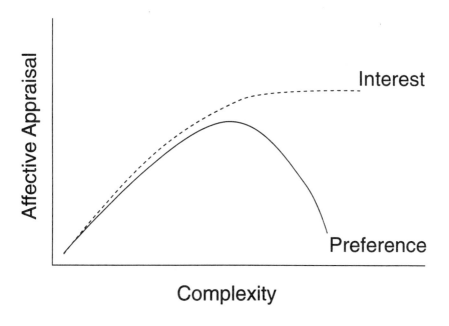

FIG. 5.3. Berlyne's (1971) view of the effect of complexity on interest and preference.

1976). They would use specific exploration to reduce their uncertainty and arousal.

Gaver and Mandler (1987) present a related argument for atypicality. According to this analysis, an individual's experience of an object, such as a building, depends on the interaction between its features and knowledge structures, or *schemas* (Mandler, 1984). We develop schemas through an active process of organizing past experience. We test new objects against our schema for that category of object. If they appear discrepant, we may expand our knowledge structure, place the objects in a different category, or create a new category. Within a basic level environmental category (such as a house), instances vary in their typicality. We see them as varying from better to worse examples of the category (Purcell, 1984, 1986; Purcell & Nasar, 1992; Wilson & Canter, 1990). When individuals experience an object that fits their schema, it looks typical or familiar, and they experience a low level of preference. Increases in discrepancy from their schema (like increases in novelty) produce increases in arousal and interest. Preference also increases with this interest and arousal up to a point. Higher levels of discrepancy would depress preference.

The Kaplans (1989) cited a potential flaw in the arousal-based models when applied to the physical environment. Because humans must navigate through the environment, cues that help them make sense of the surroundings may take on importance. The Kaplans (1989) replaced optimal level of arousal with a two-process model that has more of a cognitive flavor. Extending Gibson's (1979) idea of perceptual affordances in the environment, they argued for cognitive affordances that although related to survival, require information processing. According to them, humans needed to prefer environments that offered involvement and that made sense, or promised to make sense. Figure 5.4 displays the Kaplans' (1989) model of preferred features. In the first column, legibility and coherence contribute to preference by making environments understandable. In the second column, complexity and mystery (a deflected vista that promises further information) contribute to preference by involving the observer, inviting exploration. Coherence and complexity represent immediately available information. Legibility and mystery offer the promise of more information. As a result, the Kaplans (1989) argued that for understanding, we favor coherence and legibility, and for exploration, we favor complexity and mystery.

The theories refer to similar variables—complexity/diversity and coherence/organization—but differ in their idea of the role of arousal and cognition. Berlyne and Wohlwill place more emphasis on perception and arousal, with preference highest for a moderate level of arousal generated by a mix of diversity and structural complexity. The Kaplans take a cognitive approach, replacing arousal with information processing required to survive—the need to be involved and the need to make sense. The schema-discrepancy model agrees with aspects of the theories of Berlyne and the Kaplans. As with Berlyne, it views preference as associated with internal comparisons and moderate arousal. The use of atypicality gives a clear measure of one collative variable—novelty. Rather than having respondents judge novelty without specifying the range of stimuli for comparisons, the schema-discrepancy approach has them define the base prototypical values through judgments of goodness-of-example (Purcell, 1984; 1986; Purcell & Nasar, 1992; Rosch & Mervis, 1975). The degree of mismatch represents a measure of novelty. The model predicts a similar pattern of response to that predicted by Berlyne for novelty. The schema discrepancy model also suggests a way to achieve the Kaplans' qualities of involvement and coherence. People should experience good fit to a schema as coherent. It organizes their experience. Mismatches,

	Understanding	Exploration
IMMEDIATE	Coherence	Complexity
INFERRED	Legibility	Mystery

FIG. 5.4. The Kaplan's (1989) model of preference.

through the promise of additional information through cognitive activity to classify them, should contribute to involvement. Too much discrepancy would sacrifice coherence for involvement. Humans should prefer a moderate level of discrepancy.

ATTRIBUTES RELATED TO PREFERENCE

Research has identified five kinds of environmental attributes as relating to preferences: *order, moderate complexity, naturalness, upkeep, openness*, and *historical significance*. Liked areas tend to have these attributes, whereas disliked areas have their opposites—*disorder, low or high complexity, obtrusive man-made use, dilapidation, restriction*, and the *absence of historical significance*. Order, complexity, and openness appear to represent *formal* variables, whereas naturalness, upkeep, and historical significance appear to represent *content*, or *symbolic*, variables, but these categories remain unclear. Preference for order and openness may relate to form alone, but it may also relate to associations of the form with status. Preference for naturalness, upkeep, and historical significance may relate to their content, but it may also relate to their formal features. People may like several of these variable because of their contribution to coherence. Naturalness, good upkeep, open views, order, and historic elements enhance coherence, whereas intense uses, dilapidation, restricted movement, and disorder reduce it. According to one view (Kaplan, & Kaplan, 1982), humans may have a predisposition to favor coherence because it has fostered their survival, helping humans make sense of their surroundings so they could act to insure our safety. However, we may prefer these features for their associations with status. People do notice status and prefer "upper class" over "lower class" areas (Duncan 1973; Lynch, 1960; Royse 1969). They also make accurate judgments of social status from environmental cues (Cherulnik, 1991; Cherulnik & Wilderman, 1986; Craik & Appleyard, 1980; Sadalla, Verschure, & Burroughs 1987). They might judge places with openness, naturalness, better upkeep, compatibility (order), and historical significance as the kind that wealthier persons can afford. From an evolutionary perspective, the preference associated with status may represent a major drive and attraction for the reproductive value of status (Hogan, 1982). On the other hand, people may simply link status to income and the means to acquire desirable amenities (such as openness, naturalness, up-keep, etc.). Whatever the case, the presence of likable features will make iden-tifiable and sensuous places conveying favorable emotional meaning for many people.

Order

People like areas that have visual order, compatibility, and cohesiveness and they dislike disorder, chaos, and the lack of uniform style. Order has emerged as a prominent dimensions of human response to surroundings, and re-search consistently finds preferences associated with order and related vari-ables such as organization, coherence, fittingness, congruity, legibility, and clarity (cf. Kaplan & Kaplan, 1989; Nasar, 1988, 1989a, 1994 1997b; Ulrich, 1983; Wohlwill, 1983). Studies of preferences in two cities highlighted order as a prominent variable in preference (Nasar, 1997a). Several studies show or-ganizing variables such as legibility, identifiability, and coherence as impor-tant predictors of preference (Kaplan & Kaplan, 1989). A cross-cultural study found order as a predictor of preference for urban street scenes by both Japa-nese and United States respondents (Nasar, 1984). Clarity emerged as an im-portant predictor of the evaluative quality of housing scenes (Devlin & Nasar, 1989; Nasar, 1988b). Other work has found preference associated with increases in order. This has emerged in responses to central business dis-trict scenes and urban buildings onsite (Nasar, 1987a; Oostendorp, 1978), to photos of architectural exteriors from around the world (Oostendorp & Berlyne, 1978), to the congruity of buildings to their natural setting (Wohlwill, 1979, 1982; Wohlwill & Harris, 1980), to the compatibility of buildings to neighboring buildings (Groat, 1983, 1984), and to the coher-ence of retail signs (Nasar, 1987a).

Collative Variables

Berlyne (1971) posited collative variables as evoking arousal, uncertainty, and at a moderate level, preference. These variables involve internal compari-sons. For example, the collative variable complexity involves a comparison among the stimulus elements. More complex scenes have a larger number of different elements appearing unrelated to one another. The collative variable novelty involves a comparison between expectations and the stimulus object.

A novel scene appears discrepant from what is expected. The variable order can bring structure to collative variables. Order, discussed earlier, does not represent a collative variable, but the presence of order can provide structure, helping reduce the uncertainty from collative variables. As complexity and novelty have received the most research attention among the collative variables, this review will center on the findings for them.

Complexity (Visual Richness).   Complexity has also consistently appeared as a prominent dimension of our response to our surroundings (cf. Nasar, 1988, 1989a, 1994). This variable, also referred to as *visual richness, ornamentation, information rate, diversity,* and *variety,* involves the number of different elements and the distinctiveness between those elements in a scene. Scenes with few elements, or many similar elements, would appear relatively simple. Scenes with many distinct elements would appear more complex.

Early studies on responses to nonsense figures showed exploratory behavior and judged interest to increase with complexity (cf. Berlyne, 1971, chap. 13). Findings on real environments confirmed increases in viewing time associated with complexity (cf. Wohlwill, 1976). This finding shows stability for responses to building exteriors. Onsite judgments of interest for 20 buildings in Toronto related to building complexity (Oostendorp, 1978). For color slides of architecture, looking time, and reported interest related to one another and to complexity (Oostendorp & Berlyne, 1978). Other work has found increases in interest associated with increased complexity across two sets of housing scenes (Nasar, 1988b), and increases in excitement associated with increased complexity of retail signscapes (Nasar, 1987). The findings agree that interest increases with environmental complexity. Although lacking direct measures of arousal, the findings conform to the expectation of complexity as arousing.

The results for preference suggest a preference for moderate complexity. In studies of a variety of scenes, Wohlwill (cf. 1974, 1976) found preference to have an irregular inverted U-shaped function in relationship to (independently scaled) complexity. Other studies used artificial stimuli to control for extraneous variables present in photos of real places. In one, respondents evaluated movies of trips through scale model streets varying in diversity (cf. Wohlwill, 1976). The respondents preferred drives with moderate complexity. In another, respondents evaluated a retail signscape varied on complexity and coherence (Nasar, 1987). They preferred the scene having moderate diversity and excitement. Both studies confirmed preferences for moderate diversity (visual richness). Other research has produced contradictory findings.

However, taking into account biases in the studies (cf. Nasar, 1994), the results point to a preference for moderate complexity. The terms *diversity* and *visual richness* (cf. Kaplan & Kaplan, 1989; Wohlwill, 1976) represent complexity without negative contents such as that associated with environmental clutter and other variables that reduce order. Historical analysis of the forms of streets around the world over thousands of years confirms the desirability of complexity (Rapoport, 1990). The streets shared complex enclosing elements, many elements and textures of elements, continual variation in width, and texture and level changes underfoot.

Novelty (Atypicality).   As with complexity, research confirms increases in interest or excitement associated with novelty or atypicality (Purcell, 1986, 1995; Purcell & Nasar, 1992). People also seem to prefer moderate to low levels of novelty or atypicality, yet research has produced contradictory findings. Some studies suggest a preference for novelty (Herzog, Kaplan, & Kaplan, 1976; Nasar, 1984, 1994; Purcell, 1986) and others suggest a preference for the familiar (Canter & Thorne, 1972; Craik, 1983; Herzog et al., 1976; Kaplan & Herbert, 1988; Nasar, 1980; Kaplan, 1988; Sonnenfeld, 1966). The apparent inconsistencies result from inconsistent and inadequate ways of measuring novelty. If preference for novelty fits Berlyne's (1971) model, then the amount of novelty would affect the results, such that one study having a range of scenes up to moderate novelty might find a preference for novelty, whereas another study, with a range from moderately to extremely novel scenes, might find a dislike for novelty. In addition, the response to novelty may relate to stimulus complexity and original affect. Familiarity may moderate (or order) complexity such that people prefer familiarity in complex scenes and novelty in simpler scenes (Smith & Dorfman, 1975). When people initially dislike a scene, familiarity may further reduce preference (Mandler & Shebo, 1983). Finally, novelty and familiarity are not a continuum. They represent two distinct dimensions. *Novelty* (novel–commonplace or atypical–typical) refers more to the properties of the object or place, whereas familiarity (familiar–unfamiliar) refers more to the experience of the observer. An object or place becomes *physically* novel through having an atypical set of elements and relationships within a recognizable system, a typical set of elements in an atypical system or an atypical set of elements in an atypical system. It becomes commonplace through the reverse. You may have never experienced the commercial strip nearby my neighborhood, but if it has a similar form, elements, and relationships to other commercial strips you have experienced, you would recognize it as a commercial strip, and judge it as relatively commonplace. The observer feels familiarity with an object or place through the emotional experience. You may feel a greater sense of knowledge about and attachment to your house or immediate neighborhood than would someone living elsewhere (Brower, 1988). The object would feel more familiar to you. At the same time, you might judge the form of your house or neighborhood as novel. You may also develop familiarity through indirect experience. Although you may have never visited distant places (such as the Eiffel Tower), you may view them as familiar from your experience of them in photos or movies. This suggests the possibility that places can be familiar and commonplace or novel, and unfamiliar and commonplace or novel. Familiarity or commonplaceness may bring order, with greater meaning coming from emotional familiarity. Thus, we might expect the highest preferences to emerge for familiar places with some novelty. We might expect lower preferences for familiar but commonplace places, lower preferences for unfamiliar commonplace places, and the lowest preference for unfamiliar novel places. Variations in preference for novelty or familiarity may result from the kind of novelty measured, the context (novelty might be less desirable in housing than in a science museum), respondent's ages, and interactions with complexity and initial reaction (cf. Nasar, 1989). Furthermore, reactions to novelty and familiarity may depend on the observer's state. For example, Marans and Spreckelmeyer (1982) found that workers' feelings about the ambiance of their workplace affected their evaluations of the architectural quality of the building. Their general mood state influenced their assessment of the same familiar environment.

In a contradictory finding, Whitfield (1983) found preferences for a more typical than a less typical style. This may result from differences in content (the high vs. popular style), rather than differences in typicality in the contents. Studies researching variations within content categories found preference for moderate discrepancies from the best examples (Purcell, 1986; Purcell & Nasar, 1992). However, certain groups, such as architects, favor higher discrepancies from the shared knowledge structure than others (Purcell & Nasar, 1992, Purcell, 1995), because they develop a more differentiated knowledge structure for buildings than do others (Wilson & Canter, 1990).

Naturalness

Naturalness refers to the presence of vegetation, water, or mountains. The dimension of natural versus built up has repeatedly emerged as perhaps the most prominent in human responses to the environment (cf. Nasar, 1988, 1989a, 1994; also Herzog et al., 976, 1982). Humans see *natural* (vegetation) and *artifactual* scenes as two distinct, prominent content categories (cf. Kaplan & Kaplan, 1989). Studies have repeatedly shown nature as preferred. They showed naturalness as a predictor of preference (Nasar, 1983); the addition of vegetation to scenes as increasing preferences (Thayer & Atwood, 1978); and higher preferences for scenes with vegetation than for scenes perceived as having human intervention (Kaplan, Kaplan, & Wendt, 1972; Wohlwill, 1974, 1983). One study showed an effect on patterns of movement. Ulrich (1974) found that (other things controlled) people drove out of their way to use a parkway rather than a more direct, but less natural, expressway, presumably to experience more pleasant, natural scenery.

Beyond preference, it seems that vegetation may well strengthen the imageability of elements. Lynch (1960) reported that a great deal of planting along a path reinforced its image; and suggested that paths along water or along parks tended to be more memorable. A study of landmark qualities found the presence of nature around the building as one feature that contributed to its landmark memorability (Evans, Smith, & Pezdak, 1982).

The consistent preference for nature may relate to either the *content* (associations) or *form* of the scenes. Naturalness and vegetation may evoke favorable associations and connotative meanings associated with a scene's *content*, or nature may simply differ in *form* from the built environment. Unlike artifactual elements, natural features have more gradual changes, irregular and curvilinear lines, continuous gradation of shape and color and irregular, rougher textures (Wohlwill, 1983, p. 13). By buffering the more chaotic artifactual elements, nature may add order. Research confirms that people judge natural scenes more orderly and coherent than man-made ones.

Upkeep (Civilities)

Human beings may exhibit attention and interest in features like dilapidation, poles, wires, signs, vehicles, and undesirable land uses such as industry, referred to as physical incivilities (Skogan & Maxvield, 1981). We have seen that physical incivilities evoke fear. People dislike them and intense constructed content, and like well-kept areas. Intense uses and signs of incivilities have emerged, in open-ended questions, as having unfavorable impacts on the visual quality of two cities by residents and visitors (Nasar, 1997a). Research shows dilapidation depressing preference (Anderson, Mulligan, et al., 1983; Cooper, 1972; Marans, 1976; Nasar, 1983, 1984). Increases in the size and contrast of signs reduced preference (Nasar, 1987a); and the removal of utility poles, overhead wires, billboards or signs improves evaluations of roadside scenes (Winkel, Malek, & Thiel, 1970). Reductions in traffic relate to improvements in perceived quality of residential streets, neighborhoods, and quality of life (Appleyard, 1981; Craik, 1983; Lansing et al., 1970; Nasar, 1983). People dislike the appearance of intense uses, such as commercial and industrial facilities (Herzog et al., 1976, 1982; Wohlwill, 1982). The findings for these variables also agree with findings of preferences for coherence and for natural over man made materials. They may increase complexity at the expense of coherence thus reducing preference, or they may depress preference because of their conspicuous man-made content. Upkeep clearly represents a component of order. Maintenance and cleanliness bring order. Dilapidation and dirtiness reduce it.

Openness

Openness refers to open views. People respond favorably to the presence of open space and scenery and dislike restriction and congestion. A wider view helps the viewer to observe and make sense of a scene. A restricted view would limit this ability, and crowding and congestion would also limit one's free movement.

Evaluative maps of two cities highlighted the importance of *openness* in the evaluative image (Nasar, 1997a). In one of the earliest studies of its kind, Lynch and Rivkin (1959) had pedestrians walk around an urban block and record what they noticed. Changes in spaciousness or constriction of the streets emerged as central to the pedestrians' experience. Subsequent studies have confirmed the prominence of openness (spaciousness, density, and defined vs. undefined space) in human perception of the environment (cf. Nasar, 1988a, 1989a, 1994; Kaplan & Kaplan, 1989). The research points to preferences for defined openness, or, open but bounded space. Research has found that people prefer lower densities (Lansing et al., 1970) and that preference increases with openness (Nasar, 1984; 1988b; Nasar, Julian, Buchman et al. 1983). More importantly, research shows that people prefer moderate and defined openness (or some spatial definition) to either wide open or blocked views in both natural (Kaplan & Kaplan, 1989) and artifactual scenes (Im, 1984). Lynch (1960) pointed to the value of "visual scope" ("vistas and panoramas which increase depth of vision," p. 106) and defined space ("a strong physical form," p. 76) as strengthening the impact and memorability of nodes. Well known and well liked plazas can arise simply from the intensity of activity, but many well known and well liked streets and plazas in cities have distinctive defined spaces. For example, in a study of 192 streets from around the world, and dating from the seventh millennium BCE through 1970 CE, Rapoport (1990) found enclosed depth and width of view as common factors.

Another spatial variable deals less with the size of the view or openness, but with the *arrangement of space*. The Kaplans (1989) put forth *mystery* as preferred for its promise of new information. Deflected vistas represent one form of mystery, and ample evidence shows that people prefer deflected vistas in natural scenes (cf. Kaplan & Kaplan, 1982, 1989). It has also emerged as preferred for urban streets (Hesselgren, 1975; Rapoport, 1990). However, as we have seen in the discussion of fear, people may dislike deflected vistas in more uncertain conditions.

Historical Significance

This refers to places perceived as having historical significance. They may have historical significance or just look historical. In either case, they evoke favorable response. Several studies have found that people favor historical content. Certainly, the popularity of restored historic areas in many cities attests to the value we give to history. When researchers asked Parisians what areas they liked best, they found the Parisians preferred central historical areas (Milgram & Jodelet, 1976). They also found that historical routes were preferred in answer to a question of where you would take a last walk before going into exile. Parisians also complained frequently about modern apartments and offices replacing the greater charm of older structures. Other evidence confirms the desirability of historical significance. A survey of The Ohio State University alumni about their most liked building on campus revealed that they most liked an older building for its historical significance (Physical Facilities, Equipment and Library Committee, 1986). Several studies have found that people tend to prefer popular or vernacular styles to the high styles designed by architects and published in architectural magazines (Devlin & Nasar, 1989; Nasar, 1989b; Verderber & Moore, 1979; Whitfield, 1983). In explicit comparisons between styles, respondents from Los Angeles and Columbus, OH favored Farm and Tudor style houses (Fig. 5.5).

In a small sample study of responses to seven buildings, Marsh (1993a) found preference related to assessment of age. Non-architects showed consistent preference for the Chicago Library, a building mimicking late 19th-century Richardsonian architecture. In describing the reasons for their

FIG. 5.5. Preferred vernacular Farm and Tudor style homes (from Nasar, 1989b)© Home Planners, Inc.

preference, they referred to the mix of visual variety and order. "It keeps your eye busy taking in everything there is to see literally from bottom to top ... but they're entirely compatible.... There's a lot of different stuff, but nothing is at odds with anything else" (Marsh, p. 13). "I like the detail work.... You can tell the building is not very new—all the detail work" (p. 14). Architects also responded favorably to its historical significance, referring to the Greeks, Roman, and Palladio, but when they realized the newness of the building their evaluations turned negative (Marsh, 1993b). Historical significance also has another role. Research shows that it increases the value of a building as a landmark (Lynch, 1960; Evans et al., 1982). The preference may result from

the mix of order and visual richness, present in historic buildings, or from associations to historical content.

INDIVIDUAL AND SOCIO-CULTURAL DIFFERENCES

So far, we have considered shared evaluative response. Recall that the
interactionist perspective also suggests differences between individuals,
groups and cultures. We have seen some evidence of differences in fear and
differences in the evaluations of designers and non-designers. Other individual characteristics, such as personality, culture, internal state, and purpose,
may also affect evaluative response.

Individual Differences

Although personality theories vary from *situational* theories, emphasizing
variation in behavior across situations, to *trait* theories, emphasizing stable
characteristics of personality across situations, research findings support an
interactional perspective (Carson, 1989). Both predisposition and situation
influence behavior (cf. Carson, 1989). This suggests that personality predisposition may well affect evaluative responses to the environment (cf. Little,
1987). Researchers have found attitudes, behavior, academic performance,
and occupational choice linked to personality (Digman, 1989; Lanyon, 1984;
Myers & McCaulley, 1985). For the physical environmental, research has
found various evaluations related to McKechnie's (1977) Environmental Response Inventory (ERI). One study found differences in building evaluation
related to responses on the ERI (Gifford, 1980); another found the ERI Urbanism Scale predicted preference for urban versus rural location of practice
among optometrists (Kegel-Flom, 1976), and another found the ERI Environmental Adaptation scale predicted positive evaluation of the technological environment (Buss & Craik, 1983). Other constructs of the ERI might
also relate to environmental evaluation. For example, Pastoralism might relate to higher preferences for the natural. *Stimulus Seeking* might relate to preference for higher novelty, mystery, and complexity. *Environmental Trust* might
relate to perceptions of the security or safety of places. *Antiquarianism* might
relate to higher preferences for older and historical things. *Need Privacy* might
relate to higher preference for refuge. Other non-ERI personality dimensions also warrant attention.

   In studies dating back to the 1940s, psychologists derived 5 salient dimensions of personality (cf. Digman, 1989): *extraversion, openness to experience,
agreeableness, conscientiousness,* and *neuroticism.* Called the "Big Five," these di-

mensions have been found robust and linked to behavior (Digman, 1989). They also have precedence in young children's behavior. Observations of young children performing a variety of tasks point to recurrent patterns of behavior indicative of 3 of the Big Five personality dimensions (Gardner, 1982). Some children used copious language whereas others did the tasks silently. They vary in extraversion. Some children performed well on undefined tasks, but others displayed anxiety with these tasks, but performed better when given specific instructions to copy something. They differed in their openness to experience. Some children were person-centered and others were object-centered. They differed in agreeableness. Four of the Big Five also correlate with the dimensions of the widely used Myers-Briggs Type Indicator (MBTI, McCrae & Costa, 1989): Introversion-extraversion, sensing-intuition (or openness), thinking-feeling (or agreeableness), and judging-perceiving (conscientiousness). Research has confirmed that the MBTI is reliable, valid in predicting behavior, and correlated with other standard measures of its constructs (cf. Carlson, 1985; Myers, & McCaulley, 1985).

We need further study to determine the degree and direction of influence of these dimensions on evaluative response. For example, neuroticism that varies from tense to calm, might well relate to the sensitivity of an observer to fear-inducing features of the environment; extraversion might relate to preferences for socially interactive versus private settings; agreeableness might relate to the degree of acceptance or complaint about places; conscientiousness might relate to preferences for order and good maintenance; and openness might relate to preferences for novelty. Individuals differing on these dimensions may experience the same place differently.

An individual's internal state and adaptation level may also affect evaluative response. For example, an individual's internal state prior to rating a scene affects the rating of the scene (Gifford, 1980). Adaptation level also sets a frame of reference—influencing responses. Environmental response may depend on the kind of places typically experienced by the respondent (Sonnenfeld, 1966). The migrants' view of their new community varies based on the size of the community they had emigrated from or adapted to (Wohlwill & Kohn, 1973). Migrants from larger communities judged the new community as less noisy, polluted, lower in crime, and more safe than did residents, and migrants from smaller cities judged the reverse. A laboratory study confirmed adaptation levels effected judgments of scenes (Russell & Lanius, 1984). Cognitive set, an individual's plan for processing information, also affect preference (cf. Leff et al., 1974; Russell & Snodgrass, 1989).

Sociocultural Differences

Group differences may arise from differences in shared learning and experience across cultures and subcultures. Following Lynes (1954), Gans (1974) argued that America has distinct taste cultures, "each with its own art ... which differ mainly in ... different aesthetic standards." He described 5 taste–culture groups, distinguished primarily by education and occupation: High, upper-middle, lower-middle, low, and quasi-folk. He argued that each read different magazines, watched different shows, and lived in different areas. The model suggests differences in preference stemming from differences in experience. The groups exhibit clear differences in lifestyles and values (cf. Michelson, 1987). One study found moderate differences in connotative meanings attributed to houses by individuals from different educational and occupational groups (Nasar, 1989b). An explicit test of the model, however, found few differences between the groups, except for the high culture group (designers) who differed from all the others (Kang, 1991).

NEW DIRECTIONS

We have seen that features of the physical environment evoke shared responses for fear of crime, preference, and interest. We have also seen some processes that may differentiate responses across individuals and groups. Questions remain. Several directions in method and inquiry can enhance our knowledge for theory and practice. These include work on restorative environments, environmental simulation, meta-analysis, historiometric inquiry, evaluative mapping, and visual quality programming.

Restorative Environments

The work on environmental evaluation often assumes a deeper level effect. We might expect that improvements in the visual quality of surroundings will improve people's feelings, or *emotional reactions* (Russell & Snodgrass, 1989). Such a feeling (pleasure, excitement, calmness) involves changes in physiological state (Izard, 1977). However, few studies have gone beyond having people rate various scenes or place. Verbal measure alone may only identify what Lazarus (1984) termed *cold cognitions*, preferences that lack emotional involvement. Psychophysiological measures can capture some of the internal changes associated with emotional reactions. They can also avoid the reactive biases of verbal measures. Several studies have shown positive effects of pleasant surroundings on emotional reactions (Kasmar et al., 1968; Mintz, 1956;

Maslow & Mintz, 1956). Recent study of one environmental feature—nature—has begun to look at psychophysiological responses. The findings suggest calming and restorative responses associated with nature.

In a groundbreaking study, Ulrich (1984) observed hospital patients assigned at random to one of two rooms—one with a view of deciduous trees and the other with a view of a brick wall. Patients with a view to trees had faster postoperative recovery, fewer negative evaluations by nurses, and fewer doses of narcotic painkillers than did patients with the brick wall view. A subsequent study (Ulrich et al., 1991) found that people viewing videotapes of nature had a more rapid psychophysiological recovery from stress than did people viewing videotapes of urban scenes. Other research has found people walking through a natural environment to exhibit higher levels of restoration from stress than people walking through an artifactual one (Hartig, Mang, & Evans, 1991). Research has also observed longer term effects for an outward bound experience (Kaplan & Kaplan, 1989). In a masters thesis, one of my students stressed people, and exposed them to videotaped along one of three roads, an urban highway, an urban highway with greenery, and a parkway (Cackowski, 1999). She found that trees along the road produced a greater reduction in anger from a pretest and higher frustration tolerance. Findings have not yet clearly identified the process underlying the restorative effect.

According to one theory, the natural features have restorative effects on persons. However, a person–action–congruence model may apply. Persons experience pleasant affect when acting in accord with their traits and dispositions and negative affect when acting in contradiction to their traits and dispositions (Moskowitz & Cote, 1995). Thus, if persons have a general disposition toward selecting, seeking out, or being in natural environments, the restoration may result from the fit of the disposition, action, and setting. This means that restoration might flow not only from natural features, but also from the presence of other positively valued features reviewed. One study presented some evidence that the preference, rather than the naturalness, accounts for the restorative effect (Hartig & Korpela, 1996). In any case, the research on restorative environments makes an important public policy connection, by linking environmental appearance to human health and well-being.

Environmental Simulation

We want to generalize evaluative responses to the ordinary person's experience with real places. This suggests the desirability of obtaining onsite responses. However, the difficulty of controlling extraneous variables and getting respondents to different sites has limited the use of onsite tests. Most studies rely on various kinds of simulation. Marans and Stokols (1993) give a comprehensive overview of new simulation techniques; and Craik and Feimer (1987) offer a detailed review of the merits of various modes of simulation. Research has consistently shown that responses to color photographs and slides as accurately reflecting onsite experience, and doing so more accurately, than responses to black and white photos or drawings (cf. Stamps, 1990; also Feimer, 1984; Hershberger & Cass, 1974; Hull & Stewart, 1992; Kaplan, & Kaplan, 1989; Oostendorp, 1978; Seaton, & Collins, 1970; Shafer & Richards, 1974; Stamps, 1992).

Researchers use one of three approaches to select scenes for study. One approach involves systematically manipulating the scenes. For example, some studies systematically manipulate variables of interest on scale models and then photograph the models as stimuli (Evans et al, 1984; Nasar, 1987a; Wohlwill & Harris, 1980). By allowing the investigator to vary the experimental variables and control others, this approach can help the investigator to better identify cause. However, the results may not apply to real settings unless the simulations reflect real conditions and a realistic range of actual environments. Another approach involves sampling scenes that vary on the variable of interest, as did Kaplan, Kaplan, & Wendt (1972) when selecting natural and man-made scenes for comparison. This could yield a more realistic sample, but it may sacrifice internal validity, because other naturally occurring variables may co-vary in all of the scenes. Preselecting variables presents another problem. The preselected variable must stand out in ordinary experience for the results to have relevance to that experience. A third approach involves sampling a variety of scenes relevant to the kind of scene of interest without attempting to select scenes for the presence of an environmental feature of interest. This approach could have strong external validity, but the presence of so many variables, some interrelated, and some (such as traffic, upkeep) irrelevant to the research question interferes with establishing cause.

Computer imaging represents an alternative. It allows the investigator to digitize live images, manipulate them on the computer, and output the result as realistic color photos or videotape (Marans & Stokols, 1993). For example, we have constructed nine skylines that vary in complexity and order by importing hundreds of buildings from picture postcards, manipulating the buildings on the computer and placing them into an array that looks like a skyline. While we have not yet run a controlled test of the veracity of the simulations, I can report that several passersby have asked me what cities they were. This anecdotal evidence agrees with empirical findings. People judge the products as indistinguishable from color slides and photos of real environments (Vining & Orland, 1989). Using imaging technology, investigators can create a stimulus set that has the realism for external validity and the control for internal validity.

The lack of movement represents a limitation in all of the above simulations. What one notices and the evaluative experience of a roadside environment might depend on speed of travel. Although still photos may accurately reflect onsite experience, they probably miss some aspects of the experience of moving through place. In a pilot study, we had respondents rate slides and videotapes of scenes varying in "mystery", and we found differences in response related to the motion versus the still scenes (Heft & Nasar, 1996). The filming of movement through models, such as the Berkeley simulator represent one response to this problem (Bosselmann, & Craik, 1987; Bryant, 1991; Craik, 1993; Feimer, 1984). It is also becoming easier to create realistic environments on the computer and to simulate movement through them. One important variable identified by Berlyne (1971)—surprise—has largely gone unstudied, because of the need for movement. Surprise involves violating an expectation resulting from previous experience moving through space. Controlled simulation of movement through the environment can allow us to consider this important variable.

Meta-Analysis

When we want to structure what we know from the research evidence, we often refer to *narrative* literature reviews that integrate the findings. *Meta-analysis* also integrates the findings of previous studies, but it does so with statistics (Smith & Glass, 1977). This review of meta-analysis reflects ideas drawn from discussions on meta-analysis by Hedges and Olkin (1985), Mullen and Miller (1991) and Stamps (1997) that I refer the reader to for more detail. Meta-analysis, like other scientific research, defines the hypotheses and develops operational definitions of independent and dependent variables. Rather than collecting raw data, it collects studies of interest, and it transforms the statistics from the studies into common metrics. From those metrics, you can examine the significance and effect sizes of the combined findings. You can also examine the variability of the findings around the average effect, and the degree to which the significance levels and effects sizes vary in predictable ways. You can draw studies from journals, books, theses, dissertations, and unpublished research. Although journals may favor studies with significant findings (Chase & Chase, 1976), journals, books, and unpublished studies appear to have similar outcomes, whereas theses have weaker effects (Rosenthal, 1984). Although meta-analysis may not yield better conclusions than would a narrative review, it can enhance the precision, objectivity, and replicability of a review. The statistics increase precision; the procedures for selecting and weighting studies increase objectivity; and the explicit description of the procedures gives it replicability. Of course, the actual quality of the results depends on the care with which you define the scope of the study, define and operationalize the variables, select studies, and reconstruct the data. You can also use meta-analysis to determine how much extra data you need to achieve a certain effect size at a given probability level, or to determine the sample size needed to possibly impeach combined previous findings. Stamps (1997) has led the way in using meta-analysis for questions of visual quality. In one study, he reviewed 11 studies assessing the validity of preference responses to photographs as a predictor of onsite response (Stamps, 1990). With more than 150 environments evaluated by more than 2,400 observers, Stamps found a high correlation between preferences from photos and from the actual buildings (0.86). In another study, he evaluated design review with 500 people's responses to 400 scenes (Stamps, 1994), finding that scientific appraisals of public preferences out-performed the predictions of design review boards. He also applied meta-analysis to four of his own studies that had 170 respondents evaluating 52 scenes from different land uses and different communities (Stamps, 1995). The results showed that physical factors (scene features and content), accounted for most of the variance (90%) in response, and individual and sociocultural factors had little impact (7% and 2%, respectively). This received additional confirmation in the high correlations between various sociocultural groups. Perhaps further meta-analysis could help clarify the role of various physical features—such as novelty, complexity, and types of openness.

Historiometric Inquiry

A complete theory of evaluative responses should explain universal and longitudinal principles of preference. Unfortunately, the typical cross-sectional study, exposing individuals to stimuli and measuring their responses, may miss longitudinal effects and the process through which evaluative response holds or varies over the generations. It simply explains patterns of response for a particular period of time. If, as Lynes (1954) has argued, designers lead

popular taste such that initial public scorn changes to praise, why bother tap-
ping popular preferences? Simonton (1984) suggested the use of *historiometric
inquiry* to get at these long term patterns. *Historiometric inquiry* applies the scientific method to historical data. Thus, it defines and samples "units of
statistical analysis," operationalizes "the crucial variables under investigation,"
calculates "relationships among these variables," and uses "statistical analyses
to tease out the most probable causal connections" (p. 8), but it does so in relation to historical or archival data. For example, by examining performance records over time, Simonton identified musical masterpieces that stood the test
of time. By comparing the note structure of the masterpieces to other works
from the same time period and throughout history, he quantified attributes
that made the masterpieces different from the others. Such a scientific study of
history need not limit itself to "masterpieces" or Western culture.

Some researchers have used a historiometric approach to examining architecture and settlements. Lawrence (1986) analyzed Swiss housing forms from
1860 to 1960 to infer cultural meanings in relationship to the plans.
Martindale (1990) examined novel content in gothic architecture to identify
evolutionary trends. Rapoport (1990) sampled 192 streets from around the
world, and from the 7th millennium BCE through 1970 CE, to identify precedence for design. He also reported studies from other fields, notably a
paleosociological and landscape archaeological study that analyzed 20,000
structures in an ancient city to yield inferences about social life in the city

We have conducted two historiometric studies on architectural preferences (Nasar, 1999). We examined the frequency of citation and the
amount of space devoted to various works of architecture in five encyclo-
pedias. This developed our listing of "masterpieces" that have stood the
test of time for historians. For the 20th century, we have supplemented
this list with Starbuck's (undated) citations from 50 books about architecture from 1930 through 1945, and from 1945 through 1978. For architects, we have compiled a list from Prak's (1984) measure of the amount of
print devoted to architects in two dictionaries of architecture, and one
Who's Who book from 1963, 1975, 1977, Starbuck (undated) citations of
architects, and Brooks (undated) citations in 108 history texts. Tables 5.1
shows the resulting list of most frequently cited architects from the 15th
to the 20th century. We have used the list of masterpiece buildings to get a
preliminary evaluation of the performance of design competitions. Less
than 4% of the masterpieces result from competitions. In another study,
we had architects and non-architects evaluate photos of design competition winners and losers from a 100-year period. Both groups preferred sig-

nificantly more losers to winners, and judged significantly more losers than winners as better designs. We are presently examining the features of the buildings and architects on the lists that differentiate them from other buildings and architects of their time and from others before and afterwards. Although reliance on expert judgments of Western European and United States architecture represents a limitation, the studies serve as examples of the way such inquiry might proceed—selection of texts, sampling of citations, and the derivation of most cited works. When combined with other data and analyses, researchers can use such lists to derive principles, test theories, or generate new theories. Historiometric inquiry, used along with other methods, can provide a validity check. Where convergent findings emerge across different methods (each with their unique biases), it increases the likelihood that the findings are valid. Although some research in environmental aesthetics has used a multi-method approach (using interviews, observation of behavior and physiological measures), the methods have been constrained to the present. Historiometry adds the time dimension.

Visual Quality Programming

Our present knowledge may not provide adequate direction for decisions on appearance in various situations. Decision-makers can glean some guidelines from the research, but they may not apply to the specific situation. Perhaps, the groups or context require a unique solution. For a specific situation, you can use *visual quality programming*. This would involve the applied study of evaluative qualities suitable for the project, population, and socio-physical context. The term *visual quality programming* reflects its connection to architectural programming. As in architectural programming, the visual quality programmer investigates, develops, gathers and organizes information to produce design guidelines supportive of the goals for the facility and may evaluate the project after construction and occupancy (Sanoff, 1989). In visual quality programming, the programmer does this to produce a visual quality program or objective guidelines for the desired appearance. After completion of the design, you can conduct a follow-up evaluation to examine the performance of the program.

We demonstrated this approach for a design competition (Nasar & Kang, 1989a). A cross-section of the public ranked the five competition entries on the same appearance criteria specified by the jury as their rationale for selecting the winner. The public ranked the winning design fourth out of the five. Subsequent tests with the completed building agreed with the pre-construction evaluation of the winning entry. A campus-wide mail,

TABLE 5.1
Rankings of Fame of Architects at Various Time Periods (Nasar from Brooks)

For 20th Century from Prak (1984), most cited on the top

LeCorbusier (Charles-Edouard Jeanneret, 1887-1965)

Frank Lloyd Wright (1867-1959)

Walter Gropius (1883-1969)

Ludwig Mies van der Rohe (1886-1969)

Aalvar Aalto (1898-1976)

Eero Saarinen (1910-1961)

Louis Isadore Kahn (1902-1974)

Skidmore, Owens, and Merrill (Louis Skidmore, Nathaniel Owens, and John O. Merill)

Gerrit Rietveld (1884-1964)

Jorn Utzon (1918-)

Paul Rudolf (1918-)

Through History, Nasar (from Brooks)

Phili Cortelou Johnson (1906-)

Le Corbusier (Charles-Edouard Jeannertet, 1887-1965)

Ludwig Mies van der Rohe (1886-1969)

Walter Gropius (1883-1969)

Sir Giles Gilbert Scott (1880-1960)

Frank Lloyd Wright (1867-1959)

Henry Hobson Richardson (1938-1886)

Augustus Welby Northmore Pugin (1812-1852)

Thomas Jefferson (1743-1826)

Ribert Adam (1728-1792)

John Wood Elder (1704-1751)

Sir John Vanbrugh (1664-1726)

Nicholas Hawksmoor (1661-1736)

Sir Christopher Wren (1632-1723)

Indigo Jones (1573-1652)

Serlo Palladio (1508-1580)

Leone Battista Alberti (1404-1472)

Donato Bramante (1444-1514)

onsite interviews of passersby, and comparisons to onsite interviews to other campus buildings revealed low scores for the competition winner. Had the sponsor conducted the evaluation prior to the jury decision, the jury could have used it to inform their judgments.

For different situations, other methods might apply. Merchants and potential shoppers evaluated images of commercial signscapes manipulated on two variables relevant to a graphics code (Nasar, 1987).

Evaluative Mapping.   One special category of visual quality programming involves evaluative mapping. Just as Lynch (1960) sought community consensus on the elements that enhance the identity and structure of a city—its imageability or legibility, we can also look for community consensus on the evaluative quality of the elements. An evaluative map reveals not only the memorable features of the city but also the evaluative quality of those features. Milgram and Jodelet (1976) showed this with psychological maps of feared areas, best liked areas, and most liked streets in Paris. In studies of two cities, we had residents and visitors identify the areas whose appearance they liked and disliked in a city and give the reasons behind their evaluations (Nasar, 1997a). Overlay maps identified shared preferences and strategies for improvement of the city appearance (see Figures 5.6 & 5.7). Snodgrass and Russell, (1986) developed emotional maps for Vancouver showing four dimensions of emotional appraisals—pleasant-unpleasant, exciting-gloomy dimension, arousing-sleepy, and relaxing-distressing. Hanyu (1993, 1996) produced similar maps in response to districts in Tokyo, and in response to photos representing districts in a neighborhood in Columbus, Ohio. The evaluative image is hierarchical in that maps at smaller scales, such as a neighborhood or a block, would pick up finer grained elements than maps of a city.

Methodological Concern.   In developing a visual quality program or an evaluative map, the programmer must make choices for selecting respondents, environmental stimuli and measures of environmental features and human response. These choices involve trade-offs between what is practical, what will allow experimental control, and what will generalize to the real situation. Space constraints do not allow a full treatment of these methodological issues. However, the reader might consult a research methods text or other texts (cf. Nasar, 1997a; also Judd, Smith, & Kidder, 1991) for a more detailed discussion. For application, visual quality programming should employ realistic and relevant stimuli and measures, while minimizing loss of control.

154

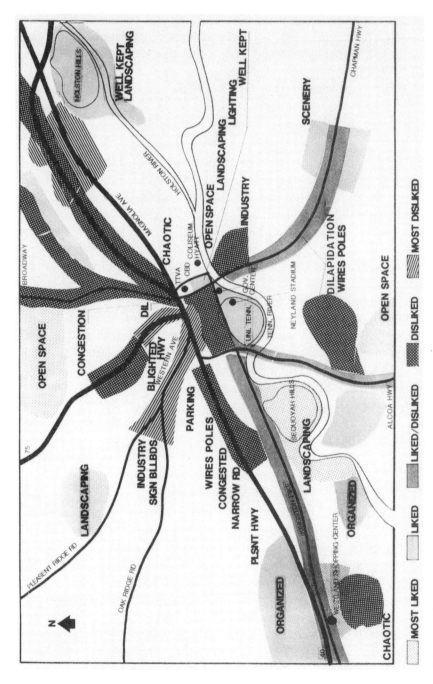

FIG. 5.6. Evaluative map of Knoxville from verbal descriptions by residents.

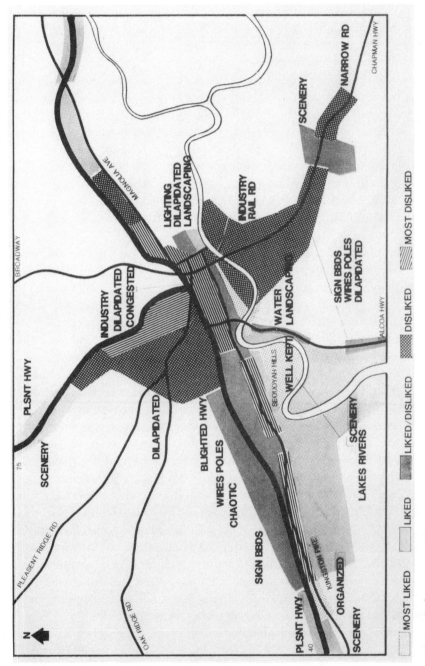

FIG. 5. 7. Evaluative map of Knoxville from visitor survey.

155

The individuals likely to experience the design represent the population to whom the program should apply. They might include all passersby, regular users of the facility, occasional visitors, and possibly funding agencies. The programmer must identify this user population or surrogates for it. For a relatively small population, the programmer could obtain responses from the full population. Otherwise, the programmer must select a sampling procedure, probability or non-probability sampling, to select respondents. Two probability sampling techniques—simple and stratified random sample—allow precise estimates for the population, but they can be difficult and time consuming to obtain. Cluster sampling can save time and still maintain good generalizability. Nonprobability tends to be most efficient, but it also tends to sacrifice the ability to generate precise estimates. An opportunity (nonprobability) sample may or may not represent the group to whom the results should apply.

I have discussed the selection of scenes and mode of presentation of scenes. Recall that computer imaging drawn from real scenes represented one approach to get experimental control and generality. Other methods may apply to a particular study situation. You also may need to measure scene attributes and human responses to the scenes. If you manipulate or select environments for variation on a scene attribute, you may need an independent measure to check the intended manipulation. For example, when we selected sites that we thought varied on prospect, refuge, and escape, we had independent observers judge each site on those characteristics to make sure that they varied, as we had speculated. You can use direct physical measures for certain attributes, such as height, depth, openness, symmetry, number of colors, or roof shape; and combine these measures to create measures of more abstract attributes. Often, you will need judgmental methods for abstract attributes (such as complexity or coherence). To reduce bias in determining the relationship between the scene attributes and evaluative experience, you should obtain the assessments of these two kinds of variables independently.

As with the environmental variables, the measures of evaluative response should reflect relevant dimensions of evaluative and connotative responses. This might include assessments of pleasantness, arousal, excitement, calmness, status, and friendliness. You can administer verbal measures, such as semantic differential scales, ranking methods, and checklists, to large numbers of people evaluating large numbers of scenes relatively quickly.

One efficient evaluative mapping strategy involves developing a random sample of the population, phoning them and asking them to define several areas that they like and that they dislike based on appearance. Follow-up questions can define the areas, find the reasons for the response, and examine other dimensions of evaluation. Although we need specific tests for evaluative maps, the research on cognitive maps indicates that such recall tasks have good reliability and validity (cf. Evans, 1980).

PROSPECTS

This chapter identified certain visual attributes that contribute to evaluative response to our physical surroundings. Respondents generally prefer structuring variables (such as compatibility, use of the typical, use of styles that are perceived as fitting a purpose), familiar and historical elements, moderate complexity, moderate discrepancies from the prototypical, defined open space, deflected vistas, and reductions in nuisances, such as traffic, dilapidation, litter, billboards, poles and wires, and incompatible land uses. Figure 5.8 shows a scene with the desired features. We have also looked at the other side of emotional appraisals to examine physical features related to fear of crime. Here we saw two levels of fear—a general climate of fear and a direct fear of victimization. Incivilities (one set of visual nuisances) evoked fears, and, at the proximate, occluding edges

FIG. 5. 8. Housing scene with some of the preferred features.

(providing concealment) and barriers to escape evoked fear. Figures 5.9 shows a scene with feared features.

For application, we must better define the linkage between judged attributes and actual physical features. We need further work in the developmental process underlying meanings and evaluative responses. This chapter has discussed several approaches to unresolved theoretical and practical issues. Historiometric inquiry can capture longitudinal trends and serve as a validity check on cross-sectional studies. Meta-analysis can help synthesize previous findings in a systematic fashion. Visual quality programming can generate appearance criteria for specific projects, and can serve as database for meta-analyses, future studies, and (in the long term) historiometric inquiries. Beyond that, researchers might improve generality by using more realistic methods. We could try to supplement verbal responses with less reactive measures, such as psychophysiological measures and observations of behavior. We can use visual imaging to create controlled realistic scenes, with animation, to enable movement. Realistic conditions may also entail connecting to public policy. Carefully chosen questions and methods can lead to advances in theory and practice, and thus improve the visual quality of the environment.

FIG. 5. 9. Scene with feared features.

REFERENCES

Americans and crime. (1994, January 23). *New York Times*, p. 5.
Appleyard, D. (1981). *Livable streets*. Berkeley: University of California Press.
Anderson, L. M., Mulligan, B. E., Goodman, L. S., & Rezen, H. Z. (1983). Effects of sounds on preferences for outdoor setting, *Environment and Behavior, 15*, 539-566.
Appleton, J. (1975). *The experience of place*. London: Wiley.
Archea, J. C. (1985). The use of architectural props in the conduct of criminal acts. *Journal of Architecture and Planning Research, 2*, 245-259.
Baum, A., Singer, J. E., & Flemming, R. (1985). Understanding environmental stress. In A. Baum & J. E. Singer (Eds.), *Advances in Environmental Psychology, Vol. 2, Methods and Environmental Psychology*. Hillsdale, NJ: Lawrence Erlbaum Associates.
Berlyne, D. E. (1971). *Aesthetics and psychobiology*. New York: Meredith Corporation.
Blake, P. (1974). *Form follows fiasco*. Boston: Atlantic Monthly Press.
Bosselmann, P., & Craik, K. H. (1987). Perceptual simulations of environments. In R. Bechtel, R. Marans, & W. Michelson (Eds.), *Methods in environmental and behavioral research*. New York: Van Nostrand Reinhold.
Brooks, S. (undated). *Index to information on individual architects in a select list of books*. Vance Bibliographies, Architecture Series, A 132.
Brower, S. (1988). *Design in familiar places: What makes home environments look good*. New York: Praeger.
Brown, B., & Altman, I. (1983). Territoriality, defensible space, and residential burglary: An environmental analysis. *Journal of Environmental Psychology, 3*, 203-220.
Bryant, K. J. (1991). Geographical/spatial orientation ability within real-world and simulated large-scale environments. *Multivariate Behavioral Research, 26*, 109-136.
Bureau of Justice Statistics. (1984). *Victim risk supplement of the National Crime Survey*. Bureau of Justice Statistics, Government Printing Office, Washington, DC.
Buss, D. M. (1995). Evolutionary psychology: A new paradigm for psychological research. *Psychological Inquiry, 6*, 1-30.
Buss, D. M., & Craik, K. H. (1983). Contemporary worldviews: Personal and policy implications. *Journal of Applied Social Psychology, 12*, 259-280.
Cackowski, J. M. (1999). *The restorative effects of nature: Implications for driver anger and frustration levels*. Unpublished masters thesis, The Ohio State University, Columbus, OH.
Calhoun, G. L., & Calhoun, J. G. (1983). Occupational stress: Implications for hospitals. In H. Selye (Ed.), *Selye's Guide to Stress Research, Vol. 3*. New York: Scientific and Academic.
Canter, D. (1969). An intergroup comparison of connotative dimensions in architecture. *Environment and Behavior, 1*, 37-48.
Canter, D., & Thorne, R. (1972). Attitudes towards housing: A cross-cultural comparison. *Environment and Behavior, 4*, 3-32.
Carp, F. M., Zawadski, R. T., & Shokron, H. (1976). Dimensions of urban environmental quality. *Environment and Behavior, 8*, 239-264.
Carlson, J. C. (1985). Recent assessments of the Myers-Briggs Type Indicator. *Journal of Personality Assessment, 49*, 356-365.
Carson, R. (1989). Personality. *Annual Review of Psychology, 26*, 393-414.
Chase, L. J., & Chase, R. B. (1976). A statistical power analysis of applied psychological research. *Journal of Applied Psychology, 61*, 234-237.
Cherulnik, P. D. (1991). Reading restaurant facades: Environmental inference in finding the right place to eat. *Environment and Behavior, 22*, 150-170.
Cherulnik, P. D., & Wilderman, S. K. (1986). Symbols of status in urban neighborhoods: Contemporary perceptions of nineteenth-century Boston. *Environment and Behavior, 18*, 604-622.

Coastal Zone Management Act (CZMA). (1972). No. 1451 (CZMA 302). Congressional hearings, and 1452 (CZMA 303) Congressional declaration of policy. Public Law, 89-454 Title III, 302, and 303, as added Public Law, 92-583.

Cooper, C. (1972). Resident dissatisfaction in multifamily housing. In W. M. Smith (Ed.), *Behavior, design and policy aspects of human habitats* (pp. 119-146). Green Bay: University of Wisconsin.

Cooper, C. (1974). The house as a symbol of self. In J. Lang, et al. (Eds.), *Designing for Human Behavior Architecture and the Behavioral Sciences* (pp. 130-146). Stroudsburg, PA: Dowden, Hutchinson, & Ross.

Craik, K. H. (1983). The psychology of the large scale environment. In N. R. Feimer & E. S. Geller (Eds.), *Environmental psychology: Directions and perspectives* (pp. 67-105). New York: Praeger.

Craik., K. H., & Appleyard, D. (1980). Streets of San Francisco: Brunswik's lens model applied to urban inference and assessment. *Journal of Social Issues, 36,* 72-85.

Craik, K. H., & Feimer, N. R. (1987). Environmental Assessment. In D. Stokols, & I Atlman (Eds.), *Handbook of environmental psychology, Volume 2* (pp. 891-917). New York: Wiley.

Devlin, K., & Nasar, J. (1989). The beauty and the beast: Some preliminary comparisons of "high" versus "popular" residential architecture and public versus architect judgments of same. *Journal of Environmental Psychology, 9,* 333-344.

Digman, J. M. (1989). Five robust trait dimensions: Development, stability and utility. *Journal of Personality, 57,* 195-214.

Duncan, J., Jr. (1973). Landscape taste as a symbol of group identity: Westchester County Village. *Geographical Review, 63,* 334-355.

Evans, G. (1980). Environmental cognition. *Psychological Bulletin, 88,* 259-287.

Evans, G., Skorpanich, M., Garling, T., Bryant, K. J., & Bresolin, L. (1984). Effects of pathway configuration, landmarks, and stress on environmental cognition. *Journal of Environmental Psychology, 4,* 323-336.

Evans, G., Smith, C., & Pezdak, K. (1982). Cognitive maps and urban form. *Journal of the American Planning Association, 48,* 232-244.

Ewald, W. R., Jr., & Mandelker, D. R. (1977). *Street graphics: A concept and a system.* McLean, VA: Landscape Architecture Foundation.

Fechner, G. T. (1876). *Vorschule der asthetik* [Preliminary aesthetics] Leipzig: Breitopf & Hartel.

Feimer, N. (1984). Environmental perception: The effect of media, evaluative context and the observer sample. *Journal of Environmental Psychology, 4,* 61-80.

Gallup Poll. (1989, March/April). Most important problem. *The Gallup Report.*

Gans, H. (1974). *Popular culture and high culture: An analysis and evaluation of taste.* New York: Basic Books.

Gardner, H. (1982). *Art, mind and brain: A cognitive approach to creativity.* New York: Basic Books.

Gaver, W. W., & Mandler, G. (1987). Play it again Sam. *Cognition and Emotion, 1,* 259-282.

Gibson, J. (1979). *The ecological approach to visual perception.* Boston: Houghton Mifflin.

Gifford, R. (1980). Environmental dispositions and the evaluation of architectural interiors. *Journal of Research in Personality, 14,* 386-399.

Goffman, E. (1971). *Relations in public. Micro studies of the public order.* New York: Harper and Row.

Goldberger, P. (1983). *On the rise: Architecture and design in a postmodern age.* New York: Times Books.

Gould, P., & White, R. (1974). *Mental maps.* Middlesex, England: Penguin.

Groat, L. (1982). Meaning in post-modern architecture: An examination using the multiple sorting task. *Journal of Environmental Psychology, 2,* 3-22.

Groat, L. (1983). A study of the perception of contextual fit in architecture. Paper presented at the 14th International Conference of the Environmental Design Research Association. Lincoln, NB.
Groat, L. (1984, November). Public opinions of contextual fit. Architecture, 73, 72-75.
Groat, L. N., & Despres, C. (1990). The Significance of Architectural Theory for Environmental Design Research. In E. H. Zube & G. T. Moore (Eds.), Advances in environment, Behavior, and design, vol. 3 (pp. 3-53). New York: Plenum.
Hanyu, K. (1993). The affective meaning of Tokyo: Verbal and non-verbal approaches. Journal of Environmental Psychology, 13, 161-172.
Hanyu, K. (1996). Visual properties and affective appraisals in residential areas. (1995, Doctoral dissertation, The Ohio State University). Dissertation Abstracts International, 56(12), p. 4978A.
Hardin, G. (1968). The tragedy of the commons. Science, 162, 1243-1246.
Hartig, T., & Korpela, K. (1996). Perceptions of environmental restorativeness as related to environmental preferences. Paper presented at the 27th International Conference of the Environmental Design Research Association, Salt Lake City, Utah.
Hartig, T., Mang, M., & Evans, G. W. (1991). Restorative effects of natural environment experiences. Environment and Behavior, 23, 3-26.
Hedges, L. V., & Olkin, I. (1985). Statistical methods for meta-analysis. Orlando, FL: Academic Press.
Heise, D. R. (1970). The semantic differential and attitude research. In G. F. Summers (Ed.), Attitude measurement. Chicago: Rand McNally.
Hershberger, R. G. (1969). A study of meaning and architecture. In H. Sanoff & S. Cohn (Eds.), EDRA 1: Proceedings of the first annual Environmental Design Research Association conference (pp. 86-100). Raleigh, NC: North Carolina State University.
Hershberger, R. G., & Cass, R. C. (1974). Predicting user responses to buildings. In G. Davis (Ed.), Man Environment Interaction: Evaluations and applications, the state of the art in environmental design research–Field applications (pp. 117-134). Milwaukee: Environmental Design Research Association.
Herzog, T. R. (1987). A cognitive analysis of preference for natural environments: Mountains, canyons and deserts. Landscape Journal, 6, 140-152.
Herzog, T. R., Kaplan, S., & Kaplan, R. (1976). The prediction of preference for familiar urban places. Environment and Behavior, 8, 627-645.
Herzog, T., Kaplan, S., & Kaplan, R. (1982). The prediction of preference for unfamiliar urban places. Population and Environment, 5, 43-59.
Herzog, T., & Smith, G. A. (1988). Danger, mystery, and environmental preference. Environment and Behavior, 20, 320-344.
Hesselgren, S. (1975). Man's perception of man-made environment. Stroudsburg, PA: Dowden, Hutchinson, & Ross.
Hogan, R. (1982). A socioanalytic theory of personality. In M. M. Page (Ed.), Nebraska Symposia on Motivation, Volume 30. Lincoln: University of Nebraska Press.
Horayangkura, V. (1978). Semantic dimensional structures: A methodological approach. Environment and Behavior, 10, 555-584.
Hull, R. B., & Revell, G. R. B. (1989). Cross-cultural comparison of landscape scenic beauty evaluations: A case study in Bali. Journal of Environmental Psychology, 9, 177-191.
Hull, R. B, & Stewert, W. P. (1992). Validity of photo-based scenic beauty judgments. Journal of Environmental Psychology, 12, 101-114.
Im, S-B. (1984). Visual preferences in enclosed urban spaces: An exploration of a scientific approach to environmental design. Environment and Behavior, 16, 235-262.
Izard, C. E. (1977). Human emotions. New York: Plenum.

Judd, C. M., Smith, E. R., & Kidder, L. H. (Eds.). (1991). *Research methods in social relations* (pp. 425–449). Fort Worth, TX: Holt, Rinehart and Winston, Inc. Fort Worth.

Kang, J. (1991). Symbolic inferences and typicality in five taste cultures. Doctoral dissertation, The Ohio State University. *Dissertation Abstracts International, 51* (12), p. 3929A.

Kaplan, R., & Herbert, E. J. (1988). Familiarity and preference: A cross-cultural analysis. In J. L. Nasar (Ed.) *Environmental aesthetics: Theory, research, and applications* (pp. 379–389). New York: Cambridge University Press.

Kaplan, S. (1995). The restorative benefits of nature: Towards an integrative framework. *Journal of Environmental Psychology, 15,* 169–182.

Kaplan, R., & Kaplan, S. (1989). *The experience of nature: A psychological perspective.* New York: Cambridge University Press.

Kaplan, S., & Kaplan, R. (1982). *Cognition and environment: Functioning in an uncertain world.* New York: Praeger.

Kaplan, S., Kaplan, R., & Wendt, J. S. (1972). Rated preference and complexity for natural and urban visual material. *Perception and Psychophysics, 12,* 354–356.

Kasmar, J. V., Griffin, W. V., & Mauritzen, J. H. (1968). Effects of environmental surroundings on outpatients' mood and perception of psychiatrists. *Journal of Consulting and Clinical Psychology, 32,* 223–226.

Kegel-Flom, P. (1976). Identifying the potential rural optometrist. *American Journal of Optometry and Physiological Optics, 53,* 259–280.

Kuller, R. A. (1972). *A semantic model for describing perceived environment.* Stockholm: National Swedish Institute for Building Research.

Lang, J. (1987). *Creating architectural theory: The role of the behavioral sciences in environmental design.* New York: Van Nostrand Reinhold.

Lansing, J. B., Marans, R. W., & Zehner, R. B. (1970). *Planned residential environments.* Ann Arbor: University of Michigan, Survey Research Center Institute for Social Research.

Lanyon, R. I. (1984). Personality assessment. *Annual Review of Psychology, 35,* 667–701.

Lawrence, R. (1986). L'espace domestique et la regulation de la vie quotidienne. *Recherches Sociologiques, 17,* 147–169.

Lazarus, R. S. (1984). On the primacy of cognition. *American Psychologist, 39,* 124–129.

Leff, H. L. (1978). *Experience, environment and human potential.* New York: Oxford University Press.

Leff, H. L., Gordon, L. R., & Ferguson, J. G. (1974). Cognitive set and environmental awareness. *Environment and Behavior, 6,* 395–447.

Lightner, B. (1993, January). A survey of design review practice in local government. (Monograph) MEMO: *Planning Advisory Service (PAS).* Chicago: American Planning Association.

Little, B. R. (1987). Personality and the environment. In D. Stokols & I. Altman (Eds.), *Handbook of environmental psychology, volume 1* (pp. 205–244). New York: Wiley.

Lorenz, K. (1964). *King Solomon's mine.* London: Methuen.

Lynch, K. (1960). *The image of the city.* Cambridge, MA: MIT Press.

Lynch, K. E., & Rivkin, M. (1959). A walk around the block. *Landscape, 8,* 24–34.

Lynes, R. (1954). *The tastemakers.* New York: Harper & Row.

Maltz, M. D., Gordon, A. C., & Friedman, W. (1990). *Mapping crime in its community setting: Event geography analysis.* New York: Springer-Verlag.

Mandler, J. M. (1984). *Stories, scripts, and scenes: Aspects of schema theory.* Hillsdale, NJ: Lawrence. Erlbaum Associates.

Mandler, G., & Shebo, B. J. (1983). Knowing and liking. *Motivation and Emotion, 7,* 125–144.

Marans, R. W. (1976). Perceived quality of residential environments: Some methodological issues. In K. H. Craik, & E. H. Zube (Eds.), *Perceiving environmental quality: Research and applications* (pp. 123–147). New York: Plenum.

Marans, R. W., & Spreckelmeyer, K. F. (1982) Evaluating open and conventional office design: *Environment and Behavior, 14,* 333–351.

Marans, R. W., & Stokols, D. (1993). *Environmental simulation: Research and policy issues.* New York: Plenum.

Marsh, T. A. (1993a). *"Seeing differently": Some observations and propositions regarding architects' and non-architects perceptions of architecture.* Paper presented at the meeting of Crossing Boundaries of Practice Conference, Cincinnati, OH.

Marsh, T. A. (1993b). Through others' eyes: An investigation of architects' and non-architects' perceptions of architecture. Unpublished master's thesis, State University of New York, Buffalo.

Martindale, C. (1990). The clockwork muse: *The predictability of artistic change.* New York: Basic Books, HarperCollins.

Maslow, A., & Mintz, N. (1956). Effects of esthetic surroundings: I. Initial short-term effects of three esthetic conditions upon perceiving "energy" and "well-being" in faces. *Journal of Psychology, 41,* 247–254.

McKechnie, G. E. (1977). The Environmental Response Inventory in application. *Environment and Behavior, 9,* 255–276.

McCrae, R. R., & Costa, P. T., Jr. (1989). Reinterpretation of the Myers-Briggs Type Indicator from the perspective of the five-factor model of personality. *Journal of Personality, 57,* 17–40.

Michelson, W. (1987). Groups, aggregates, and the environment. In E. H. Zube & G. T. Moore (Eds.), *Advances in environment, behavior, and design, vol. 1.* New York: Plenum Press.

Milgram, S., & Jodelet, D. (1976). Psychological maps of Paris. In H. Proshansky, W. Ittleson & L. Rivlin (Eds.), *Environmental psychology: People and their physical settings, 2nd edition* (pp. 104–124). New York: Holt, Rinehart & Winston.

Mintz, N. L. (1956). Effects of esthetic surroundings: II Prolonged and repeated experience in a beautiful and ugly room. *Journal of Psychology, 41,* 459–466.

Moore, G. T. (1989). Environment and behavior research in North America: History, developments, and unresolved issues. In. D. Stokols & I. Altman (Eds.), *Handbook of environmental psychology* (pp. 1359–1410). New York: Wiley.

Moskowitz, D. S., & Cote, S. (1995). Do interpersonal traits predict affect: A comparison of three models, *Journal of Personality and Social Psychology, 69,* 915-924.

Mullen, B., & Miller, N. (1991). Meta-analysis. In C. M. Judd, E. R. Smith, & L. H. Kidder (Eds.), *Research Methods in Social Relations* (pp. 425–449). Fort Worth, TX: Holt, Rinehart & Winston.

Murray, C., Motoyama, T., & Rouse, W. V. (1980). *The link between crime and the built environment.* Washington, DC: United States Government Printing Office.

Myers, I., & McCaulley, M. H. (1985). *Manual: A guide to the development and use of the Myers-Briggs Type Indicator.* Palo Alto, CA: Consulting Psychologists Press.

Nasar, J. L. (1980). *Influence of familiarity on responses to visual qualities of neighborhoods. Perceptual and Motor Skills, 51,* 635–642.

Nasar, J. L. (1983). Adult viewers' preferences in residential scenes: A study of the relationship of environmental attributes to preference, *Environment and Behavior, 15,* 589–614.

Nasar, J. L. (1984). Visual preference in urban street scenes: A cross-cultural comparison between Japan and the United States. *Journal of Cross-Cultural Psychology, 15,* 79–93.

Nasar, J. L. (1987a). Effects of signscape complexity and coherence on the perceived visual quality of retail scenes. *Journal of the American Planning Association, 53,* 499–509.

Nasar, J. L. (1987b). Environmental correlates of evaluative appraisals of central business district scenes. *Landscape and Planning Research, 14,* 117–130.

Nasar, J. L. (1988). *Environmental aesthetics: Theory, research, and applications.* New York: Cambridge University Press.

Nasar, J. L. (1988a) Urban space. Editor's introduction. In J. L. Nasar (Ed.), *Environmental aesthetics: Theory, research, and applications* (pp. 257-259). New York: Cambridge University Press.

Nasar, J. L. (1988b). Perception and evaluation of residential street-scenes. In J. L. Nasar (Ed.), *Environmental aesthetics: Theory, research, and applications* (pp. 275-289). New York: Cambridge University Press.

Nasar, J. L. (1989a). Perception, cognition, and evaluation of urban places. In I. Altman & E. H. Zube (Eds.), *Public Places and Spaces: Human Behavior and Environment, Vol. 10* (pp. 31-56). New York: Plenum.

Nasar, J. L. (1989b). Symbolic meanings of house styles. *Environment and Behavior, 21*, 235-257.

Nasar, J. L. (1994). Urban design aesthetics: The evaluative quality of building exteriors. *Environment and Behavior, 26*, 377-401.

Nasar, J. L. (1997a). *The evaluative image of the city*. Thousand Oaks, CA: Sage.

Nasar, J. L. (1997b). New developments in aesthetics for urban design. In G. Moore & R. Marans (Eds.), *Advances in Environment, Behavior and Design Volume 4: Towards the Integration of Theory, Methods, Research and Utilization* (pp. 149-193). New York: Plenum.

Nasar, J. L. (1999). *Design by competition: Making design competition work*. New York: Cambridge.

Nasar, J. L., & Fisher, B. (1993). Hot spots of fear and crime: A multi-method investigation. *Journal of Environmental Psychology, 13*, 187-206.

Nasar, J. L., Fisher, B., & Grannis, M. (1993). Proximate physical cues to fear of crime. *Landscape and Urban Planning, 26*, 161-178.

Nasar, J. L., & de Nivia, C. (1987). A post-occupancy evaluation for the design of a light pre-fabricated housing system for low income groups in Colombia, *Journal of Architectural and Planning Research, 4*, 199-211.

Nasar, J. L., & Jones, K. (1997). Landscapes of fear and stress. *Environment and Behavior, 29*, 291-323.

Nasar, J. L., & Julian, D. (1985). Effects of labeled meaning on the affective quality of housing scenes. *Journal of Environmental Psychology, 5*, 335-344.

Nasar, J. L., Julian, D., Buchman, S., Humphreys, D., & Mrohaly, M. (1983). The emotional quality of scenes and observation points: A look at prospect and refuge. *Landscape Planning, 10*, 355-361.

Nasar, J. L., & Kang, J. (1989a). A post-jury evaluation: The Ohio State University design competition for a center for the visual arts. *Environment and Behavior, 21*, 464-484.

National Environmental Policy Act (NEPA). (1969). Public Law 91-190. 83rd Stat., 852-856.

National Opinion Research Center. (1987). *General social survey (1972-1987). Cumulative codebook*. National Opinion Research Center, Chicago.

Neilson, W. A., Knott, T. A., & Carhart, P. W. (Eds.). (1960). *Webster's new international dictionary of the English language, second edition*. Springfield, MA: G & C. Merriam Company.

Newman, O. (1972). *Defensible space: Crime prevention through urban design*. New York: MacMillan.

Norberg-Schulz, C. (1965) *Intentions in architecture*. Cambridge, MA: MIT Press.

Orians, G. H. (1986). An ecological and evolutionary approach to landscape aesthetics. In E. C. Penning-Rowsell & D. Lownthal (Eds.), *Landscape means and values* (pp. 3-25). London: Allen and Unwin.

Ornstein, R. (1991). *The evolution of consciousness: of Darwin, Freud, and cranial fire—The origins of the way we think*, New York: Prentice Hall.

Osgood, C. E., Suci, C. J., & Tannenbaum, P. H. (1957). *Measurement of meaning*. Urbana: University of Illinois Press.

Oostendorp, A. (1978). The identification and interpretation of dimensions underlying aesthetic behaviour in the daily urban environment. *Dissertation Abstracts International, 40, 2,* B, 990, University of Toronto.

Oostendorp, A., & Berlyne, D. E. (1978). Dimensions in the perception of architecture: Measures of- exploratory behavior. *Scandinavian Journal of Psychology, 19,* 83-89.

Pearlman, K. T. (1988). Aesthetic regulation and the courts. In J. L. Nasar (Ed.), *Environmental aesthetics: Theory, research, and applications* (pp. 476-492). New York: Cambridge University Press.

Perkins, D. D., Meeks, J. W., & Taylor, R. B. (1992). The physical environment of street blocks and resident perceptions of crime and disorder: Implications for theory and measurement. *Journal of Environmental Psychology, 12,* 21-34.

Physical Facilities, Equipment and Library Committee. (1986). *A study of the relationship between the physical environment of the college campus and the quality of academic life.* Committee Report. Columbus: The Ohio State University.

Prak, N. L. (1984). *Architects: The noted and the ignored.* New York: Wiley.

Purcell, A. T. (1984). Multivariate models and the attributes of the experience of the built environment, *Environment and Planning B, 11,* 173-192.

Purcell, A. T. (1986). Environmental perception and affect: A schema discrepancy model. *Environment and Behavior, 18,* 3-30.

Purcell, A. T. (1995). Experiencing American and Australian high- and popular-style houses. *Environment and Behavior, 27,* 771-800.

Purcell, A. T., & Nasar, J. L. (1992). Experiencing other peoples houses: A model of similarities and differences in environmental experience. *Journal of Environmental Psychology, 12,* 199-211.

Rapoport, A. (1990). *History and precedence in environmental design.* New York: Plenum.

Riger, S. (1985). Crime as an environmental stressor. *Journal of Community Psychology, 13,* 270-281 .

Rosch, E. (1977). Human categorization. In N. Warren (Ed.), *Studies in cross-cultural psychology* (pp. 1-49). London: Academic.

Rosch, E., & Mervis, C. B. (1975). Family resemblances: Studies in the internal structure of categories. *Cognitive Psychology, 7,* 573-605.

Rosenthal, R. (1984). *Meta-analytic procedures for social research.* Beverly Hills, CA: Sage.

Ross, C. E. (1993). Fear of victimization and health. *Journal of Quantitative Criminology, 9,* 159-175.

Royse, D. C. (1969). Social inferences via environmental cues. (Doctoral dissertation, Massachusetts Institute of Technology), *Dissertation Abstracts International,* 0291(University Microfilms No. AA10221503).

Russell, J. A., & Lanius, U. (1984). Adaptation level and the affective appraisal of environments. *Journal of Environmental Psychology, 4,* 119-135.

Russell, J. A., & Snodgrass, J. (1989). Emotion and environment. In D. Stokols & I. Altman (Eds.), *Handbook of environmental psychology, vol. 1* (pp. 245-280). New York: Wiley.

Sadalla, E. K., Verschure, B., & Burroughs, J. (1987). Identity symbolism in housing. *Environment and Behavior, 19,* 569-587.

Sanoff, H. (1989). Facility programming. In E. H. Zube & G. M. Moore (Eds.), *Advances in environment, behavior, and design, Vol. 2* (pp. 239-286). New York: Plenum.

Schroeder, H. W., & Anderson, L. M. (1984). Perception of personal safety in urban recreation sites. *Journal of Leisure Research, 16,* 177-194.

Seaton, R. W., & Collins, J. B. (1970). Validity and reliability of ratings of simulated buildings. In W. S. Mitchell (Ed.), *Environmental design: research and practice, vol. 6,* 10 (pp. 1-12). Los Angeles: University of California Press.

Shafer, E. L. Jr., & Richards, T. A. (1974). A comparison of viewer reactions to outdoor scenes and photographs of those scenes. United States Department of Agriculture, Forest Service Research Paper NE 302.

Shirvani, H. (1985). *The urban design process.* New York. Van Nostrand Reinhold.

Simonton, D. K. (1984). *Genius, creativity, and leadership: Historiometric inquiries.* Cambridge, MA: Harvard University Press.

Skogan, W. G., & Maxfield, M. (1981). *Coping with crime: Individual and neighborhood reactions.* Beverly Hills, CA: Sage.

Smith, G. F., & Dorfman, D. D. (1975). The effect of stimulus uncertainty on the relationship between frequency of exposure and liking. *Journal of Social and Personality Psychology, 31,* 150-155.

Smith, M. L., & Glass, G. (1977). Meta-analysis of psychotherapy outcomes. *American Psychologist, 32,* 752-760.

Snodgrass, J., & Russell, J. A. (1986, July). *Mapping the mood of a city.* Paper presented at the 21st Congress of Applied Psychology, Jerusalem, Israel.

Sonnenfeld, J. (1966). Variable values in the space and landscape: An inquiry into the nature of environmental necessity. *Journal of Social Issues, 22,* 71-82.

Stamps, A. E. (1990). Use of photographs to simulate environments. A meta-analysis. *Perceptual and Motor Skills, 71,* 907-913.

Stamps, A. E. (1992). Perceptual and preferential effects of photomontage simulations of environments. *Perceptual and Motor Skills, 74,* 675-688.

Stamps, A. E. (1994). All buildings great and small. Design review from high rise to small houses. *Environment and Behavior, 26,* 402-420.

Stamps, A. E. (1997). *Meta-analysis in environmental research.* Paper presented at the 28th Annual Conference of the Environmental Design Research Association. Montreal, Canada.

Stamps, A. E. (1995). Beauty is in ... ? In Nasar, J. L., P. Grannis, & K. Hanyu (Eds.), *EDRA26/1995* (pp. 48-53). Edmond, OK: Environmental Design Research Association.

Starbuck, J. C. (undated). *The most depicted buildings erected in the USA between the wars.* Vance Bibliographies, Architecture Series, A34.

Starbuck, J. C. (undated). *The most depicted buildings erected in the USA since 1945.* Vance Bibliographies, Architecture Series, A34.

Stoks, F. G. (1983). Assessing urban public space environments for danger of violent crime—especially rape. In D. Joiner, G. Brimilcombe, J. Daish, J. Gray and D. Kernohan (Eds.), *Proceedings of the Conference on People and Physical Environment Research.* Ministry of Public Works and Development, Wellington, New Zealand, 331-343.

Taylor, R. B. (1989). Toward an environmental psychology of disorder: Delinquency, crime and fear of crime. In D. Stokols & I. Altman (Eds.), *Handbook of environmental psychology, vol. 2.* (pp. 951-986). New York: Wiley.

Taylor, R. B., Shumaker, S. A., & Gottfredson, S. D. (1985). Neighborhood-level links between physical features and local sentiments: Deterioration, fear of crime and confidence. *Journal of Architectural and Planning Research, 2,* 261-275.

Taylor, R. B., & Nee, C. (1988). The role of cues in simulated burglary. *British. Journal of Criminology, 28,* 396-401.

Thayer, R. L. Jr., & Atwood, B. G. (1978). Plant complexity, and pleasure in urban and suburban environments. *Environmental Psychology and Nonverbal Behavior, 3,* 67-76.

Tiffany, W. D., &. Ketchel, J. M. (1979). Psychological deterrence in robberies of banks and its application to other institutions. In J. J. Kramer (Ed.) *The role of behavioral sciences in physical security, special publication.* (pp. 81-87). National Bureau of Standards, Washington, DC.

Tooby, J., & Cosmides, L. (1990). The past explains the present: Emotional adaptations and the structure of ancestral environments. *Ethological Sociobiology*, 11, 375-424.

Tooby, J., & Cosmides, L. (1989). Evolutional psychology and the generation of culture: Part I. Theoretical considerations. *Ethological Sociobiology*, 10, 29-49.

Tooby, J., & DeVore, I. (1987). The reconstruction of hominid behavioral evolution through strategic modeling. In W. G. Kinzey (Ed.), *The evolution of human behavior: Primate models*. Albany, NY: SUNY Press.

Tunnard, C., & Pushkarev, B. (1981). *Man-made America: Chaos or control*. New York: Harmony Books.

Ulrich, R. S. (1974). Scenery and the shopping trip: The roadside environment as a factor in route choice. Doctoral dissertation, University of Michigan, 1973. *Dissertation Abstracts International*, 35 (1), 346A.

Ulrich, R. S. (1983). Aesthetic and affective response to natural environment. In I. Altman & J. F. Wohlwill (Eds.), *Behavior and the natural environment: Human behavior and environment, advances in theory and research, vol. 6* (pp. 85-125). New York: Plenum.

Ulrich, R. S. (1984). View through a window influences recovery from surgery. *Science, 224*, 420-421.

Ulrich, R. S. (1993). Biophilia and the conservation ethic. In S. R. Kellert & E. O. Wilson (Eds.), *The Biophilia Hypothesis* (pp. 73-137). Washington, DC: Island Press.

Ulrich, R. S., Simons, R. F., Losito, B. D., Fiorito, E., Miles, M., & Zelson, M. (1991). Stress recovery during exposure to natural and urban environments. *Journal of Environmental Psychology*, 11, 201-230.

U.S. Department of Justice. (1980). *Crime Prevention through Environmental Design: The Commercial Demonstration in Portland, Oregon. Executive Summary*. Washington, DC: United States Government Printing Office.

Verderber, S., & Moore, G. T. (1979). Building imagery: A comparative study of environmental cognition. *Man-Environment Systems*, 7, 332-341.

Vining, J., & Orland, B. (1989). The video advantage: A comparison of two environmental representation techniques. *Journal of Environmental Management*, 29, 275-283.

Ward, L., & Russell, J. A. (1981). The psychological representation of molar environments. *Journal of Experimental Psychology: General*, 110, 121-152.

Warr, M. (1990). Dangerous situations: Social context and fear of victimization. *Social Forces*, 68, 891-907.

Watson, D., Clark, L. A., & Tellegen, A. (1988). Development and validation of brief measures of positive and negative affect: The PANAS scales. *Journal of Personality and Social Psychology*, 54, 1063-1070.

Weber, R. (1995). On the aesthetics of architecture: A psychological approach to the structure and order of perceived architectural space. Aldershot, UK: Avebury.

Weiner, J. (1995). *The beak of the finch: A story of evolution in our time*. New York: Knopf.

Wilson, M. A., & Canter, D. V. (1990). The development of central concepts during professional education: An example of a multivariate model of the concept of architectural style. *Applied Psychology: An International Review*, 39, 431-435.

Wilson, J. Q., & Kelling, G. (1982, March). Broken Windows. *Atlantic Monthly*, 29-38.

Whitfield, T. W. A. (1983). Predicting preference for everyday objects: An experimental confrontation between two theories of aesthetic behavior. *Journal of Environmental Psychology*, 3, 221-237.

Winkel, G., Malek, R., & Thiel, P. (1970). A study of human response to selected roadside environments. In H. Sanoff & S. Cohn (Eds.), *EDRA 1: Proceedings of the 1st Environmental Design Research Association conference* (pp. 224-240). Stroudsburg, PA: Dowden, Hutchinson, & Ross.

Wise, J. A., & Wise, B. K. (1985). The interior design of banks and the psychological deterrence of bank robberies. *Proceedings of the International Conference on Building Use and Safety Technology* (pp. 74–28). Washington DC: National Institute of Building Sciences.

Wohlwill, J. F. (1974, July). *The place of aesthetics in studies of the environment.* Paper presented at the Symposium on Experimental Aesthetics and Psychology of the Environment at the International Congress of Applied Psychology, Montreal.

Wohlwill, J. F. (1976). Environmental aesthetics: The environment as a source of affect. In I. Altman and J. F. Wohlwill (Eds.), *Human behavior and the environment: Advances in theory and research, vol. 1* (pp. 37–86). New York: Plenum.

Wohlwill, J. F. (1979). What belongs where: Research on fittingness of man-made structures into natural settings. In T. C. Daniels, E. H. Zube, & B. C. Driver (Eds.), *Assessing amenity resource values* (pp. 48–53). Ft. Collins, CO: Rocky Mountain Forest and Range Experimental Station.

Wohlwill, J. F. (1982). The visual impact of development in coastal zone areas. *Coastal Zone Management Journal, 9,* 225–248.

Wohlwill, J. F. (1983). The concept of nature: A psychologist's view. In I. Altman & J. F. Wohlwill (Eds.), *Behavior and the natural environment* (pp. 5–37). New York: Plenum.

Wohlwill, J. F., & Harris, G. (1980). Responses to congruity or contrast for man-made features in natural-recreation settings. *Leisure Science, 3,* 349–65.

Wohlwill, J. F., & Kohn, I. (1973). The environment as experienced by the migrant: An adaptation-level view. *Representative Research in Social Psychology, 4,* 135–164.

Zajonc, R. B. (1984). On the primacy of affect. *American Psychologist, 39,* 117–123.

6

Models of Matching Patients and Treatment Programs

Christine Timko
Rudolf H. Moos
John W. Finney
Center for Health Care Evaluation
Department of Veterans Affairs Health Care System,
and Stanford University Medical Center

Clinicians and researchers have had a longstanding interest in the possibility of improving treatment outcomes among varied client populations by matching clients to treatments. In this chapter, we first present a general model of person–environment congruence for clients in residential treatment facilities. This model matches the client's level of functioning (in the cognitive, psychological, and social domains) with the treatment program's levels of support, performance demands, and structure. Our review of empirical work focuses mainly on models of matching psychiatric and substance abuse patients to treatment programs. We also review research on models of matching youths with conduct disorders to correctional facilities. The chapter considers some key conceptual and methodological issues that are raised by efforts to apply matching models, and by research on such efforts. Finally, we highlight some promising directions for research on patient–treatment matching.

PERSON–ENVIRONMENT CONGRUENCE MODELS

A well-known model of person–environment congruence proposed by Lawton (1989) states that a match between personal competence and envi-

169

ronmental demand is likely to result in favorable behavioral and affective outcomes. When environmental demands are either too high or too low for an individual's level of competence, maladaptive behavior and negative affect are likely to result. A component of Lawton's model, the *environmental docility hypothesis*, suggests that a given amount of objective change in demand affects low-competence people more than high-competence people. Specifically, an increase in demand should have a more negative impact on functioning among low- than among high-competence individuals. Similarly, a decline in demand should have more positive consequences for low- than for high-competence people. A companion hypothesis concerning *environmental proactivity* proposes that more competent people are better able to use environmental resources in the pursuit of their personal needs and wishes.

Moos (1997) extended Lawton's (1989) model to apply to psychiatric treatment and to other client populations in residential settings. He stated that high environmental demands should have more positive consequences for clients who are functioning well (i.e., those who have better psychosocial and cognitive skills) than for those who are functioning poorly, whereas environmental resources should have more benefit for poorly functioning clients. Specifically, a self-directed treatment climate that has high performance expectations (such as for interpersonal interaction or skills development) and relatively little structure should have the most benefit for functionally able clients. In contrast, more disturbed clients often find high performance expectations and self-direction to be disruptive, and need more support and structure. Moos points out that as clients' cognitive and psychosocial skills improve, they should be able to cope with a more demanding and less structured setting.

In support of Moos' (1997) model, Linn, Klett, and Caffey (1980, 1982) found that more sponsor-initiated activity and demands by the sponsor and by hospital social work staff were associated with a higher likelihood of relapse for impaired schizophrenic patients discharged from hospitals to foster homes. Linn et al. suggested that the key relapse-inducing factor was emotional overinvolvement. Overstimulation, produced by intrusive attempts to reactivate patients through vocational rehabilitation or social remotivation, led to unfavorable outcomes for chronic schizophrenic patients, such as manifest psychopathology and hospital readmission. In concordance with Moos' model, Linn et al. concluded that keeping such patients in the community may require treatment climates with lower expectations for performance and social involvement.

In an extension of his own model, Moos (1991, 1997) noted that supportive relationships may moderate the potentially problematic consequences of interpersonally stimulating and performance-oriented environments. That is, high levels of interpersonal stimulation and performance expectations offered in the context of high support may be beneficial for impaired clients. For example, when emphasized within a supportive milieu, a focus on practical skills training may be an additional source of stability and structure for patients with severe psychiatric disorders (Friis, 1986a; Werbart, 1992).

Another approach to person–environment congruence is Hunt's (1971) conceptual level matching model. This model describes people along the dimension of cognitive complexity, and describes the environment in terms of degree of structure. It hypothesizes that individuals at a low conceptual level (i.e., at an immature stage of development) benefit more from highly structured settings, whereas individuals at a higher conceptual level benefit more from low structure. In addition, similar to Lawton's model, the conceptual level matching model proposes that individuals with less cognitive complexity are more affected by changes in structure than are those at a more mature level.

CONCEPTUALIZING AND MEASURING THE TREATMENT CLIMATE

Many of the studies we review here focus on the social or treatment environment and have used one of the Social Climate Scales (Moos, 1994). Accordingly, we describe these scales and their conceptual rationale next.

Just as individuals have unique personalities, so do social environments. Moos has developed measures of a variety of social settings, including treatment environments (i.e., hospital-based and community-based psychiatric treatment programs), total institutions (e.g., correctional institutions for juvenile offenders), and community settings (e.g., families). These measures can be completed by both clients and staff members. Specifically, the Ward Atmosphere Scale (WAS; Moos, 1996b) and the Community-Oriented Programs Environment Scale (COPES; Moos, 1996a) assess the treatment climate of hospital-based and community-based psychiatric treatment programs, respectively. The Correctional Institutions Environment Scale (CIES; Moos, 1987) measures the social climate of juvenile and adult correctional programs, and the Family Environment Scale (FES; Moos & Moos, 1994) measures the social climates in families.

Each of the Social Climate Scales has three basic forms (Moos, 1994). The Real Form (Form R) asks people how they perceive their current social environment. The Ideal Form (Form I) asks people how they conceive of an ideal social environment. The Expectations Form (Form E) asks prospective members of an environment what they expect the environment they are about to enter to be like.

Each of these different social environments can be characterized by three broad categories of dimensions: *relationship, personal development or growth,* and *system maintenance and change. Relationship* dimensions identify the nature and intensity of personal relationships within the environment. They assess the extent to which people are involved in the environment, how much they support and help each other, and the extent to which there is spontaneity and free and open expression of affect. *Personal development* dimensions assess the basic directions along which personal growth and self-enhancement tend to occur in the particular environment. In psychiatric and correctional programs, these dimensions assess the treatment goals. *System maintenance and change* dimensions assess the extent to which the environment is orderly, clear in its expectations, maintains control, and is responsive to change.

Moos (1997) has considered how combinations of the treatment climate dimensions can be used to characterize residential programs. He points out that the meaning or interpretation of a program's score on one treatment climate dimension is complex, because it may require a consideration of the other dimensions. In general, higher scores on Involvement and Support reflect a supportive program in which patients are active and energetic and help each other and in which staff help patients. One aspect of performance expectations involves the level of interpersonal stimulation, which is captured by the treatment climate dimensions of spontaneity, personal problem orientation, and anger/aggression. An emphasis on practical orientation indicates that the program has high performance expectations; autonomy and personal problem orientation can also convey high performance expectations in terms of self-direction and self-understanding. More order/organization, policy clarity, and staff control represent more program structure, which can have a strongly supportive aspect, especially for more impaired clients and when involvement and support are high. In the next section, we examine treatment climate profiles as part of reviewing research on matching psychiatric patients to treatment settings.

MATCHING PATIENTS TO TREATMENT ENVIRONMENTS

This section reviews studies that address the issue of how to match psychiatric patients to treatment programs so as to most benefit patient outcomes. These studies are of three basic types. One type describes the real or ideal treatment environment in programs that treat patients with different levels of psychiatric impairment. Another type of study examines the relationship between treatment climate dimensions and patient outcomes, considering the level of patients' psychiatric impairment. The third type of study directly examines how interactions between patients' psychiatric impairment and programs' treatment climate contribute to patients' outcomes.

Describing the Treatment Environment of Psychiatric Programs

Coulton, Fitch, and Holland (1985) and Downs and Fox (1993) used the COPES to develop typologies of the treatment climate in residential facilities for psychiatric patients, and classified community care homes into four clusters. In Coulton et al.'s first cluster, homes scored low on support, performance demands (i.e., were low on autonomy, practical orientation, and personal problem orientation), and structure (i.e., were low on staff control). These homes provided protection but little opportunity for growth or change, and were hypothesized to be most suited for patients who can tolerate little in the way of emotional stimulation or practical demands. Downs and Fox similarly identified one type of home that provided little support and structure, but moderate performance expectations (i.e., scored moderately on autonomy and practical orientation). These were mainly single occupancy hotels that supplied just room and board, and, like Coulton et al.'s first cluster, were deemed best for clients who cannot tolerate interpersonal stimulation or practical obligations.

Coulton et al.'s (1985) second cluster was also low on socioemotional demands, but high on structure. These homes were thought to be best suited for patients who are capable of complying with rules and practical training but need only minimal emotional involvement. Downs and Fox's (1993) second type of home did not parallel Coulton et al.'s second cluster. It was high on involvement and low on both autonomy and personal expression (i.e., spontaneity, personal problem orientation, and anger/aggression). Such homes were seen as best for older clients who can comply with rules and need nurturing.

The third cluster found by Coulton et al. (1985) was high on socioemotional demands and had moderate structure. Patients best matched to these homes might need a lot of emotional support and be highly expressive, but already possess practical skills for daily living. Downs and Fox (1993) identified a type of home that was similar to Coulton et al.'s third cluster, as it was high on involvement and moderate on structure and personal expression. Homes of this type were viewed as best for individuals who desire interpersonal relationships but can bear only a moderately demanding environment.

Finally, the fourth cluster found by Coulton et al. (1985) was moderate on socioemotional demands and high on performance expectations, and may be suitable for patients who are capable of responding appropriately to both emotional stimulation and requirements for practical skills. The last of Downs and Fox's (1993) types of homes paralleled Coulton et al.'s last cluster, due to its high involvement and autonomy. These homes were seen as most appropriate for younger, goal-oriented clients who are tolerant of a stimulating environment.

Werbart (1992) classified psychiatric programs as having explorative or supportive profiles. The optimal explorative profile describes programs with intense relationships, high demands on the patients' own collaboration in the treatment process, high tolerance for anger and conflict, an emphasis on the patient's autonomy, and a minimum of rules. Specifically, such programs have high involvement, spontaneity, and personal problem orientation, moderate anger/aggression, and high autonomy and low staff control. The optimal supportive profile involves social skills training and a low emotional temperature, with limited anger and conflict, and more neutral and less intense relationships. Programs having this profile have high support, practical orientation, structure (organization and clarity), and low anger/aggression.

According to Werbart (1992), the supportive environment corresponds to psychotic patients' needs in the acute phase of illness. For such patients, the therapeutic environment should be relaxing, clear, consistent, and stably supportive. The supportive profile is found in Coulton et al. (1985) and Downs and Fox's (1993) first cluster of homes, which were low on demands for socioemotional involvement and self-direction, and so were suited to patients unable to tolerate such demands. In Werbart's (1992) model, inadequate program organization can lead to serious obstacles to the therapeutic task and promote resistance. As individuals proceed through the different phases of treatment, they need a changing balance between supportive and explorative factors in the milieu.

Coulton et al. (1985) and Downs and Fox (1993) found a balance between supportive and explorative factors in their second and third types of homes, which were deemed appropriate for moderately impaired patients. Explorative treatment assumes a milieu that integrates patients' disturbed cognitions but also does not neglect patients' needs for support. This milieu was identified in Coulton et al. (1985) and Downs and Fox's (1993) fourth cluster, in which homes were high on socioemotional involvement, goal-oriented, and seen as best for better functioning patients.

The typology research puts forth the same matching hypotheses described earlier, stating that programs with more impaired psychiatric patients should have fewer demands for interpersonal stimulation and performance and less autonomy. Friis' (1986b) study of 35 short-term psychiatric programs found that, in fact, those with more psychotic patients had less stimulation (less involvement, support, and spontaneity), fewer performance demands (less practical orientation and personal problem orientation), and less self-direction (less autonomy and more staff control). In another study of the same units, Friis (1986a) found that preferred levels of support and structure (order/organization and policy clarity) were the same on units with mostly psychotic patients and units with few psychotic patients; all patients wanted their programs to emphasize these areas. Consistent with the matching hypotheses, however, less disturbed patients wanted more stimulation (higher involvement, spontaneity, and anger/aggression) and performance expectations (practical orientation, personal problem orientation, and autonomy). Unexpectedly, they also wanted more staff control.

Treatment Climate and Patient Outcomes

Several studies have not only described different types of treatment programs, but have linked specific characteristics of treatment climates to patients' outcomes. For example, in the study cited earlier, Friis (1986a) described the Good Milieu (GM) index, assessing satisfaction with the program, staff, patients, and treatment approach. On units with psychotic patients, and on those with nonpsychotic patients, more support, practical orientation, and order/organization were associated with higher GM scores, leading Friis to conclude that both more disturbed and less disturbed patients are helped by emphasizing these areas. Possibly, when supportive programs have a focus on organization that is not unduly restrictive and expectations for skills development that vary according to clients' abilities, these aspects of the treatment climate are of general benefit for patients with quite different levels of cognitive and functional impairment (Moos, 1997).

In line with the matching hypotheses, Friis (1986a) found that less spontaneity and anger/aggression were associated with higher GM scores among psychotic patients, and more involvement and autonomy contributed to satisfaction among nonpsychotic patients. Friis suggested that psychotic and nonpsychotic patients be treated in different units that provide these different atmospheres.

Studies examining the outcome of patients' adaptation in the community provide support for Moos' (1997) matching model. Collins et al. (1985) studied psychiatric programs in which most patients were neither chronically nor severely disturbed. When programs had more anger/aggression and less order/organization, patients showed better adaptation in the community. In contrast, Klass, Growe, and Strizich (1977) studied inpatient units in which most patients had chronic schizophrenia. When there was less emphasis on anger/aggression and more emphasis on order/organization, there were fewer violent episodes involving patients, and patients stayed longer in the community after discharge.

Like Klass et al. (1977), Goldstein, Cohen, Lewis, and Struening (1988) studied programs in which most patients were chronic functionally impaired schizophrenics in acute phases of their illness. When the program was more supportive and structured and less focused on self-understanding, patients found the program more helpful and were more satisfied with it. Staff saw the program as more helpful when practical orientation and personal problem orientation were higher. According to Goldstein et al., patients may be more responsive to the emotional climate of programs, whereas staff may be more responsive to program content. In addition, as noted in research reviewed earlier, programs for acutely ill schizophrenic patients may be most helpful when they are nurturing and structured rather than focused around insight therapy and the discussion of personal problems.

Another way to focus on matching issues is to change the treatment environment and observe whether the expected effects ensue. With his colleagues, Friis (see Vaglum, Friis, & Karterud, 1985) worked with a treatment unit for psychotic patients to increase the emphasis on practical orientation and organization and decrease the emphasis on anger and aggression. These changes were made in part by discontinuing process-oriented, unstructured, and confrontational group meetings, and making staff responsible for leading meetings with clearly defined agendas. One year after the changes were made, patients were more satisfied with the program. These findings support the idea that therapeutic milieus for psychotic patients ought to have relatively little emphasis on venting affect.

Satisfaction with a program does not necessarily predict better outcomes in other areas. In this regard, Lehman and Ritzler (1976) compared two psychiatric units and found that patients on the unit with more interpersonal stimulation (involvement, anger/aggression) and performance expectations (practical orientation, autonomy) were more satisfied with the treatment climate. However, this unit also had a higher dropout rate among patients with character disorders, and a higher 1-year readmission rate, especially among neurotic patients. Lehman and Ritzler suggested that this treatment climate may have persuaded patients to seek more active and independent situations when they left the hospital, thereby placing themselves at higher risk of readmission. Moreover, high interpersonal involvement and autonomy may create a poor match for patients with character disorders, because they lack the basic levels of social cooperation and concern that are needed to function well in such treatment environments.

Notwithstanding these findings on the potential negative effects of high involvement and performance expectations, even seriously ill patients may benefit from interpersonal stimulation and self-direction in the context of a highly supportive program that does not make too many practical demands. Two programs treating patients newly diagnosed with schizophrenia were compared by Wendt, Mosher, Matthews, and Menn (1983). In comparison to the general hospital program, the community-based psychosocial program was more supportive (higher on involvement, support, and policy clarity), but also more interpersonally demanding (higher on spontaneity and personal problem orientation) and self-directed (higher on autonomy, lower on order/organization and staff control). In addition, it was lower on practical orientation. Real–ideal discrepancies on the treatment climate dimensions were much smaller for the psychosocial program. Few differences were found between the two programs in patients' symptomatology up to 2 years postadmission, but the psychosocial program was favored on several measures of community adjustment. These results suggest that these acutely ill patients may have been better matched to the more active psychosocial program.

Coulton, Holland, and Fitch (1984b) studied chronically mentally ill individuals who were discharged from a psychiatric hospital to community homes. After living for 1 month in the community home, patients and staff completed measures of the patient's needs and the home's demands or resources with respect to each COPES dimension. A home environment that focused more on autonomy and personal problems than the patient could handle, allowed less spontaneity than the patient needed, and had either too much or too little order/organization was associated with hospital readmission.

In a companion study, Coulton, Holland, and Fitch (1984a) followed the patients who remained in their community homes for at least 4 months. For the dimensions of autonomy, anger/aggression, and staff control, and especially order/organization, a discrepancy between the patient and environment in either direction had a negative effect on patient adjustment to the community home. The negative effects of autonomy were stronger when too much autonomy was required of the patient. For practical orientation, negative effects occurred only when there were too many performance demands; too few demands did not seem to reduce patient adjustment. Too little emphasis on personal problem orientation was associated with deterioration. Taken together, Coulton's studies provide support for Lawton's (1989) person–environment congruence model in that environmental deviations in either direction from an individual's level of competence were maladaptive; in addition, more performance demands appeared to be especially difficult for more impaired patients, whereas having too few demands was problematic, but less so, for better functioning patients.

Interactions Between Patients' Psychiatric Impairment and Treatment Climate

Some research has empirically examined the extent to which the direction and strength of associations between the treatment milieu and patient outcomes depend on patients' psychiatric status. Segal and Aviram (1978) described the ideal psychiatric treatment environment as putting more emphasis on support, interpersonal interaction, performance expectations, self-direction, and structure. This type of stimulating and demanding environment seemed to motivate relatively asymptomatic patients to become more involved in activities in the community. In contrast, it motivated more symptomatic patients to become more involved in activities within the program.

In a study of psychiatric and substance abuse treatment programs, we (Timko & Moos, 1998) found that, among groups of patients with minimal psychiatric impairment, the extent to which programs emphasized support, interpersonal stimulation, or practical orientation had only a slight positive association with patients' more frequent use of community resources. Among groups of patients at a moderate level of psychiatric impairment, more emphasis on each of these three areas bore a stronger positive relationship to patients' activity. Finally, among groups of patients with more severe psychiatric impairment, more program emphasis on support or interpersonal or practical demands was strongly related to more frequent activity in

the surrounding community. Similarly, more emphasis on practical orientation was associated most strongly with more participation in program services and better functioning (as rated by program observers) among the most
impaired groups of patients.

There are two noteworthy aspects of our results. First, our findings regarding patient activity in the community did not agree with those of Segal and
Aviram (1978), who found that a stimulating and demanding environment
was a stronger predictor of community activity among patients who were less
disturbed than among more disturbed patients. Segal and Aviram's measure
of community activity included, in addition to the frequency with which patients used community services, assessments of how easy or difficult it would
be for patients to arrange to use community and other services on their own.
Possibly, the levels of support, interpersonal stimulation, and practical orientation in our sample of programs were sufficient to enable impaired patients
to use services once they were made available, but would still be insufficient
to enable impaired patients to personally arrange for those services.

In addition, our findings did not appear to confirm the matching hypotheses in that more impaired, rather than more intact, patients seemed to benefit most from more interpersonal stimulation and practical orientation. We
thought this finding might be due to the supportiveness of the context
within which interpersonal expression and practical orientation were emphasized. In fact, programs with more interpersonal stimulation and practical demands were also higher on support. These results confirm Moos'
(1991, 1997) conceptual model suggesting that impaired individuals may
benefit from highly expressive and performance-oriented environments if
the treatment milieu also provides high levels of support. Our results also fit
with Lawton's (1989) environmental docility hypothesis that functionally impaired individuals are more influenced by environmental factors than are
functionally competent individuals.

Lehmann, Mitchell, and Cohen (1978) studied interactions between psychiatric patients' needs for support and involvement, self-direction, and
structure, and the extent to which a hospital program and patients' subsequent community residences met those needs. Each patient assessed his or
her own needs, as well as the hospital and community resources and demands. Across patients, in comparison to community residences, the hospital was evaluated as providing more support and involvement. Patients with
serious and frequent symptoms had a good hospital but poor community fit,
and stayed longer periods in the hospital and shorter periods in the community. In contrast, patients with few symptoms had a poor fit between their

needs and the hospital environment, and a good fit in the community; these patients had short hospital and long community stays. These results are consistent with hypotheses that impaired patients need a more supportive environment.

Summary

The research just reviewed identified programs that emphasized support and structure, and put less emphasis on performance expectations, including self-direction and demands for interpersonal interaction. On the whole, these programs were most beneficial for relatively impaired psychiatric patients. In contrast, programs that put more emphasis on socioemotional and performance demands tended to be more helpful for clients with better cognitive and psychosocial functioning. The findings also support hypotheses that too many demands are more detrimental for impaired patients, than are too few demands for well-functioning clients, and that generally, less competent individuals are more influenced by the treatment climate than are more capable persons. However, if the program offers a supportive milieu, interpersonal and performance demands may benefit most patients, even those who are quite impaired. In the next section, we review research that focuses more on matching patients to treatment orientations than to treatment environments.

MATCHING PATIENTS TO TREATMENT ORIENTATIONS

The literature on psychiatric and substance abuse care describes different models of treatment, such as therapeutic community, psychodynamic, rehabilitation, social learning, and Alcoholics Anonymous (AA)/12-step. Treatment orientations represent perspectives associated with one or more of these broad treatment models, but are more specific and thus reflect more clearly the actual goals and activities that underlie a program. Treatment orientations consist of combinations of goals and activities that are determined in part by staff training and experience, and, at a higher level of abstraction, by current beliefs about effective treatment (Swindle, Peterson, Paradise, & Moos, 1995). The research is scattered with few replicated findings, but studies show that particular treatment orientations may be especially appropriate for particular groups of patients. Some of the key results of these studies are similar to the findings regarding matches between patients and treatment environments; for example, more structure benefits more impaired clients.

Kadden, Cooney, Getter, and Litt (1989) examined patient matching using a mix of structure and treatment orientation in the therapeutic setting. They assigned alcohol and drug abuse patients completing a residential program to one of two types of aftercare. More impaired patients (i.e., higher levels of psychopathology and sociopathy) had better outcomes after more highly structured coping skills training, whereas less disturbed patients benefited more from interactive therapy that emphasized the immediacy and spontaneity of interactions. Follow-up at 18 months posttreatment confirmed these findings (Cooney, Kadden, Litt, & Getter, 1991), and later analysis of the data extended the findings to two patient subtypes (Litt, Babor, Delboca, Kadden, & Cooney, 1992). Type B patients, who were more impaired (i.e., had more psychopathology, severe alcohol dependence, familial alcoholism, a predisposing personality profile, and an early onset of alcohol problems), fared better in cognitive-behavioral therapy, whereas the less impaired type A patients did better in interactive therapy.

Based on the encouraging results of these and other studies (see Mattson et al., 1994), NIAAA conducted a large-scale multisite clinical trial. More than 1,700 patients were randomly assigned to three treatment conditions (twelve-step facilitation, motivational enhancement therapy, and cognitive-behavioral skills training) to explore matching hypotheses relating to 10 different characteristics (e.g., motivation to change, cognitive impairment, sociopathy). The results (Project MATCH Research Group, 1997) suggested that matching on one patient characteristic—psychiatric severity—might improve the effectiveness of outpatient treatment. Specifically, patients low in psychiatric severity had more abstinent days after twelve-step facilitation (TSF) treatment than after cognitive-behavioral therapy; neither treatment was clearly superior for clients with higher levels of psychiatric severity. The Project MATCH group suggested that psychiatrically disturbed patients might react less well to some of the components of the TSF treatment. Notably, the TSF intervention was designed to foster active participation in the interactive fellowship activities of AA.

The Project Match (1997) and Kadden (Cooney et al., 1991; Kadden et al., 1989; Litt et al., 1992) findings agree with the general matching hypothesis that demands for interpersonal interaction are difficult for impaired patients, and of positive value for well-functioning patients. Impaired patients need more structure in the treatment setting. As we review in the next section, the finding that impaired clients benefit most from more structure in the treatment milieu has been replicated in studies of client-treatment matching for youths with behavior problems.

MATCHING YOUTHS WITH CONDUCT DISORDERS
TO CORRECTIONAL PROGRAMS

Researchers have developed several typologies in attempts to classify youths with conduct disorders. Some of these typologies have been used as a basis for matching youths to correctional programs. Generally, the typologies classify youths according to their level of maturity, and programs according to their level of structure.

Conceptual Level Matching

One approach to matching youths to correctional programs is based on Hunt's (1971) conceptual level matching model, which was described briefly at the beginning of the chapter. Hunt described three stages of conceptual development for youths ages 12 through 18. Stage A, the least mature developmental stage, is characterized by the failure to internalize parental and cultural values and standards for right and wrong and by a self-centered, anti-authority stance. Stage B involves the internalization of parental and societal norms and values; this stage is pro-authority, in that the child looks to others to see how to behave. Stage C youths are less reliant on authority and use internally generated guidelines for their behavior.

As noted earlier, the conceptual level matching model categorizes clients along the dimension of conceptual complexity, and treatment settings on degree of structure. Structured program environments are staff-controlled and are specific with regard to program content and expectations for client behavior. Consistent with the Lawton (1989) and Moos (1997) person–environment models, this model hypothesizes that low conceptual level youths (Stage A) profit more from a highly structured treatment approach, whereas high level youths (Stage C) both benefit more from low structure, and are less affected by changes in structure.

In a test of the conceptual level matching model, Brill (1978, 1980) studied adolescent boys who were matched or mismatched to two residential treatment programs according to their conceptual level and the structure of the programs. He used Moos' CIES to propose environmental profiles varying in structure. Programs with high structure were supportive, clear, and well-organized, high on practical orientation, and low on expressiveness, autonomy, and personal problem orientation. Low structure programs had the converse profile.

Immature boys (Stage A) who were assigned to the high structure program (i.e., the program scoring higher on the CIES dimensions representing structure) were considered matched; immature boys who were assigned to the low structure program were considered mismatched. More mature boys (Stage B) who were assigned to the lower structure program were considered matched, whereas those who were placed in the high structure program were considered mismatched. The boys' progress was monitored during treatment and after their return to community placement.

In the immature group, compared to matched boys, mismatched boys had twice as many problem behavior incidents and more days truant from the program. Among the more mature boys, matching did not affect treatment outcomes. As Lawton's (1989) model would predict, matching may be more crucial for immature boys, who can function adequately only under high-structure conditions. Among immature boys, environmental structure and support compensate for their inability to structure their own experience, resulting in fewer frustrations and the development of new coping responses to problem situations. Also consistent with Lawton's (1989) model, Brill (1978) noted that more mature boys may function more adequately under varied environmental conditions. The prediction of a decrement in performance for individuals placed in conditions with more structure than is theoretically desirable may apply more clearly to Stage C youths, who may deteriorate with high structure; this did not happen with the moderately mature Stage B boys.

Leschied, Jaffe, and Stone (1985) obtained results that were consistent with Brill's (1978) for low conceptual level (CL) problem youths. Specifically, low CL youths in a high structure setting functioned more independently than did low CL youths in a low structure program. In contrast to Brill, Leschied et al. found that, in comparison to matched high CL youths, mismatched high CL youths (i.e., placed in a residence with high structure) received more staff discipline and spent more time out of the program due to disciplinary problems. Matched high CL youths showed more positive adjustment (responsibility and social control) as rated by program observers. Because Leschied et al.'s high structure program was more constrained and secure than Brill's high structure program, Leschied et al.'s mature youths may have been more frustrated by not being able to display their own abilities in self-control.

Other conceptual schemes are broadly similar to the conceptual level approach. For example, Veneziano and Veneziano (1986) used an MMPI classification system to identify a "characterological" group of youths who displayed the signs of what, at the adult level, is antisocial personality disorder. Such individuals lack internal controls, but function well in highly structured environments that supply external controls for their behavior. They should respond best to a structured program of rules and activities. In contrast, a "neurotic" group, and a group with no signs of psychopathology, would be most likely to benefit from intensive psychotherapy or from group counseling. Veneziano and Veneziano pointed out the potential usefulness of the classification system from a treatment management perspective.

Interpersonal Integration Matching

Another system for matching juvenile offenders to programs draws on the developmental conceptual model termed Interpersonal Integration. Jesness (1971) developed an inventory to assess an individual's level of Interpersonal Integration (I-level) as well as sets of recommended treatment techniques and therapeutic environments for individuals at different levels. A particular "I-level" designation indicates a level of social maturity that is based on the respondent's understanding of social roles and interactions.

Of the seven I-levels, most youthful offenders are functioning at an I-2 (focus is on self; poor planning and reflective skills; impulsive; poor interpersonal relationships), I-3 (focus is more on others; accepts set of values that is quite rigid), or I-4 (reflective, understanding of others, own value system) level. These three I-levels parallel Hunt's (1971) CL Stages A, B, and C. Treatment plans for I-2 youths are to provide an unambiguously structured environment and make concrete demands for progress. For I-3 individuals, treatment encourages identification with adults and increased social competence, while making clear the program's structure and penalties for unacceptable behavior. Treatment for I-4 youths involves eliminating the delinquent self-concept with individual counseling to develop insight into and resolve internal conflicts, develop interpersonal skills, and encourage self-responsibility.

A set of "differential-treatment studies" based on the I-level concept were conducted with juvenile offenders in the California Youth Authority (Warren, 1983). In one project, the home atmosphere established by group home parents was matched to the needs of I-level subtypes. Matching for the most immature and dependent youths (e.g., I-2s) consisted of placement in a protective home; middle-maturity youths (I-3s) were placed in a containment home providing very high structure; and higher maturity (I-4) youths who needed an atmosphere of relative freedom were placed in a boarding home. Matching was associated with reduced recidivism for all three groups, but the boarding home was particularly successful in benefiting high-maturity youths.

Leschied and Thomas (1984) used both the I-level and CL models in a study of "hard-to-serve" problem youths. Most of these youths fell at the more immature end of psychosocial development, as measured by I-level and CL scales. Immature youths were matched to a highly structured, behaviorally-oriented program, whereas more mature youths were placed in a less structured program that emphasized peer responsibility and working through personal feelings with a focus on planning for the future. At 3-month and 1-year follow-ups, these matched mature and immature youths committed fewer additional criminal offenses, were less likely to be residing in correctional facilities, and had lower recidivism to residential treatment than other hard-to-serve treated groups that were not matched to correctional programs. Leschied and Thomas suggested gradually exposing problem youths to greater independence and autonomy following residential treatment.

Social Systems Matching

Recent research with problem youths has shown that client–treatment matching can lead to improvements in the family environment, which in turn lead to better outcomes. Much of this type of work has used Multisystemic Therapy (MST; Henggeler & Borduin, 1990), which is based on Bronfenbrenner's (1979) social ecological model. Within MST, the primary purpose of assessment is to understand the fit between the identified youth's problems and his or her broader systemic context. The success of MST in the treatment of antisocial behavior in adolescents is attributed in part to the match between MST intervention foci and empirically identified correlates or causes of antisocial behavior.

MST is a family- and home-based treatment approach that directly addresses the intrapersonal factors assessed in the I-level and CL models, as well as familial and extrafamilial (peer, school, and neighborhood) factors that are known to be associated with adolescent conduct problems. The ongoing transactions between familial and extrafamilial systems are also targeted for intervention. Because different combinations of these factors are relevant for different adolescents, MST interventions are individualized and flexible. Specific MST techniques used to obtain objectives vary in accordance with the strengths and weaknesses of the particular youth, family, school, and so on, as well as with the strengths and weaknesses of the particular therapist.

At the first MST session (usually conducted with the parents or guardians, the identified problem youth, and his or her siblings), a primary goal is for the therapist to gain an understanding of the systemic context of the presenting problems. More specifically, the therapist attempts to determine how these problems fit with the individual characteristics of the family members, the nature of family relations, and the many extrafamilial variables that can be linked with the presenting problems. The strengths and weaknesses of the youth and of the systems of which she or he is a part are identified, vis à vis the problem behavior. For example, a youth's delinquent behavior may be linked with problematic characteristics of several systems: use of ineffective discipline strategies by parents and teachers, inadequate parental monitoring, support for delinquent behavior by peers and siblings, and youth impulsivity.

Systemic strengths used to promote therapeutic change may be the parents' and teachers' general competence and concern for the child, the siblings' concern, the parents' strong social support network, the child's high status among peers, and the child's athletic abilities. In addition, the interrelations among some systems may contribute to the problem behavior or be used to help ameliorate it. For example, antagonism between the parents and the teacher may exacerbate the child's problems. In general, the therapist's task is to design a set of interventions that build on the existing strengths of the various systems and/or that help to develop new strengths that can be used to promote behavior change.

The content of the therapeutic interventions depends on the results of the initial assessment. Because different combinations of intrapersonal and systemic factors are relevant for different adolescents and families, treatment is directed only at those factors that are most pertinent. For example, in using MST with juvenile offenders, the nature of the interventions varies for each family and may include family therapy, school intervention, peer intervention, individual therapy with a family member, and/or marital therapy. The therapist may also need to provide interventions that target the transactions between two or more systems. A common focus is the interface between family and school. A therapeutic goal may be to open intersystem communication channels between parents and teachers and gain collaboration on mutually desired goals.

The benefits of MST's problem-intervention matching approach were demonstrated by Mann, Borduin, Henggeler, and Blaske (1990), who used MST with problem adolescents and their families. The goals of the interventions were to increase structure, cohesion, and warmth, and decrease conflict within the family. These positive changes in the family milieu were associated with decreased psychiatric symptomatology among the adolescents. Subsequently, MST was compared with usual services in the treatment of youths who had committed serious offenses and their families (Henggeler, Melton, & Smith, 1992). In comparison with youths who received usual services, youths who received MST had fewer arrests and self-reported offenses and spent an average of 10 fewer weeks incarcerated. In addition, families in MST reported increased cohesion in the family milieu and decreased youth aggression in peer relations.

Borduin et al. (1995) examined the 4-year effects of MST vs. individual therapy among youths at high risk for committing additional crimes. The findings clearly demonstrated the impact of MST on key family correlates of antisocial behavior. Specifically, MST had highly favorable effects on the family climate (increased cohesion, support, and adaptability, and decreased conflict and hostility). MST also resulted in decreased symptomatology in parents and decreased behavior problems in the youths. Youths treated with MST were significantly less likely than comparison counterparts to be rearrested within 4 years after treatment termination, and, when rearrested, had committed significantly less serious offenses. Criminal behavior may have been influenced primarily by strengthening the family such that the deleterious effects of association with deviant peers were buffered.

Summary

Hunt's (1971) conceptual level matching model and Jesness' (1971) interpersonal integration level model both classify youths on an immature–mature continuum. Immature youths do better in structured settings, whereas more mature youths may be less affected by the environment, unless it is on the extreme structured end of the unstructured–structured continuum. Henggeler and Borduin's (1990) MST considers the maturity level of youthful offenders, and also considers the environmental context composed of family, peers, and school. Outcome evaluations of MST have found that problem–intervention matching is an effective approach to helping youths with delinquency problems.

CONCEPTUALIZING MATCHING MODELS

We have reviewed matching models based on the program characteristics of treatment environment and treatment orientation. Lawton's (1989) model proposed that a match between personal competence and environmental demand results in positive affective and behavioral outcomes. Mismatches created by too-high demand are especially detrimental for poorly functioning individuals. Well-functioning people are better able to utilize the environmental resources that are available to them. Hunt (1971) also proposed that a match between clients' competence, reflected in their maturity, and environmental resources and demands, reflected in environmental structure or lack of it, produces good outcomes. Like Lawton, Hunt stated that less competent individuals are more affected by changes in demand than are more able individuals. Finally, Moos (1997) similarly proposed that high demands are likely to be detrimental for poorly functioning clients—that is, unless they occur in a supportive context. In contrast to Lawton, Moos emphasized that environmental resources, such as greater support and structure, are more beneficial for poorly functioning than for well functioning clients.

Broadly speaking, the empirical findings reviewed in this chapter support Hunt's (1971) model regarding outcomes of maturity–structure matching, as well as Moos' (1997) model describing the benefits of demand for intact clients, and of resources for impaired individuals. Studies that pertained to Lawton's (1989) conceptualization were also generally supportive. However, much of the empirical research on patient–treatment matching for psychiatric patients is not directly germane to Lawton's model because his formulation is relatively complex. For example, researchers have not yet determined how to assess that a match exists between personal competence and environmental demands, that demands are too high or too low, or that a change has occurred in demand such that low-competence individuals may be negatively affected. Until these issues are resolved, Lawton's model cannot be fully tested.

One needed line of work on person–environment matching is to better understand the resource and demand qualities of each of Moos' (1997) treatment climate dimensions covering the relationship, personal growth, and system maintenance domains. For example, although support is typically characterized as a resource, the personal attention of supportive staff members and patients may be experienced as demands for interpersonal involvement. Similarly, a program's emphasis on practical orientation is usually viewed as a demand, but may be considered a supportive and structured resource by patients who would have difficulty learning new skills and planning for community life on their own. Further development of Moos' (1997) theory should focus on the program contexts and personal characteristics of clients that define the resource and demand aspects of the treatment climate dimensions.

Another issue for future research is to examine models in terms of whether the client outcomes considered involve mood and satisfaction or performance criteria. Of course, these sets of outcomes are not independent, as each may affect the other. As Lehman and Ritzler (1976) found, however, more satisfaction does not necessarily predict better performance. Resources such as support in the treatment environment may be especially likely to influence affective states and satisfaction with the program and with life in general. Demands may be more likely to affect performance-related outcomes, such as the development of basic living and interpersonal skills, work-related or vocational functioning, and length of clients' stay in the community after discharge.

To understand more fully the congruence between clients' characteristics and program demands and resources, researchers need to examine the selection processes that affect the extent to which clients are matched to treatment settings. Many facilities select and place clients on the basis of their level of functioning, which tends to enhance the congruence between clients' competence and the treatment setting. Programs serving more impaired patients tend to emphasize support and other resources; those serving more intact residents tend to emphasize demands (Moos & Lemke, 1994). Patients may choose to leave a program in which the demands for performance are lacking in challenge. Because less competent individuals may function optimally within a narrower range of environmental conditions than more intact individuals, selecting a suitable program may become more difficult with greater impairment.

Ideally, a systematic approach to selecting a treatment program for a particular client should involve the treatment climate as well as the treatment orientation domains (Hser, 1995b), and the entire spectrum of services should be available to meet patients' needs. Current research, however, cannot support an empirically-based systematic referral with this kind of sophistication, and few communities offer the full range of treatment options. Research is needed to enhance matching with each type of program characteristic. Researchers need to use common measures of program characteristics and patients' functioning across studies so that results can be compared and interpreted. In addition, matching research is needed to expand and examine the issues of problem–service, client–staff, and client–client matching.

Problem-Service Matching

The work of McLellan and his colleagues suggests that the difficulty of identifying and replicating patient–treatment orientation matches in the substance abuse treatment field is due to the fact that the patient and treatment variables examined in many studies have been too molar. In an early retrospective study, McLellan, Woody, Luborsky, O'Brien, and Druley (1983) recruited substance abusing veterans from several inpatient and outpatient programs. Patients with severe psychiatric problems fared poorly in all programs, in contrast to those with the lowest severity, who showed consistent improvement regardless of program. Patients with moderate psychiatric severity and severe employment and family problems at admission to treatment showed better outcomes in service-intensive inpatient programs during treatment and 6 months postadmission than they did in less intensive outpatient programs.

Based on these findings, McLellan et al. (1983) prospectively matched alcoholic- or drug-dependent patients having milder psychiatric, employment, and family problems to lower intensity programs, and those with more severe problems to higher intensity programs. Compared to mismatched patients, matched patients had better 6-month outcomes; in addition, during treatment, matched patients were rated as more motivated for treatment, stayed in treatment longer, and had fewer irregular discharges.

Subsequently, McLellan et al. (1997) revised their approach to patient–treatment matching by targeting the services available at each program to address specific problems presented by the patient at treatment admission. They called this approach *problem-service matching*. It resembles MST's problem–intervention matching strategy for youths with conduct disorders. In a test of the problem–service matching model, patients were randomly assigned to a standard-care condition or a matched-care condition. In the matched-care condition, patients who had significant problems in the areas of psychiatric health, family/social relations, and/or employment received a minimum of three individual sessions from a professionally trained staff person appropriate to the target problem area. Matched patients were less likely to drop out of treatment early and, at a six-month follow-up, had better outcomes than standard-care patients. Additional research focused on quantifying dose-response functions between service provision and patient outcomes would suggest both the types and amounts of targeted services that are needed to achieve good outcomes (Hser, 1995b).

Client-Staff Matching

One way to match patients to programs is to capitalize on staff members' interpersonal styles, attitudes, and expectations. Brill (1978) suggested that it may be beneficial to match immature delinquent youths with staff members and therapists who have a directive interpersonal style, and more mature youths with nondirective staff members. Matching by staff members' styles and clients' maturity levels may be most appropriate when the staff member is responsible for creating the primary treatment approach for individuals in his or her caseload.

Staff members' interpersonal styles were seen as potentially important by Condry (1987), who studied a residential facility for adolescent girls with behavior problems. In this program, implementation of an environment suitable for I-2 youths was generally accomplished in that the daily environment was highly organized and behavior expectations were concrete. However, implementation of an I-3 climate was only partly accomplished. Opportunities to analyze interpersonal issues among residents were limited, but residents did have to adapt to authority figures and the penalties for inappropriate behavior were specific and quickly applied. I-4 treatment techniques were the least well implemented. The program's emphasis was not consistent with the I-4 youth's problems, which center on issues of individual growth, self-knowledge, self-control, and responsibility.

As a solution, Condry suggested selecting staff with interpersonal styles that are appropriate for the I-level of residents they treat. Her suggestion is based on the Jesness Manual (1974), which recommends hiring staff who have interpersonal styles fitting with clients' I-levels, rather than attempting to develop those styles. In the program Condry studied, staff were selected for an interpersonal style that was appropriate for I-2 and I-3 individuals; that is, they were willing to exert control over the residents. Staff members treating I-4 youths need to be conceptually complex and to be conversant with alternative treatment techniques. In particular, they need to expand learning opportunities for I-4 residents in order to provide more responsibilities and opportunities to develop skills. For example, I-4 youths may serve as teaching assistants or tutors in the program or complete internships outside the facility. An environment with fewer external controls is more appropriate for I-4 youths, and is good preparation for their return to community living.

With respect to client–staff matching in the substance abuse treatment field, McLachlan (1972, 1974) tested the hypothesis that alcoholic inpatients functioning at a higher conceptual level (i.e., more independent, empathic, and cognitively complex—see Hunt, 1971) would respond better to less structured therapists at a similar conceptual level, whereas patients functioning at a lower conceptual level would fare better when treated by more structured therapists with lower conceptual levels. In comparison to mismatched patients, matched patients had better drinking outcomes up to 16 months posttreatment. Hser (1995a) points to potential interactions among treatment variables by noting that the nature of client-staff interactions may vary with differences in program characteristics. For example, Hser hypothesizes that staff or therapist characteristics may have more impact on patient outcomes in programs that are less structured.

Client–Client Matching

A question raised by research on patient–treatment matching is whether patients should be treated only among patients with similar impairment levels, or whether matching can take place and be even more beneficial in a program in which patients are heterogeneous with respect to their impairment levels. In other words, should poorly and well functioning patients be treated in separate programs, or can one program meet the needs of a heterogenous group of patients?

A related question concerns whether patients need to move to new treatment settings as their functional levels improve. As patients' functioning improves, their needs change. For example, Lehmann et al. (1978) found that psychiatric patients' needs for social contact, social support, and responsibility increased with their time in the hospital. Can patients' needs be met sufficiently if they remain in the same program as they make progress toward their treatment goals? Researchers have noted the importance of moving patients through more demanding treatment climates as they get better and closer to discharge (Leschied & Thomas, 1984; Werbart, 1992).

As our review indicates, the answers to these questions probably depend on the patients' specific level of functioning and the specific treatment environment or orientation. Too little support and structure and too many demands for interpersonal and work skills are detrimental for poorly functioning patients, whereas too much support and structure and too few demands are detrimental for well functioning patients. Well functioning patients may be less affected by program mismatches, especially when supportiveness, structure, and demands are not extreme. Furthermore, demands may be acceptable for poorly functioning patients if the program also offers support and handles performance demands in a personalized fashion.

Research should determine how large the mismatches between functioning and support and performance demands have to be, for less and more impaired patients to be negatively affected. As Coulton et al. (1984a) have noted, some mismatch between individual need or competence on one hand

and environmental resources and demands on the other may stimulate personal growth. Possibly, gaps are beneficial in some areas but not in others. For example, individuals who fit well with a nondemanding environment may be making little progress toward fuller reintegration into the community. Large patient–program mismatches may cause the patient to be seen as disruptive to the program or as uncooperative. Further specification is needed regarding those patient–program characteristics in which congruence is essential to satisfactory patient adjustment versus those in which discrepancies may be beneficial.

The tension between matching an individual's current needs as well as his or her needs to achieve future-oriented goals was noted by Reitsma-Street (1988; Reitsma-Street & Leschied, 1988) in reviewing the conceptual level matching model and its use with troubled youths. She distinguished between contemporaneous matching (i.e., routines appropriate to get through a day with minimal overt problems) and developmental matching (i.e., environmental characteristics promoting changes within the youth so that she or he has a better chance of staying out of trouble on discharge). Contemporaneous person–environment matching is important for stable management and personal satisfaction, whereas developmental matching is necessary for challenge and individual growth. In discussing how staff can promote environmental characteristics that are both contemporaneously and developmentally matched to youths' needs, Reitsma-Street recommended a highly structured program that balances the current need for specific and consistent expectations with the future need for flexible responses to individual situations. She labeled this concept of balancing *structured flexibility*.

CONCLUSION

In conducting future evaluations, special attention should be paid to how treatment programs' characteristics, such as their social environment, treatment orientation, and services, and staff and client characteristics, may differentially impact on different clients' functioning and life contexts when they return to the community. It is important to consider how formal and informal services may maintain improvements in psychological, social, and cognitive functioning, and how they may help to restructure clients' family, social, and work contexts. The most active and powerful ingredients of treatment may be those that improve the match between clients' abilities and the support and performance demands offered in these multiple community settings.

ACKNOWLEDGMENT

Preparation of this chapter was supported by Department of Veterans Affairs Health Services Research and Development Service funds and by NIAAA Grant AA06699. We thank Molly Kaplowitz for valuable help with the literature review.

REFERENCES

Borduin, C. M., Mann, B. J., Cone, L. T., Henggeler, S. W., Fucci, B. R., Blaske, D. M., & Williams, R. A. (1995). Multisystemic treatment of serious juvenile offenders: Long-term prevention of criminality and violence. *Journal of Consulting and Clinical Psychology, 63,* 569–578.

Brill, R. (1978). Implications of the Conceptual Level Matching Model for treatment of delinquents. *Journal of Research in Crime and Delinquency, 15,* 229–245.

Brill, R. (1980). Guiding staff to create environments facilitating treatment. *The Differential View, 10,* 47–60.

Bronfenbrenner, U. (1979). *The ecology of human development.* Cambridge, MA: Harvard University Press.

Collins, J. F., Ellsworth, R. B., Casey, N. A., Hyer, L., Hickey, R. H., Schoonover, R. A., Twemlow, S. W., & Nesselroade, J. R. (1985). *Journal of Clinical Psychology, 41,* 299–308.

Condry, S. (1987). Therapy implementation problems in a residence for delinquents. *Journal of Applied Developmental Psychology, 8,* 259–272.

Cooney, N. L., Kadden, R. M., Litt, M. D., & Getter, H. (1991). Matching alcoholics to coping skills or interactional therapies: Two-year follow-up results. *Journal of Consulting and Clinical Psychology, 59,* 598–601.

Coulton, C. J., Fitch, V., & Holland, T. P. (1985). A typology of social environments in community care homes. *Hospital and Community Psychiatry, 36,* 373–377.

Coulton, C. J., Holland, T. P., & Fitch, V. (1984a). Person–environment congruence and psychiatric patient outcome in community care homes. *Administration in Mental Health, 12,* 71–84.

Coulton, C. J., Holland, T. P., & Fitch, V. (1984b). Person–environment congruence as a predictor of early rehospitalization from community care homes. *Psychosocial Rehabilitation Journal, 8,* 24–37.

Downs, M. W., & Fox, J. C. (1993). Social environments of adult homes. *Community Mental Health Journal, 29,* 15–23.

Friis, S. (1986a). Characteristics of a good ward atmosphere. *Acta Psychiatrica Scandinavica, 74,* 469–473.

Friis, S. (1986b). Factors influencing the ward atmosphere. *Acta Psychiatrica Scandinavica, 73,* 600–606.

Goldstein, J. M., Cohen, P., Lewis, S. A., & Struening, E. L. (1988). Community treatment environments: Patients versus staff evaluations. *The Journal of Nervous and Mental Disease, 176,* 227–233.

Henggeler, S. W., & Borduin, C. M. (1990). *Family therapy and beyond: A multisystemic approach to treating the behavior problems of children and adolescents.* Pacific Grove, CA: Brooks/Cole.

Henggeler, S. W., Melton, G. B., & Smith, L. A. (1992). Family preservation using multisystemic therapy: An effective alternative to incarcerating serious juvenile offenders. *Journal of Consulting and Clinical Psychology, 60,* 953–961.

Hser, Y. (1995a). Drug treatment counselor practices and effectiveness. *Evaluation Review, 19*, 389-408.

Hser, Y. (1995b). A referral system that matches drug users to treatment programs: Existing research and relevant issues. *The Journal of Drug Issues, 25*, 209-224.

Hunt, D. E. (1971). *Matching models in education*. Toronto: Ontario Institute for Studies in Education.

Jesness, C. F. (1971). The Preston typology study: An experiment with differential treatment in an institution. *Journal of Research in Crime and Delinquency, 8*, 38-52.

Jesness, C. F. (1974). *Classifying juvenile offenders: The sequential I-level classification manual*. Palo Alto, CA: Consulting Psychologists Press.

Kadden, R. M., Cooney, N. L., Getter, H., & Litt, M. D. (1989). Matching alcoholics to coping skills or interactional therapies: Posttreatment results. *Journal of Consulting and Clinical Psychology, 57*, 698-704.

Klass, D. B., Growe, G. A., & Strizich, M. (1977). Ward treatment milieu and posthospital functioning. *Archives of General Psychiatry, 34*, 1047-1052.

Lawton, M. P. (1989). Behavior-relevant ecological factors. In K. W. Schaie & C. Schooler (Eds.), *Social structure and aging: Psychological processes*. Hillsdale, NJ: Lawrence Erlbaum Associates.

Lehman, A., & Ritzler, B. (1976). The therapeutic community inpatient ward: Does it really work? *Comprehensive Psychiatry, 17*, 755-761.

Lehmann, S., Mitchell, S., & Cohen, B. (1978). Environmental adaptation of the mental patient. *American Journal of Community Psychology, 6*, 115-124.

Leschied, A. W., Jaffe, P. G., & Stone, G. L. (1985). Differential response of juvenile offenders to two detention environments as a function of conceptual level. *Canadian Journal of Criminology, 27*, 467-476.

Leschied, A. W., & Thomas, K. E. (1984). Effective residential programming for "hard to serve" delinquent youth: A description of the Craigwood program. *Canadian Journal of Criminology, 26*, 161-177.

Linn, M. W., Klett, C. J., & Caffey, E. M. (1980). Foster home characteristics and psychiatric patient outcome. *Archives of General Psychiatry, 37*, 129-132.

Linn, M. W., Klett, C. J., & Caffey, E. M. (1982). Relapse of psychiatric patients in foster care. *American Journal of Psychiatry, 139*, 778-783.

Litt, M. D., Babor, T. F., Delboca, F. K., Kadden, R. M., & Cooney, N. (1992). Types of alcoholics: II. Applications of an empirically derived typology to treatment matching. *Archives of General Psychiatry, 49*, 609-614.

Mann, B. J., Borduin, C. M., Henggeler, S. W., & Blaske, D. M. (1990). An investigation of systemic conceptualizations of parent-child coalitions and symptom change. *Journal of Consulting and Clinical Psychology, 58*, 336-344.

Mattson, M. E., Allen, J. P., Longabaugh, R., Nickless, C. J., Connors, G. J., & Kadden, R. M. (1994). A chronological review of empirical studies matching alcoholic clients to treatment. *Journal of Studies on Alcohol*, Supplement No. 12, 16-29.

McLachlan, J. F. C. (1972). Benefit from group therapy as a function of patient-therapist match on conceptual level. *Psychotherapy, Theory, Research and Practice, 9*, 317-323.

McLachlan, J. F. C. (1974). Therapy strategies, personality orientation and recovery from alcoholism. *Canadian Psychiatric Association Journal, 19*, 25-30.

McLellan, A. T., Grissom, G. R., Zania, D., Randall, M., Brill, P., & O'Brien, C. P. (1997). Improved outcomes from problem-service "matching" in substance abuse patients: A controlled study in a four-program, EAP network. *Archives of General Psychiatry 54*, 730-735.

McLellan, A. T., Woody, G. E., Luborsky, L., O'Brien, C. P., & Druley, K. A. (1983). Increased effectiveness of substance abuse treatment: A prospective study of patient-treatment "matching." *The Journal of Nervous and Mental Disease, 171*, 597-605.

Moos, R. H. (1987). *Correctional Institutions Environment Scale manual* (2nd edition). Palo Alto, CA: Mind Garden.

Moos, R. H. (1991). Connections between school, work, and family settings. In B. J. Fraser & H. J. Walberg (Eds.), *Educational environments: Evaluation, antecedents, and consequences* (pp. 29–53). Oxford, England: Pergamon.

Moos, R. H. (1994). *The Social Climate Scales: A user's guide* (2nd edition). Palo Alto, CA: Consulting Psychologists Press.

Moos, R. H. (1996a). *Community-Oriented Programs Environment Scale manual* (3rd edition). Palo Alto, CA: Mind Garden.

Moos, R. H. (1996b). *Ward Atmosphere Scale manual* (3rd edition). Palo Alto, CA: Mind Garden.

Moos, R. H. (1997). *Evaluating treatment environments: The quality of psychiatric and substance abuse programs*, 2nd edition. New Brunswick, NJ: Transaction.

Moos, R. H., & Lemke, S. (1994). *Group residences for olde adults: Physical features, policies, and social climate*. NY: Oxford.

Moos, R. H., & Moos, B. S. (1994). *Family Environment Scale manual* (3rd edition). Palo Alto, CA: Consulting Psychologists Press. Project Match Research Group (1997). Matching alcoholism treatments to client heterogeneity: Project MATCH posttreatment drinking outcomes. *Journal of Studies on Alcohol, 58*, 7–29.

Reitsma-Street, M. (1988). A pilot participant observation study of the environment in a program for young offenders from a conceptual level matching model perspective. *Journal of Offender Counseling, Services, and Rehabilitation, 12*, 77–93.

Reitsma-Street, M., & Leschied, A. W. (1988). The conceptual-level matching model in corrections. *Criminal Justice and Behavior, 15*, 92–108.

Segal, S., & Aviram, U. (1978). *The mentally ill in community-based sheltered care*. NY: Wiley.

Swindle, R. W., Peterson, K. A., Paradise, M. J., & Moos, R. H. (1995). Measuring substance abuse program treatment orientations: The Drug and Alcohol Program Treatment Inventory. *Journal of Substance Abuse, 7*, 61–78.

Timko, C., & Moos, R. H. (1998). Outcomes of the treatment climate in psychiatric and substance abuse programs. *Journal of Clinical Psychology, 54*, 1137–1150.

Vaglum, P., Friis, S., & Karterud, S. (1985). Why are the results of milieu therapy for schizophrenic patients contradictory? An analysis based on four empirical studies. *The Yale Journal of Biology and Medicine, 58*, 349–361.

Veneziano, C., & Veneziano, L. (1986). Classification of adolescent offenders with the MMPI: An extension and cross-validation of the Megargee Typology. *International Journal of Offender Therapy and Comparative Criminology, 30*, 11–23.

Warren, M. Q. (1983). Applications of interpersonal-maturity theory to offender populations. In W. S. Laufer & J. M. Day (Eds.), *Personality theory, moral development, and criminal behavior* (pp. 23–50). Lexington, MA: DC Heath.

Wendt, R. J., Mosher, L. R., Matthews, S. M., & Menn, A. Z. (1983). Comparison of two treatment environments for schizophrenia. In J. G. Gunderson, A. O. Will, & L. R. Mosher (Eds.), *Principles and practice of milieu therapy* (pp. 17–33). NY: Aronson.

Werbart, A. (1992). Exploration and support in psychotherapeutic environments for psychotic patients. *Acta Psychiatrica Scandinavica, 86*, 12–22.

7

Working Lives in Context: Engaging the Views of Participants and Analysts

Allan W. Wicker
Rachel A. August
Claremont Graduate University

All systematic attempts to understand or explain human experience and behavior entail assumptions about the nature and importance of people's relationships with their environments. Often, these assumptions are hidden, and are not thoughtfully examined (cf. Slife & Williams, 1995). In environmental psychology, researchers and theorists have a special obligation to examine and reflect on their underlying assumptions regarding person–environment transactions, because such events are a core concern of the field (cf. Craik, 1996).

In this chapter, we follow a naturalistic research strategy called *substantive theorizing* (Wicker, 1989), that entails close, empirically grounded scrutiny of assumptions, concepts, and propositions (also see Blumer, 1969, chap. 1). The term *theorizing* is used to stress that theory building is an evolving, continually developing process. Our empirical focus here is the work lives of ordinary people, as revealed in their own personal accounts. Specifically, we draw on work narratives from nationals and expatriates who live and work in Ghana, West Africa, and from late-career women in the United States.

A major section of the chapter outlines our developing framework for seeking to understand workers and their social and physical environments. In the discussion, we juxtaposed the perspectives of people whose working

197

lives are being examined with the studied, but more distant, views of researchers and theorists. Although these perspectives are sometimes believed to be incommensurate, incompatible, and even contradictory, we considered the prospects for engaging them in a way that would yield a more comprehensive grasp of person–environment relationships.

Also imbedded in attempts to study person–environment relationships are potentially troubling epistemological issues. We consider one of them, the matter of how researchers can "know" other persons and their environments, particularly when the social situations and backgrounds (e.g., age, gender, race, or culture) of the two parties are notably different. We draw on our own experiences to illustrate aspects of the issue and make several practical suggestions for researchers.

We begin with our rationale for selecting work as the substantive domain where to examine person–environment relationships.

OUR SUBSTANTIVE DOMAIN:
WORK AND WORK STORIES

Why is Work an Appropriate Focus?

Initial Considerations. In a previous article, Wicker (1989) argued that conceptual and theoretical development by social and environmental psychologists, and other social scientists, should entail their making frequent reference to actual happenings, in particular, concrete sectors of the empirical world. Wicker advocated examining naturally occurring events for clues to how potentially generalizable human processes unfold in natural settings.

Wicker (1985) encouraged theorists to reflect on what might be appropriate criteria for selecting a domain to develop their ideas. One criterion suggested was the domain's significance to large numbers of people. Work fits this requirement extremely well, although its boundaries are quite broad. The domain of work can usefully serve as a testing ground for considering the central issues in person–environment psychology. If the issues can be understood in relation to the perceptions and experiences of workers, and in the contexts that workers perform their duties, we can have confidence that we are addressing topics where there are potentially nontrivial applications. In this chapter, we aspire to use the domain of *work* to inform, shape, and condition our theoretical statements about people and their environments.

Our strategy of using informal, context-bound thought trials, observations, personal accounts, and other information to assess conceptual ideas reflects our judgment that *theories of the middle range* represent an appropriate, and probably best, strategy for conceptual development in social and environmental psychology and related fields. Grand, formal, context-free theories sound attractive when pronounced, but are often of little or no value for applications, and in any case, can be evaluated only in specific contexts. The distance between their general constructs and concrete applications is often so great as to be almost unbridgeable, and the number of plausible concrete referents of the constructs in empirical work is often so large they make any claim of theoretical support barely credible. Weick (1989) summarized the argument this way: "To look for theories of the middle range is to prefigure problems in such a way that the number of opportunities to discover solutions is increased without becoming infinite" (p. 521).

Indeed, *work* is in some ways too broad a concept, but it provides an orienting context—where we begin. From general considerations of work, we move to specific workers whose cases we will draw on to filter, assess, and illustrate the points we make regarding person-environment relationships.

It should be noted that, in light of United States, and indeed, world history, defining work in psychological or social terms and theorizing about it are inescapably value-laden, even political, actions. Issues of *power, equity*, and *hegemony* are intertwined with work in most individuals' conceptions, although for many, the linkages may be more latent than manifest. Yet, as Neff noted, with regard to work, "each of us has his own vantage point—his own particular ax to grind" (p. 1). Our own vantage point will become more evident as we proceed.

Conceptualizing the Work Domain.   One of the themes of this chapter is that sharp, firm boundaries and definitions, and static, mechanical, or linear conceptions of events are hard to sustain, when one engages in substantive theorizing. Nevertheless, some specifications are appropriate, and a good place to start is with the concept of work.

After examining various meanings, Ransome (1996) defined work as a "purposeful activity which is seen in some way expedient, requiring mental and/or physical exertion, carried out in exchange for 'payment'" (p. 36). Ransome noted that in contemporary Western society, work is largely public in nature, officially recognized for legal and tax purposes, and payment for work typically takes the form of salary, wages, or a working entrepreneur's profit. Although payment seems to be the essential criterion in contemporary usage, Ransome considered a purely economic perspective simplistic because it disregards important, dynamic aspects of work, such as shaping of personal

identity, expression of creativity, and the development of social ties and social standing.

Ransome's characterization of work as expedient and effortful, and his
recognition of personal and social functions that work serves for the individual, seem appropriate for incorporation in our own developing conception of work. Although the data we consider in this chapter are exclusively
from paid workers, we do not limit our conception of work to activities
where payment is given. For example, we consider maintaining a house-
hold and caring for one's children as work. As will be evident in later sections of this chapter, we emphasize the contextual nature of work.
Productive activities commonly regarded as work are conceived and enacted in social environments, including work settings, families, informal social groups, trades and occupations, and various organizations and
institutions. We believe an attempt to understand human work must consider people's relationships to such groups, including the degree that individuals internalize and enact the groups' values and prescriptions (cf. Neff,
1985, p. 40; Wicker, 1987, pp. 623-626). To study work conceived this way
is to study person-environment relationships.

The Significance of Work in Human Affairs.   Before presenting our
research in synthesizing work and key issues in person-environment psychology, we offer several additional reasons why we believe this domain is appropriate for substantive theorizing. The justifications are, necessarily, selective
and incomplete.

Numerous areas of research and evidence indicate that work is fundamental to human social existence. In earliest human history, engaging in productive activity was indistinguishable from living; people had to exert constant
energy and attention to simply survive (Neff, 1985, p. 26). Even today, for
many groups and individuals, a similar condition exists.

The great social theorists have recognized the importance of work, although they have ascribed different meanings to it. Marx assigned the highest significance to work, or the means of production from, which, he said,
human consciousness and the structures of society derive. For followers of
Marx, then, any attempt to understand how people relate to their environment must start with human labor.

For Freud (1961), work was a means where socially unacceptable impulses
could be channeled in ways that did not threaten the individual. Work also
served to establish and maintain social relationships, and provided essential
protections and benefits that individuals could not obtain in isolation. Thus,

both Marx and Freud recognized work as a link to other people and a basis for community.

Another reason for studying work is its ubiquitous nature: Much of an individual's waking time is spent at the workplace, and work settings comprise substantial portions of the environments afforded by communities. Although now somewhat dated, comprehensive studies of two small towns, one in Kansas and one in Yorkshire, England, illustrate this point. Barker and Schoggen (1973) found that behavior settings staffed and run by employees represented more than two thirds of the total extent of each town's public environments (p. 137). And more than 86% of the time people spent in the public sector of the community was spent in settings staffed by paid employees (p. 298).

On a far grander scale, recent social and economic developments in the world's industrially advanced countries are leading to what has been called "an irreversible transition in the organization of work" (Ransome, 1996, p. 140). Technological advances, organizational restructuring, downsizing in all sectors of our economy, and other broad-scale events are changing the nature of people's jobs, their relationships to their employers, and the meanings they attach to work. A report of a recent national survey that documented these and other trends called for greater "focus on the quality of the work environment, on social relationships at work, and on the general culture of the workplace—whether it be the corner drugstore, a factory, or an office.... " (Galinsky, Bond, & Friedman, 1993, p. 2). We examine such issues in this chapter.

First, however, we introduce our respective projects and two people whose work stories are among the data we have used as "filters" in substantive theorizing about person–environment relationships.

WORK STORIES

Two Naturalistic Studies of Work

The narratives we use next to illustrate central issues in person–environment psychology are drawn from two larger projects that explored the lives of working people. In the first project, Ghanaian workers and expatriates were interviewed about their work, with emphasis on the activities carried out in doing the job. In the second project, U.S. late-career women of various ethnic backgrounds were interviewed about their work histories, daily work experiences, and thoughts about their retirements. These projects follow a tradition of collecting workers' stories, illustrated by Studs Terkel's classic book, *Working* (1974), and by other works including Lasson (1971), Schroedel (1985), Xinxin and Ye (1987), and Blackwell and Seabrook (1996).

Although we dealt with samples of workers from two different countries, we do not consider this chapter a "cross-cultural" report. Specifically, we have not presumed that the cases in each data set are equivalent, to be contrasted only with cases in the other set. We explicitly reject such dichotomous thinking in favor of a more complex view that is elaborated on in the following sections of this chapter. We aspire to be "culturally aware," and to be sensitive to similarities and differences among the individuals both within and across the data bases (cf. Moghaddam, 1996, p. 57).

We next describe how the narratives were collected and the kinds of information obtained. Further details of the Ghanaian study are available online (Wicker, 1996b), where the full text of 50 work narratives are currently posted. See August (1996) for specifics on the study of U.S. late-career women.

The Ghanaian narratives were derived from interviews with 97 Ghanaian workers, and 30 expatriates, who live and work in Ghana. These interviews were collected during Wicker's assignment to the University of Ghana as a Fulbright scholar during 1993 and in two follow-up visits. Three students at the University of Ghana were trained to conduct the interviews with Ghanaian workers, that occurred in English when possible, or in a language spoken by both interviewer and worker. The sample includes workers from a wide range of jobs, including traditional healer, village chief, yam trader, butcher, nurse, cycle repairman, and member of parliament. The interviews with expatriates were conducted by Wicker and his assistants; these foreigners to Ghana are also a diverse group, both in country of origin and type of work. They included a Zairian Roman Catholic missionary, the American director of an agricultural development agency, and a Hungarian pediatrician. In the interviews with Ghanaians and expatriates, interviewers sought to learn various aspects of the individual's work, including his or her duties, feelings toward work, relationships with work associates, and how work affected their personal and family life.

The interviews with U.S. late-career women were conducted during the second half of 1995, and early 1996, as August's dissertation research. Twenty-one women with diverse ethnic backgrounds were interviewed about their work lives. All were late-career women who were seriously considering retiring within 5 years. Because August was interested in examining occupational differences in work experiences, she included women from three occupation groups: nursing, public school teaching, and private practice mental health therapy. The women held a variety of jobs within those occupations, including nurse's aide, nurse manager, reading specialist, vocational education teacher, Jungian analyst, and a therapist who specialized in counseling for women. August interviewed each woman on three occasions, and dealt with these topics, respectively: (a) work history and family experiences (e.g., favorite jobs, career interests in high school, family influences on career choices, marital history, significant events in work life), (b) details of present job and retirement plans (e.g., duties, rewarding and frustrating aspects of their work, relationships with work associates, effects of work on home life, planning for retirement, factors affecting retirement decisions), and (c) meaning ascribed to work (e.g., personal definition of work, wisdom accumulated from working, contributions made in work life, relationship of personal life to work life, how gender, ethnicity, and age affected work life, conceptions of "retired persons.")

Interviews with both the Ghanaian and late-career women ordinarily lasted one hour, although some took much longer. Interviews were conducted at a place convenient for the worker, typically homes and workplaces. Interviewers took detailed notes during and following each interview. In neither study was the sample of workers statistically representative of a specified population. Our intent was to explore the breadth and depth of selected workers' experiences.

We briefly describe next two workers, whose stories are drawn on throughout this chapter, to illustrate various points we wish to make. The two individuals were chosen, in part, because they differ from one another in several significant ways (nationality, gender, age, occupation, marital history, and educational level) and, in part, because their stories are relatively rich in straightforward examples of our points. Readers must understand that these are sample cases, and our theoretical work with the narratives has not focused on these cases more than numerous other cases available to us.

A Ghanaian Butcher.   Zoore is a single man in his late 20s. For the past 8 years, he has followed his father's trade as a butcher. He lives and works in a suburb of Accra, the capital city located on the coast in the south of Ghana. Previously, he was a farmer in the Ashanti Region in central Ghana. His home town is in northern Ghana, where he completed primary school and where his parents remain. Zoore resides in a single room in a detached, domestic servant's quarters. He prefers being a butcher to farming, particularly because, he says, "there is no blessed day that I fail to get money into my pockets, unless I don't find an animal to kill." His work requires him to take animals to the slaughter house, kill them quickly, and skin them or burn their hair off. He then cuts the meat into small portions that he sells at a stand near the slaughter house.

Proud of his trade, Zoore perceives several benefits to being a butcher. He is assured of "pocket money," and he "stands the chance of meeting many people, especially young ladies, whom one can make friends with." He is particularly mindful of women at this point in his life; he hopes he will soon be able to marry one of the "beautiful spinsters" he has met through his work. He also enjoys being self-employed. He is "not subject to the supervision of a boss," nor does he need to adhere to a rigid schedule. Zoore is committed to killing healthy animals, cutting good-sized pieces of meat for his customers, and treating customers tactfully. He has some concerns about his work, including competition from sellers of imported meat, and problems he would face if he were to become very sick and unable to work. He is irritated by the local butcher's association, that does him very little good and whose leaders have "all developed double bellies out of our moneys" (dues paid by the butchers).

An African American Teacher.   Maria is a divorced woman in her late 50s. She has been a vocational education teacher for the past 30 years, although she began her work life as a secretary. She grew up in Tennessee, where her father was a railroad laborer, and her mother was a domestic worker who "took care of a rich family's kids, and kind of cooked." Maria has lived in various places since then, including Florida, where she held her first job, in Chicago, where she "had a lot of relatives," and now resides in California.

Maria "loves teaching," particularly because she provides instruction in skills such as word processing and accounting, where students can see immediate applications. She also appreciates that her day brings variety; teaching a new lesson each day, and dealing with variations in her students' moods and needs, keeps her work stimulating. Maria is an active member of both the Human Rights Committee and the Curriculum Committee of her school, is on the State Council of Teachers, and is president of her school district's large teachers' union. Being able to "affect change" in the district pleases her, but Maria is cautious of her clout. "You have to be careful when you're a leader," she says, "because you have people who will follow you." She became very active in the teacher's union after separating from her spouse, and was subsequently surprised by all she had to offer as well as the positive reactions she received from other teachers.

Maria expressed concerned with several aspects of her work, including the degree that educators and students must cope with the "ills of society" that spill into the classroom. She also worries that, as she gets older, she may face "a big change in my energy" that would make it difficult for her to teach. Presently, she is disturbed by the sexism and racism she often encounters, particularly from leaders on Board of Education, but feels "you just can't let that hold you back."

We return to Zoore and Maria's working lives numerous times in the following section, as we next consider person-environment relationships in more general terms.

CONCEPTUALIZING THE PERSON-ENVIRONMENT RELATIONSHIP

Point of View

In our attempt to understand the person-environment relationship, we find it necessary to grapple with the fundamental issue of *point of view*. We aspire to bring together the perspectives of participants such as Zoore and Maria—the targets of study who sense, interpret, and act in relationship to their environments and the perspectives of analysts—those who stand apart from participants and their immediate environments and seek to make sense of their actions and circumstances.

Zoore's and Maria's accounts of their work depict the perspectives of themselves as participants. Such data, however, represent a somewhat degraded summary of lived human experience. They are degraded, to an unknown extent, by "filtering screens" (memories, selection of content to be related, ability to communicate) of narrators, interviewers, and editors. Although the accounts are imperfect, we take them as our best available source of participant information.

We should note that some scholars have argued that first-person accounts do not necessarily need to be analyzed. They believe it is sufficient to "give voice and standing" to people whose perspectives and expressions of meaning would not otherwise be heard. Such people are typically the marginalized, less privileged members of a society. It is a service to the intellectual community, some scholars have argued, to provide a channel of free expression to people who have been "constructed" by others, and who have had to adopt the language and assumptions of dominant groups in order to be heard (cf. Sampson, 1993; Shakespear, Atkinson, & French, 1993; Rappaport, 1995).

We are sympathetic with the above arguments. The Ghanaian work narrative has been made available on the Internet for use by students and scholars, as stated earlier, for these and other reasons. But we also believe that further processing (analysis) of the workers' stories is appropriate, and that such efforts can enhance the impact of the perspectives expressed. Reports of analyzed narratives typically will reach audiences that first person accounts would not. Of course, the potential downside is that analysts may further degrade the core ideas and meanings expressed in the primary documents.

Analysts vary widely in their approaches to understanding participants and their environments. One important way they differ is in their *orienting frameworks*—some may begin by looking for instances of well-articulated categories derived from formal models or theories, whereas others may apply only fuzzy and largely implicit categories and assumptions. We assume that no analyst begins with a blank slate. Our favored approach is one where analysts begin by articulating their existing framework, and then seek to assess and modify it, as they register and process new information from the empirical social world (cf. Blumer, 1969; Wicker, 1989).

Background. In the next section, we sketch our developing framework (as analysts) for the person–environment relationship in the context of work. Before doing so, we present some brief background on the point of view issue.

As readers may know, much of Lewin's (1951) work was based on analysts' representations of the participant's view of a situation, that is, the life space. However, Lewin's work with social change projects led him to see the value of another kind of data: representations of events and circumstances in the social and physical world that are in the *boundary zone* of the life space, and that can impinge on it. Lewin considered such additional nonpsychological data to be necessary for forecasting change and for predicting the life course of individuals. He advocated the development of a "psychological ecology" to address such matters (cf. Bonnes & Secchiaroli, 1995, chap. 2).

Lewin's call was answered by two of his associates, Barker and Wright, whose work led to the founding of ecological psychology. Their basic environmental unit, the *behavior setting*, is a conception of the immediate context of human actions.

Behavior settings are small-scale social/physical systems with a number of defining characteristics, including a definite time and place locus, a regularly occurring behavior pattern, and a close linkage between the behaviors of people and the physical objects in the setting. In Barker's conception, although people are essential components of settings, they are largely interchangeable; settings do not depend on particular individuals. Examples include a second-grade class, a court session, and a basketball game (for more details on behavior settings see Schoggen, 1989; Wicker, 1984).

Although people's actions are essential features of behavior settings, Barker (1987) forcefully argued that participants are not the best, or even necessarily appropriate, sources of information on setting-level events. Outside analysts are needed to comprehend, and if desired, induce change in settings, Barker stated, because participants take a *particularistic view* of setting events. In other words, Barker believed that people who are intricately linked to a subset of elements in a system typically see only those elements, and not the larger picture.

Two types of representation are being contrasted here. One is the analyst's characterization of the participant's perspective, exemplified by a sketch of a person's life space. The terms of representation (regions, valence, and so on) are those of the analyst, but the particulars are, presumably, reflections of the psychological situation of the person analyzed. The other representation, exemplified by Barker's conception of behavior settings, is the analyst's characterization of *his or her own* perspective on designated persons (participants) and their environments. Barker regarded each kind of representation as legitimate, yet considered them incompatible and unbridgeable. Some researchers and scholars have attempted to address this problem of incommensurability (e.g., Fuhrer, 1990; Wicker, 1989, 1992) that we will discuss later in the chapter.

Our developing framework for person–environment relationships in the context of work is sketched below; it builds on Wicker's previous efforts to apply the organizing model (Weick, 1979) to behavior settings (Wicker, 1992). The framework is a work in progress, not a completed, or static, theory (cf. Wicker, 1989; Craik, 1996).

Our Developing Framework

The Person.   We believe that people generally have a need to arrive at explanations for much of what they encounter; they are continually engaged in sense-making. We also believe that there are substantial differences among individuals in the kinds of events where they seek explanations, and in the number of iterations of their sense-making efforts. For example, virtually all workers feel a need to understand their personal responsibilities on the job, although some people want to know a lot more about their duties, and the social and physical relationships they are embedded in, than do others. And, workers differ in the kinds of information they seek about various other events and circumstances in the workplace and beyond; for some, relationships among work associates may be the greatest concern, whereas for others, work equipment may be a primary interest.

When workers describes their job and explain how it affects their family, for example, they are providing an account that makes sense to them. The narrative draws on their prior knowledge and beliefs about their physical and social world (Weick, 1979, calls this cognitive reservoir a *cause map*), and how they relate to that world. That is to say, they select and relate portions of retained wisdom from past sense-making efforts; (this process is further described next). For example, in Zoore's mind, his reduced contributions to his parents in the North are justified because frozen meat is imported into Ghana. Due to competition from sellers of such meat, whose prices are lower, Zoore's profits, and thus his discretionary funds, are reduced, leaving him less to share with his parents.

Individual and Social Sense-Making.   The process where people formulate accounts that are acceptable (i.e., make sense) to them is both *individual* and *social*. This process entails a series of "sense-making cycles" (Wicker, 1992). As they go about their daily lives, people are exposed to a vast array of events, only some that they attend to. The particular environmental events that they notice depend on their existing *cause maps*—their prior understandings about the world. Once noticed, events are further scrutinized and given meaning in light of what one already knows and believes about relevant parts of the world—that is, the events are interpreted by screening them through the individual's cause maps. If a given event can be readily interpreted, the person will then respond to, or ignore it, based on what seems appropriate given their understanding of what it represents; in this case the sense-making cycle is completed. But if the event is not readily understandable, that is, cannot be easily assimilated in their cause map, they may undertake further attempts to comprehend it, that is, engage in further sense-making cycles. An individual might, for example, further examine the event itself, attend to other related events, or ask another person for their interpretation. The new information is then processed, as described here, until some satisfactory interpretation and response is arrived at, and the person's cause map is modified to accommodate the additional information. Subsequent interactions with similar events will be affected by the individual's modified cause map.

As suggested here, people often consult others in search of acceptable accounts for events. In work settings, and in other social groupings, a degree of consensual sense-making and collective wisdom develops; it serves to screen subsequent events affecting the group, guides their responses to those events (cf. Weick, 1979; Wicker, 1992). Zoore's cause map, linking importation of frozen meat with the possibility of selling freshly slaughtered products at a profit, is likely shared by his fellow butchers. The cause maps of Zoore and the like-minded butchers are not exact copies of one another, however; they undoubtedly include some distinct and some common concepts and beliefs, and vary in degree of differentiation. At least some of their social interactions are devoted to arriving at more overlapping cause maps.

Our narratives indicate that people's cause maps related to work often include characterizations of the self and others in terms of age, gender, and marital status. These three distinctions are evident in the perspectives of individuals and social groups, both in the Ghanaian and United States samples. Two other demographic characteristics seem to be differentially salient in the two samples: Ethnicity in the U.S. and literacy in Ghana. August (1996) explored ways that these characteristics affected the work lives of the women she interviewed. For example, referring to her work as a union officer, Maria said that a woman has to:

> get out there and just run for things like the males do. Discriminated against because you're a woman is the same thing as being discriminated against because you're Black. Or you get a double whammy against you I guess, but you can't let that hold you back.

Zoore's frequent references to "young ladies" reflects his status as a young unmarried male. In Northern Ghana, where he comes from, young adults his age would usually already be married and have a family. In another narrative, a Ghanaian man hired as a laborer complained of being assigned "women's work" (cleaning rooms) because of his age. Illiterate workers in Ghana often noted the advantages that literacy afforded to their trade or profession. We address these distinctions later.

People's Long Term Pursuits.   At various times in their lives, people may engage in the pursuit of one or more major life goals. The major life goals of many people relate to work and career achievements. Workers may seek to accomplish distant, but verifiable, outcomes for themselves; the accomplishment of these goals may entail the performance of numerous and diverse tasks, may take one to a variety of settings, and may require sustained, motivated effort (Wicker, 1992). Such goals may be regarded as distinctive aspects of people's cause maps: People may have, in their minds, elaborate schemes that include intermediate steps, or subgoals, and beliefs about how they may be accomplished. Over time and place, as people undertake these steps and interpret their results in sense-making cycles, their cause maps are continually modified.

For Zoore, getting married and having a family seem to be a major life goal, and his work as instrumental in achieving it. His assessment of the benefits of being a butcher is made this way: "Above all, I have been able to establish very good friendships with a number of beautiful spinsters here in town, one of whom I hope to marry in the course of time." Another Ghanaian narrator, a clothing designer and producer, aspired to market his clothing in Europe and North America. His narrative revealed an elaborate comprehension of the necessary steps and potential blockages, to attain this goal.

The Environment.   The above descriptions of segments of work narratives in terms of the sense-making model and people's major life goals are examples of our (analysts) characterizing the participants' perspectives. The characterization of Zoore's situation includes reference to various features of his environment: the meat he sells, the buying public, Ghana's importation laws. In his narrative, Zoore refers to numerous other features of his physical and social world. If we were to adhere to the role of the analyst who seeks to communicate the participant's perspective, our task would be to extract these contextual features and represent them in some way, such as aspects of the participant's cause map. The same procedure applied across a subset of our narratives (e.g., those from late-career nurses or Ghanaian entrepreneurs) would produce a set of environmental features that are recognized by participants in the sample. Such an endeavor would be informative and worthwhile; it is part of the plan for analyzing the Ghanaian narratives. Indeed, many environment and behavior researchers regard participants' accounts as valid representations of their environments and of their relationships with those environments, and some of them also believe that the accounts are sufficient for theorizing (for a discussion of the phenomenological approach to the person–environment relationship, see Bonnes & Secchiaroli, 1995, chap. 5).

Our position is that although such accounts are useful and necessary, they are not sufficient. They are likely to yield a fragmented, largely incoherent construal of the social–physical world. The studied efforts of the outside analyst, on the other hand, may present more coherent, bounded structures, although they are likely to leave out important aspects of the views of participants. Of course, how a person's world is constructed through sense-making may resemble in various ways the construals of analysts, and those convergences are worthy of reflection and study. But—and this is Barker's point—the resemblance is not sufficient to justify reliance only on subjective reports of environments and person–environment relationships. He argued that there is a well-structured "pre-perceptual environment" that is evident to outside analysts who carefully examine the immediate milieu or surrounding socio-physical system of the individual: the behavior setting.

Multiple Dynamic Normative Systems

We believe that Barker's argument should be extended to other types of milieus, that is, to other normative social systems that, like behavior settings, afford opportunities and impose obligations on people within them.[1] And although knowledge of these systems can and should be obtained from participants, studious nonparticipant observers and analysts can provide perspectives that contribute to the understanding of participants, their multiple environments, and participants' relationships with those environments.

In our developing framework, person–environment relations are more complex than Barker described. In addition to the behavior setting, we believe that these systems represent significant environments of workers, and thus deserve attention: trade or occupational groups, employing organizations, families, informal social groups, localities, and society at large.[2]

We regard all of these systems as *social constructions* of their participants. That is, the patterned relationships that constitute the respective structures of these systems derive from previous interactions among the people within them (cf. Wicker, 1996a). And, although at any given moment these systems may appear to be stable, closer examination will reveal that they are in constant flux, due to changes in inputs from outside the systems and the complex interpersonal dynamics that sustain them. Somewhat paradoxically, certain patterns of participants' actions may be more discernible by analysts whose aloof stance affords a different, and perhaps more leisurely or encompassing perspective, than participants.

---

[1] We have deliberately avoided using the term *culture* for these systems, in favor of the more descriptive term, *normative social system* (see Clausen 1996 for a discussion of uses of the term *culture*).

[2] Bronfenbrenner (1979) has proposed a multi-system model representing the "ecology of human development" that shares some features with our developing conception of work environments.

By definition, *normative systems* prescribe certain actions and prohibit oth ers. There are variations within systems of the same kind, and any given sys tem will be perceived and responded to in different ways by its variou participants. For example, some work behavior settings are more constrictive than others. Maria seemed to have more latitude in establishing classroon routines than did some other teachers, whose lesson plans were scrutinized Workers may also vary in the degree they regard a given system to be con straining. For example, Zoore seemed to accept readily an obligation to senc money to his parents in the north, although other workers in similar situa tions did not express such concerns about their families.

People are variously positioned in the multiple systems they inhabit. Some workers regard their immediate workplace as centrally important, and are less concerned with prescriptions of their trade or occupation, for example. For other workers, the opposite may be true. And just as normative systems are in flux, so too are the relationships of workers to those systems, both in terms of the individual's position in any one system, and of the locus of the individual across several systems. For example, the reduced centrality of Maria's family system after she and her husband separated led her to become active in a professional group (the teachers' union).

At this stage in our development of an environmental framework of multi ple normative systems, some important issues need to be more fully ad dressed. One is the how the various systems we have identified, and that we discuss next, are related to one another. Another is what forces motivate or drive these systems. Satisfactory answers to these disarmingly simple ques tions are unlikely to be very simple; complications abound. To illustrate, the scale of the systems range from small, less inclusive social arrangements (be havior setting, family, informal social group) to larger and more inclusive ar rangements (trade or occupational group, employing organization, locality, society at large). Some of the systems are embedded in others (e.g., family and informal social groups may be embedded in locality; each of the other sys tems is within the society at large), although other systems are not fully en compassed or encompassing, but overlapping (e.g., trade or occupational group and employing organization). At this point, we are not ready to accept without modification the conception of Barker (see Schoggen, 1989) and of Bronfenbrenner (1979) of multiple systems being completely nested "like a set of Russian dolls" (Bronfenbrenner, 1979, p. 3). Among the complications in regard to the second issue is the following: The driving forces for some sys tems have been postulated to operate at more than one level; Barker specifies as driving mechanisms of behavior settings, for example, individuals' needs to achieve various personal goals, and extra-personal setting forces to carry out the setting program (Barker, 1987).

We believe the systems specified here are significant environments of workers, and that analysts' considerations of them will yield more comprehensible accounts of person–environment relationships.

We next comment briefly on the 7 types of normative systems, from an analyst's perspective. These systems constitute our orienting framework of the environments of workers. Although their work lives are carried out within these systems, workers are often unaware of the systems' structural and dynamic properties.

Work Behavior Settings.   Workers' behavioral routines within bounded workspaces, and in relationship to other people and to physical objects, comprise their *work behavior settings.*[3] Maria's accounting class, and the slaughter shed and grounds where Zoore worked, are examples. Barker conceived of these small-scale environmental systems largely in functional terms. In his view, system-level operating and maintenance mechanisms provide the output and stability that characterize behavior settings (Schoggen, 1989).

Wicker (1989, 1992) subsequently recast these mechanisms in terms of the sense-making activities of participants, and suggested that social–emotional considerations should supplement the functional view of settings. That is, workers do not simply carry out their tasks as components of a machine; they also converse, joke, construct meanings of events unrelated to the work program, and develop emotional ties that constitute part of the normative system we call a work behavior setting. To illustrate, Zoore and his fellow butchers carried out the usual tasks in the slaughter shed where they worked, but also regarded one another as brothers who shared food and jokes. They also honored the senior butcher by addressing him using an honorific name. We also believe that analysts who develop greater familiarity with particular work settings, such as ethnographers might achieve, can discern from their observations deeper, symbolic aspects of settings that can further increase our understanding of these environments (see e.g., Rosen, 1985, and Schultz, 1991).

We regard workplace behavior settings as the primary environmental system to be considered in understanding worker–environment relationships, for several reasons. The day-to-day activities and experiences of all workers

---

[3]Face-to-face work groups are considered to be part of the work behavior setting that also includes temporal, physical, and spatial features (see Wicker, 1987, p. 617).

take place within, and in relation to, these systems. Behavior settings are workers' most immediate social-physical environments. In contrast to more inclusive environmental systems, conditions within behavior settings are difficult for participants to escape if they remain on the job; the setting reality is typically their reality, regardless of the situation elsewhere. Behavior settings may also mediate the effects of other, larger normative systems, such as one's trade or occupation, and the employing organization. For example, codified norms such as policies and established practices of these larger units have their point of application within work settings, and it is at the setting level that workers experience them.

Trade or Occupation.   The primacy of behavior settings notwithstanding, other normative systems are important in characterizing worker-environment relationships. Among them is the worker's trade or occupational group—the body of workers who perform similar tasks, and who know themselves and are known by others for the type of work they do. In seeking to understand the situations of Zoore and Maria, we are aided considerably by knowing that he is a butcher and she is a teacher. Analysts' knowledge of the teaching profession and the butchering trade, that may include duties, training, current professional issues, occupational associations, status of these occupations in society, and the like, gives them a different, and more encompassing perspective than that of participants. (See Trice, 1993, for an extended discussion of occupational normative systems in industrially developed societies like the U.S.)

In developing countries such as Ghana, particulars regarding occupational groupings differ somewhat from those in industrialized countries. For example, farming and other work in the informal sector, such as petty trading, craft work, and vehicle driving, encompass larger proportions of the population, and are differentiated into distinctive categories related to status and wealth. For example, cash crop farmers, such as cocoa growers, are contrasted with farmers, whose crops are used to feed their families (Oyeneye & Peil, 1993). And due to economic stringency, workers in developing countries are increasingly diversifying from public and formal sector jobs, like clerical work and teaching, to take on additional, informal sector jobs such as petty trading and farming (Seppala, 1996).

Employing Organization.   Most workers in industrialized societies, as well as workers in the formal sector of developing countries, are participants in another significant normative system: the organization that employs them. For present purposes, we consider organizations as social units that are larger than a single behavior setting, and that are staffed by people who comprise more than one face-to-face work group. In the United States, the typical organization is, of course, much larger. For Maria, the school district is her employing organization. For Zoore, whose work is in the informal sector, there is no employing organization, as he pointed out with satisfaction in his narrative.

The salience and significance of organization level norms and practices seem to have increased in recent years, perhaps in part because leaders of many organizations have become more self-reflective about institutional goals and purposes. In capitalist countries, where competition is prevalent, many private enterprises have engaged management experts to help make their organizations distinctive in a variety of ways: by drafting mission statements and strategic plans, adopting programs of organizational change, such as Total Quality Management and re-engineering, and by actively promoting certain values and images of their firms, such as being "lean," "efficient," "client-centered," and using "leading edge technology." In the United States, numerous organizations in the public and nonprofit sectors have embraced similar strategies.

Paralleling these developments over the past decade, organizational researchers have produced a huge amount of literature on "organizational culture" and "organizational climate," (cf. Denison, 1996). There is also a growing amount of literature on the "psychological contract" between workers and employers (cf. Rousseau, 1995), reflecting, perhaps, workers' concerns about some of the consequences of organization-level changes (cf. Galinsky, Bond, & Friedman, 1993).

Our conception of organization-level normative systems leads us to focus on organizational policies and practices; the rhetoric, metaphors, and symbols used by top management in communicating to employees about the organization, including its purposes goals, and actions; and any organization-wide values and practices of employees as they carry out their jobs. (As noted earlier, we regard work behavior settings as a more appropriate level than the organization per se, for examining many organizational events.)

The Family.   In human affairs, and human development generally, *the family* is the primary normative system. From our perspective, the family is of particular importance for some of the same reasons that the work behavior setting is: its immediacy to the person, and its role in mediating inputs and values from more inclusive systems, including society at large. To speak of a person's relationship to an organization, or their position in a society without considering more proximal, mediating social systems is, in our view, to neglect much of what is essential to understanding person–environment relationships.

Kinship systems, including families of origin and of procreation, provide opportunities to participants and impose obligations on them, and the values of these social systems permeate other life domains, including work[4] (cf. Oyeneye & Peil, 1993, ch. 5). For some people, work and family are inseparable domains. The two seem more distinct in industrialized societies, but there are notable exceptions, including family businesses (cf. Wicker & Burley, 1991).

Knowledge of the prevailing kinship and family systems in a worker's culture can contribute greatly to understanding the relationships of that worker to their environment. In Ghana, for example, male children traditionally learned and practiced their father's trade, and even if they did not live with their extended family, they were obliged to help support their parents and other relatives. Recently, and particularly in urban areas, family and kinship ties have become more "compressed," (i.e., obligations are becoming more narrowly focused on the nuclear family), to the exclusion of more distant relatives (Nukunya, 1992). However, from a Western perspective, family ties in Ghana still seem strong. To illustrate, although Zoore moved to a different region of the country to farm, he soon took up his father's trade of butchering, and he seems to have readily accepted the obligation to send money to his parents on a regular basis. Another example of the interdependence of family and work in Ghana is the traditional practice of child care by members of the extended family, allowing women relatives to carry out a trade or occupational duties.

Family obligations to provide for the material and social–emotional needs of one's spouse and children represent an important context for work in all societies. Conflicting obligations of work-centered systems (work behavior setting, trade or occupation, employing organization) and the family system are often a source of stress for workers, as has been documented by much research. For example, providing care for parents or grandchildren conflicted with the work of several women in August's (1996) study. Yet, work and family systems can also be mutually supporting, and can serve as alternative means of rewards and self-expression. A therapist suggested that counseling

---

[4]Some ethnic groups in Ghana have *matrilineal* kinship systems and others have *patrilineal* systems; these distinctions are not considered in the present discussion.

had made her a better wife and mother, and Maria discovered her talent for leadership when she began union activities after separating from her husband.

Informal Social Groups.   For some people, groups of close friends serve many of the functions of family. We include this type of normative system here because both of our samples included narratives indicating that small groups, whose members were neither family nor coworkers, sometimes were important in participants' work lives. Typically, the groups were made up of peers, although we would also include in this category, mentoring and support groups made up of people of different status.

In August's research, peer groups sometimes included role models—women who were in professions that the participants subsequently entered. Peer groups also were often sources of job-related information and support; this was true, for example, of some therapists in private practice, who relied on friends within their profession to discuss cases and "cover" for them, should clients need emergency attention when they were away (August, 1996).

The Ghanaian participants typically did not emphasize the importance of such friendship groupings; those that did tended to mention fellow church members. In contrast, expatriates in Ghana frequently mentioned groups from outside their work settings. Peace Corps volunteers, for example, whose families were inaccessible, often spoke of informal social groups composed of other volunteers.

Locality.   We believe it is necessary to include in our scheme of normative systems, a level more inclusive than a family or informal social group, yet less inclusive than an entire national society. We use the term *locality* for this level. Although the defining characteristics of localities, such as regions, cities, city neighborhoods, towns, and villages, are typically more difficult to specify than other normative systems we are considering,[5] these systems often figure significantly in the ways that workers relate to their environments, and thus they merit our attention (cf. Blunt, 1983, chap. 3).

Localities are frequently associated with distinctive cultural groups having their own languages, rituals, and other practices, further complicating the problem of defining these normative systems. In fact, the matter is more com-

---

[5]For an extended discussion of the problem of scale in characterizing social organization, see Groenhaug, 1978.

plex than that. In ethnic groupings, there are further divisions, including ethnic subgroups, clans, and lineages, whose norms and practices may be relevant at one time or another, depending on the issue (cf. Nukunya, 1992, p. 225). We are admittedly glossing over numerous meaningful distinctions by our use of a single construct, the locality. We include it to signal a level that a contemporary Western perspective might neglect or overlook.

Analysts' characterizations of localities afford us greater understanding of the actions of workers attached to those localities, and provide us a basis for interpretation of first hand accounts referring to themselves and others in terms of locality. Numerous examples are found in the Ghanaian narratives; Zoore, for example, said that if he should win a substantial amount of money in the lottery, he would send it to his father to buy land for building a house in his home town in the north. Ghanaians' ties to home villages are so strong that city dwellers often identify their parents' village as their home town, although they have never lived there, and even if it is in a neighboring country. Zoore also noted that he and his fellow butchers were close "even though we do not all come from the same region." Regional and ethnic differences are emphasized in the stereotypes that groups hold of others; these views affect the actions of workers, including for example, hiring decisions (cf. Blunt & Popoola, 1985).

Locality is also important in the United States, although it has been less emphasized by social science researchers. References to the "bible belt," "new south," "rust belt," and the like are, of course, regional distinctions. In her narrative, Maria referred to segregation in a town where she first worked ("the Blacks lived on one side") and to Blacks' migration to the north ("the better way of life, or their salvation, was Chicago").

The Larger Society.   Here, we refer essentially to nation-level normative systems, that are more internally variable and harder for analysts to characterize incisively than smaller-scale systems. Some credible attempts have been made, however, and they provide useful reference points for our attempts to understand the lives, experiences, and social worlds of workers. For example, Kohls' (1984) listing of the "values that Americans live by" includes a number of concepts that can help us understand the experiences of workers. They include such values as personal control over the environment, change, equality, future orientation, competition and free enterprise, productive activity, practicality and efficiency, and materialism/acquisitiveness. We are not aware of any similar list for Ghana, but it would likely include such shared African values as courtesy, generosity, self-control, mutual respect, honoring of elders, and obeying the law (Blunt, 1983, p. 36).

A nation's laws and policies, including those dealing with economic and labor issues, represent a significant normative context in which workers operate (cf. Obeng-Fosu, 1991). For example, certain practices of the Ghanaian government, and other employers in Ghana, have weakened salaried workers' ties to their extended families, by limiting accommodation provisions and fringe benefits to the nuclear family (Nukunya, 1992, pp. 156–157). The Ghanaian government's steps toward freer international trade are directly linked to Zoore's concern that imported frozen meat is hurting his business. And government health inspectors can declare a carcass diseased and order its burial, causing Zoore or his fellow butchers to lose their investment in the animal. Maria's activities in the teachers' union can likewise be better understood in the context of industrial relations laws in the U.S. that permit workers to strike, and that govern actions by employers and unions.

Demographic Considerations In Normative Systems

When we discussed our conception of the person, we mentioned that individuals often characterize themselves and others in terms of age, gender, marital status, ethnicity, and literacy. These distinctions are also made, sometimes in codified form, in the normative systems just discussed. For example, in the organization where the Ghanaian laborer complained about having to clean rooms instead of doing "men's work," there was a policy of giving older workers less physically demanding jobs. Family and kinship systems and localities typically have strong norms about division of labor by gender and age. Certain trades and occupations may set literacy and marital status qualifications. And, national laws may give preference to people in hiring or in training programs based on ethnicity. The point we wish to make with these examples is that these distinctions cut across both personal and environmental domains: Not only does the individual see him- or herself in terms of these characteristics, the normative systems that comprise his or her environment impose different obligations and opportunities based on them.

Engaging The Views Of Participants And Analysts

We have covered a broad set of concerns in a limited space. But neither the expansive scope of the normative systems sketched earlier, nor the brevity of the discussion, should detract from this basic message: By engaging participants' and analysts' viewpoints, scholars can potentially achieve a deeper understanding of people in their social-physical contexts than if they either limit themselves to one of them, or, regard the two viewpoints as separate, largely unrelated, parallel approaches. In the present case, workers' stories about their work lives bring us close to lived human experience. They can reveal what are to participants the most salient aspects of their social-physical world. However, these perspectives are fragmentary, and even if pieced together, they yield an unnecessarily incomplete comprehension of the person and their environment. It seems unlikely, for example, that analyses of participants' life spaces would ever have yielded the behavior setting concept. Analysts who study the encompassing systems of persons (or at least what analysts have conceptualized as the encompassing systems), provide knowledge that can further inform scholars and help them render more sophisticated, comprehensive accounts. Of course, analysts' contributions should be critically examined, and in many cases, selectively drawn on.

It is, admittedly, easy to wish for and advocate more encompassing and finely articulated knowledge claims arising from the joining of contrasting perspectives, or paradigms. It is more difficult to suggest ways that researchers might proceed in order to achieve the postulated benefits. Fortunately, others have grappled with this issue in a related context, namely, contrasting approaches to organizational culture (e.g., Denison, 1996; Schultz & Hatch, 1996). Schultz and Hatch (1996) suggest a two-step mental strategy: first, deliberately positioning oneself outside both paradigms to note their contrasts and connections (p. 550), and second, engaging the identified contrasting qualities, such as clarity and ambiguity or stability and instability, in a kind of dialectical interplay that facilitates the construction of a more complex characterization—one that retains both of the contrasting qualities. They further argued that this placing of contrasting constructs in "interdependent tension" (p. 550) allows the researcher to understand each more fully. Schultz and Hatch said that the strategy "permits a more sophisticated approach to the analysis and interpretation of empirical data" (p. 552).

We have not yet subjected our work narratives to this kind of analysis, but the Schultz and Hatch interplay approach seems promising. For example, in our domain of interest, two contrasting assumptions are that only participants can know their social worlds, and that only analysts can know them (participants' social worlds). A more complex reconstruction would be that neither participants nor analysts can know the social worlds fully, that each can know some parts of those worlds better than the other, that some participants may comprehend normative systems much as some analysts do, and that some analysts may experience participants' social worlds in much the same ways as some participants do.

An example from previous research may be used to illustrate something of the interplay process and its possible benefits. In an extended series of bi-weekly interviews with a woman who was organizing a new business (a coffee shop), Wicker (1992) obtained the woman's unfolding story of the founding. Her biweekly accounts included descriptions of her activities since the previous interview and what she planned to do next. One of the analytic tools that Wicker brought to the investigation was *action theory* (e.g., Hacker, 1985), that emphasizes that planful action requires organizing goals into superior and subordinate levels, and identifying and executing the proper sequencing of the lesser goals to achieve the higher order goals. Stepping aside from both the founder's and the action theory perspective, one can recognize a common emphasis on goal achievement. But the accounts of how progress is made were quite different. Action theory presented a rational analysis and orderly sequencing of actions leading to the goal, whereas the founder's account seemed at times to portray almost random action, little or no attention to sequencing, and frequent diversion from tasks, often due to outside demands, but sometimes also due to motivational lags of the founder. Reflection on these commonalities and contrasts was helpful in formulating a view of planning and implementation that included aspects of both perspectives: a hierarchy of goals and sequencing of actions can be discerned, and may be essential, but the couplings are much looser, and suffer from more interference than rational analysis acknowledges.

Similar applications of the interplay strategy to the work narratives are planned, and are expected to yield refinements to the orienting conceptual framework we have outlined here.

Thus far in the discussion we have skirted a matter that we now wish to address more directly: the question of how researchers can come to know other people and their situations. This question has deep philosophical as well as very practical aspects. In the following section, we offer a few reflections and suggestions based on our research.

KNOWING OTHERS

Many writers have noted the difficulties analysts face when attempting to understand people who are, in various ways, unlike themselves. These attempts are generally grounded in the epistemological assumptions of the theoretical

perspectives that researchers embrace, such as empiricism, rationalism, social construction, and hermeneutics (cf. Slife & Williams, 1995). Even those
who wish to comprehend broadly may not be able to differentiate the individual's perspective from that of the larger cultural community (cf.
Rosenwald and Ochberg, 1992). And, when analysts occupy positions of
dominance relative to those they seek to know, significant and possibly
even insurmountable barriers may exist (cf. Okeke, 1996; Overaa, 1995).
In recognition of these and other concerns, Campbell (1996) called for "an
epistemology and methodology which explains how, and to what degree,
knowing the other is possible, as well as the common errors made in the attempt" (p. 169).

The Relationship Of the Analyst
To the Participant

Ecological Distance and Knowing.   Our developing person–environment framework provides a way of thinking about one aspect of the
epistemological question, namely, the relationship of the analyst to the participant. We have characterized participants as active sense-makers, whose
cognitive schemas, or cause maps, serve as filters for their experiences and the
accounts they give of their working lives. Participants were also represented as
capable of pursuing and achieving major long term goals in their lives. And
we have suggested that each individual can be viewed as being situated in a
distinctive series of normative social systems that comprise their environment. That is, each person can be viewed as occupying a particular niche
within what can be termed an *ecological network*. Each person has a unique
pattern of relationships with family, friends, work groups, and organizations;
major life pursuits; and specific ethnic, gender, occupational, and national
identities.

Researchers who seek to understand others also have niches in their own
distinctive ecological networks. This common framework provides a basis for
thinking about the relationship between researchers and participants. For
any given researcher and the person they wish to know, a kind of "ecological
distance" can be imagined, based on the details of their respective ecological
networks, and their niches in them. When the distance is smaller, the researcher is likely to grasp more of the participant's point of view. When it is
larger, knowing the other becomes more difficult. To illustrate, August had
little background about Ghanaian gender relationships when she first read

Zoore's narrative. To her, Zoore appeared to view women as either commodities to be obtained in exchange for hard work, or as temptresses. However, Zoore's intense focus on potential marriage partners can be understood by knowing that in Ghana, families and children are highly valued, and that it is unusual for someone of his age to be single. Most of his peers have already completed what is seen as an essential developmental step—marriage—and Zoore would like to follow this cultural norm. Although August is quite similar to Zoore in some respects—both are single people in their late 20s who work in a profession similar to one of their parents—August's position as a member of a culture where many people in their 20s are not married created initial barriers to understanding Zoore's view of women with regard to his work life.

This way of thinking about the problem of knowing others has an advantage over dichotomous representations such as "participant–analyst" and "insider–outsider:" Degrees of communality of various particular kinds are considered (cf. Okeke, 1996). Continuing the previous illustration, although some aspects of Zoore's work life may have been easily comprehensible to August because of their commonalties, others are less comprehensible because of their dissimilarities.

In seeking to understand others, analysts need to be particularly reflective about their theoretical and methodological assumptions and their broader belief systems. The cognitive schemas that researchers carry with them are, in part, derived from their own previous research and the traditions in which they were trained. Achieving the status of researcher may have represented for many the achievement of a long sought goal that required heavy personal investment and strong commitment to a particular belief system. Even if they attempt to do so, such researchers cannot simply blot out prior interpretations of the subject matter they investigate. Observations unavoidably will be selected, at least in part, on knowledge carried from their professional learning, that for many, may have been the achievement of a major life goal (cf. Knorr-Cetina, 1981, cited by Overaa, 1996).

An illustration of this difficulty in our own research can be noted. In analyzing Maria's narrative, August initially noted Maria's perception of being discriminated against because of her ethnicity. This is not an unexpected finding; others have noted the pervasive negative attitudes toward women of color embedded in the American culture (Cox, 1993; Duckitt, 1992), and that these attitudes cause many to feel devalued, powerless, and discriminated against in the workplace (Bell, Denton, & Nkomo, 1993; Gilkes, 1990). However, on closer scrutiny, it is clear that Maria does not have only negative associations with her ethnicity. She also perceives being an African American woman as a challenge, and this attitude is a prime motivating force in her work. This more positive construal of her ethnicity could have been easily overlooked in light of the accrued knowledge August carried from earlier learning.

Ecological Distance and Disclosing. The ecological distance between analysts and participants may affect not only what the analyst can come to understand, but also what participants are willing to reveal. This seemed to be the case at one point in August's interview with Maria. In explaining why she moved from Florida to New York, Maria said it was because the new city would be "the better way of life, the salvation." She then asked, with some indignation, "Are you familiar with the migration?" as if she expected that August would not understand what she was referring to—the migration of African Americans from the south to urban areas in the north. After making this statement, Maria quickly moved to another topic. One interpretation of her abrupt shift is that Maria had judged that a major life goal she had successfully pursued could not be adequately communicated to August, given their different ethnic backgrounds and ages.

Greater ecological distance may not always result in less disclosure, however. In Ghana, some kinds of distance, particularly education and age, seemed to enhance cooperation and willingness to disclose personal information. Interviewers' reports indicate that Ghanaian workers were sometimes swayed to tell their stories by the knowledge that they were contributing to a University project. Also, in Ghana, older people seemed to feel obligated to respond to younger people who sought information from them. Regarding other dimensions, such as language, dialect, and locality, closeness, rather than distance, seemed to increase cooperation and disclosure.

Increasing Rapport With Participants. Researchers can make deliberate steps to reduce the apparent ecological distance between themselves and participants when it seems to be a barrier. Interviewers who communicate a serious interest in people's lives, and particularly in their pursuit of major life goals, are more apt to create situations where participants will want to make themselves known.

In our experience, participants tend to disclose more about themselves when they recognize a common bond with the interviewer. Interviewers can often facilitate the process by making the bond explicit. To illustrate, because August shared few obvious links with her interviewees beyond their gender—they were of different ages, occupations, and familial contexts—she made deliberate efforts to communicate commonalities. She often told therapists that her mother is a therapist; she told nurses that she lived with several nurses during college; and she told teachers that an intimate friend of hers is a teacher. These gestures provided them a link, and suggested that August might have some practical basis for understanding their experiences. Interviewers can also listen for, and call attention to, commonalities that may not be obvious initially, such as being from the same region or having the same religious faith, or sharing of long term aspirations.

When participants are interviewed at work or at home, their behavior settings may include objects such as photographs, posters, or decorative items that indicate personal interests and backgrounds that interviewers share. Indeed, in both of the projects described in this chapter, we obtained descriptions of the settings where interviews took place, including notes about availability (or lack of availability) and comfort level of furniture, level of lighting, amount of background noise, presence of others, and additional, similar factors.

Even if settings do not provide ways of further bonding with participants, they can help researchers assess how far "inside" the participant's world they were able to get. August, for instance, found that a particularly noisy air conditioner that was in operation during one interview made it difficult to establish good communication between herself and the woman she was interviewing. The noise acted as a barrier, requiring both parties to choose between speaking very loudly, or speaking at a normal volume and not being fully comprehended. Neither was conducive to getting inside the interviewee's world.

The problem with the noisy air conditioner illustrates a more general point: the need for interviewers to monitor their interviews, both within and across sessions, and to act appropriately to preserve or enhance the quality of the information they are getting, and ultimately, their potential for knowing. For instance, when August first began her interviews, she tended to use the same "technique" with each participant. She asked each woman the same questions in the same manner, and attempted to derive parallel information from each of them. Soon, however, August realized that for some women, she could get the desired information by asking very direct questions about specific events, whereas for others, she should ask open-ended, general questions, and give her interviewees time to make free associations to them. For instance, in her first interview with Maria, August asked open-ended, general questions about the course her career had taken, and Maria responded ex-

pansively. However, on reviewing the transcript prior to the second interview, August noted a need for more detailed information in several places.
Marla's responses did not always contain the information necessary to derive
a detailed work history, the intended outcome of that interview. Thus, in the
second and ensuing interviews, August asked more direct and specific questions. By changing her style, she was able to obtain the kind of information
she sought. Some of August's other participants, however, were not as comfortable with this approach, and responded better to questions asked in a less
pointed manner.

The above example illustrates a principle that researchers who undertake
qualitative research should keep solidly in mind: people differ in all kinds of
ways, including some that researchers must be aware of—and adjust to—if they
are to gain the information they seek. For example, it became obvious to August that the women she interviewed differed greatly in the degree that they
had previously reflected on their careers and what work meant to them. Part
of her task was to assess how much any respondent had thought about the
matters she wanted to know, and to adjust her interviewing style accordingly.
Wicker had the same experience when interviewing expatriates in Ghana.
Some interviewees felt they had accumulated wisdom that others should
know, and they were expansive and forceful in relating it. Others had to be
coaxed to provide similar information.

The practical implications of individual differences for knowing people
extend beyond interviewing techniques, of course. In the next section, we
briefly consider some implications of human differences for selection of research participants.

Knowing Multiple Others

Earlier in this chapter, we suggested that researchers can achieve greater understanding of person-environment relationships by juxtaposing the perspectives of participants and analysts. The idea of seeking out and then
engaging different points of view to arrive at a more complex, and more complete representation, is applicable to work stories as well.

To illustrate, in the first dozen or so interviews of Ghanaian workers, people were outspoken in their disdain for the trade associations and labor unions that represented them. They typically saw these groups as ineffectual,
and their officials as living well on their dues. (Recall Zoore's contempt for
the butcher's association; among other things, he blamed it for not being
able to get a reliable water supply at the slaughter shed.) This led Wicker to

ask one of the interviewers to obtain the story of a union official. His account indicated pleasure in the opportunity to develop leadership skills and to meet government officials, resignation at the minimal compensation he receives for his efforts, and annoyance that members do not attend union meetings or recognize the conditions in society that limit what the union can do for them.

The decision to obtain work stories from expatriates in Ghana was also based on this principle of gaining multiple viewpoints. The expatriates, like the Ghanaians, work and live in Ghana. But they are from different cultures, and thus, provide perspectives on working that are useful in comprehending the people and their environments. For example, the ways that an expatriate pediatrician and an illiterate yam trader see safety and health issues in a local market are quite different; the pediatrician's concerns are for sanitation, whereas the trader mentions heart pains from sitting for long periods and physical strain from carrying heavy loads of yams. (A more extended illustration and claim for the value of narratives from multiple points of view is found in Wicker, 1996a).

Complicating the Analyst. We have represented people as sense-makers of objects, conditions, and events in their lives. We have further suggested that people attend to, interpret, and respond to happenings in different ways, depending on their cognitive schemas or cause maps, including those representing their major life pursuits. These cognitive structures constitute the residuals of past experience, that is, people's retained wisdom (cf. Heider, 1958; Weick, 1979). We have also noted that the retained wisdom of researchers includes their current beliefs about the phenomena they study, the theories they embrace, and the methods they use. We endorsed Schultz and Hatch's (1996) strategy of researchers' bringing into interplay contrasting elements of apparently opposing perspectives as a means of increasing their comprehension of phenomena. The presumed mechanism is reorganization of the researcher's conceptual scheme such that it is more complicated, and thereby, capable of comprehending greater complexity in the phenomena he studies (cf. Weick, 1979).

Applied to the present concern of knowing others, the implication for researchers is to "be of several minds" when seeking to understand participants. In that way, they may be able to grasp subtleties and nuances that previously escaped them. They may, for example, come to appreciate that a worker can validly express inconsistent and contradictory feelings about her retirement within a single interview, as August came to realize.

In a similar vein, Fineman (1991) observed that "if I think deeply about what work 'means' to me (and you, the investigator, allow me to) I can report the following:

> 1. I have good days and bad days. Sometimes I feel I'm really making headway; other times I do not. What happened to me this morning was peculiar ... "
> 2. My emotions fluctuate. At 9:15 a.m. on Monday mornings I'm not my best. At 11 a.m. I can be happier, depending who knocks on my door ...
> 3. What happened last night at home, and what might happen tomorrow, affects my tolerance and motivation.... " (p. 167)

Fineman also suggested that one can find in contemplative expressions about work experience "some of the essential qualities of experienced meaning. We articulate a world of ephemeral images, struggles, and competing emotion ... " (p. 167)

Our point is that complicated researchers are more likely to seek or consider data that communicate such details, and they are better able to understand work in these terms. At the same time, we strongly believe that they could and should thoughtfully consider other forms of data, such as formal surveys of work attitudes, and interpret them in light of their understanding of how those responses were generated.

RECAPITULATION

In substantive theorizing there are few natural breaking points or boundaries, and a sense of completion is rarely appropriate. We do not believe that we have arrived at such a place in our explorations in person–environment psychology. There are always additional matters to consider, further qualifications to make, ideas that should have been incorporated but were not. A conclusion is not yet in order, although a brief recapitulation may be.

In this chapter, we have attempted to illustrate the viability of naturalistic inquiry as a means of theorizing about person–environment relationships. Our approach, *substantive theorizing*, presumes that close scrutiny of a limited domain of human activity can yield important insights that broader surveys might miss. Human work, as revealed in the stories of Ghanaians, expatriates in Ghana, and late-career American women, has been our substantive domain. We drew on the narratives of two workers, a young Ghanaian man whose trade is butchering, and an African American woman teacher in her late 50s, to illustrate the point of view of participants (i.e., those who most directly experience the events that are to be understood). We contrasted the participant viewpoint with that of the analyst, who stands outside the events but wishes to comprehend them.

As analysts, our characterization of persons and environments has been presented. We described persons as seekers of explanations for events that matter to them, and we described mechanisms that people engage in sense-making, both on their own and in collaboration with others. Individuals may also engage in long term pursuits that draw on current understandings, and that over time, lead to more complicated conceptual maps of their worlds. We briefly discussed seven normative social systems that our professional backgrounds and exposure to the work narratives lead us to believe are significant environments in people's working lives: work behavior settings, trade or occupational groups, employing organizations, families, informal social groups, locality, and society at large. We argued that deliberate attempts to engage the views of participants and analysts has the potential of yielding fuller understanding, than reliance on either alone.

We also briefly discussed the issue of interpersonal "knowing," particularly, how analysts may come "to know" participants. The concept of *ecological distance*, or the degree of commonality of the work and life situations of analysts and participants, may be helpful to researchers reflecting on knowing and disclosing. We conclude this section on interpersonal knowing by advocating that researchers seek out multiple, divergent viewpoints from participants, and that they also attempt to complicate their own conceptual schemes, in order to grasp subtleties in the phenomena that they study.

ACKNOWLEDGMENTS

The research described in this chapter was supported in part by a grant from the Fletcher Jones Faculty Research Fund at Claremont Graduate University, and a Fulbright grant to Allan W. Wicker, and by grants from the John Randolph Haynes and Dora Haynes Foundation, and the Datatel National Scholars Foundation, to Rachel A. August. We are indebted to the women and men who shared stories of their work with us in our respective projects. The dedicated service of Philip Awekeya, Ebenezer Mensah, and Stephen Obiri-Yeboah, interviewers for the Working in Ghana Project, is gratefully acknowledged.

We received helpful comments on an earlier draft of this manuscript from Kenneth H. Craik, Richard H. Price, Norman D. Sundberg, and Kathleen O'Brien Wicker.

REFERENCES

August, R. A. (1996). *Career retrospectives: Late career women's reflections on the experiences and meanings of work and retirement.* Unpublished doctoral dissertation, Claremont Graduate University, Claremont, CA.

Barker, R. G. (1987). Prospecting in environmental psychology. In D. Stokols & I. Altman (Eds.), *Handbook of environmental psychology* (Vol. 2, pp. 1413–1432). New York: Wiley.

Barker, R. G., & Schoggen, P. (1973) *Qualities of community life.* San Francisco: Jossey-Bass.

Bell, E. L., Denton, T. C., & Nkomo, S. (1993). Women of color in management: Toward an inclusive analysis. In E. A. Fagenson (Ed.) *Women in management* (pp. 105–130). Newbury Park, CA: Sage.

Blackwell, T., & Seabrook, J. (1996). *Talking work: An oral history.* London: Faber & Faber.

Blumer, H. (1969). *Symbolic interactionism.* Englewood Cliffs, New Jersey: Prentice-Hall.

Blunt, P. (1983). *Organizational theory and behavior: An African perspective.* New York: Longman.

Blunt, P., & Popoola, O. E. (1985). *Personnel management in Africa.* London: Longman.

Bonnes, M., & Secchiaroli, G. (1995). *Environmental psychology.* London: Sage.

Bronfenbrenner, U. (1979). *The ecology of human development.* Cambridge, MA: Harvard University Press.

Campbell, D. T. (1996). Can we overcome worldview incommensurability/relativity in trying to understand the other? In R. Jessor, A. Colby, & R. A. Shweder (Eds.), *Ethnography and human development: Context and meaning in social inquiry* (pp. 153–172). Chicago: University of Chicago Press.

Clausen, C. (1996). Welcome to postculturalism. *American Scholar, 65,* 379–88.

Cox, T., Jr. (1993). *Cultural diversity in organizations.* San Francisco: Berrett-Koehler.

Craik, K. H. (1996). Environmental psychology: A core field within psychological science. *American Psychologist, 51,* 1186–1187.

Denison, D. R. (1996). What IS the difference between organizational culture and organizational climate? A native's point of view on a decade of paradigm wars. *Academy of Management Review, 21,* 619–654.

Duckitt, J. (1992). *The social psychology of prejudice.* New York: Praeger.

Fineman, S. (1991). The meaning of working? *European Work and Organizational Psychologist, 1,* 166–173.

Freud, S. (1961). *Civilization and its discontents.* New York: Norton. (Original work published 1930)

Fuhrer, U. (1990). Bridging the ecological-psychological gap: Behavior settings as interfaces. *Environment and Behavior, 22,* 518–537.

Galinsky, E., Bond, J. T., & Friedman, D. E. (1993). *The changing workforce: Highlights of the national study* (Report No. W93-01). New York: Families and Work Institute.

Gilkes, C. T. (1990). "Liberated to work like dogs!": Labeling black women and their work. In H. Y. Grossman & N. L. Chester (Eds.), *The experience and meaning of work in women's lives,* (pp. 165–188). Hillsdale, NJ: Lawrence Erlbaum Associates.

Groenhaug, R. (1978). Scale as a variable in analysis. In F. Barth (Ed.), *Scale and social organization,* (pp. 78–121). Oslo: Universitetsforlaget.

Hacker, W. (1985). On some fundamentals of action regulation. In G. P. Ginsburg, M. Brenner, & M. von Cranach (Eds.), *Discovery strategies in the psychology of action* (pp. 63–84). London: Academic.

Heider, F. (1958) *The psychology of interpersonal relations.* New York: Wiley.

Kohls, L. R. (1984). *The values Americans live by.* Unpublished manuscript.

Lasson, K. (1971). *The workers: Portraits of nine American jobholders.* New York: Grossman.

Lewin, K. (1951). *Field theory in social science.* New York: Harper.

Moghaddam, F. M. (1996). Training for developing-world psychologists: Can it be better than the psychology? In S. C. Carr & J. F. Schumaker (Eds.), *Psychology and the developing world* (pp. 49–59). Westport, CT: Praeger.

Neff, W. S. (1985). *Work and human behavior* (3rd ed.). New York: Aldine de Gruyter.

Nukunya, G. K. (1992). *Tradition and change in Ghana: An introduction to sociology.* Accra: Ghana Universities Press.

Obeng-Fosu, P. (1991). *Industrial relations in Ghana.* Accra: Ghana Universities Press.

Okeke, P. E. (1996). Postmodern feminism and knowledge production: The African context. *Africa Today, 43,* 223–234.

Overaa, R. (1995). *Interpretation of other life worlds: An essay on the construction of gendered world versions.* (Geography in Bergen, Series A, No. 215) Bergen, Norway: Department of Geography, Norwegian School of Economics, University of Bergen.

Oyeneye, O. Y., & Peil, M. (1993). *Consensus, conflict, and change in African societies: A sociological introduction.* Birmingham: Centre of West African Studies, Birmingham University.

Ransome, P. (1996). *The work paradigm.* Aldershot, England: Avebury.

Rappaport, J. (1995). Empowerment meets narrative: Listening to stories and creating settings. *American Journal of Community Psychology, 23,* 795–807.

Rosen, M. (1985). Breakfast at Spiro's: Dramaturgy and dominance. *Journal of Management, 11,* 31–48.

Rosenwald, G. C., & Ochberg, R. I. (1992). Introduction: Life stories, cultural politics, and self-understanding. In G. C. Rosenwald & R. L. Ochberg (Eds.), *Storied lives: The cultural politics of self-understanding* (pp. 1–18). New Haven, CT: Yale University Press.

Rousseau, D. M. (1995). *Psychological contracts in organizations: Understanding written and unwritten agreements.* Thousand Oaks, CA: Sage.

Sampson, E. E. (1993). Identity politics: Challenges to psychology's understanding. *American Psychologist, 48,* 1219–1230.

Schoggen, P. (1989). *Behavior settings: A revision and extension of Roger G. Barker's Ecological Psychology.* Stanford, CA: Stanford University Press.

Schroedel, J. R. (1985). *Alone in a crowd: Women in the trades tell their stories.* Philadelphia: Temple University Press.

Schultz, M. (1991). Transitions between symbolic domains in organizations. *Organization Studies, 12,* 489–506.

Schultz, M., & Hatch, M. J. (1996). Living with multiple paradigms: The case of paradigm interplay in organizational culture studies. *Academy of Management Review, 21,* 529–557.

Seppala, P. (1996, November). *Entrepreneurship and diversification: The decline of professionalism in Tanzania.* Paper presented at the meeting of the African Studies Association, San Francisco.

Shakespear, P., Atkinson, D., & French, S. (Eds). (1993). *Reflecting on research practice.* Buckingham, England: Open University Press.

Slife, B. D., & Williams, R. N. (1995). *What's behind the research? Discovering hidden assumptions in the behavioral sciences.* Thousand Oaks, CA: Sage.

Terkel, S. (1974). *Working: People talk about what they do all day and how they feel about what they do.* New York: Pantheon.

Trice, H. M. (1993). *Occupational subcultures in the workplace.* Ithaca, NY: ILR Press.

Weick, K. E. (1979). *The social psychology of organizing* (2nd ed.). Reading, MA: Addison-Wesley.

Weick, K. E. (1989). Theory construction as disciplined imagination. *Academy of Management Review, 14,* 516–531.

Wicker, A. W. (1996a). *Work narratives: A potentially useful tool for evaluators and planners.* [Unpublished manuscript.].

Wicker, A. W. (1996b). *The "Working in Ghana" Project*. [On-line]. Available: http://www.cgsweb.cgs.edu/~wickera/working.html.

Wicker, A. W. (1992). Making sense of environments. In W. B. Walsh, K. H. Craik, & R. H. Price (Eds.), *Person environment psychology: Models and perspectives* (pp. 157–192). Hillsdale, NJ: Lawrence Erlbaum Associates.

Wicker, A. W. (1989). Substantive theorizing. *American Journal of Community Psychology, 17,* 531–547.

Wicker, A. W. (1987). Behavior settings reconsidered: Temporal stages, resources, internal dynamics, context. In D. Stokols & I. Altman (Eds.), *Handbook of Environmental Psychology* (Vol. 2, pp. 613–653). New York: Wiley.

Wicker, A. W. (1985). Getting out of our conceptual ruts: Strategies for expanding conceptual frameworks. *American Psychologist, 40,* pp. 1094–1103.

Wicker, A. W. (1984). *An introduction to ecological psychology*. New York: Cambridge University Press.

Wicker, A. W., & Burley, K. A. (1991). Close coupling in family-work relationships: Making and implementing decisions in a new family business and at home. *Human Relations, 44,* 77–92.

Xinxin, Z., & Ye, S. (1987). *Chinese lives: An oral history of contemporary China*. New York: Pantheon.

8

The Lived Day of an Individual: A Person–Environment Perspective

Kenneth H. Craik
University of California at Berkeley

LIFE AS QUOTIDIAN:
THE LIVED DAY AS A UNIT OF STUDY

Murray (1938), identified the life history as the "long unit" in the study of persons in transaction with their various environments. Indeed, the life history remains an ultimate challenge for providing a comprehensive, integrative account of an individual's existence (Runyan, 1982). However, the obvious paucity of detailed observational records for an entire life course remains a daunting, and perhaps inevitable, limitation of life historical analysis. In this sense, life history analysis remains closer to history than to observational science (Craik, 1996; Lowenthal, 1985, 1996). Certainly, a complete naturalistic field recording of an individual's lifelong environmental transactions is far beyond our current scientific capabilities.

The other extreme in the study of person–environment relations is embodied in the temptation to capitulate to these limitations and settle for too narrow a window of observation, one that severely attenuates the living, ongoing, temporal sequence of person–environment transactions. Records of conduct such as: 'the person made a set of thorough lecture notes,' or 'the person gave a forceful presentation during the group discussion' may fuel important scientific inquiry, but may be too brief and encapsulated to afford

233

full understanding of the texture of an individual's life, while the tracking of a work career, for example, may be too abstracted from the everyday ongoing context of person's life.

The recognition that informs lived day analysis is that lives are lived day by day, one day at a time, from day to day, day after day, day in and day out. Lives as we experience them are inherently quotidian (Craik, 1993).

As Barker and Wright persuasively argued in their pioneering *One Boy's Day* (1951), the lived day constitutes a natural diurnal segmentation of life. The lived day captures a broad temporal frame within which a person's experience and conduct develop. The lived day incorporates transitions from setting to setting. And the lived day is inclusive and encompassing, providing a reminder to us of the unselected, unanticipated, ordinary features of daily existence. These humdrum details of a person's day may be just what is overlooked by current theoretical orientations and research. Thus, the lived day of an individual can be advanced as a moderately long and fitting unit of observation for contextual field studies of person–environment transactions. The purpose of this chapter is to explore this possibility and articulate a set of key questions generated by the structure of this analytic problem.

LIVED DAY ANALYSIS
AND PERSON–ENVIRONMENT PSYCHOLOGY

This chapter advances two major contributions that lived day analysis can make to the development of person–environment psychology. First, it argues that lived day analysis offers a heuristically productive context for exploring the descriptive tasks accomplished by behavior-setting, goal, and trait concepts in depicting situated everyday conduct. Acknowledging that these conceptual systems are distinctive is only a first step toward theoretical clarification (Pervin, 1994). Beyond that recognition, we must evolve a better understanding of what conceptual jobs each of these approaches performs and interrelates in describing the events in a person's lived day. We will find that these approaches are not mutually exclusive tools for depicting everyday person–environment transactions: One is not forced to choose between, for example, being a goal-oriented theorist and a trait theorist. Furthermore, lived day analysis highlights the close contextual interplay among these conceptual systems. Thus, we must not only attend to the theoretical structure and options specific to each conceptual arena (e.g., behavior-setting theory, motivational-goal theory, dispositional-trait theory) but also aspire to the higher order of comparative conceptual analysis required by person–environment theory.

Second, lived day analysis contributes to the intellectual project of articulating a person–environment psychology by providing a basis for mapping its conceptual frontiers. The focal point of our field may remain the contextual description and understanding of situated person–environment transactions and the ways they are sequenced and nested in the course of persons' lived days. However, we discover that careful consideration of lived days opens up new, and less well explored, territories of inquiry. Two major questions deal with how information generated by the events of an individual's lived day circulates throughout the person's community, and by what means and to what extent that information is retained over time. Another central question is how we can monitor the spreading impacts and consequences of those events of a person's lived day throughout the community and over time.

Analysis of Lived Days

Lived day analysis seeks to describe and understand the lived days of individuals in the context of their occurrence. The descriptive task is to secure a comprehensive record that is more or less continuous and unselective. Thus, the endeavor can be sharply contrasted with daily time sampling approaches. Important advances in such experience sampling are being made, through the use of beeper devices and other techniques, in the study of targeted phenomena, such as self-reported activities, emotional states, and stressful events (Tennen, Suls, & Affleck, 1991). In order to convey the distinctively inclusive characteristics of lived day depiction, the cases of Raymond Birch, Leopold Bloom, and Lorna Dodge are presented.

To begin to explore the analytic agenda in the study of the lived days of individuals, we address four basic questions. First, what happened? That is, how do we depict where and when the events of the day took place, and what options do we possess in characterizing the nature of those events? Second, who knew about the events of the individual's day? That is, how do we monitor the ways that news about everyday events is, or is not, circulated throughout the person's social network? Third, what impact did the events of the day have on the various components of that person's ecological niche? That is, how do we conduct a socio-environmental impact analysis of a person's lived day? And finally, how long does representation of the individual's lived day persist? That is, what are the decay processes in autobiographical memory, collective recollection, and even documentary records, with regard to any given lived day of any individual?

Three Approaches to Depicting the Lived Days of Individuals

Before sketching issues in the analytic agenda of lived day inquiry, the characteristics of this unit of study must be examined. The following three cases illustrate some of the descriptive facets and methodological options entailed in depicting the lived days of individuals.

The Lived Day of Raymond Birch

In *One Boy's Day*, Barker and Wright (1951) present the complete text of one of the person-centered behavior specimen records prepared at their Midwest Psychological Field Station in Oskaloosa, KA. The endeavor exemplified their research program, aimed at escaping from the confines and constraints of the psychological laboratory and studying persons in the ordinary contextual influences of their everyday lives.

On April 26, 1949, a relay team of eight observers, working in a sequence of 30 minute periods, set out to depict 7-year-old Raymond Birch's lived day. They recorded, in writing, Raymond's directly observable behavior and their own on-the-spot impressions and inferences concerning Raymond's perceptions, motives, and feelings. "The observers wished to recreate for others the behaviors of Raymond and the situation which confronted him as they experienced them" (Barker & Wright, 1951, p. 8).

Following each 30-minute period of observation, the researchers then dictated their observations for an audiotape record. Another researcher at this dictation session would then interrogate the observer regarding any unclear or thin aspects of the report. Based on these behavior reports, the full text for Raymond Birch's lived day, from 7:30 a.m. until 8:32 p.m., required 422 pages of the 1951 volume documenting this classic field study.

The Lived Day of Leopold Bloom

Any consideration of the lived days of individuals must note June 16, 1904. In *Ulysses*, recognized as a masterpiece of 20th-century literature, James Joyce (1922) evoked the lived day of 38-year-old Leopold Bloom, from approximately 8 a.m. that morning until 2 a.m. the next morning. June 16 is now celebrated each year in Dublin as Bloomsday by Joyce scholars and aficionados, as well as by the Irish tourist board.

The modernist novel, exemplified by *Ulysses*, represented a shift from a single-ascendant, authorial point of view, to the accommodation of multiple points of view (Levitt, 1972; Thomas, 1978-79). Thus, we are offered accounts of some events of Bloom's day and his conduct, as seen by young friend Stephen Dedalus, his wife Molly, and other Dubliners found at the Ormond Hotel's dining room and bar, at the office of the *Evening Telegraph* newspaper, at Barney Kiernan's pub, and at other behavior settings encountered in the course of Bloom's specific wanderings throughout that city on that day (Hart & Knuth, 1975). Later, we return to examine the impact on Bloom's reputation in Dublin of a series of events throughout the day involving Leopold Bloom, Bantam Lyons, Mr. Lenehan, and the fates of 'Sceptre' and 'Throwaway' in the Ascot Gold Cup horse race. Through Joyce's innovations in narrative technique, we are permitted to enter Bloom's lived day through his own consciousness, not only the experience of his environmental transactions, but the ongoing associations, fantasies, daydreams, autobiographical memories, and so forth evoked by them. With these multiple perspectives, Joyce's portrait of Bloom's lived day differs, importantly, from Barker and Wright's depiction of Raymond Birch's lived day, which is made from the single vantage point of a detached, but interested, observer.

The Lived Day of Lorna Dodge

My own interest in studying the lived days of individuals is excited by the increasing availability of miniature, portable, hand-held battery pack videorecorders and wireless microphones. With use of video research techniques, a comprehensive audiovisual record can be made of a person's lived day from early morning until late evening.

Video recordings of the lived days of individuals have the advantage of tracking everyday conduct through the person's typical range of behavior settings. The videorecording presents an advance over the behavior specimen records of the Midwest Psychological Field Station in providing permanent preanalytic documentation. Unlike the case of *One Boy's Day*, subsequent analyses of video records are not limited to, or dependent on, a single verbal depiction of the lived day's episodes. Instead, an immediate visual, as well as auditory, record affords access to the 'look' of the person's transactions with other individuals in the sequence of settings encountered in the course of the day. Thus, the events of a lived day can be subsequently described and analyzed from multiple perspectives generated by a variety of observers and conceptual orientations.

Obviously, following a person around with a videorecorder all day has its inherent constraints as a field study method, particularly with regard to its reactivity. In our explorations with the technique, we encouraged the person whose day is being videorecorded to interact spontaneously with the videoresearch team members, rather than pretending the team members are somehow not on the scene. Thus, the videorecording project and staff become components of the lived day itself, along with its more usual ingredients. It remains existentially inescapable that the person must somehow live through the day, structure the day's activities and tasks, and deal with the other persons and settings encountered along the way. The person can be followed and recorded from setting to setting, indoor and outdoor, in public as well as private places, under conditions of more or less continuous monitoring. Of course, participants can go 'off camera' at any time they choose. The video camcorder, with millions sold each year, has become an often seen, if not ubiquitous, feature of public and private settings in contemporary society.

Although much remains to be explored regarding use of the technique, it is clear that a remarkably comprehensive video record of the lived day of an individual is now socially and technologically feasible. As Ginsburg (1985) opined, the video camcorder may become as important a tool for the analysis of everyday human action "as the microscope proved to be for the biological laboratory sciences" (pp. 262-263).

Comparative Analysis of Lived Day Depictions

Figure 8.1 compares the depictions of the lived days of our three individuals. In each case, the name is fictional. Raymond Birch is a pseudonym for the lad whose lived day April 26, 1949 is preserved in *One Boy's Day*, whereas Bloom, we remind ourselves, is a fictional character whose lived day of June 16, 1904 in Dublin is portrayed in Joyce's *Ulysses*. Lorna Dodge is a pseudonym for a young manager in a large electronics firm whose lived day on December 4, 1990 constituted our second video research study. In all three cases, the depiction of the day is, more or less, continuous, although not entirely so. The lived days of Birch and Bloom are portrayed in verbal written accounts, whereas the video record of Dodge's lived day retains the visual and auditory context where any number of different verbal accounts might be generated.

Two major points of view can guide the depiction of an individual's lived day—the *outside* vantage point of those who can observe the individual's conduct and the *inside* vantage point of the focal individual (see Hogan & Roberts, this volume). Bloom and Birch's lived days are similar in the type of record generated—a more or less continuous verbal account, but they differ

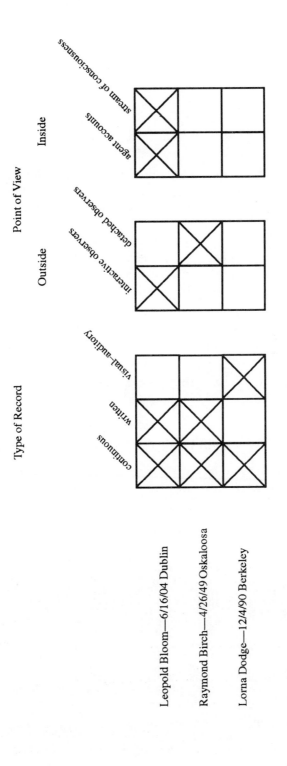

Figure 8.1 Modes of depicting the lived day of an individual.

239

dramatically in two ways. First, the two depictions differ in the status of observers providing the outsider accounts of the person's conduct. In the case of Bloom's observers, they are spontaneously engaged interactants and onlookers going about the business of their own day that intersects only occasionally with that of Bloom. Although the Midwest Psychological Field Station observers are also *in situ*, and occasionally interact with Raymond, they are explicitly research-oriented, engaged in the professional task of recording Raymond's conduct and circumstances during April 26. Second, through his literary techniques, Joyce offered us access to Bloom's ongoing consciousness as he moved through June 16. In the account of Bloom and Dedalus' visit to Bella's whorehouse, for example, several pages presenting Bloom's associations, fantasies, and musings occur between one sentence uttered by Bella and her next sentence. Nothing of this kind of inside point of view is found in Barker and Wright's account of *One Boy's Day*.

The video record of Lorna Dodge's lived day on December 4 is presented from the perspective of the detached eye of the videorecorder. Supplementary retrospective accounts can be gathered immediately from interactants and from the focal individual, but that person's stream of consciousness will remain elusive.

THE LIVED DAY:
SOMETHING HAPPENED—WHERE, WHEN, AND WHAT?

A thorough video recording of an individual's lived day yields a miniature historical archive. *Something has happened.* What has happened has now indeed occurred, and it is there to be portrayed, reconstructed and analyzed in some fashion. However, environmental psychologists, along with journalists, wish to know *where* and *when* as well as *what*. Lenntorp (1978, p. 164) offers a graphic device for depicting a minimal person–environment perspective on a lived day (Fig. 8.2). Lenntorp's attention to the geotemporal locus of human action traces the sequence of places (dwelling-to-workplace-to-bank-to-workplace-to-post office-to-dwelling) as well as time and duration. The question of what happened at these various times and places is more complicated.

Conceptual Systems for Categorizing
the Episodes of a Lived Day

A major heuristic value of the analysis of an individual's lived day is that it establishes a context for comparing alternative conceptual systems for catego-

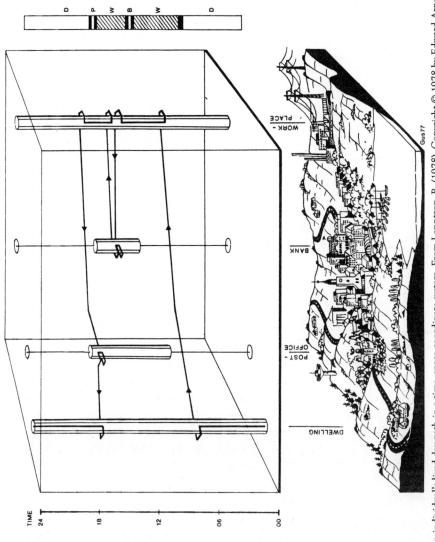

FIG. 8.2 An individual's lived day path in a time–space coordinate system. From Lenntrop, B. (1978). Copyright © 1978 by Edward Arnold, London. Reprinted with permission.

rizing *what* happened during the day. Of course, we have endless ways of coding or categorizing human actions (Collett, 1980). A set of actions can be classified as *obligatory activities* (e.g., work tasks, home chores) or *leisure activities* (e.g., watching television, travels) (Robinson, Andreyenkov, & Patruskev, 1988). At a more microanalytic level, a set of behaviors can be classified as the components of a greeting—the sighting of another, the head toss, the approach, the head dip, the close salutation, and so forth (Kendon, 1985).

For our purposes, three major conceptual systems, currently prominent in environmental and personality psychology, warrant attention, namely, behavior setting concepts, goal-oriented concepts, and trait concepts. We are sometimes asked to choose among these conceptual systems. But are they mutually exclusive? Must we declare ourselves as ecological psychologists versus goal-analytic psychologists versus trait psychologists (Pervin, 1994)? Or do these conceptual systems simply perform different jobs for us in the categorization of everyday transactions with the environment? How much do they overlap or diverge? We use video records of the lived days of individuals to begin to sort out these issues systematically. In doing so, we expect to learn a good deal about what happened in the course of a person's day, and also about the comparative attributes of these conceptual systems.

Episodes Categorized Within
Behavior Setting Concepts

Taking a person–environment perspective on an individual's lived day decisively moves us out of the research laboratory, interview room, and even assessment center, and into the sequence of behavior settings encountered by Raymond Birch, Leopold Bloom and Lorna Dodge. Table 8.1 illustrates a few of the behavior settings through which each of them moved during the course of their lived days. In this sense, the Lenntorp diagram can be delineated in more contextual detail by substituting specific behavior settings for his more institutional place units. Raymond Birch's behavior settings were all located in a few blocks of his dwelling, Bloom's behavior settings spanned most of Dublin, whereas Dodge's behavior settings were dispersed across at least three cities in the San Francisco area.

Behavior settings are identified by their standing pattern of behavior, in conjunction with their geotemporal locus and physical milieu (Barker, 1968; Schoggen, 1989; Wicker, 1987; this volume). Thus, one way to depict systematically the episodes of an individual's lived day is to categorize those act–episodes that count as the person's participation in the collective, and more or

TABLE 8.1
Selected Lived Day Behavior Settings

Leopold Bloom	Raymod Birch	Lorna Dodge
Home: breakfast	Home: breakfast	Home: breakfast
Turkish and Warm Bath	Courthouse lawn	Car commute
Glasnevin Cemetery	School: halls and cloakroom	Firm: workstation
Evening Telegraph office	School: art period	Firm: staff meeting
Ormond Hotel dining room and bar	School: arithmetic seatwork	Car commute
Barney Kiernan's pub	School: playground	Espresso cafe
Maternity Hospital	School: oral reports	MBA student lounge
Sandymount strand	School: story period	University library
Bella's brothel	Vacant lot	Shop
Cabman's shelter	Neighbor's yard	Home: supper
Home: 7 Eccles Street	Home: supper time	Home: children's bedtime

less coordinated, actions that constitute the programs of various specific behavior settings.

Behavior setting concepts are useful because they tell us one compelling and essential part of the story of each person–environment transaction. That is, they situate it in its pertinent geographical-temporal setting, and the resources associated with the setting's specific purposive program.

Episodes Categorized Within Goal-Oriented Concepts

A second major approach to categorizing the act–episodes of a lived day is in terms of the person's goals, projects, pursuits, serials, strivings, and tasks (Cantor & Zirkel, 1990; Emmons, 1986; Little, 1983, this volume; Murray, 1938; Pervin, 1989; Wicker, 1992). That is, a person's daily conduct can be seen as organized by a set of strivings whose goals are typically pursued in the form of temporally extended life tasks and personal projects.

Wicker (1992) has reported a case study of a major life pursuit of a person, namely, Abby's efforts to start a small retail business. Wicker illustrates how

TABLE 8.2
Behavior Settings Relevant to Abby's Café Project

Real Estate Developer's Office

Bank

Architectural Firm

Contractor's Office

Construction and Equipment Suppliers

Electric Utility Office

Board of Health

Leased Space as Construction Site

Leased Space as Cafe—Open for Business

Adapted from Wicker, 1992.

its multitude of subgoals and subtasks take her, over many days and even months, to a wide variety of behavior settings (Table 8.2).

On a given day, Abby might move from her future cafe (an interior renovation site), to the Board of Health to check on her permit, then to the electric utility office to see about delays in connecting the service to her shop, and so on. Of course, Abby's personal goals for a given lived day would encompass more than simply moving ahead her coffee shop project, and all of these tasks must be scheduled and interwoven.

In addition to this sequential property, personal goals are typically organized in a hierarchical structure that links specific actions to various tasks and projects, and to each other (Little, 1983; Rommetveit, 1980). Furthermore, extended projects, such as a courtship, can be analyzed from the standpoint of culture and the environment (Altman, Brown, Staples, & Werner, 1992). Thus, specific personal projects must be located in a more general cultural context. For example, Abby's project of starting a small business would likely take quite different form in contemporary Moscow than it did in southern California. In summary, the specific act–episodes of an individual's lived day can be categorized into hierarchical structures of goals, tasks, and projects.

Goal concepts are useful because they locate a person–environment transaction in the purposive schema of its various participants, linking it to plot lines of temporally dispersed past and intended transactions.

Episodes Categorized
Within Trait Concepts

The third significant system for categorizing the events of an individual's lived day is offered by ordinary language trait concepts. Indeed, my initial impetus for videorecording lived days of persons derived from a longstanding interest in following up *One Boy's Day* with a trait-oriented analysis of 'One Introverted Boy's Day' or 'One Dominant Girl's Day' (Craik, 1976, 1990). Although we typically assess traits by self-report personality scales or self and peer ratings, the proof has seemed to me to lie in identifying the situated, observable, everyday conduct that serves as the basis for trait judgments and assessments.

Categorizing act–episodes in trait concepts may be surprising to some colleagues, may even seem a bit odd. Traits refer to persons, do they not? Yes, trait concepts are usually considered with reference to attributes of individuals, but they can also be used to characterize specific human actions (Buss & Craik, 1983a; Wiggins, 1997). Buss and I have delineated a two-step process, where trait concepts are first applied in categorizing specific act–episodes, and then applied in assessing persons according to their dispositional act trends. In doing so, we have adopted the British philosopher Stuart Hampshire's (1953) formulation of traits, or personal dispositions, as summarizing statements (Craik, 1997; Hampshire, 1953). In asserting that Mary is dominant, for example, we are claiming that over a period of observation "the term dominant is the right word to summarize the general trend of Mary's conduct" (Hampshire, 1953). Thus far, we have been primarily examining the notion that trait concepts can be analyzed usefully as categories of situated acts and unpacking the meaning of specific trait constructs by identifying the kind of everyday act–episodes deemed to be prototypical or exemplary of a given trait construct (Buss & Craik, 1983a, 1984a, 1984b, 1985, 1987, 1989; Shopshire & Craik, 1996).

With video records of the continuous flow of a person's day-long conduct, we can begin to identify when and how specific traits are being manifested. Shopshire and I have begun to examine the complexities of categorizing the episodes of an individual's lived day on the basis of trait concepts (Craik, 1994; Shopshire, 1990; Shopshire & Craik, 1996).

To cite one example, in the midst of videorecording the lived day of undergraduate Linda Martinez, we realized it would be useful to audiotape, at least, a lecture by one of her professors who had declined to welcome our videocamera into his classroom. Linda immediately offered to help: she found her audiorecorder in her dorm room, and on the way to this class she stopped to purchase a tape for recording the lecture, and at the end of the class she handed us the completed audiorecord. Her videorecorded conduct will likely be judged by a research panel of viewers as prototypical for trait constructs such as cooperative and initiating.

Trait concepts are useful because they group specific person–environment transactions into descriptive categories that are widely employed in everyday life to interpret and anticipate the act trends of other individuals and their social implications for the community.

Note that trait categorizations can be made for all of the act-episodes of a videorecorded lived day, including actions taken by others. For example, one person's lived day may be characterized by many dominant acts by others, whereas another individual might be surrounded throughout the day by agreeable acts by others. In this way, a trait analysis of a focal individual's day-long interpersonal environment can be rendered, as well as the trait analysis of the video research participant's own trends in conduct (Buss, 1985).

Viewed alone, behavior setting, goal-oriented, and trait concepts cannot tell the whole story about a set of person–environment transactions. However, in combination, they each contribute distinctively toward a fuller account. In addition, we will find that each conceptual system poses its own particular array of methodological issues. In summary, a program of research will be necessary to clarify the many procedural issues in categorizing the episodes occurring in the lived day of an individual in our three conceptual systems.

Procedural Issues
in Episode Categorization

Analyzing ongoing, spontaneous, situated human action entails a host of general procedural issues (Bakeman & Ginsburg, 1981; Barker, 1963; Collett, 1980; Cranach, Machler, & Steiner, 1985; Ginsburg, 1985) as well as those specific to each conceptual system. One advantage of videorecordings is that research panel members can individually view and review the videorecords, identifying and classifying episodes according to a given conceptual system, and providing judgments whose composite reliabilities can be statistically gauged (Gosling, John, Craik, & Robins, 1997; Ware & Craik, 1997). In addition, certain distinctive procedural issues are generated by each conceptual system.

Behavior Setting Concepts

With regard to behavior setting concepts, we must determine which act–episodes are properly categorized in the concurrent setting's standing pattern of behavior, and those that are to be recognized as incidental to the behavior setting's program. As Wicker (1992) noted, not all conduct is necessarily part of an identifying behavior setting program. For example, as Linda Martinez walked along Shattuck Avenue in downtown Berkeley during her video-recorded lived day, she was suddenly, directly, and persistently challenged by a well-dressed elderly woman: "What does it mean in English - plot? P-L-O-T?" "It means a story—a story line ... " Linda initially responded. As it turned out, this meaning was not the one being sought—instead, something more conspiratorial appeared to be of concern. Is Linda's engagement in this slightly bizarre exchange to be classified as a component of the program of a specific behavior setting that can be identified with this particular urban intersection? For example, is this spot a regular gathering place for this woman or other troubled individuals? We would have to study this site over time to make a determination, following the K-21 guidelines provided by ecological psychology (Barker, 1968).

Goal-oriented Concepts

In regard to goal-oriented concepts, the research panel must identify what the individual is trying to do, in terms of goals and intentions, and assign act–episodes to categories of tasks, projects, pursuits, and so on.

The hierarchical structure of goal-oriented concepts must also be deployed. For example, when Lorna Dodge was conducting a staff meeting, nested with that task, she was engaged in the subtask of establishing plans for the unit's Christmas party. In this way, videorecordings of lived days of individuals offer a new context for systematic comparison among such purposive concepts as strivings, personal projects, and goals—an endeavor that has just gotten underway with the use of self-report methods (Kaiser & Ozer, 1994; Ware & Mendelsohn, 1996).

Trait Concepts

An array of procedural alternatives must be evaluated in the trait categorization of act–episodes. Is it recommended to instruct members of a research panel to nominate and identify instances of the manifestation of any trait concept, as they view the video record of an individual's lived day, or should they be assigned to observe one particular trait at a time, such as dominance, and instructed to search for any prototypic instance of it in the video record. Or perhaps, it is better to segment the video record into more or less discrete episodes, and instruct the research panel to sort these relatively decontextualized episodes, into a fixed array of trait categories, such as those of the Five Factor Model (FFM) of personality structure (i.e., extraversion, agreeableness, conscientiousness, emotional stability, openmindedness) (John, 1990). Comparative analyses of these options is required.

Supplementing the Lived
Day Video Record

Gathering supplementary documentation of the lived day videorecord con-stitutes yet another major undertaking. Several supplementary approaches appear to be feasible and valuable.

First, the focal individual can be invited to view the video record and pro-vide several forms of 'insider' retrospective accounts of the ongoing act–epi-sodes (Nielsen, 1963; Robins & John, 1997). At one level, the individual can make action identifications (e.g., "What were you doing at this point?" Vallacher & Wegner, 1985) and recall as much as possible of concurrent in-tentions and action-related cognitions (Cranach et al., 1985). The person can also be asked to categorize each act-episode of the day in hierarchies of per-sonal projects, goals, and strivings (e.g., "Which of your personal projects are involved in what you were doing at this point?" (Emmons, 1986; Little, 1983, this volume; Vallacher & Wegner, 1985), as well as into trait categories. In a subsequent viewing of the video record, the individual might attempt to re-call emotional states, impressions of interactants and settings, and any associ-ations, memories, or reveries that were experienced concurrent with each act-episode. Finally, from an idiographic vantage point, individuals can be asked to make their own assignments of the episodes from the lived day videorecording to trait categories (Buss & Craik, 1983a; Krahe 1992).

Second, interactants and onlookers can be mobilized to supply compara-ble insider accounts of their own actions and reactions to the conduct of the focal individual. The lived day's full cast of characters is typically indeterminant until the day's activities unfold. One research team member with a second camcorder might be assigned to lag behind and videorecord brief interviews with casual interactants and onlookers, and persons with more substantial roles might be interviewed subsequently in a fashion simi-lar to that proposed for the focal individual. It is noteworthy that these possibilities are almost endless, but pragmatic constraints can be acknowledged by seeking information primarily related to the three conceptual systems we compare.

Every method of psychological investigation suffers from its particular forms of systematic bias. To the extent that the focal individual is enlisted in post-video commentaries and interpretations, the influence of social desirability bias must be examined—just as it must with regard to the conduct that has been videorecorded. Similarly, to the extend that acquaintances and onlookers from the focal individual's community and lived day happenings are recruited to provide commentaries, their possible bias toward bolstering or denigrating other actors in the lived day's events must be considered. As with other methods of study, such as standard assessment situations and self-report personality scales and inventories, systematic research can provide the means for gauging biases of these kinds.

Why go to these ambitious efforts to supplement what is already contained in the video record of the individual's lived day? Why not be content with categorizations made by research panels viewing the rich documentation of the day's events? After all, research panels viewing the videorecord are capable of making judgments concerning action identifications, can isolate tasks undertaken during the day, and can estimate what the standing pattern of behavior of the various settings are likely to be.

At least two major reasons can be given for seeking supplementary accounts from the focal individual, and from key interactants and onlookers, in reconstructing the person's lived day. First, analysts of situated human action have increasingly recognized that pluralistic points of view may generate multiple descriptions of the same act–episode that in turn may lead to different categorizations in our three conceptual systems (Borkenau, 1986; Buss & Craik, 1984b, 1989; Feinberg, 1965; Rommetveit, 1980; Vallacher & Wegner, 1985). That is, a specific action is an event identified 'under a description' (Anscombe, 1979). We must examine how invariant, for example, trait categorizations of act–episodes are across descriptions (a) made from the point of view of detached observers, (b) derived from in situ interactants and onlookers, and (c) informed by retrospective insider accounts provided from the point of view of the agent of the action.

Barker and his associates (Barker & Wright, 1955; Barker, Schoggen, & Barker, 1955) classified episodes in the day-long behavior specimen records of Raymond Birch and other children of the Midwest into a number of trait-like 'action modes,' such as dominance, aggression, and nurturance. However, trait categorization based only on the detached point of view of outside observers can be seen as problematic; we are now expected to address the issue of multiple vantage points, as well as the relative prototypicality of act-episodes for specific trait constructs (Buss & Craik, 1983a; Gosling et al., 1997).

The second rationale for supplementary points of view, concerns their value in testing and sustaining alternative interpretations and categorizations in the comparative analysis of conceptual systems.

Comparative Analyses of Episode Categorizations

An important function of video records of the lived days of individuals lies in providing an arena for examining, systematically, how certain conceptual approaches to human action interrelate.

You will recall that Linda Martinez offered to audiotape a lecture she was scheduled to attend during her videorecorded lived day. On the way from the lecture hall she stopped to purchase an audio tape. The only clerk in the shop had become intensely engaged in a telephone conversation. Despite the unannounced arrival of the video research team as well as Linda, the clerk continued his telephone chat while completing the entire purchase script with Linda, through taking of cash payment, tending the receipt, offering a paper bag, etc., with barely a word to his customer, but with just a hint of an acknowledging smile at the end of the exchange.

First, this act-episode is classified as part of the program of the behavior setting of a small retail shop, albeit with a telephonic twist. Second, from the direct evidence of the video record, the event can be categorized as one component of Linda's goal-oriented task of recording the lecture, and that task might be categorized as part of her personal project of participating in our video research explorations. Finally, Linda's nonchalant quickness in picking up cues to the clerk's nonverbal invitation to an almost entirely pantomimed transaction, may lead a research panel of observers to place this act-episode in the trait category of social sensitivity.

Note that this instance of social sensitivity is carried out in a goal-oriented task (purchasing a tape) located in a hierarchically broader goal-oriented task (recording the lecture) that can be categorized in the trait concept of helpfulness. Furthermore, this instance of social sensitivity is occasioned by a slight departure of the shop clerk from the standing pattern of behavior of that setting.

Lorna Dodge's visit to a new coffee shop conveys a more complex variation on the same theme while highlighting the important information value of seemingly incidental episodes. After visiting the university library as part of her MBA personal project, Lorna stopped to purchase coffee beans on the way to picking up her children and preparing supper. She parked her car in a row of angled parking spaces across from the coffee shop. As the group moved toward the crosswalk, Lorna noticed that the driver's door of another car had been left wide open and expressed concern that it was perhaps at risk of being stolen. After hesitating and commenting that she often wonders what to do about such matters, she closed the car door. A member of the videorecording team then mentioned he would like a cup of coffee, and Lorna, who had earlier stopped for a cafe latte at an espresso shop, offered to get him her free cup of coffee that came with the purchase of coffee beans. At the same time, she spotted the new shop across the street and headed toward it. On entering, she explored, commented on the new coffee shop, gossiped, and reminisced with the clerk about what became of the previous shop (a revered ice cream parlor) and its owners, completed her purchase, talked to a little boy, and left.

Although Lorna performed the basic, standing pattern of behavior for this setting (i.e., select purchase, place order, make payment, secure free cup of coffee), her visit became multigoaled, and manifested several personality traits. Indeed, my undergraduate students, in a personality assessment course, readily nominated exemplars of each of the domains of the Five-Factor model of personality trait structure (Digman, 1990; John & Robins, 1993). Selected examples included: for Extraversion: (a) elicited from, and shared with the clerk, childhood memories of the ice cream parlor, (b) talked with a little boy; for Agreeableness: (a) offered her free cup of coffee to another, (b) expressed positive, approving affect about the new shop's decor; for Conscientiousness: (a) closed the car door, (b) followed through to get the free cup of coffee, plus a cover for the cup; for Neuroticism (vs. Emotional Stability): (a) uttered a high-strung "there! there! there!" in locating the new shop across the street, (b) expressed dismay at 'loss' of the ice cream parlor; and, for Openness: (a) browsed curiously along all the display shelves, (b) commented on the interior design of the shop. The breadth of trait concepts pertinent to the events of a single episode in Lorna's day is emphasized by their relevance across the Five-Factor personality domain.

The overall usefulness of our three alternative conceptual systems becomes apparent, even for unanticipated events, like the encounter with the open car door. What emerges as particularly important is the need for systematic analysis of the mutual relevance and the distinctive conceptual jobs performed by these significant categorization systems.

Joint Categorizations and Testing
Hypotheses about Conceptual Systems

Joint categorizations in three conceptual systems offer a means of examining hypotheses about how the conceptual systems themselves differ. It can be argued, for example that goal-oriented concepts primarily serve a function for the agents of action. Goal-oriented concepts, such as tasks and projects, facilitate the organization of an individual's conduct and provide cognitive steering, and control of actions (Cranach et al., 1985; Little, 1983; Pervin, 1989). It can also be argued that, in contrast, trait concepts primarily serve functions for observers of the actions of others. To say in a summarizing fashion that a person, over a period of observation, has shown a general trend of conscientiousness in their conduct, can be viewed as carrying important information to the individual's community. A person with a reputation for conscientiousness, for example, might be assigned the responsibility of night sentry for a village, or as an accountant for a firm, because he or she is considered, based on this evidence, as having shown a suitability for achieving collective purposes of that kind (Borkenau, 1990; Buss, 1991; Buss & Craik, 1985, 1986; Craik, 1996, 1997; Hogan, 1982; Hogan & Roberts, chap. 1, this volume).

These assertions imply that the most important information about an action from the standpoint of goal-oriented concepts is information about what the person is trying to do, and how that goal fits into a hierarchical structure of tasks, projects, and so on. In contrast, the most important information about an action, from the trait standpoint, has to do with the results of actions and what consequences they hold for the agent, other persons, and the community at large. Indeed, trait concepts would function poorly as observer tools if they required full, valid knowledge of the entire array of ongoing personal intentions and goals of the agent of the actions. In everyday life that kind of information may be much less immediately evident to observers than is information about the likely results of actions. For example, the act: 'taking charge after the accident' is generally seen as prototypically dominant (Buss & Craik, 1984a) and entails some discernible impact on the event (e.g., aid is mobilized for the injured; proper record taking is completed, etc.). Other individuals on the scene might also have had the personal goal of taking charge of the situation but those efforts were unnoticed and ineffectual, with the upshot being that the actions may likely be described in other ways, and categorized according to trait concepts other than dominant.

Thus far, we have dealt with three major approaches to describing what may have happened during the course of an individual's lived day. Yet a broadly contextual person-environment perspective requires us to address additional questions that move us toward the frontiers of such analysis. First, who knows what occurred during the person's lived day? Second, what per-˙ son-environment impacts might a particular lived day have had? Third, in what ways, if at all, might specific lived days of individuals be subsequently recollected in their community?

WHAT'S NEW? WHO KNOWS?

A central challenge for a person-environment perspective is to locate an individual's lived day in a community that constantly notes and communicates social information. We must examine who took notice of what events. Did anyone else notice? How did others on the scene interpret those events they did attend to? What did they recollect and pass on to third parties? At the end of the day, what kind of portrait of our individual's lived day might be reconstructed, simply and only by subsequently gathering accounts from the cast of characters encountered through the course of that day?

Take, for example, Leopold Bloom as he walked along Westland Row in Dublin about midmorning on June 16 and encountered Bantam Lyons, who asked to borrow his newspaper to check on the horse races. Bloom actually gives his newspaper to Lyons, saying he was just going to "throw it away," in any case. Lyons misinterprets this phrase as a betting tip: the horse Throwaway is running later that day in the Ascot Gold Cup. Shortly after 5 p.m., Bloom is conversing with a group at Barney Kiernan's pub. During the chat, Lenehan brings the news that the 20 to 1 Throwaway has won the Gold Cup race. This means nothing to Bloom, who has no interest in betting, but means a lot to some of the others present, who had put their money on the favorite Sceptre. Bloom goes off on an errand to the nearby courthouse. In his absence, Lenehan, apparently having heard from Bantam Lyons, spreads the mistaken idea about Bloom's supposed betting tip. The group discussion continues in some outrage that Bloom has furtively gone off to collect his winnings, too mean-spirited to stand them a round of drinks in celebration before doing so (Blamires, 1988; Joyce, 1922).

Here is an event whose misinterpretation circulates socially around Bloom, without his awareness, but with some detriment to his reputation. This vivid instance may represent an extreme case in some respects, but it does highlight questions about what social information is generated by an individual's lived day, how that information is dispersed and circulates among various interactants and onlookers, how it is communicated further in the individual's community, and how it contributes to that person's reputation.

The amount of social information generated by a particular lived day of a person is, in part, a function of the degree and pattern of attention that interactants and onlookers bestow on that individual's presence and conduct. Indeed, on a moment to moment basis, how informative is an individual's conduct to others? The phenomenon of the FASTFORWARD impulse is pertinent to this issue (Craik, 1993). Despite the considerable effort that must be devoted to gathering video records of the lived days of individuals, as our research team initially viewed them, we paradoxically found ourselves tempted to many points to press the fast forward button on our television monitor. Thus, at this impressionistic, precategorization stage, many stretches of a person's lived day (e.g., Linda Martinez walking from her dorm to a classroom) seemed quite uninformative in relation to others. Is it the case that, rather than being characterized by a steady, even flow of information, a person's lived day is punctuated by especially revealing, or consequential episodes? By focusing our own research programs only on these critical, but rather rare, happenings in daily life, are psychologists inadvertently engaged in a conspiracy to make persons and their social life appear more interesting and intriguing than they really are (Craik, 1993)? Perhaps our scientific tendency to neglect the ordinary, humdrum aspects of daily life reflects some limitations in the conceptual systems we have formulated thus far for categorizing everyday person–environment transactions. Detailed categorization of the act–episodes in the video records of actual lived days of individuals will clarify these issues.

We anticipate that of the wealth of potential information generated by an individual's lived day, only a selective amount becomes effective social information, heeded and considered by others in the person's everyday community. Furthermore, given the diverse vantage points and limited viewing periods of various interactants and onlookers, this social information is also dispersed in an uneven, only partially overlapping fashion. Indeed, it is unlikely that this fragmented, scattered information generated by the lived day of a person is ever integrated in any comprehensive way. Yet, in its partial and dispersed form, some of this social information will circulate through gossip, chat, and more formal channels in the person's social network, and may become the basis for significant extensions or revisions of the individual's reputation in society at large (Bromley, 1993; Craik, 1985; 1996; Emler, 1990). Understanding this entire process is an important goal in achieving a person–environment perspective on an individual's lived day.

IMPACT ANALYSIS: WHAT A DIFFERENCE A DAY MAKES

When we move from questions of what happened and who noticed to the issue of what impact the events in a person's lived day have made, we must broaden our conceptual framework, from categorization systems for video-recorded act–episodes, to dynamic systems formulations to trace the impacts of episodes on persons and their varied and interrelated environments (Pervin, 1992; Wicker, 1993, chap. 7, this volume).

For example, in Wicker's (1992) case study of the establishment of a small retail business, Abby's Cafe, he reported:

> In one instance, Abby spoke with a man at the electric utility office about a delay in connecting electric service at her construction site. He attributed the delay to slowness of the "little gals" in another office. Although she was quite busy, Abby took the time to point out to the man the sexist nature of his remark and to suggest a more appropriate way of referring to the women." (p. 180)

With regard to episode categorization, making and responding to inquiries can be seen as a component of the standing pattern of behavior for this setting. For Abby, the episode constitutes one of many tasks in her personal project of starting her retail business. Challenging the sexist remark might also be categorized as (a) an effort to change a feature of the behavior setting, (b) a task in Abby's personal striving for the goal of a nonsexist society, and (c) a prototypically assertive act. A video record of the episode would likely provide a viewing panel with the basis for additional trait categorizations, such as persuasive, indignant, or friendly.

In regard to impact analysis, a continuing delay in connecting electric service might immediately require rescheduling of an array of other project-related tasks, such as installation of kitchen equipment, and so forth. Beyond the direct impact on the restructuring of this personal project, the delay might be seen to affect Abby's perception of the project with regard to its difficulty, effort required, and probability of success. Emmons (1986), Little (in press) and others have shown that the way personal strivings are perceived along these dimensions is related to the subjective well-being of the individual.

In parallel fashion, it is possible that unbeknown to Abby, her complaint about the delay in service may have placed an institutional record keeping Complaint Index over the threshold for the reassignment of additional staff resources to that function. Thus, this act–episode might yield organizational impact as well as impact on this specific behavior setting. Finally, Abby's chal-

lenge to the sexist remark at the utility office might directly have a successfully persuasive impact on this staff member's subsequent conduct and,
depending on his influence in the setting, an indirect impact on the general
social climate of that utility office.

The interaction between Abby and the utility office highlights a number
of difficult issues in conducting a lived day impact assessment. First, although the immediate results of human actions are typically apparent in the
observational context, the longer term consequences are not, and require
subsequent detective work. The video record provides a basis for assessing
some results of Abby's actions—for example, her inquiry about the delay was
effectively conveyed to the staff member—but whether the organization later
reassigned staff resources to this particular function, of course, is not immediately evident. We would not learn from the episode itself how the delay will
restructure Abby's own personal project, alter her perceptions of it, or affect
her sense of well-being. A person–environment impact assessment is necessarily an open-ended, incomplete story; at the end of any lived day, its longer
term consequences remain indeterminant until they unfold, and can be
tracked and gauged.

Second, interactants in encounters of this kind are themselves often unlikely to gain knowledge of later consequences of the episode. The staff members will probably not learn about how the delay affected Abby's project, nor
is Abby ever likely to discover the possible impacts of her actions on the behavior setting and organization. In this sense, the feedback process with regard to person–environment impacts may be quite loosely structured in
everyday life. At the same time, we must recognize that each day brings some
news of the consequences of prior actions. In her conduct as a manager at her
workplace, Lorna Dodge ensured that she was provided with ample information of this type, through her constant rounds of telephone calls, email, and
staff meetings.

Third, for researchers to track the person–environment impacts of a single
lived day of a person is a formidable undertaking. For Abby, we must gauge
the extent that each and every act-episode of her lived day facilitated or hin-
dered any of her various personal projects and strivings, factor in resultant
changes in her perceptions of the projects, monitor her affective responses,
mobilize a dynamic systems formulation of how all of these variables interact,
and so forth. To conduct a parallel impact assessment of all of the settings of
Abby's lived day would require a major effort. We must initially identify the
various relevant levels and kinds of environmental systems (e.g., behavior settings, work organizations, families, public institutions) in order then to ana-

lyze the functioning state of each system of her ecological niche and to gauge the impact on each of them of the day's act-episodes involving Abby.

To say that a person-environment impact assessment of a lived day of an individual is exceedingly difficult is not to say that such case studies are impossible, or unworthy of our research efforts. On the contrary, the undertaking would certainly be enlightening. However, it raises an important question about the scope of person-environment psychology (Walsh et al., 1992). Our mission is certainly to study the immediate person-environment transactions of the sort captured in a videorecord. But are we also committed to tracking impacts through personality systems and socio-environmental systems as well (Craik, 1972; Hogan & Roberts, chap. 1 this volume; Mayer, 1995; McCrae & Costa, 1995; Mischel & Shoda, 1995; Wicker, chap. 7 this volume)? The answer, of course, is yes: We must explore such frontiers of person-environment analysis, however vast they may now seem to be.

THE END OF A DAY: ON A TREADMILL TO OBLIVION?

Fred Allen, the great radio comedian, entitled a volume of his memoirs *Treadmill to Oblivion* (1954). In commenting on what he considered the ephemeral nature of his art, Allen lamented:

> When a radio comedian's program is finally finished, it slinks down memory lane into the limbo of yesterday's happy hours. All that the comedian has to shown for his years of work and aggravation is the echo of forgotten laughter. (p. 240)

An historical geographer, Hugh Prince (1978), voicing a similar view, noted that his own scholarly efforts: "to record and interpret the past may delay but cannot prevent the past receding into oblivion" (pp. 36-37).

We have already seen that a person lives in an environment of social information as well as one of behavior settings and boulevards. Of the total amount of potential information generated by an individual's lived day, just a relatively small proportion seems to be socially noted, and that meager information is dispersed among members of the individual's community and is unlikely to be reintegrated. When day is done, what is the likely fate of such information that has managed to capture the attention of others and exists socially? How rapidly and in what patterns will the information of a day's events recede into oblivion? Weeks or years hence, what information, if any, about that particular lived day might still be recollected, and under what circumstances?

To address these issues, we must first consider the sense of history of the various lived day participants (Lowenthal, 1985; 1996). Has the focal individual or any of the interactants or onlookers maintained records of the day's events, for example, in the form of letters, email, diaries, and journals?

Second, the nature of autobiographical memory is relevant. To what extent is autobiographical memory organized by calendar dates, types of episodes, tasks and projects, or by day-long narrative reconstructions? As a start, we might supplement our video records by requesting the focal individual and key interactants provide subsequent accounts of the entire lived day at different later points in time (Rubin, 1986).

As biographers, life history analysts, and historians point out (Carr, 1986; McAdams, 1988; Mink, 1978; Runyan, 1988; Sarbin, 1986), the narrative form is an especially useful cognitive instrument to depict sequences of episodes and events. Study of the ways that individuals organize narrative reconstructions of a lived day may provide an important bridge; between accounts of the textures of daily life and the trajectories of life stories. Systematic comparisons should be made of narrative constructions taken at different time intervals from a videorecorded, lived day. In particular, how are relatively routine, nondirectional, repetitive, and quasi-repetitive actions handled by these narrative accounts (Gould, 1995; Newtson, 1994)? Do these quotidian episodes tend to fall by the wayside of recall? What kind of plot structures are employed for retrospective lived day accounts, and how might they differ from those used in life stories (Gergen & Gergen, 1983; McAdams, 1993)?

Third, we can examine how information generated by an individual's lived day recurs in the context of collective remembering. In what social occasions and settings, under what circumstances, and for what purposes might some remnant of that particular lived day be subsequently recalled by others (Connerton, 1989; Middleton & Edwards, 1990)? Tracking the entire future appearances of an individual's lived day in society may not be feasible. However, we can take beginning steps in this kind of inquiry. For example, as we compile archives of the video records of lived days, we search for episodes that entail recollections drawn from persons' previous lived days.

APPRAISAL OF THE LIVED DAY AS A UNIT OF ANALYSIS

In light of this examination of the structure of research issues generated by the analysis of the lived days of individuals, the viability of the lived day as a unit of analysis must now be reviewed and critiqued.

From a scientific standpoint, taking the lived day of an individual as a unit of analysis can be seen to have heuristic value, in challenging us to encompass in our study of person–environment relations all of a person's situated daily experience and conduct, the humdrum as well as the momentous. In addition to being conceptually apt, from a person–environment perspective, analysis of lived days has become increasingly more feasible from am methodological standpoint. Video research techniques, supplemented by more traditional methods of self report and interview, can now yield valuable quasi-historical records for the comparative analysis of alternative conceptual systems for categorizing everyday episodes of person–environment transactions. They also provide a starting point, and a basis, for tracking the information generated by an individual's lived day throughout the person's community and over time, and for assessing person–environment impacts of a lived day's events.

At the same time, the evidence is neither ample nor strong at the moment that either an individual or an individual's community attends to the lived day as a spontaneous unit of intention, observation, or recollection. First, we must determine the extent that the temporal unit of the day is a structuring element for organizing personal goals and strivings. Second, we must examine the degree that the lived day as such may serve as an organizing focus of recollection for the individual. Does it extend beyond a narrative response to the dinnertime query: "How was your day?" Are a few end of day reveries, and perhaps a diary entry, a typical extent of lived day retrospection? Third, with regard to an individual's community of observers, vantage points on a person's lived day are typically dispersed among different interactants and onlookers, who grant varying, fluctuating amounts of attention to episodes featuring any given person's conduct (Barker & Wright, 1955; Barker, Schoggen, & Barker, 1955; Craik, 1985). Through chats and gossip, some of this dispersed information may be integrated into story lines (Bergmann, 1993). However, a concerted effort to pull together an account of an individual's entire lived day may indeed be an infrequent occurrence, outside of police investigations of missing persons, murders, and so forth (e.g., Stephen, 1988).

Detailed empirical research examining the ways that the lived day may or may not be an artificial unit of analysis, will be scientifically productive. Furthermore, the unit of the lived day remains sufficiently meaningful that the request to provide a narrative account of a prior lived day constitutes a sensible task to most persons, as, we have found, does our request to videorecord an entire lived day.

How do we go about employing our systems to categorize lived day episodes, narrative structures, dynamic systems formulations, and other conceptual tools, for organizing and portraying the diverse forms of information generated by a single lived day of an individual? How do we deploy the ingredients of our person-environment perspective to move beyond Barker and Wright's preanalytic *One Boy's Day?* How do we establish criteria for gauging our progress in this type of undertaking (Runyan, 1988). The case history offered a valuable synthesizing and stocktaking exercise in many realms of inquiry (Barker et al., 1955; Bromley, 1986; Murray, 1938). Similarly, for person-environment psychology, the recording, reconstruction, and interpretation of a lived day of an individual holds similar heuristic advantages.

In this endeavor, we need not be so foolhardy as to enter into all-out competition with James Joyce. Nonetheless, consideration of *Ulysses* highlights certain issues and lessons in organizing information generated by the lived day of an individual. The use of multiple points of view is an obvious analytic as well as narrative tool. *Ulysses* reminds us that we should seek to depict the inside point of view as well as diverse outside points of view. *Ulysses* locates the person in a network of physical, cultural, and social environments that encompasses the recollection and transmission of information via chat, gossip and other reputational vehicles. *Ulysses* illustrates that individuals are embedded in a web of layered environments about which they gain only partial information, and that are loosely structured with regard to person-environment impacts and feedback. And *Ulysses* strongly demonstrates that the narrative form is a cognitive instrument that can powerfully complement our conceptual systems for the categorization of lived day episodes and events. And of course, we are no longer restricted to the written narrative: video and cinematic techniques for editing and scripting visual-auditory records can also be deployed for these purposes.

But what about context? Through various literary devices, Joyce introduced an enormous amount of information about the personal past of the characters of Bloom and his associates. Through Bloom's extraordinarily rich imagination, the cultural history of Dublin is also evoked. So much contextual material is presentthat the Joyce scholar Kenner (1972) was willing to speculate about episodes that took place on June 16, but were not directly depicted in *Ulysses*, such as the 4 p.m. assignation between Bloom's wife Molly and Blazes Boylan. Kenner stood ready to be proven wrong about who moved the furniture in the Blooms' flat that day "if enough evidence can be marshalled" against his reading (Thomas, 1978-79, p. 87). Costello (1981) has been more foolishly emboldened to extrapolate a full-scale biography of

Bloom, extending beyond June 16, 1904 to his death on Sunday January 31, 1937 (run down by a Ford motor car in Clanbrassil Street).

On the basis of our more humble video records of an individual's lived day, should we entertain kindred aspirations—to depict an urban culture in a lived day? Or discern a life history in a lived day? "To see a world in a grain of sand ... And eternity in an hour" (Blake, 1989)? Probably not. We must begin with the information derived from the video record itself and augmented by strategic, conceptually guided supplementary accounts. The point, after all, is not that the novelist has outdone us at what we are seeking to do, or that we should forsake our commitment to systematic analysis and understanding for the artistic freedom of imaginative literature.

Rather, what can be advocated is that we turn our attention to detailed analysis of the lived days of individuals, deploying our conceptual systems for categorizing the events of the day, examining the incidence and nature of what happens in the everyday lives of persons in their ordinary environments, and in doing so, refine our concepts and increase our grasp of how the days and lives of persons can be depicted and understood.

Finally, in gathering video records of the lived days of individuals, we must deal with certain reactive effects on the researchers themselves. Specifically, it would be useful to identify an worthy ego ideal for such lived day analysts. Are we merely Orwell's (1949) Big Brother, snooping on our fellow citizens? Are we government agents conducting security surveillances (U. S. Senate, 1985)? Are we voyeurs? Does any more favorable and inspiring cultural role model exist for us? A attractive nominee might be apparent already: that is, the reader of *Ulysses*. In our type of research, we must aspire to capture and depict the lived days of individuals with the same density of detail, comprehensiveness, and humanistic generosity of spirit that we, as the reader, are granted access by James Joyce to the lived day of Leopold Bloom's June 16, 1904.

ACKNOWLEDGMENTS

I wish to note the sustained encouragement and insights I have gained from Michael Shopshire concerning lived day analysis, and the benefits of conversations with Peter Borkenau, David M. Buss, Samuel D. Gosling, Brian R. Little, David Lowenthal, Daniel J. Ozer, Kurt Pawlik, Richard W. Robins, and Aaron P. Ware on matters discussed in this chapter. I also salute the members of our pioneering video research team: Sigal Barsade, Douglas Creed, Corinne Kosmitzki, Brent Roberts, Michael Shopshire, and Michal Strahilevitz. We are indebted to the two participants referenced briefly in this chapter; by their pseudonyms of Lorna Dodge and Linda Martinez. Finally, support is gratefully acknowledged from the Committee on Research, and the Institute of Personality and Social Research, at the University of California at Berkeley.

Sections of this chapter were derived from an invited address to the Division of Population and Environmental Psychology at the annual meeting of the American Psychological Association in San Francisco, August 16, 1991.

REFERENCES

Allen, F. (1954). *Treadmill to oblivion.* Boston: Little, Brown.

Altman, I., Brown, B. B., Staples, B., & Werner, C. (1992). A transactional approach to close relationships: Courtship, weddings, and placemaking. In W. B. Walsh, K. H. Craik, & R. Price (Eds.), *Person–environment psychology* (pp. 193–242). Hillsdale, NJ: Lawrence Erlbaum Associates.

Anscombe, G. E. M. (1979). "Under a description." *Nous, 13,* 219–233.

Bakeman, R., & Ginsburg, G. P. (1981). *The use of video in the analysis of human action.* Unpublished report, Department of Psychology, University of Nevada, Reno.

Barker, R. G. (1963). *The stream of behavior.* New York: Appleton Century Crofts.

Barker, R. G. (1968). *Ecological psychology: Concepts and methods for studying the environment of human behavior.* Stanford, CA: Stanford University Press.

Barker, R. G., Schoggen, M., & Barker, L. S. (1955). Hemerography of Mary Ennis. In A. Burton (Eds.), *Case histories in clinical and abnormal psychology, Volume II. Clinical studies of personality* (pp. 768–808). New York: Harper & Row.

Barker, R. G., & Wright, H. F. (1951). *One boy's day: A specimen record of behavior.* New York: Harper & Row.

Barker, R. G., & Wright, H. F. (1955). *Midwest and its children.* Evanston, IL: Row & Peterson.

Bergmann, J. R. (1993). *Discreet indiscretions: The social organization of gossip.* New York: Aldine de Gruyter.

Blake, W. (1989). Auguries of innocence. In H. W. Stevenson (Ed.), *Blake, the complete poems.* (2nd ed.). London: Longman.

Blamires, H. (1988). *The new Bloomsday book: A guide through Ulysses, 2nd ed.* London: Routledge.

Borkenau, P. (1986). Toward an understanding of trait interrelationships: Acts as instances for several traits. *Journal of Personality and Social Psychology, 51,* 371–381.

Borkenau, P. (1990). Traits as ideal-based and goal-derived social categories. *Journal of Personality and Social Psychology, 58,* 381–396.

Borkenau, P., & Ostendorf, F. (1985). Retrospective estimates of act frequencies: How accurately do they reflect reality? *Journal of Personality and Social Psychology, 52,* 626–638.

Bromley, D. P. (1986). *The case study method in psychology and related disciplines.* Chichester: Wiley.

Bromley, D. P. (1993). *Reputation, image and impression management.* Chichester: Wiley.

Buss, D. M. (1985). The act frequency approach to the interpersonal environment. *Perspectives in Personality, 1,* 173–200.

Buss, D. M. (1991). Evolutionary personality psychology. *Annual Review of Psychology, 42,* 459–492.

Buss, D. M., & Craik, K. H. (1983a). The act frequency approach to personality. *Psychological Review, 90,* 105–125.

Buss, D. M., & Craik, K. H. (1983b). The dispositional analysis of everyday conduct. *Journal of Personality, 51*, 393–412.

Buss, D. M., & Craik, K. H. (1984a). Acts, dispositions and personality. In B. A. Maher, & W. B. Maher (Eds.), *Progress in experimental personality research: Normal processes, Volume 11* (pp. 241– 301). New York: Academic Press.

Buss, D. M., & Craik, K. H. (1984b). *The act: Notes.* Berkeley, CA: Institute of Personality and Social Research, University of California.

Buss, D. M., & Craik, K. H. (1985). Why not measure that trait? Alternative criteria for identifying important dispositions. *Journal of Personality and Social Psychology, 48*, 934–946.

Buss, D. M., & Craik, K. H. (1986). The act frequency approach and the construction of personality. In A. Angleitner, A. Furnham, & G. Van Heck (Eds.), *Personality psychology in Europe, Volume II* (pp. 143–156). Berwyn, PA: Swets North America.

Buss, D. M., & Craik, K. H. (1987). Acts, dispositions and clinical assessment: The psychopathology of everyday conduct. *Clinical Psychology Review, 6*, 141–156.

Buss, D. M., & Craik, K. H. (1989). On the cross-cultural examination of acts and dispositions. *European Journal of Personality, 3*, 19–30.

Cantor, N., & Zirkel, S. (1990). Personality, cognition and purposive behavior. In L. A. Pervin (Ed.), *Handbook of Personality: Theory and Research* (pp. 135–164). New York: Guilford.

Carr, D. (1986). Narratives and the real world: An argument for continuity. *History and Theory, 25*, 117–131.

Connerton, P (1989). *How societies remember.* New York: Cambridge University Press.

Collett, P. (1980). Segmenting the behavior stream. In M. Brenner (Ed.), *The structure of action.* (pp. 150–167). New York: St. Martin's Press.

Costello, P. (1981). *Leopold Bloom: A biography.* Dublin: Gill and Macmillan.

Craik, K. H. (1972). An ecological perspective on environmental decision-making. *Human Ecology, 1*, 69–80.

Craik, K. H. (1976). The personality research paradigm in environmental psychology. In S. Wapner, S. Cohen, & B. Kaplan (Eds.), *Experiencing environments* (pp. 55–80). New York: Plenum.

Craik, K. H. (1985). Multiple perceived personalities: A neglected consistency issue. In E. E. Roskam (Ed.), *Measurement and personality assessment* (pp. 333–338). New York: Elsevier Science.

Craik, K. H. (1990). Environmental and personality psychology: Two collective narratives and four individual story lines. In I. Altman & K. Christensen (Eds.), *Environment and behavior studies: Emergence of intellectual traditions* (pp. 141–168). New York: Plenum.

Craik, K. H. (1993). Accentuated, revealed, and quotidian personalities. *Psychological Inquiry, 4*, 278–280.

Craik, K. H. (1994). Manifestations of individual differences in personality in everyday environments. In D. Bartussek & M. Amelang, (Eds.), *Fortschritte der Differentiellen Psychologie und Psychologischen Diagnostik: Festschrift zum 60, Geburtstag von Kurt Pawlik* (pp. 19–25). Gottingen, Germany: Hogrefe.

Craik, K. H. (1996). The objectivity of persons and their lives: A noble dream for personality psychology? *Psychological Inquiry, 7*, 326–330.

Craik, K. H. (1997). Circumnavigating the personality as a whole: The challenges of integrative methodological pluralism. *Journal of Personality, 65*, 1087–1111.

Cranach, M. von, Machler, E., & Steiner, V. (1985). The organization of goal-directed action: A research report. In G. P. Ginsburg, M. Brenner, & M. von Cranach (Eds.), *Discovery strategies in the psychology of action* (pp. 19–61). New York: Academic Press.

Digman, J. M. (1990). Personality structure: The emergence of the five-factor model. *Annual Review of Psychology, 41*, 417–440.

Emler, N. (1990). A social psychology of reputation. In W. Stroebe, & M. Hewstone (Eds.), *European review of social psychology, Volume I* (pp. 171-193). New York: Wiley.

Emmons, R. A. (1986). Personal strivings: An approach to personality and subjective well-being. *Journal of Personality and Social Psychology, 51*, 1058-1068.

Feinberg, J. (1965). Action and responsibility. In M. Black (Ed.), *Philosophy in America*. London: George Allen & Unwin.

Gergen, K. J., & Gergen, M. M. (1983). Narratives of the self. In T. R. Sarbin, & K. E. Scheibe (Eds.), *Studies in social identity* (pp. 254-273). New York: Praeger.

Ginsburg, G. P. (1985). The analysis of human action: Current status and future potential. In G. P. Ginsburg, M. Brenner, & M. von Cranach (Eds.), *Discovery strategies in the psychology of action* (pp. 255-279). New York: Academic Press.

Gosling, S. D., John, O. P., Craik, K. H., & Robins, R. W. (1997). Do people know how they behave? Self-reported act frequencies compared with on-line codings by observers. *Journal of Personality and Social Psychology, 74*, 1337-1349.

Gould, S. J. (1995). Cordella's dilemma. In S. J. Gould. *Dinosaur in a haystack: Reflections in natural history* (pp. 123-132). New York: Harmony Books.

Hampshire, S. (1953). Dispositions. *Analysis, 14*, 5-11.

Hart, C., & Knuth, L. (1975). *A topological guide to James Joyce's Ulysses*. Colchester: A Wake Newsletter Press, Department of Literature, University of Essex.

Hogan, R. (1982). A socioanalytic theory of personality. *Nebraska Symposium on Motivation, 30*, 55-89.

John, O. J. (1990). The "Big Five" factor taxonomy: Dimensions of personality in the natural language and in questionnaires. In L. A. Pervin (Ed.), *Handbook of personality: Theory and research* (pp. 66-100). New York: Guilford.

John, O. J., & Robins, R. W. (1993). Gordon Allport: Father and critic of the five-factor model. In K. H. Craik, R. Hogan, & R. N. Wolfe (Eds.), *Fifty years of personality psychology* (pp. 215-236). New York: Plenum.

Joyce, J. (1961/1922). *Ulysses*. New York: Random House (Original work, Paris: Shakespeare and Company).

Kaiser, R. T., & Ozer, D. J. (1994). Personal goals and the Five-Factor model of personality. Presented at the annual meetings of the American Psychological Association, Los Angeles.

Kendon, A. (1985). Behavioural foundations for the process of frame attunement in face-to-face interaction In G. P. Ginsburg, M. Brenner, & M. von Cranach (Eds.), *Discovery strategies in the psychology of action* (pp. 229-253). New York: Academic Press.

Kenner, H. (1972). Molly's masterstroke. *James Joyce Quarterly, 10*, 19-28.

Krahe, B. (1992). *Personality and social psychology: Towards a synthesis*. London: Sage.

Lenntrop, B. (1978). A time-geographic simulation model of individual activity programmes. In T. Carlstein, D. Parkes, & N. Thrift (Eds.), *Human activity and time geography* (pp. 162-180). London: Edward Arnold.

Levitt, M. P. (1972). A hero for our time: Leopold Bloom and the myth of Ulysses. *James Joyce Quarterly, 10*, 132-146.

Little, B. R. (1983). Personal projects: A rationale and method for investigations. *Environment and Behavior, 14*, 273-309.

Little, B. R. (1987). Personality and the environment. In D. Stokols & I. Altman (Eds.), *Handbook of environmental psychology, Volume I* (pp. 206-244). New York: Wiley.

Little, B. R. (in press). Personal project pursuit: Dimensions and dynamics of personal meaning. In P. T. P. Wong & P. S. Fry (Eds.) *Handbook of personal meaning: Theory, research and applications*. Mahwah, NJ: Lawrence Erlbaum Associates.

Lowenthal, D. (1985). *The past is a foreign country*. Cambridge, England: Cambridge University Press.

Lowenthal, D. (1996). *Possessed by the past: The heritage crusade and the spoils of history.* New York: Free Press.

Mayer, J. D. (1995). A system-topics framework and the structural arrangement of systems in and around personality. *Journal of Personality, 63,* 459-493.

McAdams, D. P. (1993). *The stories we live by: Personal myths and the making of the self.* New York: Morrow.

McCrae, R. R., & Costa, P. T. (1995). Trait explanation in personality psychology. *European Journal of Personality, 9,* 231-252.

Middleton, D., & Edwards, D. (Eds.). (1990). *Collective remembering.* Newbury Park, CA: Sage.

Mink, L. O. (1978). Narrative form as a cognitive instrument. In R. H. Canary & J. Kozicki, (Eds.), *The writing of history: Literary forms and historical understanding* (pp. 129-150). Madison: University of Wisconsin Press.

Mischel, W., & Shoda, Y (1995). A cognitive-affective system theory of personality: Reconceptualizing situations, dispositions, dynamics, and invariance in personality structure. *Psychological Review, 102,* 246-268.

Murray, H. A. (1938). *Explorations in personality.* New York: Oxford University Press.

Newtson, D. (1994). The perception and coupling of behavior waves. In R. R. Vallacher & A. Novak (Eds.), *Dynamical systems in social psychology* (pp. 139-167). New York: Academic Press.

Nielsen, G. S. (1963). The method of self-confrontation. In R. W. White (Ed.), *The study of lives: Essays on personality in honor of Henry A. Murray* (pp. 123-141). New York: Atherton Press.

Orwell, G. (1949). *Nineteen eighty-four, a novel.* London: Secker & Warburg.

Ozer, D. J., & Buss, D. M. (1991). Two views of behavior: Agreement and disagreement among marital partners. In D. J. Ozer, J. M. Healy, Jr., & A. J. Stewart (Eds.), *Perspectives in personality* (Volume III, pp. 91-106). London: J. Kingsley, Ltd.

Pervin, L. A. (Ed.). (1989). *Goal concepts in personality and social psychology.* Hillsdale, NJ: Lawrence Erlbaum Associates.

Pervin, L. A. (1993). Pattern and organization: Current trends and prospects for the future. In Craik, K. H., Hogan, R., & Wolfe, R. N. (Eds.), *Fifty years of personality psychology* (pp. 69-84). New York: Plenum.

Pervin, L. A. (1994). A critical analysis of current trait theory. *Psychological Inquiry, 5.* 103-113.

Prince, H. (1989). Time and historical geography. In T. Carlstein, D. Parkes, & N. Thrift (Eds.), *Making sense of time* (pp. 17-37). New York: Wiley.

Robins, R. W., & John, O. P. (1997). Self-perception, visual perspective and narcissism: Is seeing believing? *Psychological Science, 8,* 37-42.

Robinson, J. P., Andreyenkov, V. G., & Patruskev, V. D. (1988). *The rhythm of everyday life: How Soviet and American citizens use time.* Boulder, CO: Westview Press.

Rommetveit, R. (1980). On "meanings" of acts and what is meant and made known by what is said in a pluralistic social world. In M. Brenner (Ed.), *The structure of action* (pp. 108-149). New York: St. Martin's Press.

Rubin, D. C. (Ed.). (1986). *Autobiographical memory.* Cambridge, England: Cambridge University Press.

Runyan, W. M. (1982). *Life histories and psychobiography; Explorations in theory and method.* New York: Oxford University Press.

Runyan, W. M. (1988). Progress in psychobiography. *Journal of Personality, 56,* 285-326.

Sarbin, T. R. (Ed.). (1986). *Narrative psychology: The storied nature of human conduct.* New York: Praeger.

Schoggen, P. (1989). *Behavior settings: A revision of Roger G. Barker's Ecological Psychology*. Stanford, CA: Stanford University Press.

Shopshire, M. (1990). *Some old and new act notes: Problems and issues from a study of hypothetical conduct*. Berkeley, CA: Unpublished report, Institute of Personality and Social Research, University of California.

Shopshire, M. S., & Craik, K. H. (1996). An act-based conceptual analysis of obsessive-compulsive, paranoid, and histrionic personality disorders. *Journal of Personality Disorders, 10*, 203-218.

Stephen, A. (1988). *The Suzy Lamplugh story*. London: Faber & Faber.

Tennen, H., and Suls, J., & Affleck, G. (1991). Personality and daily experience: The promise and the challenge. *Journal of Personality, 59*, 313-337.

Thomas, B. (1978-1979). Not a reading of, but the act of reading *Ulysses. James Joyce Quarterly, 16*, 81-93.

U. S. Senate (1988). *Federal government security clearance programs*. Washington, DC: U.S. Government Printing Office.

Vallacher, R. R., & Wegner, D. M. (1985). *A theory of action identification*. Hillsdale, NJ: Lawrence Erlbaum Associates.

Walsh, W. B., Craik, K. H., & Price, R. H. (Eds.). (1992). *Person–environment psychology: Models and perspectives*. Hillsdale, NJ: Lawrence Erlbaum Associates.

Ware, A. P., & Craik, K. H. (1997). Judgments of humorousness: The role of confirmatory and disconfirmatory acts. In J. Burmudez, B. De Raad, J. De Vries, A. M. Perez-Garcia, A. Sanchez-Elvira, & G. L. Van Heck (Eds.), *Personality psychology in Europe, Volume 6* (pp. 76-80). Tilburg: University of Tilburg Press.

Ware, A. P., & Mendelsohn, G. A. (1996 July). *The influence of structural components on the elicitation and analysis of goals*. Presented at the meetings of the European Association for Personality Psychology, Ghent, Belgium.

Wicker, A. W. (1987). Behavior settings reconsidered: Temporal stages, resources, internal dynamics, context. In D. Stokols & I. Altman, (Eds.), *Handbook of Environmental Psychology, Volume 1* (pp. 613-653). New York: Wiley.

Wicker, A. W. (1992). Making sense of environments. In Walsh, W. B., Craik, K. H., & Price, R. W. (Eds.), *Person–environment psychology: Models and perspectives* (pp. 157-192). Hillsdale, NJ: Lawrence Erlbaum Associates.

Wiggins, J. S. (1997). In defense of traits. In R. Hogan, J. Johnson, & S. Briggs (Eds.), *Handbook of personality psychology* (pp. 95-115). New York: Academic Press.

9

Modeling and Managing Change in People–Environment Transactions

Daniel Stokols
H. C. Clitheroe, Jr.
Mary Zmuidzinas
University of California, Irvine

OVERVIEW

Environmental psychology, and the field of environment-behavior studies (EBS) more generally, examine the dynamic transactions between people and their everyday, sociophysical environments (Bechtel, 1997; Proshansky, Ittelson, & Rivlin, 1976). These everyday environments include people's homes, neighborhoods, work, and community settings. In keeping with Lewin's (1936) *action research* orientation, research in environmental psychology integrates the scientific goals of analyzing and explaining the nature of people-environment transactions, with the more practical goal of enhancing—even optimizing—people's relationships with their surroundings through effective strategies of urban planning and environmental design (cf., Stokols, 1978; Weisman, 1983).

This chapter is focused on a particular facet of human-environment transactions, namely, the circumstances surrounding fundamental changes in the structure and subjective qualities of people's relationships with their surroundings. The issue of change is central to the study of people-environment transactions, since transactional relationships involve dynamic and reciprocal influences between individuals and groups, on the one hand, and their sociophysical environments, on the other. Thus, in contrast to linear models of environment and behavior, the transactional perspective assumes that continual changes are inherent in the nature of people's relationships with their environments, and that these changes vary considerably in their scope, magnitude, behavioral, and health consequences (cf., Altman & Rogoff, 1987; Ittelson, Proshansky, Rivlin, & Winkel, 1974).

Although transactional models of environment and behavior emphasize the centrality of change in people's relationships with their surroundings, much research in environmental psychology reflects a *nontransformational perspective*—one that emphasizes the relative stability of people's relationships with their environments. To the extent that the structure and subjective qualities of people's environments remain relatively stable, the observation of reliable links between environmental conditions and behavior is more straightforward. However, when people's everyday surroundings are dynamic and unstable, the links between environment and behavior are more situation-specific (i.e., limited to the particular settings and events where they are observed), and less generalizable to other situations and settings.

Over the past 10 to 15 years, research in environmental psychology has begun to give greater attention to *transformational perspectives* on environment and behavior (Saegert, 1987; Stokols, 1988). In contrast to nontransformational approaches, the transformational perspective assumes that certain forms and phases of people-environment transaction are highly prone to rapid change and instability. Transformational analyses are explicitly concerned with those factors that influence the relative stability or instability of people's relationships with their environments. For example, the transformational perspective assumes that fortuitous events play an important role in shaping patterns of people-environment transaction. Moreover, transformational analyses emphasize deviation-amplification optimization processes in people-environment transaction, equilibrium maintenance and normalization (cf., Maruyama, 1963; Stokols, 1978).

The growing interest in transformational analyses of environment and behavior is consistent with certain societal events and concerns that have surfaced in recent years. Since the early 1980s, we have become more aware of the rapidity and scope of global environmental changes (e.g., atmospheric ozone depletion, global warming); sizable demographic shifts in the ethic composition and aging of the population; the evolution of information technologies (e.g., desktop computing, the Internet, and World Wide Web) that have fundamentally altered the ways in which people work and communicate with each other; and the increasing globalization and fragility of the world's economy (cf., Mitchell, 1995; Stern, 1992; Stokols, 1995). Clearly, we live during an era of profound environmental and societal change. The salience of this change has prompted researchers to direct their attention toward the development of more effective strategies for modeling and managing environmental and behavioral change processes (e.g., Ashton, Grey, & Barnard, 1986; Prochaska & DiClemente, 1986; Silver & DeFries, 1990; Thietart & Forgues, 1995).

Whereas many psychological theories (e.g., theories of learning, perception, social behavior, and human development) have focused on the links between environmental conditions and behavior, environmental psychology brings a distinctively different perspective to the study of environment and behavior. First, environmental psychology gives greater attention to molar units of the environment, such as people's homes, neighborhoods, and work settings than other areas of psychology that have focused more exclusively on micro-level stimuli and events (Craik, 1973; Stokols, 1983). Second, many, if not all theories in environmental psychology, construe people-in-environments as dynamic systems characterized by certain qualities and varying degrees of interdependence (Barker, 1968; Wapner, 1987). Examples of *transactional constructs* that denote composite qualities of interdependence between people and their surroundings are conditions of *under- and over-staffing in behavior settings* (Barker, 1968; Wicker, McGrath, & Armstrong, 1972); *person–environment fit* or *congruence* (Caplan & Harrison, 1993; Michelson, 1976); *defensible space* (Newman, 1973); *urban overload* (Milgram, 1970); and *place identity* (Proshansky, Fabian, & Kaminoff, 1983).

In this chapter, we are concerned primarily with modeling and managing *transactional change* that is, altered patterns of interdependence among individuals, groups, and their sociophysical milieus. We are less concerned with purely intrapersonal or environmental changes—for example, those that occur in individuals as the result of physiological or developmental processes, or in the physical structure of environments, as a result of erosion or routine wear and tear. However, intrapersonal or environmentally based changes that lead to a restructuring of people's relationships with their surroundings are relevant to the present analysis. For instance, transformations of the physical environment triggered by purely geographic forces (e.g., earthquakes, floods) that subsequently promote fundamental and persisting changes in people's relationships with their surroundings, are encompassed by this analysis. Similarly, developmental transitions such as graduation from college, marriage, or retirement that substantially alter patterns of people-environment transaction (e.g., through geographic relocation or changes in one's social networks) are relevant here as well.

Throughout this chapter, we distinguish between subtle and routine changes in people-environment transactions, and those that reflect substantial and demonstrable departures from the status quo (cf., Clitheroe, Stokols, & Zmuidzinas, 1998). The unique contribution of environmental psychological theories is that they provide a vocabulary for describing significant patterns of interdependence between people and their environments, and a corresponding set of criteria for determining whether fundamental shifts have occurred in the strength or quality of interdependence between particular individuals and their surroundings. These theories also specify certain behavioral and cognitive processes that mediate changes in the relationships between people and their environments, and a variety of behavioral, psychological, and health sequelae of these shifts. Finally, many transactional theories offer practical guidelines for enhancing the quality of people's relationships with their surroundings through proactive, strategic changes in environmental design, interpersonal relationships, and organizational structure.

The next section outlines several qualities of interdependence between people and their environments identified in earlier theories. These theories are grouped according to three levels of analysis: (a) *the individual* or micro level, focused on the transactions between individuals and their environments; (b) *the organizational* or *meso level* of analysis, pertaining primarily to the interdependencies among the members of groups, and between groups and their sociophysical milieu; and (c) *the community* or *macro level* of analysis that focuses on the qualities of interdependence existing between the members of a population, and the sociocultural and geographic conditions of the community where they reside.

Whereas earlier theories in environmental psychology have identified key dimensions of people-environment transaction, and processes of transactional change occurring at micro, meso, and macro levels of analysis, little attention has been given in prior research to the development of more integrative, cross-level models of change. In an earlier analysis, Stokols (1988) defined *transformational theories* as "those that explain the circumstances under which people-environment transactions are likely to undergo fundamental and demonstrable change" (p. 238). He also noted examples of transformational theories in environmental psychology, including Wapner's

(1981) analysis of the processes where people prepare for and cope with environmental transitions such as residential relocation; Wicker's (1987) analysis of the lifecycles of behavior settings; and Saegert's (1987) discussion of the ways in which researchers prompt social change through the very process of studying the relationships between people and their surroundings. However, earlier research has stopped short of developing more integrative formulations of transformative change—for example, models that span micro, meso, and macro levels of change, and incorporate constructs from multiple theories so as to provide a more complete portrayal of simultaneous and interrelated change processes.

The prospects for developing more integrative, multi-level theories of transactional change are addressed later in the chapter. We also consider some of the practical implications of developing more integrative theories of change for community problem-solving and environmental design. First, however, we review earlier conceptualizations of people–environment transaction, and models of transformative change, at the micro, meso, and macro levels of analysis. Our review of previous theories is by no means exhaustive, but it does provide an overview of several constructs that have been developed to depict important facets of human–environment transaction.

QUALITIES OF INTERDEPENDENCE BETWEEN PEOPLE AND THEIR ENVIRONMENTS

The qualities of interdependence posited by transactional theories are typically represented by hypothetical constructs that are not immediately observable in objective terms (MacQuorqodale & Meehl, 1948; Spence, 1944). These constructs denote composite qualities of situations and settings (Stokols, 1987) and, as such, provide a kind of short-hand representation of people–environment relationships that is inherently incomplete (i.e., leaves out many objective details of the relationships). Transactional theories focus on delimited aspects of situations and settings that are of central concern to the theorist. They highlight systemic qualities of people–environment relationships that are often subjective in nature and not immediately apparent to objective observers. It is through the interpretive lens provided by the theory that these psychologically significant, composite qualities of people's relationships with their environments are revealed.

As will be evident from our discussion of environment–behavior theories, the potential complexity of people's relationships with their surroundings increases from micro to macro levels of analysis. Whereas micro-level theories are focused on the transactions between single individuals and their surroundings, meso-level analyses examine group-environment transactions and, thus, encompass the interrelationships among group members (social interdependencies), as well as connections between groups and their physical milieu (Stokols & Shumaker, 1981). Similarly, macro- or community-level analyses encompass a greater number and range of individuals, groups, organizations, physical environments, and the structural linkages among them, than are subsumed by meso- or micro-level analyses of person- and group-environment transactions.

Micro-Level Theories
of Person–Environment Transaction

Several lines of research on individuals' transactions with their environments are rooted in the concept of *behavior–environment congruence*, or how a situation or setting accommodates the goals and needs of its users (cf., Lawton & Nahemow, 1973; Michelson, 1976; Wicker, 1972). Early analyses of congruence (or *person–environment fit*) focused on the degree of match between a particular personal need (e.g., an employee's desire for a challenging job) and a corresponding environmental condition (e.g., the actual complexity of one's job). Subsequent analyses offered broader conceptions of congruence reflecting the overall level of fit between a person's diverse goals and activities, and the opportunities available for meeting those goals in the multiple environments comprising his or her *life domains, overall life situation* or *daily activity system* (cf., Chapin, 1974; Magnusson, 1981; Michelson, 1985; Stokols, 1979; Swindle & Moos, 1992).

An important, widely studied aspect of person–environment congruence is the degree that individuals are able to cope effectively with the environmental demands they encounter in their day-to-day lives. The term *stress*, refers to a state of imbalance in a person elicited by an actual or perceived disparity between environmental demands and one's capacity to cope with them (Lazarus, 1966; Selye, 1956). The experience of stress signals a reduced and possibly inadequate level of congruence that is manifested through a variety of physiological, emotional, and behavioral responses. Conditions of the sociophysical environment (e.g., airport noise, traffic congestion, air pollution, interpersonal conflict) operate as *stressors* to the extent that they tax or exceed a person's adaptive resources (cf., Evans, 1982).

Transactional theories have identified certain environmental and psychological factors that are crucial in facilitating or hindering individuals' efforts to accomplish their goals and plans while avoiding stress (Lazarus & Launier,

1978). Glass and Singer's (1972) research demonstrated that individuals' perceptions of *environmental control* and *predictability* enable them to cope more effectively with urban stressors. Their experimental studies offered compelling evidence that short term laboratory exposure to unpredictable and uncontrollable events (e.g., the onset of noise) can trigger adverse *behavioral aftereffects* (including reduced tolerance for frustration and task effectiveness) that persist even after the initial stressors have subsided (cf., Cohen, 1980).

Other research has shown that when exposure to unpredictable or uncontrollable situations is prolonged, a debilitating syndrome of *learned helplessness* can occur (Schulz & Hanusa, 1978; Seligman, 1975). For example, *technological disasters* (e.g., the radioactive and chemical contamination at Three Mile Island and Love Canal) are events occurring at the community level that provoke chronic anxiety and distress in exposed individuals because the health effects of these events can be catastrophic but are difficult to gauge in the short run (Baum, Fleming, & Davidson, 1983). Routine exposure to aircraft noise has been linked to physiological stress and symptoms of learned helplessness among children attending schools under the flight paths of busy airports (cf., Cohen, Evans, Stokols, & Krantz, 1986; Evans, Bullinger, & Hygge, 1998). Also, *involuntary relocation* from private residences to institutional care settings has been found to promote higher rates of depression and death among the infirm elderly (Pastalan, 1980). And other studies have found significant links between the magnitude and number of *stressful life events* (e.g., divorce, job loss, death of a loved one, legal conflict) experienced by a person during a given period, and the severity of physical illness and psychiatric symptoms observed in the individual (Dohrenwend & Dohrenwend, 1974; Holmes & Rahe, 1967).

Whereas individuals' perceived control over their surroundings is an important facet of behavior–environment congruence, environmental controllability may not be a necessary feature of supportive environments. Kaplan (1983), for example, has distinguished between *controllable, supportive*, and *restorative* environments. He observes that events in many environments are beyond individuals' personal control, yet the situation or setting can be quite compatible with a person's goals and activities. Under these circumstances, one's sense that "things are under control" may be more crucial than the belief that "things are under my personal control."

Kaplan notes that supportive environments do not necessarily afford individuals complete control over personal outcomes, but they do facilitate their efforts to accomplish important goals and activities. According to Kaplan

(1983), *supportive environments* are those where choice and the information necessary for making choices are readily available. *Restorative environments* comprise a special category of supportive settings that not only facilitate people's efforts to accomplish important goals and plans, but also foster activities that are intrinsically enjoyable. A defining feature of restorative environments is that they afford individuals opportunities for experiencing fascination with their surroundings and a sense of "being away" from the routine pressures and distractions of everyday life. Also, restorative settings promote a sense of coherence that has been found by Antonovsky (1979) to be a key aspect of person–environment transaction that enables individuals to cope successfully with stressful life events. Supportive and restorative environments, as defined by Kaplan, are conducive to activities involving relaxation and thoughtful contemplation. Thus, they facilitate individuals' efforts to formulate important life goals and to develop systematic plans for accomplishing their *personal projects* (Little, 1983)—patterns of coordinated action carried out by persons over extended periods and across multiple settings that are directed toward achieving their goals and aspirations.

The analyses noted here of congruence, stress, environmental controllability, predictability and supportiveness offer several useful constructs for describing qualities of person–environment transaction. At the same time, other theories and research have focused on the ways that individuals become strongly attached to and dependent on particular places. The construct of *place identity*, for example, was conceptualized by Proshansky (1978; Proshansky, Fabian, & Kaminoff, 1983) as

> those dimensions of self that define the individual's personal identity in relationship to the physical environment by means of a complex pattern of conscious and unconscious ideas, beliefs, preferences, feelings, values, goals, and behavioral tendencies and skills relevant to this environment (p. 155).

Place identity highlights the critical role played by physical environments in shaping individuals' development over the lifespan and their overall sense of self. Consistent with Proshansky's analysis of place identity, Cooper (1974) observed the important ways that individuals' home environments reflect and reinforce their sense of self. Similarly, Fried's (1963) study of slum dwellers forced to move from their original neighborhood to a new environment, revealed the syndrome of grief and distress that often occurs when one's physical and emotional ties to a particular place are disrupted.

Bronfenbrenner's (1979) *ecology of human development* model is broadly concerned with the ways that environmental conditions and transactional processes occurring in multiple settings influence a wide range of developmental outcomes over the lifespan. Bronfenbrenner's theory examines developmental processes and outcomes not only in a specified environment (e.g., the *microsystem* of the home, school, or workplace), but also the ways that functional links between two or more settings (i.e., the *mesosystem*, *exosystem*, and *macrosystem*) influence individuals' development over the lifespan. At the microsystem level, research by Wachs and Gruen (1982) demonstrated that infants' cognitive development is enriched within home environments that are highly responsive to the child and provide shelter from distracting stimuli (cf., Wohlwill & Heft, 1987). Bradley and Caldwell (1976) found that children's cognitive and social development is enhanced by residential environments that provide an ambiance of family cohesion and harmony. And Kohn and Schooler (1982) observed significant links between the substantive complexity of adult workers' job environments and measures of their intellectual flexibility and personal autonomy gathered 10 years later. Thus, it appears that the transactional qualities of *environmental responsiveness, protection from distraction, challenge and complexity* are conducive to positive developmental outcomes among different age groups.

The theoretical analyses summarized above underscore the psychological and developmental significance of people's attachment to those places that are prominent in their overall life situation. They also reveal certain forms of interdependence between people and places whose disruption can provoke a variety of adverse behavioral, emotional, developmental, and health outcomes. Moreover, the analyses raise questions about the possible impacts of certain societal conditions, such as our growing reliance on digital communications and virtual environments (cf., Blanchard, 1997; Negroponte, 1996). These social and technological trends, conceivably, could reduce people's opportunities for active engagement in face-to-face settings and weaken their ties to work environments, educational settings, and public places (e.g., Meyrowitz, 1985; Noam, 1995; Stokols, 1999). We return to these issues of technological change and place attachment later in the chapter. In the next section, however, we consider meso-level theories in environmental psychology that focus on the transactions between groups, organizations, and their physical environments.

Meso-Level Theories of People–Environment Transaction

A number of theoretical constructs have been developed by environmental psychologists to describe important dimensions of group–environment transaction. One of the most influential of these analyses is Barker's (1968; Barker, 1978) *theory of behavior settings*. Barker defines the behavior setting as an ecobehavioral system comprised of group members, a program of group activities, and a physical milieu. Behavior settings are characterized by recurring patterns of activity that take place within specific temporal and spatial boundaries. Settings strive to maintain equilibrium by achieving optimal levels of staffing, reflecting a balance between the number of members admitted to the setting, on one hand, and the number of roles available to them, on the other. *Under-staffing* occurs when there are too few members to staff the roles required for maintaining the setting at an optimal level. *Over-staffing* prevails when the number of group members exceeds the number of roles available to them in the setting (Wicker, McGrath, & Armstrong, 1972). Studies of behavior settings have shown that conditions of under-staffing within small versus large schools, and within small versus large churches, create forces among group members toward participation in leadership roles and core activities of the setting (Wicker, 1969; Willems, 1967). The stronger claim of small, under-staffed organizations on their members has important implications for personal development and well-being, as well as for group cohesion, productivity, and viability (cf., Barker, 1968; Wicker, 1987).

Barker's analysis of behavior settings emphasized their "preperceptual" or objective features, rather than their subjective qualities. Yet, subsequent research has examined the influence of members' perceptions and motivations on the functioning of behavior settings. For example, Wicker (1987) examined the *lifecycles of behavior settings* and the ways that members' motivations, goals, and personalities influence the formation, maintenance, and eventual dissolution of organized settings. Also, whereas much of the research inspired by Barker's theory of behavior settings focused on the measurement of social and behavioral phenomena (e.g., adaptive reactions to conditions of understaffing in groups) rather than on the physical features of settings, later analyses have examined the processes that groups are affected by and, in turn, influence their physical milieu.

In Stokols' (1981) analysis of *group x place transactions*, the physical environment is construed both as an antecedent of behavior and as a sociocultural product—i.e., as the material reflection of collective activity and affiliation, and as a repository of shared social meanings. Accordingly, settings can be characterized with regard to their *social imageability*, or capacity, to evoke vivid, widely shared social meanings among group members. Business managers, for example, often incorporate physical symbols of company and team identity (e.g., team photographs, award certificates, motivational signage) in an effort to enhance the social imageability and organizational climate of the workplace (Ornstein, 1990; Steele, 1986; Wells, 1997).

Another facet of group–environment transaction is *place dependence*, or the degree group members perceive the major functions of their setting to be exclusively tied to a particular location (Stokols & Shumaker, 1981). Elaborating on the ideas of place dependence and social imageability, Stokols and Jacobi (1984) conceptualized *temporal orientations of groups* as "the actual and perceived links between past, present, and future generations of group members, and between the group and particular environments (p. 311)." For example, *traditional behavior settings* (e.g., the Wailing Wall in the Old City of Jerusalem; Plymouth Plantation in Massachusetts) are those where recurring patterns of group activity and symbolic meanings of the environment perpetuate and strengthen the ties between current members, an historical referent group, and a specific location. A variety of other criteria for classifying diverse behavior settings in terms of their core functions and features are provided by Price and Blashfield (1975).

In addition to the analyses of behavior settings and group x place transactions, other theories have examined qualities of social cohesion in organized groups and the ways that the physical features of settings influence informal social contacts, friendship formation, and group members' sense of security or fear of crime. Constructs pertaining to social cohesion and support in group settings include Moos' (1976) conceptualization of *social climate* in institutional, occupational, and school environments; the level of *management concern* for employees' well-being in work organizations (Roethlisberger & Dickson, 1939); and Stokols' (1992) analysis of *conflict-prone and conflict-resistant organizations*, defined in terms of the environmental arrangements and social conditions in organizations that either predispose members to chronic conflict and health problems or, alternatively, make the occurrence of those difficulties less likely. In an important series of field experimental studies, Sherif (1958) found that intergroup conflicts can be stemmed by creating *superordinate goals* relating to the physical environment shared by competing groups—e.g., the goal of resolving an environmental crisis that threatens the well-being of both groups' members. These analyses highlight conditions of the social environment that either promote or hinder the smooth functioning of groups and organizations (cf., Walsh, Price, & Craik, 1992).

At the same time, architectural and spatial features of settings can strongly influence patterns of social interaction and the quality of group members' attachments to particular places. For instance, Festinger, Schachter, & Back

(1950) found that *physical proximity* between the front doors of neighbors' apartments in a married student housing complex at MIT, strongly predicted the frequency of their informal social contacts, development of enduring friendships, shared political attitudes, and common patterns of consumer behavior. Also, Baum and Valins (1977) observed that the *architectural design* of college dormitories significantly affected residents' susceptibility to crowding stress and interpersonal conflict, with suite-design dorms affording more effective territorial regulation, and stress avoidance than corridor-design dorms.

The architectural and site planning features of group environments also influence residents' feelings of security and fear of crime. Newman (1973) defined *defensible space* as "the range of mechanisms—real and symbolic barriers, strongly defined areas of influence, and improved opportunities for surveillance—that combine to bring an environment under the control of its users" (p. 3). Territorial markers of ownership, effective site planning of apartment complexes, and clearly defined boundaries between public, semi-public, and private spaces are environmental features that enhance defensible space and residents' sense of security (cf., Alexander et al., 1977); whereas *physical incivilities* such as graffiti, litter, and poorly maintained landscaping and streets are conditions that undermine defensible space, heighten residents' fear of crime, and create greater opportunities for motivated offenders to commit crimes in the area (cf., Altman, 1975; Nasar & Fisher, 1993; Perkins, Wandersman, Rich, & Taylor, 1993; Taylor, 1988).

Some of the constructs noted here pertaining to group–environment transactions (e.g., the behavior setting, social imageability, crowding and distraction, group conflict and cohesion) have been extended from micro- and meso-scale analyses of settings, to macro-level studies of people–environment transactions within larger-scale areas such as neighborhoods, public places, and urban regions. Other concepts that are uniquely relevant to community-scale analyses (e.g., social capital, social traps, environmental justice, global sustainability, and the community planning strategies of New Urbanism) have been developed as well. We turn now to a review of these macro-level analyses of people's relationships with their community environments.

Macro-Level Theories of People–Environment Transaction

Bronfenbrenner (1992) defines the *macrosystem* context of human development as "the overarching pattern of micro-, meso-, and exosystems characteristic of a given culture, subculture, or other broader social context, with particular reference to the developmentally instigative belief systems, resources, hazards, life styles, opportunity structures, life course options, and patterns of social exchange that are embedded in each of these systems" (p. 228). The macrosystem encompasses not only the individual settings in a person's life, but also clusters of two or more interconnected settings that jointly influence one's developmental outcomes; for example, the home–school *mesosystem* of a child, or the *exosystem* linking a child's home environment and his or her parents' workplaces—the latter being settings that affect the child even though he or she does not directly participate in them.

The macrosystem construct is valuable because it suggests various strategies for describing and understanding people's transactions with their large scale environments (e.g., the opportunity structures and patterns of social exchange afforded by a community). Barker and Schoggen's (1973) research on *qualities of community life*, for example, compared an American and English town in terms of the relative number, diversity, and productivity of all behavior settings observed in each community. They developed several measures for describing macro-level qualities of people–environment transaction including the *urb*, i.e., the number, occurrence, and duration of a town's behavior settings, and the range of behavioral opportunities available or "at hand" to community members each year. Also, the *productivity index* of a community denotes the cumulative person-hours of participation required to operate and maintain community settings for a one-year period, and the extent to which inhabitants are engaged in crucial roles in those environments.

Barker and Schoggen's (1973) analysis of community life is highly relevant to Putnam's (1995) conceptualization of *social capital*, or "those features of social organization such as networks, norms, and social trust that facilitate coordination and cooperation for mutual benefit" (p. 67). Based on analyses of extensive survey data, Putnam concluded that Americans' participation in civic organizations (e.g., neighborhood associations, political action groups) has declined since the 1980s, and that these trends signal an erosion of social capital in the United States. In light of Putnam's findings, Barker and Schoggen's research suggests that the availability of a sufficient number and diversity of behavior settings in a city or town may encourage residents to participate actively in social networks and civic organizations, thereby strengthening social capital in the community as a whole. Thus, the behavior setting may be a crucial building block for promoting social capital.

A number of theories have identified physical features of environments that promote or hinder social cohesion in communities. For instance, Carr,

Francis, Rivlin, and Stone (1992) suggested that citizens' participation in *public places* (such as historical sites, town squares, urban plazas, cultural centers, regional parks, playgrounds, shopping malls) is an important barometer of community cohesion and civic engagement. They offer several design and programming guidelines for ensuring that public places are responsive to occupants' needs for security, comfort, aesthetic enjoyment, collective identity, discovery and exploration (cf., Sommer, 1983). Also, proponents of the New Urbanism (Calthorpe, 1993; Duany & Plater-Zyberk, 1991; Katz, 1995) have outlined principles of urban design for establishing compact, cohesive communities—for example, by making retail services and recreational facilities accessible to residents within a short walk from their homes, and by situating civic buildings in central, highly visible areas of the town.

The strategic placement of civic buildings, historical landmarks, and public parks in urban areas can enhance the *legibility* or *physical imageability* of cities, i.e., the extent that they are easily remembered and navigated by residents and visitors (Lynch, 1960). A conceptualization of social imageability at the community level was provided by Milgram and Jodelet (1976) in their study of Parisians' cognitive maps of Paris. Their research highlighted the widely shared symbolic and historical meanings conveyed by the urban environment. The physical legibility and social imageability of cities may be important contributors to residents' sense of security, participation in public places, and levels of social cohesion within the community as a whole.

Milgram's (1970) analysis of *urban overload*, on the other hand, posits that exposure to excessive social and physical stimulation in large cities (e.g., noise, crowding, traffic congestion) undermines residents' responsiveness to others' needs and erodes the civility and cohesiveness of urban communities. Milgram's conceptualization of overload and its detrimental effects on city life is consistent with Wirth's (1938) earlier theory of urbanism that emphasized the impersonality and blasé attitude of city dwellers. Appleyard's (1981) research on "livable streets" also focuses on a socially corrosive condition of large cities: automobile traffic in residential neighborhoods. Appleyard found a significant inverse correlation between the daily *volume of automobile traffic* on residential streets and the level of social contact among neighbors living on the same city block. In effect, high volume traffic was associated with a shrinkage of social life in the community.

Another line of research in environmental psychology has examined the effects of human behavior on the quality and sustainability of the physical environment (cf., Gardner & Stern, 1996; Geller, Winett, & Everett, 1982). Stern (1992), for example, has analyzed the behavioral underpinnings of *global environmental changes* such as the depletion of the earth's ozone layer, and the warming of the earth's surface through the production of green-house gasses. According to Stern, certain behavior patterns, such as the consumption of fossil fuels in households and organizations, are significantly linked to atmospheric ozone depletion and global warming (e.g., fuel consumption for personal transportation accounts for over 20% of US carbon dioxide emissions). Stern further suggests that a combination of technological and public policy strategies, such as improving levels of automobile fuel efficiency and developing corporate incentives to promote employee ridesharing and other environmentally protective behaviors, will be needed to reduce or reverse adverse global environmental changes.

Platt's (1973) analysis of social traps offers a theoretical basis for devising effective public policies to enhance environmental quality and sustainability. Social traps arise because individuals are typically motivated to pursue their own, short-term financial benefits without regard for the longer term public interest. According to Platt, a *social trap* occurs when there is an opposition between highly motivating short-term rewards or punishments for a given behavior (e.g., purchasing a luxurious, fuel-inefficient car) and the long-run consequences of that action. He outlines certain strategies for alleviating social traps and their adverse effects on environmental quality and resource conservation. Disincentives for engaging in environmentally injurious behavior can be applied, e.g., by levying higher excise taxes on the purchase of fuel-inefficient cars. Alternatively, incentives can be added to encourage *environmentally protective behavior*, e.g., by providing higher speed lanes and enhanced parking privileges for multipassenger vehicles. Similarly, Everett, Hayward, and Meyers (1974) found that the provision of tokens redeemable for retail products and services to passengers on specially marked city buses led to a 150% increase in rates of bus ridership (relative to baseline rates) in a college community.

A particularly insidious social trap is environmental injustice and inequity (Bullard, 1990). *Environmental injustice* occurs when people of color living in low income minority communities are exposed to higher levels of environmental contamination and stress than nonminority residents who live in more affluent neighborhoods (cf., Clark Atlanta University Environmental Justice Resource Center, 1998; University of Michigan Environmental Justice Resource Center, 1998). The differential exposure of low income minority groups to toxins and stressors can result from intentional discriminatory actions on the part of community leaders (e.g., unequal enforcement of environmental protection laws in different parts of the community); or through the neglect and disinterest of affluent communities that pursue their own, short-term economic interests and neglect the longer term, detrimental effects of environmental inequities on public health and community cohesion.

The micro-, meso-, and macro-level theories summarized next offer a useful starting point for developing more integrative, cross-level analyses of transactional change (see Table 9.1). In the final sections of the chapter, the prospects for developing more comprehensive strategies for modeling and managing change in people–environment transactions are discussed.

DEVELOPING MORE COMPREHENSIVE
AND ROBUST STRATEGIES FOR MODELING
AND MANAGING TRANSACTIONAL CHANGE

Before we can hope to develop predictive theories and prospective interventions for modeling and managing change in people–environment relationships, at least two important tasks must be addressed. First, it is necessary to develop taxonomic terms for identifying and categorizing key aspects of human–environment transaction and criteria for calibrating change processes and their outcomes at varying analytic levels (e.g., micro, meso, and macro levels). Efforts to develop predictive theories in the behavioral, social, and physical sciences generally are preceded by a taxonomic phase where descriptive terms for classifying important units of analysis are established (cf., Altman, 1968; Price & Blashfield, 1975). Second, owing to the enormous diversity and complexity of human–environment relationships, the formulation of more integrative analyses of transactional change processes and outcomes can be facilitated by identifying a set of organizing principles, or conceptual strategies, to guide future theory development efforts. We address these concerns in the forthcoming sections of the chapter.

Classifying Important Dimensions of People-Environment
Transaction and Categories of Transactional Change

The theoretical terms and qualities of interdependence outlined in Table 9.1 comprise a nonexhaustive, but reasonably representative, list of conceptual concerns that have guided environment–behavior research over the past several years. An inspection of this list of constructs reveals that some denote (a) *structural aspects of people-place transactions* whose valence is neutral (e.g., micro-, meso-, exo- and macro-system contexts of development; behavior set-

TABLE 9.1

Theoretical Terms Describing Qualities of Interdependence Between People and Their Environments

Level of Analysis	Form of Interdependence Between People and Their Environments
Micro-level	person–environment congruence or fit
	physiological and psychological stress
	environmental controllability
	environmental predictability
	learned helplessness
	restorative environment
	supportive environment
	personal projects
	place identity and attachment
	microsystem contexts of development
Meso-level	behavior setting
	under- and over-staffing
	lifecycles of behavior settings
	group x place transactions
	social imageability of settings
	place dependence
	temporal orientations of groups
	social climate of organizations
	conflict resistant/prone organizations
	superordinate goals
	defensible space
Macro-level	macro, meso, and exosystems of development
	the *urb* productivity index of community behavior settings
	physical legibility and social imageability of cities
	"New Urbanist" community design
	social capital
	urban overload
	social trap
	technological and natural disasters
	global environmental change and sustainability
	environmental injustice and inequity

tings; the urb measure of community settings). Others pertain to (b) *desirable or undesirable qualities of interdependence* between people and their surround-ings (e.g., person-environment fit vs. incongruence; conflict-resistant vs. conflict-promotive organizations; social capital and superordinate goals vs. social traps and environmental injustice). Still others reflect (c) *positive or neg-ative outcomes* of people-environment transactions (e.g., psychological resto-ration and sense of coherence vs. physiological/psychological stress and learned helplessness). Finally, some of the terms reveal the contrast between (d) *intentional, planful efforts of people to improve the quality of their transactions with the environment* (e.g., carrying out personal projects, creating defensible space, designing communities in accord with New Urbanist principles), ver-sus (e) *unintentional, dramatic changes in people-environment transactions* that challenge the adaptive capacities of individuals and groups (e.g., technologi-cal and natural disasters, adverse global environmental change).

Given the diversity of theoretical concerns addressed in environmental psy-chology, how valuable are the constructs outlined in Table 9.1 as a basis for de-veloping more integrative, robust strategies for modeling and managing transactional change? First, these constructs offer useful taxonomic criteria for categorizing situations and settings according to the *quality* (valence) and *strength of connection* between particular people and places (e.g., situations characterized by low vs. high levels of person-environment congruence; weak vs. strong levels of place identity among individuals vis-à-vis their sur-roundings; or low vs. high levels of place dependence between groups and their environments). They also reflect the *varying levels of structural complexity* inherent in people-environment transactions, ranging from the transitory ex-periences of individuals involved in brief, momentary situations occurring within infrequently visited places (low complexity), to the more enduring pat-terns of transaction among groups, organizations, and their environments that recur on a regular basis in specified locations and time intervals (higher com-plexity). In relation to modeling and managing change processes, these taxo-nomic dimensions of people-environment relationships suggest baseline criteria for calibrating levels of change in transactional states—for example, *changes in the quality or valence* of people's interactions with their surround-ings; the *strength of connection* between particular individuals or groups and a specified environment; and the *structural complexity* of situations and settings. Clearly, multiple quantitative and qualitative measures are required to assess these diverse criteria of change in people-environment transactions.

Second, the grouping of transactional terms according to different levels of analysis suggests the possible value of combining certain constructs across the micro-, meso-, and macro-analytic levels to yield more comprehensive analyses of change processes, and their impacts on individual well-being, group cohesion, organizational productivity, and qualities of community life. For example, in attempting to understand and change macrosystem conditions such as the level of social capital within a community, it may prove useful to incorporate micro- and meso-scale constructs in developing environmental design and public policy strategies aimed at promoting citizens' involvement in social networks. Thus, ensuring that a sufficient number and diversity of behavior settings and restorative environments are made available to the members of a community may expand their opportunities for civic participation and stress reduction, thereby strengthening social capital in the community as a whole. Alternatively, to anticipate the micro-level changes associated with community-wide conditions such as urban overload, technological disasters, and environmental injustice, it may be instructive to consider the ways that these macro-level phenomena undermine the quality of group x place transactions and person–environment fit, thereby promoting stress and learned helplessness among individuals exposed to these events.

Third, the constructs listed in Table 9.1 provide a set of interpretive "filters" for anticipating the consequences of powerful societal forces whose effects are likely to be seen at each level of human–environment transaction. The trend toward societal aging in many regions of the world, for example, implies that a larger number and diversity of behavior settings oriented toward an older population will be required in future years. Also, the criteria for establishing supportive and restorative environments vary across different age groups, so the task of identifying cohort-sensitive guidelines for environmental design will become increasingly important in the context of societal aging. Moreover, the pronounced cultural and ethnic diversity of certain regions in the United States (e.g., in South Florida, Texas, Arizona, and California) raises questions about the efficacy and generalizability of community initiatives designed to strengthen social capital and social imageability in urban environments. In light of these trends, it is reasonable to ask whether community-wide efforts to promote social capital, social imageability, and a greater mix of urban behavior settings will benefit all subgroups of the population; or, instead, could widen the rift between advantaged and disadvantaged groups in society. It may be necessary in the coming years to establish culturally specific interventions for enhancing social capital, environmental imageability, and civic participation among the diverse subgroups that coexist in large urban communities.

Similarly, the profound social and psychological changes engendered by the rapid growth of the Internet and World Wide Web are being felt at all levels of human–environment transaction. For instance, many computer users complain that they are now inundated by a surfeit of electronic communications (e.g., email, voice mail) and beset by feelings of chronic information overload and stress. At the same time, as more people spend greater amounts of time on computer-mediated transactions, their opportunities for engaging in face-to-face discourse with others and participating in public places may dwindle (cf., Kraut, Patterson, Lundmark, Kiesler, Mukopadhyay, & Scherlis, 1998; Meyrowitz, 1985; Noam, 1995; Stokols, in 1999), thereby undermining social cohesion at the community level.

The nature of social interaction and civic participation has been changed radically by the emergence of *virtual communities* (Blanchard & Horan, 1998). Many individuals are redirecting their energies away from participation in face-to-face settings toward greater involvement in *virtual behavior settings*—electronic sites on the Internet that develop a symbolic sense of space or place through the sustained computer-mediated communications among participants in those sites (Blanchard, 1997). The cumulative impact of these micro- and meso-level change processes on macrosystem conditions such as the levels of social capital within particular communities remains an open, empirical question. For example, the differential access to computers and online services that currently exists among affluent and nonaffluent groups in society exemplifies a social trap or environmental inequity that will need to be redressed as a prerequisite for strengthening social capital at the community level (cf., Stokols, 1999; U.S. Department of Commerce, 1995).

Also, in relation to Bronfenbrenner's (1979, 1992) conception of the micro-, meso-, and exosystems of development, the emergence of virtual behavior settings has given rise to a new category of mesosystems, reflecting the links between place-based and virtual environments (Stokols, 1999). These relations between virtual environments and their place-based host settings can be complementary, contradictory, or neutral. To the extent that mesosystem links between real and virtual settings are contradictory (e.g., an employee at a company engages in recreational web surfing when at work, thereby arousing resentment among coworkers and their supervisor), a variety of disruptive outcomes can be expected to occur within the host setting at both personal and group levels.

In summary, the theoretical constructs reviewed earlier provide a useful set of taxonomic terms for describing important dimensions of human–environment transaction, and criteria for gauging changes in the quality, magnitude, and complexity of people's relationships with their surroundings. Moreover, they suggest the value of incorporating previously separate constructs into cross-level models of transactional change, e.g., those that account for the micro- and meso-scale consequences of societal conditions; and those that track the influence of micro- and meso-scale events on qualities of community life. Finally, these constructs offer a set of interpretive lenses for anticipating, and possibly modifying, the impacts of major societal trends at individual, organizational, and community levels of human–environment transaction.

In the concluding section, we offer a set of conceptual strategies intended to facilitate the development of more comprehensive and robust analyses of transactional change, and effective interventions for managing change processes and outcomes.

Conceptual Strategies for Modeling and Managing Transactional Change

1. Delimit the contextual scope of transactional analyses. Efforts to model and manage transactional change require that the spatial, temporal, and sociocultural scope of a particular analysis be specified (cf., Stokols, 1987). The complexity of people–environment transactions, and the range of potential change processes to be considered, increase as analyses move from micro to meso, and from meso to macro, levels. Also, given that the relationships between people and their surroundings are continually in flux, the criteria for determining what constitutes a significant change process or an outcome of such change depends on the time interval specified for a particular analysis. Whether an analysis of transactional change is disaggregated by socioeconomic or cultural subgroups (or, alternatively, is assumed to apply uniformly to the entire population) has an important bearing on how changes in people–environment relationships are defined and measured. Macro-level changes in social capital, for example, can be defined and measured for the community as a whole or in relation to particular subgroups of the population. It is essential that researchers and change agents be clear at the outset about the contextual scope and boundaries of their analyses.

2. Clearly identify the transactional states, change processes and outcomes to be explained. A theoretical analysis or intervention program, to be feasible, must identify those aspects of human–environment transaction that will be examined most closely, and what indices of transactional change processes and outcomes will be given highest priority. At the micro level, for example, changes in perceived congruence for an individual might be designated as the focal issue, with self report measures of person-environment fit and stress outcomes receiving closest scrutiny by the researchers. At the meso-level, researchers may be more interested in identifying circumstances that influence the establishment, structural change, or termination of behavior settings (Wicker, 1987). Community planners, on the other hand, may be more interested in developing macro-scale guidelines for urban design that afford high levels of environmental legibility (Katz, 1995; Lynch, 1960).

The methods and measures used to assess different aspects of human-environment relationships, and the processes and outcomes of transactional change, must be tailored to the focal concerns and purposes of the study at hand. Because the qualities of people's connections to their environments are so diverse, it is unlikely that an all-encompassing metatheory of transactional change can be developed. More realistically, effective efforts to model and manage changes in people-environment relations will require a variety of theoretical formulations, each of which is uniquely suited to understanding the particular array of circumstances existing within a given category of situations or settings.

3. Develop cross-level models of transactional change.   Delimiting the contextual scope and focal concerns of an analysis does not preclude opportunities for incorporating constructs drawn from multiple levels into broader formulations of transactional change. Cross-level analyses will be of wider contextual scope than single-level theories, yet the former may afford greater parsimony and conceptual leverage for understanding certain aspects of people's relationships with their milieu. For instance, the most powerful leverage points for enhancing person-environment fit and reducing psychological stress may be located at the group or setting level, rather than at the micro scale of intervention. Reducing social conflict by establishing superordinate goals, improving organizational climate, or expanding the number of meaningful roles available to setting members are strategies that can enhance individuals' perception of person-environment fit and bolster their resistance to stress. Similarly, successful efforts to increase social capital at the community level may require meso-scale interventions, such as organizing a greater number and diversity of behavior settings in various parts of the community, reducing levels of conflict in community organizations, or creating defensible space in residential areas. As these examples suggest, efforts to model and manage transactional change can benefit from strategic integration of theoretical constructs spanning multiple levels of analysis.

4. Target high-impact transactions and change processes.   Both single- and multi-level analyses of transactional change become more powerful to the extent that they capture important qualities of human–environment transaction, and identify high impact strategies for promoting desirable change processes and outcomes (Stokols, 1996, in press). For example, organizational managers act as intermediaries of transactional change because they have the capacity to promote conflict or cooperation among group members, and to influence the emotional and physical well-being of many individuals by virtue of their administrative position and authority. Analyses that target key decisionmakers in organizations and communities, and suggest ways of ensuring that their actions will strengthen rather than undermine social cohesion, exemplify high impact models and change strategies.

Also, previous analyses of environment and behavior indicate that the settings and domains comprising an individual's overall life situation are associated with different levels of psychological importance, and that certain settings exert a disproportionate influence on the person's development and well-being (cf., Magnusson, 1981; Swindle & Moos, 1992). These assumptions are central to Proshansky's (1979) theory of place identity, and Wapner's (1981) analysis of how people establish environmental "anchor points" as a secure base of operations when they move to a new residential environment. High-leverage analyses of human–environment transactions and change processes focus on those settings and domains in people's lives that exert greatest impact on their behavior and well-being, and elucidate strategies for promoting and maintaining desirable transactional states in these salient life domains.

A stressful job, for example, can engender a variety of unhealthful coping behaviors in employees, such as smoking, alcohol abuse, and a sedentary lifestyle imposed by the demands of overtime work. Behavior–change strategies aimed at improving the individual's health habits (e.g., smoking cessation, substance abuse, joining a neighborhood fitness center) are likely to be ineffective unless sources of stress in the individual's work environment are eliminated or reduced. In this example, the occupational environment is identified as the most strategic target for change processes aimed at improving the individual's overall well-being.

5. Account for interdependencies between the physical and social features of environments. Transitory encounters with an unfamiliar environment reflect low levels of interdependence between occupants and the physical and social attributes of the place. On the other hand, long standing patterns of people–environment transaction that recur regularly in a familiar location are characterized by high levels of interdependence between individuals and the social, organizational, and physical features of the setting. In the context of more structured and enduring settings, the physical and social attributes of environments are closely intertwined, and jointly influence members' behavior and health outcomes.

In business environments, for instance, displaying physical symbols of corporate achievement, photographs of team members, and signage that reinforces employees' identification with the company exemplify changes in the physical environment whose ultimate purpose is to promote social outcomes—i.e., team cohesion and organizational effectiveness (cf., Ornstein, 1990; Steele, 1986; Wells, 1997). Similarly, in the context of residential neighborhoods, defensible space guidelines for environmental design are implemented to promote positive psychological and social outcomes, for example, enhanced sense of security and informal contacts among neighbors (Newman, 1973).

As noted earlier, however, certain conditions of the physical environment, such as high levels of vehicular traffic, substantially reduce the cohesiveness of urban neighborhoods (Appleyard, 1981). Furthermore, the disproportionate exposure of minority groups to environmental toxins and stressors can be traced to social-structural conditions in society—for instance, the racially discriminatory practices of regulatory officials and the neglect of these problems by more affluent groups in the community. Future analyses of transactional change will be strengthened to the extent that they address important linkages between the physical and social features of settings, organizations, and communities.

CONCLUSIONS

Accelerated rates of global environmental change, societal aging, and digital communications have heightened levels of contextual "turbulence" in recent years (Clitheroe et al., 1998; Emery & Trist, 1965; Stokols, 1999). In the face of these macro-system perturbations, it becomes all the more crucial to devise robust models of human–environment transaction and effective strategies for managing transactional change. We have reviewed several transactional constructs in an effort to identity *taxonomic criteria* for categorizing transactional states, change processes and outcomes; and *conceptual guidelines* for developing more integrative, cross-level analyses of transactional change. The proposed guidelines highlight important qualities of people-environment transaction and address interrelations among the physical and social features of certain situations and settings.

Our discussion of these issues has identified some potentially useful directions for future theory development and research. Subsequent analyses will need to address certain concerns that are beyond the purview of this chapter, including the role of fortuitous events in triggering unanticipated, unintended changes in people's relationships with their surroundings; and the theoretical and practical difficulties inherent in attempting to anticipate and prepare for these fortuitous events. We have not discussed the complex research design and measurement issues posed by the development of cross-level models of transactional change. Our principal goal is to identify taxonomic criteria and conceptual strategies as a foundation for constructing more comprehensive models of transactional change. We are hopeful this chapter will provide a useful, albeit preliminary, framework for future research on transactional change.

REFERENCES

Alexander, C., Ishikawa, S., Silverstein, M., Jacobson, M., Fiksdahl-King, I, & Angel, S. (1977). *A Pattern Language.* New York: Oxford University Press.

Altman, I. (1968). Choicepoints in the classification of scientific knowledge. In B. P. Indik & F. K. Berrien (Eds.), *People, groups, organizations* (pp. 47–69). New York: Columbia University Press.

Altman, I. (1975). *Environment and social behavior: Privacy, personal space, territory, and crowding.* Monterey, CA: Brooks/Cole.

Altman, L., & Rogoff, B. (1987). World views in psychology and environmental psychology: Trait, interactional, organismic, and transactional perspectives. In D. Stokols & I. Altman (Eds.), *Handbook of Environmental Psychology* (pp. 7–40). New York: Wiley.

Antonovsky, A. (1979). *Health, stress, and coping.* San Francisco: Jossey-Bass.

Appleyard, D. (1981). *Livable streets.* Berkeley: University of California Press.

Ashton, J., Grey, P., & Barnard, K. (1986). Healthy cities: WHO's New Public Health Initiative. *Health Promotion, 1,* 319–324.

Barker, R. G. (1968). *Ecological psychology: Concepts and methods for studying the environment of human behavior.* Stanford, CA: Stanford University Press.

Barker, R. G. (1978). *Habitats, environments, and human behavior.* San Francisco: Jossey-Bass.

Barker, R. G., & Schoggen, P. (1973). *Qualities of community life.* San Francisco: Jossey-Bass.

Baum, A., Fleming, R., & Davidson, L. M. (1983). Natural disaster and technological catastrophe. *Environment and Behavior, 15,* 333–354.

Baum, A., & Valins, S. (1977). *Architecture and social behavior: Psychological studies of social density.* Hillsdale, NJ: Lawrence Erlbaum Associates.

Bechtel, R. B. (1997). *Environment and behavior: An introduction.* Thousand Oaks, CA: Sage.

Blanchard, A. (1997). *Virtual behavior settings: An application of behavior setting theories to virtual communities.* The Center for Organizational and Behavioral Sciences, The Claremont Graduate University, Claremont, CA.

Blanchard, A., & Horan, T. (1998). Virtual communities and social capital. *Social Science Computer Review, 16,* 293-307.

Bradley, R. H., & Caldwell, B. M. (1976). Early home environment and changes in mental test performance in children from 6 to 36 months. *Developmental Psychology, 12,* 93-97.

Bronfenbrenner, U. (1979). *The ecology of human development.* Cambridge, MA: Harvard University Press.

Bronfenbrenner, U. (1992). Ecological systems theory. In R. Vasta (Ed.), *Six theories of child development: Revised formulations and current issues* (pp. 187-249). London: Jessica Kingsley Publishers.

Bullard, R. D. (1990). *Dumping in Dixie: Race, class, and environmental quality.* Boulder, CO: Westview Press.

Calthorpe, P. (1993). *The next American metropolis: Ecology, community, and the American Dream.* New York: Princeton Architectural Press.

Caplan, R. D., & Harrison, R. V. (1993). Person-environment fit theory: Some history, recent developments, and future directions. *Journal of Social Issues, 49,* 253-275.

Carr, S., Francis, M., Rivlin, L. G., & Stone, A. M. (1992). *Public space.* New York: Cambridge University Press.

Chapin, F. S., Jr. (1974). *Human activity patterns in the city: Things people do in time and in space.* New York: Wiley.

Clark Atlanta University Environmental Justice Resource Center (1998). *Foundations of environmental justice.* [On-line] Available: Http://www.ejrc.cau.edu/ejrc.

Clitheroe, H. C., Jr., Stokols, D., & Zmuidzinas, M. (1998). Conceptualizing the context of environment and behavior. *Journal of Environmental Psychology, 18,* 103-112.

Cohen, S. (1980). Aftereffects of stress on human performance and social behavior: A review of research and theory. *Psychological Bulletin, 88,* 82-108.

Cohen, S., Evans, G. W., Stokols, D., & Krantz, D. S. (1986). *Behavior, health, and environmental stress.* New York: Plenum.

Cooper, C. (1974). The house as symbol of the self. In J. Lang, C. Burnette, W. Moleski, & D. Vachon (Eds.), *Designing for human behavior* (130-146). Stroudsburg, PA: Dowden, Hutchinson & Ross.

Craik, K. H. (1973). Environmental psychology. *Annual Review of Psychology, 24,* 403-422.

Craik, K. H. (1977). Multiple scientific paradigms in environmental psychology. *International Journal of Psychology, 12,* 26-31.

Dohrenwend, B. S., & Dohrenwend, B. P. (1974). *Stressful life events: Their nature and effects.* New York: Wiley.

Duany, A., & Plater-Zyberk, E. (1991). *Town and town-making principles.* New York: Rizzoli.

Emery, F. E., & Trist, E. L. (1965) The causal texture of organizational environments. *Human Relations, 18,* 21-32.

Evans, G. W. (Ed.) (1982). *Environmental stress.* NY: Cambridge University Press.

Evans, G. W., Bullinger, M., & Hygee, S. (1998). Chronic noise exposure and physiological response: A prospective study of children living under environmental stress. *Psychological Science, 9,* 75-77.

Everett, P. B., Hayward, S., & Meyers, A. W. (1974). The effects of a token reinforcement procedure on bus ridership. *Journal of Applied Behavioral Analysis, 7,* 1-10.

Festinger, L., Schachter, S., & Back, K. (1950). *Social pressures in informal groups.* NY: Harper.

Fried, M. (1963). Grieving for a lost home. In L. Duhl (Ed.), *The urban condition* (pp. 151-171). New York: Simon & Schuster.

Gardner, G. T., & Stern, P. C. (1996). Environmental problems and human behavior. Boston, MA: Allyn & Bacon.

Geller, E. S. (1991). Where's the validity in social validity? Journal of Applied Behavior Analysis, 24, 189-204.

Geller, E. S., Winett, R. A., & Everett, P. B. (1982). Preserving the environment: New strategies for behavior change. New York: Pergamon.

Glass, D. C., & Singer, J. E. (1972). Urban stress. New York: Academic Press.

Holmes, T. H., & Rahe, R. H. (1967). The Social Readjustment Rating Scale. Journal of Psychosomatic Research, 11, 213-218.

Ittelson, W. H., Proshansky, H. M., Rivlin, L. G., & Winkel, G. H. (1974). An introduction to environmental psychology. New York: Holt, Rinehart, & Winston.

Katz, P. (1995). The new urbanism: Toward an architecture of community. New York: McGraw-Hill.

Kohn, M. L., & Schooler, C. (1982). Job conditions and personality: A longitudinal assessment of their reciprocal effects. American Journal of Sociology, 87, 1257-1286.

Kraut, R., Patterson, M., Lundmark, V., Kiesler, S., Mukopadhyay, T., & Scherlis, W. (1998). Internet paradox: A social technology that reduces social involvement and psychological well-being? American Psychologist, 53, 1017-1031.

Lawton, M. P., & Nahemow, L. (1973). Ecology and the aging process. In E. Eisdorfer & M. P. Lawton (Eds.), Psychology of adult development and aging. Washington, DC: American Psychological Association, 619-674.

Lazarus, R. S. (1966). Psychological stress and the coping process. New York: McGraw-Hill.

Lazarus, R. S., & Launier, R. (1978). Stress-related transactions between person and environment. In L. A. Pervin & M. Lewis (Eds.), Internal and external determinants of behavior (pp. 287-327). New York: Plenum.

Lewin, K. (1936) Principles of topological psychology. (F. & G. Heider, Trans.). New York: McGraw-Hill.

Little, B. (1983). Personal projects: A rationale and method for investigation. Environment and Behavior, 15, 273-309.

Lynch, K. (1960). The image of the city. Cambridge, MA: MIT Press.

MacCorquodale, K., & Meehl, P. E. (1948). On a distinction between hypothetical constructs and intervening variables. Psychological Review, 55, 95-107.

Magnusson, D. (1981). Wanted: A psychology of situations. In D. Magnusson (Ed.), Toward a psychology of situations: An interactional perspective. Hillsdale, NJ: Lawrence Erlbaum Associates.

Maruyama, M. (1963) The second cybernetics: Deviation-amplifying mutual causal process. American Scientist, 51,164-179.

Meyrowitz, J. (1985). No sense of place: The impact of electronic media on social behavior. New York: Oxford University Press.

Michelson, W. H. (1985). From sun to sun: Daily obligations and community structure in the lives of employed women and their families. Totowa, NJ: Rowman & Allenheld.

Michelson, W. H. (1976). Man and his urban environment: A sociological approach. 2nd ed. Reading, MA: Addison-Wesley.

Milgram, S. (1970). The experience of living in cities. Science, 167, 1461-1468.

Milgram, S., & Jodelet, D. (1976). Psychological maps of Paris. In H. M. Proshansky, W. H. Ittelson, & L. G. Rivlin (Eds.), Environmental psychology. 2nd ed., (pp. 104-124). New York: Holt, Rinehart, & Winston.

Mitchell, W. J. (1995). The city of bits: Space, place, and the infobahn. Cambridge, MA: MIT Press.

Moos, R. H. (1976). The human context. New York: Wiley.

STOKOLS, CLITHEROE, ZMUIDZINAS

Nasar, J. L., & Fisher, B. (1993). "Hot spots" of fear and crime: A multi-method investigation. *Journal of Environmental Psychology, 13,* 187–206.

Negroponte, N. (1996). *Being digital.* New York: Vintage Books.

Newman, O. (1973). *Defensible space: Crime prevention through urban design.* New York: Macmillan.

Noam, E. (1995). Electronics and the dim future of the university. *Science, 270,* 247–249.

Ornstein, S. (1990). Linking environmental and industrial/organizational psychology. In C. L. Cooper & I. T. Robertson (Eds.), *International Review of Industrial and Organizational Psychology, Volume 5* (pp. 195–228). Chichester, England: Wiley.

Pastalan, L. (1980 September). Relocation, mortality, and intervention. Paper presented at the Annual Convention of the American Psychological Association.

Perkins, D. D., Wandersman, A., Rich, R. C., & Taylor, R. B. (1993). The physical environment of street crime: Defensible space, territoriality, and incivilities. *Journal of Environmental Psychology, 13,* 29–49.

Platt, J. (1973). Social traps. *American Psychologist, 28,* 641–651.

Price, R. H., & Blashfield, R. K. (1975). Explorations in the taxonomy of behavior settings: Analyses of dimensions and classifications of settings. *American Journal of Community Psychology, 3,* 335–351.

Prochaska, J. O., & DiClemente, C. C. (1986). Toward a comprehensive model of change. In W. R. Millner, & N. Heather, (Eds.), *Treating addictive behaviors: Processes of change* (pp. 3–27). New York: Plenum.

Proshansky, H. M. (1978). The city and self-identity. *Environment and Behavior, 10,* 147–169.

Proshansky, H. M., Fabian, A. K., & Kaminoff, R. (1983). Place Identity: Physical world socialization of the self. *Journal of Environmental Psychology, 3,* 57–83.

Proshansky, H. M., Ittelson, W. H., & Rivlin, L. (Eds.), (1976). *Environmental psychology: People and their physical settings.* (2nd ed.). New York: Holt, Rinehart, & Winston.

Putnam, P. D. (1995). Bowling alone: America's declining social capital. *Journal of Democracy, 6,* 65–78.

Roethlisberger, F., & Dickson, W. (1939). *Management and the worker.* Cambridge, MA: Harvard University Press.

Saegert, S. (1987). Environmental psychology and social change. In D. Stokols & I. Altman (Eds.), *Handbook of environmental psychology, Volume 1* (pp. 99–128). New York: Wiley.

Seligman, M. E. P. (1975). *Helplessness: On depression, development, and death.* San Francisco: W. H. Freeman.

Seyle, H. (1956) *The stress of life.* New York: McGraw Hill.

Sherif, M. (1958). Superordinate goals in the reduction of intergroup conflicts. *American Journal of Sociology, 63,* 349–356.

Shulz, R., & Hanusa, B. H. (1978). Long-term effects of control and predictability-enhancing interventions: Findings and ethical issues. *Journal of Personality and Social Psychology, 36,* 1194–1201.

Silver, C., & DeFries, R. (1990). *One earth, one future: Our changing global environment.* Washington, DC: National Academy of Sciences.

Sommer, R. (1983). *Social design: Creating buildings with people in mind.* Englewood Cliffs, NJ: Prentice Hall.

Spence, K. W. (1944). The nature of theory construction in contemporary psychology. *Psychological Review, 51,* 47–68.

Steele, F. I. (1986). *Making and Managing High-Quality Workplaces: An Organizational Ecology.* London: Teacher's College Press.

Stern, P. C. (1992). Psychological dimensions of global environmental change. *Annual Review of Psychology, 43,* 269–302.

Stokols, D. (1978). Environmental psychology. In M. R. Rosenzweig & L. W. Porter (Eds.), *Annual Review of Psychology*. Palo Alto, CA: Annual Reviews, 29, 253–295.

Stokols, D. (1979). A congruence analysis of human stress. In I. G. Sarason & C. D. Spielberger (Eds.), *Stress and anxiety*, Vol. 6 (pp. 27–53). New York: Wiley.

Stokols, D. (1981). Group x place transactions: Some neglected issues in psychological research on settings. In D. Magnusson (Ed.), *Toward a psychology of situations: An interactional perspective*. Hillsdale, NJ: Lawrence Erlbaum Associates, 393–415.

Stokols, D. (1983). Editor's introduction: Theoretical directions of environment and behavior research. *Environment and Behavior, 15*, 259–272.

Stokols, D. (1987). Conceptual strategies of environmental psychology. In D. Stokols and I. Altman (Eds.), *Handbook of environmental psychology* (pp. 41–70). New York: Wiley.

Stokols, D. (1988). Transformational processes in people-environment relations. In J. E. McGrath (Ed.), *The social psychology of time* (pp. 233 252). Beverly Hills, CA: Sage.

Stokols, D. (1990). Instrumental and spiritual views of people–environment relations. *American Psychologist, 45*, 641–646.

Stokols, D. (1992). Conflict-prone and conflict-resistant organizations. In H. Friedman (Ed.), *Hostility, coping, and health*. Washington, DC: American Psychological Association, 65–76.

Stokols, D. (1995). The paradox of environmental psychology. *American Psychologist, 50*, 821–837.

Stokols, D. (1996). Translating social ecological theory into guidelines for community health promotion. *American Journal of Health Promotion, 10*, 282–298.

Stokols, D. (1999). Human development in the age of the internet: Conceptual and methodological horizons. In S. L. Friedman & T. D. Wachs (Eds.), *Measuring environment across the lifespan: Emerging metkhods and concepts* (pp. 327–356). Washington, DC: American Psychological Association.

Stokols, D. (in press). Theory development in environmental psychology: A prospective view. In S. Wapner, J. Demick, H. Minami, & T. Yamamoto (Eds.), *Theoretical perspectives in environment-behavior research: Underlying assumptions, research problems, and methodologies*. New York: Plenum.

Stokols, D., & Jacobi, M. (1984). Traditional, present-oriented, and futuristic modes of group-environment relations. In K. J. Gergen & M. M. Gergen (Eds.), *Historical social psychology* (pp. 303–324). Hillsdale, NJ: Lawrence Erlbaum Associates.

Stokols, D., & Shumaker, S. (1981). People in places: A transactional view of settings. In J. Harvey (Ed.), *Cognition, social behavior and the environment* (pp. 441– 488). Hillsdale, NJ: Lawrence Erlbaum Associates.

Swindle, R. W., Jr., & Moos, R. H. (1992). Life domains in stressors, coping, and adjustment. In W. B. Walsh, K. H. Craik, & R. H. Price (Eds.), *Person-environment psychology: Models and perspectives* (pp. 1–33). Hillsdale, NJ: Lawrence Erlbaum Associates.

Taylor, R. B. (1988). *Human territorial functioning*. New York: Cambridge University Press.

Thietart, R. A., & Forgues, B. (1995). Chaos theory and organization. *Organization Science, 6*, 19–31.

University of Michigan Environmental Justice Resource Center (1998). *Background: The problem of disproportionate burdens*. [Online]. Available: Http://www.umich.edu/~snre492/index.html.

U.S. Department of Commerce (1995). *Falling through the net: A survey of the "have nots" in rural and urban America*. [Online]. Available: Http://www.ntia.doc.gov/ntiahome/fallingthru.html.

Wachs, T. D., & Gruen, G. (1982). *Early experience and human development*. New York: Plenum.

Walsh, W. B., Price, R. H., & Craik, K. H. (1992). Person–environment psychology: An introduction. In W. B. Walsh, K. H. Craik, & R. H. Price (Eds.), *Person–environment psychology: Models and perspectives* (pp. 243–269). Hillsdale, NJ: Lawrence Erlbaum Associates.

Wapner, S. (1987). A holistic, developmental, systems-oriented environmental psychology: Some beginnings. In D. Stokols & I. Altman (Eds.), Handbook of environmental psychology, Volume 2 (pp. 1433–1465). New York: Wiley.

Wapner, S. (1981). Transactions of persons-in-environments: Some critical transitions. *Journal of Environmental Psychology*, 1, 223–239.

Weisman, G. D. (1983). Environmental programming and action research. *Environment and Behavior*, 15, 381–408.

Wells, M. (1997). *Personalization of workspace and employee well-being.* Unpublished doctoral dissertation, School of Social Ecology, University of California, Irvine.

Wicker, A. W. (1987). Behavior settings reconsidered: Temporal stages, resources, internal dynamics, context. In D. Stokols & I. Altman (Eds.), *Handbook of Environmental Psychology, Volume 1* (pp. 613–653). New York: Wiley.

Wicker, A. W. (1972). Processes which mediate behavior–environment congruence. *Behavioral Science*, 17, 265–277.

Wicker, A. W. (1969). Size of church membership and members' support of church behavior settings. *Journal of Personality and Social Psychology*, 13, 278–288.

Wicker, A. W., McGrath, J. E., & Armstrong, G. E. (1972). Organization size and behavior setting capacity as determinants of member participation. *Behavioral Science*, 17, 499–513.

Willems, E. P. (1967). Sense of obligation to high school activities as related to school size and marginality of student. *Child Development*, 38, 1247–1260.

Winett, R. A., Moore, J. F., & Anderson, E. S. (1991). Extending the concept of social validity: Behavior analysis for disease prevention and health promotion. *Journal of Applied Behavior Analysis*, 24, 215–230.

Wirth, L. (1938). Urbanism and the American way of life. *American Journal of Sociology*, 44, 1–24.

Wohlwill, J. F., & Heft, H. (1987). The physical environment and the development of the child. In D. Stokols & I. Altman (Eds.), *Handbook of Environmental Psychology*, 281–328. New York: Wiley.

10

Person–Environment Psychology: A Summary and Commentary

W. Bruce Walsh, PhD
The Ohio State University

Kenneth H. Craik
University of California, Berkeley

Richard H. Price
University of Michigan

The chapters in this volume, by major contributors to the field, provide readers with an excellent opportunity to catch up on important theoretical developments. The authors address the question of how best to formulate and examine relationships between people and their everyday environments. This question is central to the fields of environmental, personality, clinical, counseling, industrial, and social psychology, and indeed, provides a basis for promoting integration among these fields.

The fact that each of these influential authors are working on the general theoretical problem, affords an exceptional opportunity to gauge the extent that a resolution of the problem can be discerned. In this summary and commentary, it seems relevant and sensible to address these comparative issues: Are the models of person–environment relations different, and if so, what are their distinctive elements? And, what are the implications of system concepts for person–environment psychology?

MODELS OF PERSON-ENVIRONMENT RELATIONS: DIVERGENCES

In this chapter, we focus on the differences among the person-environment models. The different theories are compared and contrasted on a number of dimensions.

Reinforcement

As in our first book (Walsh, Craik, & Price, 1992), we have found the relative importance of reward or reinforcement as a determinant of behavior is emphasized explicitly in some of the models and implicitly in others. The so-called "law of effect" states that only those responses that are accompanied by a reward or the experience of pleasure, or satisfaction will be retained or learned. Hogan and Roberts (chap. 1) along with Holland (Walsh & Holland, 1992) support the well documented view that people choose activities and interactions that are consistent with their identities and avoid activities and interactions that are discordant or incongruent with their identities. Stated differently, as noted by Holland, *complementary*, or *congruent person-environment links* are viewed as reinforcing and satisfying. Uncomplimentary person-environment links are thought to be punishing and contribute to change. Individual's past choice of situations predicts future involvement in those situations. There is substantial evidence indicating that reinforced preferences for situations, as assessed with interest measures, predict occupational membership, occupational tenure, occupational change, and college major choice. Hogan and Roberts noted that these preferences are extraordinarily stable over time, and the reason is that people choose, define, and specialize particular types of situations depending on their identities, and identities are quite stable over time.

A well known model of person-environment congruence proposed by Lawton (1989) states that a match between personal competence and environmental demand is likely to result in favorable behavioral and affect outcomes. When environmental demands are either too high or too low for an individual's level of competence, maladaptive behavior and negative affect are likely to result. Moos (1997) has extended Lawton's model to apply to psychiatric treatment and to other client populations in residential settings. Timko, Moos, and Finney (chap. 6) state that high environmental demands should have more positive consequences for clients who are functioning well than for those who are functioning poorly, whereas environmental resources and support should have more benefit for poorly functioning clients. Specifically, a self-directed treatment climate with high performance expectations and relatively little structure, should have the most benefit for functionally able clients that find this environment to be rewarding. In contrast, more disturbed clients often find high performance expectations and self-direction to be disruptive, and need more support and structure to have a rewarding experience.

Schneider, Smith, and Goldstein (chap. 3) suggested that people are attracted to organizations with characteristics that match their own personalities. The match is viewed as being rewarding, satisfying, and instrumental in attaining highly valued outcomes. There is also evidence that people are likely to leave organizations that do not fit or match their personalities. These authors believe that environments or organizations consciously select and promote individuals who tend to resemble the personality attributes of the dominant coalition in the culture.

According to Little (chap. 4), human well-being is postulated as being influenced by stable aspects of the person, such as trait and temperamental variables, and stable aspects of the environmental context. For example, well-being is influenced directly by *extraversion* (positively) and *neuroticism* (negatively), in part because these stable traits are strongly associated with the experience of positive and negative affect. Extraverts characteristically seek out situations that are stimulating and therefore, congruent with their needs, and lead to enhanced well-being and reinforcement. The direct effect of environmental variables on well-being is also well established. Stressful environments affect well-being and tend to extract psychological costs even during adaptation. In his theoretical framework Little (chap. 4) focused on a unit of analysis termed *personal projects*. Personal projects are influenced by personal and contextual variables in dynamic interaction. The completion of personal projects tends to contribute to adaptation and well-being and a pervasive sense of reinforcement.

Wapner and Demick (chap. 2) viewed *reinforcement* as one of many processes underlying change in the balanced status of the person-in-environment system. Because their focus on change is characterized developmentally (e.g., a developmentally advanced person-in-environment system state is described as differentiated and hierarchically integrated), they are concerned with processes that underlie the achievement of that state. Wapner and Demick believe reinforcement is one of a number of processes that probably contribute to achieving that outcome. Stated differently, optimal development involves a differentiated, hierarchically integrated person-in-environment system with flexibility, freedom, self mastery, and the capacity to shift from one mode of person-in-environment relationship to another, as required by goals, demands of the situation, and the instrumentalities available. Reinforcement appears to be a meaningful concept in facilitating this process.

Wicker and August (chap. 7) suggested that in the pursuit of major life goals, *cause maps* (cognitive structures) lead to sense making cycles (sensing, interpreting, and acting) that reduce uncertainty about environmental events. Wicker and August implicitly suggested that reduction in uncertainty about environmental events will reinforce the sense-making process and influence behavior and the interpretation of environmental events.

Craik, (chap. 8), similar to Little (chap. 4), Pervin (1992), and Wicker and August (chap. 7) noted that the individual's goals, projects, pursuits, striving, and tasks are relevant in analyzing the act–episodes of a lived day for an individual. Implicitly, Craik suggested that the pursuit of goals and projects is self reinforcing in terms of the process and long term rewarding in terms of the eventual outcome. Similar to Pervin (1992), Craik assumed that specific goal directed activities are terminated when the goal is achieved to a satisfactory extent, when achievement does not seem realistic, or through some kind of disruption of the person–environment process.

Nasar (chap. 5) noted that research has identified 6 kinds of environmental attributes as relating to preference (arousal): *order, moderate complexity, naturalness, upkeep, openness,* and *historical significance*. Liked areas tend to have these attributes; disliked areas have their opposites: disorder, low or high complexity, obtrusive manmade use, dilapidation, restriction, and the absence of historical significance. Liked areas tend to have perceived attributes that are reinforcing, whereas disliked areas do not.

Genetic Factors and the Environment

The role of heredity and environmental factors in individual functioning has long been an issue of debate. A substantive body of research over the years has indicated that individual functioning is determined to some extent by inherited factors. This work has been carried out in the areas of intelligence, schizophrenia, depression, temperament, altruism, and aggressiveness. Magnusson and Törestad (1992) point out that, within the limits set by inherited factors, there are large potentialities for change, due to the interaction with environmental factors. These authors and others (Angoff, 1988) noted that an inherited predisposition for a certain type of behavior does not mean that it cannot be changed by environmental factors.

In this context, Wapner and Demick (chap. 2) strongly reject biological reductionism that assumes functioning is determined completely by the biological structure and state of functioning of the organism. Wapner and Demick take the position that differing levels of integration must be considered in any analysis of psychological functioning. The assumption that an individual functions at multiple levels of integration means that both genetic and environmental factors must be taken into account. Nasar (chap. 5) suggested that personality predisposition may well effect evaluative responses to the environment and implicitly suggests a genetic component. Nasar suggested that nature and nurture determine individual functioning and that genetic factors demonstrate large potential for change due to the interaction with environmental factors. Little (chap. 4) suggested that at one level individuals are characterized by relatively fixed traits or natural inclinations. By natural Little referred to behavior strongly rooted in temperamental characteristics or in traits with a genetically linked biological base. For example, Little and others (Eysenck, 1987) suggested that individuals differ in the biological disposition of extraversion. Hogan and Roberts (chap. 1), in the context of socioanalytic theory, indicated that people are primarily motivated by a small number of unconscious biological needs. Our history has suggested that the need for social acceptance, status, predictability, and meaning enhance our chances for survival and reproductive success. The remaining theorists (Craik (chap. 8); Schneider, Smith, & Goldstein (chap. 3); Timko, Moos, & Finney (chap. 6); Wicker & August (chap. 7)) similar to Wicker (1992), Swindle and Moos (1992), Peterson (1992), and Altman et al. (1992) in our first volume, placed little emphasis on genetic factors. In summary, Wapner, and Demick and Nasar, suggested that nature and nurture determine individual functioning, and genetic factors demonstrate large potential for change. Little, and Hogan and Roberts, indicated that genetic factors, although susceptible to environmental influence, are central to individual functioning.

Prediction in Person–Environment Psychology

Several chapters have again raised the prospect that adequate person–environment models will require abandonment of the goal of prediction in person–environment psychology. Different models seem to take quite different approaches to this issue. There continues to be a questioning of positivist assumptions that, in the past, were accepted almost without question. Wicker and August (chap. 7) follow a naturalistic research strategy called *substantive theorizing* that entails close, empirically grounded scrutiny of assumptions, concepts, and propositions. The term *theorizing* is used to stress that theory building is an evolving, continually developing process. The empirical focus of Wicker and August is on the work lives of ordinary people, as revealed in their personal accounts. A primary aim is to acquire a detailed, idiographic understanding and communicate that understanding. Prediction and control are viewed as unlikely, secondary outcomes of the research. Research designs and measures are not determined prior to the researcher's exposure to a life domain. Instead, they are formulated as the researcher encounters the events to be understood. Wicker and August noted that in substantive theorizing, conceptual and theoretical development is regarded as a continually evolving process, and qualitative research methods are frequently used because of their flexibility and sensitivity.

A primary aim for Craik (chap. 8) is to acquire a detailed, idiographic understanding of the lived day of an individual in the context of behavior settings, goals and pursuits, and trait concepts. Stated differently, Craik is concerned with what happened in an individual's lived day; who knew about the events of the individual's day; what impact the events of the day had on the individual; and how long the representation of the individual's lived day persists. The descriptive task is to secure a comprehensive record using video research techniques and then analyze this record using behavior setting, goal, and trait concepts.

Little's (chap. 4) social ecological perspective shows the importance of completing personal projects in explaining and predicting human well-being and adaptation. The completion of personal projects, according to Little, may contribute to adaptation and well-being. More specifically, free traits and personal contexts (restorative niches) facilitate the pursuit of personal projects and a sense of adaptation and well-being. In terms of assessment methods, Little uses narrative sketches and videotapes. The videotape technique provides a record of what actually goes on in a daily life, the narrative sketch technique provides a person's construal of the significance of context in the life story, and merging these two techniques forms what Little called *idio-tape analysis*. In idio-tape, analysis individuals are asked to write down the images and scenes of objects that they feel are important to understanding their lives. After respondents generate a set of images, they are asked to comment on the significance of each image with respect to the quality of their lives and general well-being.

Wapner and Demick (chap. 2) see advantages and limitations to the natural science approach and the human science approach. The natural science approach is focused on observable behavior and explanation in terms of cause-effect relations and scientific experimentation is the appropriate methodology. In contrast, the human science perspective specifies as its goal the understanding of experience, or the explication of structural relationships, pattern, or organization that specifies meaning. The human science approach carries out qualitative analysis through naturalistic observation, and empirical, phenomenological methods. Wapner and Demick noted that although the natural science approach may be characterized by precision and reliability, it may suffer from lack of validity. In contrast, the human science approach may be characterized by validity, it may suffer from lack of precision and reliability. Thus, the authors concluded that both these approaches to understanding complement each other and both need to be fostered. In their view holistic, ecologically oriented research is a necessary complement to more traditional laboratory work.

The remaining authors presented models consistent with the positivist paradigm. They suggested the tangible world can be understood, and to some extent controlled, by seeking to discover causal relations with research designs and measures that are determined prior to the researcher's exposure to a life domain. For example, the Timko, Moos, and Finney (chap. 6) model matches the client's level of functioning (in the cognitive, psychological, and social domains), with the treatment programs' levels of support, performance demands, and structure. Moos predicted that as clients' cognitive and psychosocial skills improve, they will be able to cope in more demanding, less structured settings. Moos further predicts that supportive relationships may moderate the potentially problematic consequences of interpersonally stimulating and performance oriented environments.

The central proposition of Attraction-Selection-Attrition theory (Schneider, Smith, and Goldstein, chap. 3) is the prediction that organizations tend toward homogeneity of personality. The consequences of the predicted homogeneity and the boundary conditions where homogeneity is a positive or negative force for organizational effectiveness remain empirical questions. These authors hypothesized that later in an organization's life cycle good person-environment fit may have negative consequences. However, early in an organization's life cycle, good person-environment fit may yield the harmony and cooperation required for early effectiveness.

Hogan and Roberts (chap. 1) suggested that *identity* (personality from the actor's perspective) translates into *reputation* (personality from the observer's perspective) because each identity dictates a certain self-presentational style and lifestyle. For example, helping the poor supports an altruistic identity; driving an exotic car supports a sporty identity; and publishing scholarly articles supports an intellectual identity. Thus, Hogan and Roberts use reputation to predict other's behavior and use identity to explain it. However, they are careful to note that within each individual the two aspects of personality are related. People use their identities to decide whether and how they will interact with others, and how they interact with others creates their reputations.

Nasar suggested that the perceived visual quality of our surroundings has important impacts on human experience and behavior. It can evoke strong emotions like delight or fear, act as a stressor, and lead us to make inferences about places and people. It may also influence our behavior, leading us to avoid or go to certain places. Thus, he would suggest that our perceptions of physical environments tend to influence our behavior. He further noted that perceived visual quality arises from the person, the environment, and the ongoing interaction between the two. It may vary with biology, personality, social cultural experience, goals, expectations, internal, and external factors.

In summary, Wicker and August, Craik, Little, and to some extent, Wapner and Demick (similar to Wicker, Altman et al., Pervin, Magnusson and Törestad in our first volume) imply that the interpretive approach to here-and-now naturalistic studies of human behavior, in context, suggests a perspective for inquiry that calls in question the relevance of a singular focus on prediction. These authors have suggested that in interpretive, here-and-now naturalistic studies of human conduct, the goal of prediction presumably loses some of its importance.

Concept of the Person

The theories vary considerably in their conceptualization of the person. The Attraction- Selection-Attrition model (Schnieder, 1987) assumed an extreme, person-based position on the nature of organizational behavior, a position that emphasizes the *attributes* (traits) of people as the defining characteristic of an organization and the fundamental determinants of organizational behavior. Thus, Schnieder, Smith, and Goldstein (chap. 3) viewed the person in terms of *traits*. Based on these personal traits, competencies, interests, and values individuals tend to actively and purposefully seek environments that complement and reinforce their personal trait makeup.

Timko, Moos, and Finney (chap. 6) conceived of the individual in terms of cognitive, psychological, and social domains. They are primarily concerned with the client's level of functioning in these domains. These authors suggested along with Lawton (1989) that a match between *personal competence* (traits) and *environmental demand* is likely to result in favorable behavioral and affective outcomes. When environmental demands are either too high or too low for an individual's level of competence, maladaptive behavior and negative affect are likely to result.

In Nasar's model (chap. 5), the personal dispositions of those forming perceptions of the environment are key elements, and personality predisposition tends to influence evaluative responses to the environment. More specifically, perceived visual quality of environments (linking personality predispositions and their physical environment), facilitate an evaluative image that influences meaning and behavior. Other characteristics of individuals, such as culture, internal state, and purpose, may affect perceived evaluative responses.

Wapner and Demick (chap. 2) defined the person aspect of the person-in-environment system with respect to levels of integration, and so assume that the person is comprised of mutually defining biological–physical (e.g., health), psychological–intrapersonal (e.g., self-esteem), and social–cultural (e.g., role at work, family member) aspects. They further regard individuals as active, striving, purposeful, goal oriented agents, capable of spontaneously structuring, shaping, and construing their environments in various ways, and acting from their own experience.

Hogan and Roberts (chap. 1) conceived of individuals in terms of their identities and their reputations. Identities tell us how people want to be perceived by their motives, goals, and values. Reputations tell us how people are perceived and predict how they may behave. For example, being seen as helping the poor (reputation) supports an altruistic identity.

Wicker and August (chap. 7) introduced the concepts of *cause maps* and *major life pursuits* for the occupants of behavior settings. The person is analyzed in terms of major life goals. The pursuit of a major life goal is a person-initiated sense making process that extends over time and place operationalized through cause maps. Cause maps (cognitive structures) lead to sense-making cycles (sensing, interpreting, acting) that reduce uncertainty about environmental events.

Little (chap. 4) suggested that at one level individuals are characterized by relatively fixed traits suggesting that human behavior may be ordered and measured along dimensions of defined traits. But at another level people act on the basis of what he calls *free traits*. Free traits are culturally scripted patterns of conduct that are carried out as part of a person's project and commitments independently of that person's natural inclinations (fixed traits). Little's person concept then includes fixed traits and free traits in pursuing important questions about human well-being.

In the Craik model (chap. 8), the person is analyzed in terms of *major* as well as *quotidian goals* (the inside perspective) and *traits* (the outside perspective). As with Wicker, Pervin and Little, the pursuit of goals is a person initiated sense making process that extends over time and place. As with Hogan and Roberts, Craik also conceived of a person in terms of trait concepts as elements of a person's reputation. His belief is that the individual's behavior can be ordered and assessed along trait categories (Buss & Craik, 1983).

In summary, Schneider et al., Timko et al., and Nasar view the person in terms of personality attributes, personal competencies, and personality predispositions. Wapner et al., Hogan et al., Wicker et al., and Little and Craik, in whole or in part, all conceptualize the person in terms of life goals (motives, values, projects, pursuits, major life goals). Thus, the two major themes emerging are traits and life goals.

Measurement of the Person

The theories offered in this volume use a variety of methods to operationalize their concepts of *the person*. Schneider, Smith, and Goldstein (chap. 3) conceived of the individual in terms of their defined traits. They believe that human behavior may be ordered and measured along dimensions of defined traits and factors. Thus, the individual is operationally defined by responses to traditional inventories of personality, interests, values, and competencies. They would suggest individuals tend to move toward environments or organizations that they perceive to have trait compositions similar to their own.

Timko, Moos, and Finney (chap. 6) conceived of the individual in terms of the cognitive, psychological, and social domains. Operationally, they are concerned about the person's level of functioning in these domains. The authors do not comment, but one may assume that these traits may be assessed in a variety of different ways. For example, intelligence tests, personality inventories, and social support inventories would seem to be appropriate. It is most important in the assessment to determine the client's level of cognitive, psychological, and social functioning and how that functioning may appropriately fit into different residential treatment facilities.

Little (chap. 4) believes there are strong links between personality traits and well-being. To operationally define his person concepts of fixed traits and free traits he uses the Five-Factor model of personality. These are neuroticism, extraversion, openness to experience, agreeableness, and conscientiousness (John, 1990). Little suggested the prediction, understanding, and promotion of well-being is enhanced by the use of the Big Five factors as fixed and free traits influenced by contextual factors in the pursuit of personal projects and goals. The Big Five factors can be assessed using observer-based trait ratings and various self report inventories, such as the NEO Personality Inventory (John, 1990; Costa & McCrae, 1992).

For Hogan and Roberts (chap. 1), *identity* and *reputation* are central to the concept of the person. The identity concept is operationally defined by means of self stories or stories actors tell about themselves regarding their motives, goals, and values. Hogan and Roberts noted that these self stories are idealized self images or identities. They are unique to each individual, and as a result, are hard to measure. Reputations are operationally defined in terms of the Five-Factor model of personality. The Five-Factor model can serve to profile reputation in terms of extraversion (self confidence), adjustment (social impact), agreeableness (charm), conscientiousness (trustworthiness), and intellectual openness (intellectual talent). The Big Five factors can be assessed by use of observer-based trait ratings and various self-report inventories, such as the NEO Personality Inventory (John, 1990; Costa & McCrae, 1992). As noted here, reputations tell us how individuals are perceived and predict how they are likely to behave.

In the Nasar model (chap. 5), people are operationally defined by their predispositions. According to Nasar, our personality and environmental predispositions tend to influence our perceptions (evaluative images) and may be operationally defined by the Big Five factors of personality, the Environmental Response Inventory (ERI) (McKechnie, 1977) and scales of the Myers Briggs Type Indicator (MBTI); (Myers & McCaulley, 1985; Myers, 1987). The MBTI may be scored for four pairs of scales: extraversion versus introversion, sensing versus intuition, thinking versus feeling, and judgment versus perception.

Wicker and August (chap. 7) conceived of the person in terms of major life goals (pursuits). The pursuit of a major life goal is a sense making process operationalized by cause maps. Cause maps and sense making cycles reduce uncertainty about environmental events. To learn about individual cause maps and sense making cycles, Wicker and August have used informal, context bound interviews, observations, personal accounts and other information. This qualitative, idiographic definition of the person has proved informative about people's actions and interpretations of environmental events.

In analyzing a person's lived day Craik (chap. 8) suggested a person's major life goals and traits are significant. Goals and traits are central to the concept of the person. Much of the pattern and organization of behavior may be understood in terms of the individual's life goals and everyday behaviors when categorized in trait terms. Operationally, video records are analyzed to identify an individual's goals, traits, and behavior.

Wapner and Demick (chap. 2) assume that *the person-in-environment system* is the unit of analysis with mutually defining aspects of person and environment. According to these authors, treating the person-in-environment as the unit of analysis has the advantage that it corresponds to and represents the complexity of the real life situation. It further suggests analysis of the individual's behavior and experience in a variety of contexts. Specifically, they conceptualized the individual (as a system at various levels of integration, meaning biological, psychological, social, and cultural), individual in group, individual in organization, and organization in environment systems. Stated differently, Wapner and Demick assume that the person-in-environment system operates as a unified whole so a disturbance in one part affects other parts and the totality. Wapner and Demick do not address the issue of operational definitions. They imply that we need to know about the person's health, self-esteem and roles in the context of the physical environment, interpersonal environment, and the rules and regulations of society.

In summary, the two major themes of traits and life goals are operationalized in a variety of different ways by the theorists. To operationalize the trait concept suggested by Schneider et al. and Timko et al. self-report inventories are used. The individual's traits are defined by responses to traditional inventories of personality, competencies, interests, and values. Little, Hogan and Roberts, Craik, and Nasar in part define the person using the Five-Factor model of personality. Wicker and August, Little and Craik in part conceptualize the person in terms of life goals. To assess the concept, they use the interview, observation, personal accounts, and video records. Wapner and Demick indicated that we need to know about health, self-esteem, and roles of the person, but no specific operational definitions are suggested. An interesting emerging trend in the theories discussed here is the use of the Five-Factor model of personality to operationally define the person.

Concept of the Environment

There is considerable variation in how these theories conceive of the environment. The primary concept of the environment, for Nasar (chap. 5) is the physical features. The physical characteristics, and the form of these characteristics in the environment, is the primary stimulus. To Nasar, the perceived visual quality of these physical characteristics (surroundings) has important impacts on human experience and behavior.

Timko, Moos, and Finney (chap. 6) recognized a central role for appraisal and how one perceives the environment. Just as individuals have unique personalities, so do social environments. Thus, their approach is primarily concerned with how our perceptions of environments tend to influence our behavior. When appraisals of environmental demands are either too high or too low for an individual's level of competence, maladaptive behavior and negative affect are likely to result.

For Little, the environment is viewed in terms of *personal contexts*. Personal contexts are the idiosyncratically construed objects, situations, settings and circumstances of our daily lives. At another level, Little identified two other environmental concepts he terms *restorative niches* and *specialization niches*. A restorative niche is a place or setting, often at a very micro level, where individuals may escape in order to restore their first natures. The Little model predicts that the perceived availability of a restorative niche will be a key factor in mitigating the strain of free trait behavior. Clearly, a niche that is restorative for one individual may not be for another. Specialization niches are settings where individuals with specialized orientations are given full opportunity to have those propensities expressed and valued.

Schneider et al. (chap. 3), and Hogan and Roberts (chap. 1) similar to Holland, tend to believe that people make the environment. Thus, for Schneider et al., the environment is viewed in terms of the atmosphere created by the people who dominate a given setting; that is, the dominant features of an environment depend on the typical traits or characteristics of its members. A driving force in shaping this psychological environment is the personality of an organization's founder. Schneider (1987) viewed the founder as a central determinant of organizational behavior.

Hogan and Roberts (chap. 1) suggested the dominant features of an environment or situation are dependent on the *agendas* and *roles* that translate into expectations. The agenda is defined in terms of the project or the theme to be carried out. Roles are the parts we play in carrying out the agenda. If people know the agenda for an interaction and the roles that they and others will be assuming, they can formulate expectations about the other's behavior, and about the other's expectations regarding their behavior. According to Hogan and Roberts (chap. 1) most people generally comply with expectations when they are aware of them because noncompliance has implications for their reputations and they know this. Knowing the rules of the game encourages one to complete the interaction and lowers the level of anxiety associated with the experience. On the other hand, to the degree that the person is unclear about the roles, agendas, and expectations that operate in an interaction, they will be stressed.

Barker conceptualized the environment in terms of *behavior settings*. Behavior settings are small-scale social physical systems with a number of defining characteristics, including a definite time and place locus, a regularly occurring behavior pattern, and a close linkage between the behaviors of people and the physical objects in the environment. For Barker (1968), behavior settings are concrete environmental realities. They contain internal regulating mechanisms, or rules that act to preserve their programs. People who occupy settings are often the target of these behavioral rules. Behavioral rules tend to link the person and the behavior setting. Wicker (1992) expanded the behavior setting framework to include the entire life cycle of behavior settings, including their creation, growth, decline, and eventual demise. In this volume, Wicker and August suggested that Barker's argument should be extended to other types of milieus that is, to other normative social systems that like behavior settings, afford opportunities and impose obligations on people in them. Thus, they suggest that person–environment relationships are more complex than Barker described. In addition to the behavior setting, they believe that additional systems represent significant environments of workers, and deserve attention, including: trade or occupational group, employing organization, family, informal social groups, locality, and society at large. Wicker and August regard all of these systems as social constructions of their participants.

Craik (chap. 8), similar to Barker, and Wicker and August (chap. 7), conceptualized the environment in terms of behavior settings. According to Craik, behavior setting concepts are useful because they tell us an essential part of the story for each person–environment transaction. They place the person–environment transaction within a meaningful geographical temporal setting and indicate the resources associated with the setting's specific purposive program. Stated differently, behavior settings contain internal regulating mechanisms or rules that act to preserve their programs. People who occupy settings are often interpreted as the targets of those behavioral rules.

Analogous to the Wapner and Demick (chap. 2) conceptualization of person, these authors assume that the environmental aspect of the person-in-environment system is comprised of mutually defining physical (e.g., natural and built enforcement), interpersonal (e.g., spouse, friend, coworker), and sociocultural (e.g., rules and regulations of society) aspects. Again, Wapner and Demick do not focus on the person or on the environment per se, but rather, consider the person and the environment relationally as part of one whole.

In summary, Nasar, Little, and Timko et al. tend to conceptualize the environment in terms of *perceptions*. The environment is as it is perceived, and the way one perceives the environment tends to influence the way one will behave in that environment. Schnieder et al. and Hogan et al. suggest that people tend to make the environment. The environment is conceived and defined in terms of the people who dominate the situation. According to Wicker and August, and Craik, behavioral rules and standards tend to link people and environments. People who occupy environments and settings are often the target of these rules and standards.

Measurement of the Environment

The theories use a wide range of techniques to operationalize their concepts of the environment. The Nasar (chap. 5) approach is primarily concerned with how our perceptions of environments tend to influence our evaluations and subsequent behavior. Perceived visual quality of environments facilitate an evaluative image that influences meaning and behavior. The perceived visual qualities facilitate the development of evaluative images (pleasantness, arousal, excitement, and relaxation) that facilitate meaning and behavior. Thus, we want the perceived visual quality of the environment to describe and evaluate the physical environments, but in addition, we want to understand how the perceptions tend to influence the way individuals behave in that environment. This may be done (understanding the perceptions) using the Environmental Response Inventory (McKechnie, 1977) that makes an assessment of how a person, or group of persons, think about and relate to the everyday physical environment. Here the emphasis is on assessing personality and environmental predispositions.

The Timko, Moos, and Finney (chap. 6) perspective is based on the general principle that the way one perceives the environment tends to influence the way one will behave in that environment. Just as individuals have unique personalities, so do social environments. Moos has developed measures of a variety of social settings, including treatment environments, total institutions, and community settings. These measures may then be completed by both clients and staff members. An important finding of the Moos work over the years, is that very different social environments may be described by some common sets of dimensions associated with three somewhat global categories. The broad categories of dimensions are relationship, personal development or growth, and system maintenance and change.

For Schneider, Smith, and Goldstein (chap. 3) the dominant features of an environment depend on the typical characteristics of its members and the personality of an organization's founder is a driving influence in shaping the perceived environment. To operationally define the environment, the founder's goals are implemented through the organization's practices, policies, and structure and result in the selection of individuals who to some extent match the founder's personality style. According to this theoretical framework potential employees are attracted to the founder and to the environment he or she has created. This leads to the selection of individuals for the environment that tend to match the way the founder thinks and behaves.

For Hogan and Roberts (chap. 1) the environment is defined by people in terms of their agendas and roles. Roles or parts people play are operationalized by what the authors call the big three (status, affiliation, and intimacy). They suggest no specific measurement technique. Agendas are operationally divided into public and private components. The public components are operationally defined in terms of Holland's types (Realistic, Investigative, Artistic, Social, Enterprising, and Conventional). Thus, there are 6 public agendas for interactions in general. We can get together and fix something (Realistic), analyze something (Investigative), decorate something or entertain someone (Artistic), help someone (Social), manipulate or persuade someone (Enterprising), or regulate something (Conventional). The private component of agendas involve seeking three basic goals: seeking *status*, *acceptance*, and *predictability*. For the private agenda component no specific operational definition is suggested.

Wicker and August (chap. 7) believe that Barker's argument should be extended to other types of milieus that is, to other normative social systems that, like behavior settings, afford opportunities and impose obligations on people in them. In this context, they suggest 7 normative social systems they believe are significant environments in people's working lives. The authors noted that the scale of the systems range from small, less-inclusive social arrangements (behavior setting, family, informal social group) to larger, more inclusive arrangements (trade or occupational group, employing organization, locality, society at large). They noted that some of the systems are embedded in others. At this point, Wicker and August (chap. 7) conclude that the systems specified are significant environments of workers, and that analysts' considerations of them will yield more comprehensive accounts of person–environment relationships. In this context, assessment should include the views of participants and analysts (individuals who stand outside the events, but who wish to comprehend them) in order to produce a fuller understanding of the social systems.

As previously noted, Craik (chap. 8) conceptualized the environments in terms of *behavior settings*. Behavior settings are small scale social systems composed of people and physical objects configured in such a way as to carry out a purpose or program of activities within specifiable time and place boundaries. For example, when in church we behave "church." Thus, behavior settings contain rules that act to preserve their programs. The behavioral rules tend to link the person and the behavior setting. To operationally define behavior settings, in the Craik model (chap. 8) video records for an individual's lived day are observed to track the behavior settings when the target person moves and interacts distinctively.

Narrative sketches and videotapes provide effective and complementary methods for assessing the personal contexts of people's lives in Little's model (chap. 4). The latter provided a record of what actually goes on in a person's daily life, and the former provides a person's construal of the significance of context in their life's story. An additional operational definition involves the merging of the two assessment techniques (videotaping and life stories) by having individuals process an imaginary videotaping of their personal contexts. The essential idea in *idiotape analysis* is that individuals are asked to write down the images, scenes, or objects that they feel or perceive to be important to understanding their lives.

Again, Wapner and Demick (chap. 2) assume that the person-in-environment system is the unit of analysis with mutually defining aspects of person-in-environment. As noted earlier, the authors indicate that treating the person-in-environment as the unit of analysis has the advantage in that it corresponds to and represents the complexity of the real life situation. This assumption has figured significantly in their research over time. Specifically, it has led to conceptualizing the individual (as a system at the various levels of integration), individual in group, individual in organization, and organization in environment systems. As noted earlier, Wapner and Demick also assume that the person-in-environment system operates as a unified whole, so a disturbance in one part effects other parts, and the totality.

In summary, Nasar operationally defines the environment in terms of perceived visual quality (pleasantness, arousal, excitement and relaxation) using self-report measures. In addition, he suggests the use of the Environmental Responses Inventory (ERI) for assessing dispositions toward selective perceived visual qualities of the environment. The ERI is a person centered assessment that focuses on self reports about personality and environmental predispositions. Timko, Moos and Finney also define the environment in terms of the individual's perceptions. This definition uses a number of self-report inventories developed by Moos and his colleagues. For Hogan and Roberts, the environment is defined by people in terms of their agendas and roles. Status, affiliation and intimacy are used to describe roles and agendas are defined using Holland's environmental models. Schnieder, Smith and Goldstein suggested that people make the environment, and the personality of an organization's founder is a driving influence in shaping the perceived environment. The founder's goals are implemented through the organizations practices, policies, and structure. According to Wicker and August and Craik, behavioral rules and standards tend to link people and environments. To learn about the behavioral rules, they use a variety of idiographic techniques (including video records) and naturalistic observations. Little used narrative sketches, videotapes, and idiotape analysis to assess the personal contexts of people's lives. Wapner and Demick conceptualized the environment in terms of the physical, interpersonal and the sociocultural aspects, but suggest no explicit methods or operational definitions for assessment purposes.

The Person–Environment Relationship

As in our first volume, all of the models focus on the reciprocal transaction between the person and the environment. However, they do have different ways of conceptualizing the person–environment relationship and the consequent outcomes for the individual. In the Nasar (chap. 5) model, perceived visual quality of environments links personality predispositions and physical environments, and facilitates an evaluative image that influences meaning and subsequent behavior. Evaluative images include pleasantness, arousal, excitement, and relaxation. It is the human perception and evaluation of the physical environment that gives it meaning. Nasar suggested the evaluative image arises from the person, the environment, and the ongoing interaction between the two, and may vary with biology, personality, social–cultural experience, goals, expectations, and internal and external factors.

Timko, Moos, and Finney (chap. 6) formulated an integrative person–environment framework that suggested people and environments reciprocally influence each other. The *conceptual model* posits an environmental system that is composed of levels of support, performance demands, and structure. The *personal system* encompasses a person's resources in terms of cognitive, psychological, and social functioning. The person–environment model suggests that a good match of the client's level of functioning with the treatment program (environmental demands) will facilitate adaptative behavior and a favorable outcome. For example, programs that emphasize support and structure, and put less emphasis on performance expectations, were most beneficial for relatively impaired psychiatric patients. In contrast, programs that put more emphasis on social, emotional, and performance demands tended to be more helpful for clients with better cognitive and psychosocial functioning. The findings also support the hypothesis that less competent individuals are more influenced by the treatment climate than are more capable persons. However, if the treatment program offers a supportive milieu, interpersonal and performance demands may benefit most patients, even those who are quite impaired. In summary, Timko, Moos, and Finney are primarily concerned with how perceptions and environments tend to influence adaptative behavior and well-being.

Schnieder, Smith, and Goldstein (chap. 3) suggest that good person–environment fit (the individual has the characteristics that are similar to the characteristics of the persons in the environment or the organization) may result in positive outcomes for the individuals over the short term, mainly in terms of adjustment, satisfaction, and commitment. However, these authors further suggested that research indicates that over the long term, this cycle may yield homogeneity in thinking, decision making and action. Thus, Attraction-Selection-Attrition theory proposes that for organizational and longitudinal outcomes, good fit may be detrimental to organizational health. Stated differently, good fit may yield the harmony and cooperation required for early organizational effectiveness, but later in an organization's life cycle that good fit may have negative consequences. In practice, these authors suggested that homogeneity may be useful in the early stages of an organization's life cycle to promote growth through harmony, collegiality, and unified focus on the organization's initial goals. But over time, a shift toward heterogeneity (at least in the perspectives, backgrounds, and personalities of principal decision makers) will tend to increase the likelihood of an accurate assessment of an organization's strategic environment.

Hogan and Roberts (chap. 1) viewed behavior as a function of the person and the situation, although they tend to emphasize the person in this formation. They believe that what we do at a given time depends on our identities, the part or role we are playing in an interaction, and the agenda for the interaction. Behavior is the function of what we do to support our identities; what we do to honor our role obligations; and what we are required to do in terms of the agenda if we want the interaction to continue. Stated differently, a person–environment relationship involves a person's identity, the role they must play, the agenda, and the implications for the person's reputation. Hogan and Roberts further noted three outcomes of the reciprocal transaction between the person and the environment. First, the individual can accommodate to the other person and try to get along with them. Second, the individual can compete with the person and try to out perform them. Third, the individual may withdraw from the interaction.

Little (chap. 4) suggests that *fixed* and *free traits* (e.g., as defined by the five personality factors) and *personal contexts* (e.g. restorative niches) defined by narrative sketches and videotapes, facilitate the pursuit of personal projects and a sense of adaptation and well-being. To the extent that people are engaged in personal projects that are meaningful, well structured, supported by others, efficacious, and not too stressful, their well-being is enhanced and the person–environment process is rewarding.

Wicker and August (chap. 7) attempted to illustrate the viability of naturalistic inquiry as a means of theorizing about person–environment relationships. Their approach, substantive theorizing, presumes that close scrutiny of a limited domain of human activity can yield important insights that broader surveys might miss. Human work, as revealed in the stories of Ghanaians, expatriates in Ghana and American late-career women has been their substantive domain. In the main, they have represented people as sense makers of objects, conditions, and events in their lives. They further suggested that people attend to, interpret, and respond to events in different ways, depending on their *cognitive schemas*, or *cause maps*, including those representing their major life pursuits. The authors further suggested that although engaging in long term pursuits, conceptual maps of their worlds become more complicated. In this context, Wick and August suggest 7 normative social systems they believe are significant environments in people's working lives: work behavior settings, trade or occupation group, employing organization, family, informal social groups, locality, and society at large. To explore the person–environment relationship, Wicker and August contrasted the participant viewpoint with that of the analyst, who stands outside the events, but who wishes to comprehend them.

Craik (chap. 8) suggested that understanding individual–environment transactions involves the interplay among traits, goals, and behavior settings. On the individual side we have goals (the inside perspective) and personality traits (the outside perspective). The environment is defined in terms of behavior settings, and it seems likely that behavior settings are implicated in the actions of people as they pursue major life goals. Behavior settings link people and environments according to behavioral rules and individual pursuits. Personality traits may be viewed as facilitating or thwarting the pursuit of life goals in a behavior setting context. Operationally this person–environment behavioral process is video recorded during the lived day of an individual. The traits, goals, and behavior settings may then be analyzed in terms of the ongoing person–environment process.

Wapner and Demick (chap. 2) conceptualized adaptation as a congruent person-in-environment system state consisting of optimal relations between the person and/or the environment. The assessment of adaptation is carried out through an examination of the structural characteristics of the person-in-environment system as a whole. The more differentiated and hierarchically integrated a system is, in terms of its parts and of its means and ends, the more highly developed it is said to be. Optimal development entails a differentiated and hierarchically integrated person-in-environment system with flexibility, freedom, self-mastery, and the capacity to shift from one mode of person-in-environment relationship to another as required by goals, demands of the situation, and the instrumentalities available. Wapner and Demick go on to discuss less organized systems according to the orthogenetic principle defining development. These include a *dedifferentiated* person-in-environment state, *differentiated* and *isolated* person-in-environment states, and *differentiated* and *in conflict* person–environment states.

Theory of Action

It seems possible to classify various person–environment models or paradigms in at least four general theories of action. For definition purposes, a *theory of action* is defined as a way of identifying the prime mover or the locus of action in a model or theory. First, there is a set of traditions that focus primarily on the person, and is oriented to individual, purposive, relational action. These theories focus, by and large, on individual motivation, need, and satisfaction, or the pursuit of some goal. Most often the environment primarily becomes a task environment where individual goals or aspirations are pursued. The models of Hogan and Roberts (chap. 1) and Little (chap. 4) tend to be consistent with this theory of action. Hogan and Roberts viewed the individual as a purposeful, active agent with specific motives, goals, and values. In that context, they believe that people choose activities and interactions that are consistent with their identities and avoid activities or interactions that are discordant, or inconsistent, with their identities, motives, and goals. The authors further noted that people's past choices of situations tend to predict their future involvement in situations. Substantial evidence indicates that

preferences for environments, as assessed with interest inventories, effectively and accurately predict occupational membership, tenure, and change.
These preferences tend to be stable over time because people choose, define,
and specialize in particular types of environments depending on their identities (motives, goals, and values). Little (chap. 4) analyzes the person in terms
of fixed and free traits defined by the Big Five personality factors, and views
behavior as a function of the person (fixed and free traits) and the environment (restorative niches), although he primarily emphasizes the person component. The theory focuses on the completion of personal projects that
contribute to adaptation and well-being. According to Little, fixed and free
traits, and restorative niches, facilitate the pursuit of personal projects and a
sense of adaptation and well-being.

A second general theory of action is one where the individual is primarily
responding to demands or contingencies in the external environment. The
emphasis is primarily on the stimulus environment as a controlling context
of behavior. Timko, Moos, and Finney (chap. 6) conceptualized the person in
terms of *cognitive, psychological,* and *social functioning,* and are concerned with
how perceptions of environment (levels of support, performance demands,
and structure) tend to influence adaptive behavior and coping responses. In
other words, how we perceive the social climate will tend to influence our
adaptive behavior. In ways similar to the Timko, Moos, and Finney model
(chap. 6), the emphasis in the Nasar model (chap. 5) is primarily on the stimulus environment as a controlling context of behavior. Nasar conceptualizes
the person in terms of *personality predispositions,* and is concerned with how
our perceptions of physical environments facilitate an evaluative image that
influences meaning and behavior. Stated differently, the perceived visual
quality of the environment links personality dispositions and the physical environment. The evaluative images formed based on these perceptions tend to
influence subsequent meaning and behavior. How we perceive the environment (pleasant, arousing, exciting, or relaxing) tends to influence our view
and subsequent behavior of that environment.

A third theoretical tradition emphasizes *matching,* or, *fit,* between the individual and the environment as a primary mechanism or dynamic. Often, it is
not clear how this matching takes place (either by shaping on the one hand or
by selection on the other) but, nevertheless, fit and congruence become a major explanatory story line in this theoretical frame. The Schneider et al., Hogan et al., and Wapner et al. models seem to be the most consistent with this
theory of action. In the Schneider, Smith, and Goldstein model (chap. 3) person–environment fit emphasizes the attributes of people as the defining char-

acteristics of an organization and the foundation of determinants of organizational behavior. According to these authors, good fit may yield positive outcomes for individuals over the short term, but over the long term, this cycle may yield homogeneity in thinking, decision making, and action. Hogan and Roberts (chap. 1) suggested that people choose activities and interactions that are consistent with their identities and avoid interactions inconsistent with their identities, motives, goals, and values. These performances, as noted earlier, tend to be stable over time, and the reason is because people tend to choose particular types of environments depending on their motives and goals. Wapner and Demick (chap. 2) focused on change that is characterized developmentally (e.g., a developmentally advanced person-in-environment system state is described as deferentiated and hierarchically integrated). Thus, they are concerned with the adaptation process that underlies the achievement of this state. Wapner and Demick conceptualized adaptation as a congruent person-in-environment system state consisting of optimal relationships between the person and the environment. In their transactional approach, the person and environment parts must be treated relationally as part of one whole. Thus, the assessment of adaptation is carried out through the examination of the structural characteristics of the whole person-in-environment system.

Finally, there is a fourth theoretical tradition that may be described as emergent, interpretive, and social constructionist in orientation. This tradition focuses primarily on the way that actors in the social environment interpret their current circumstances and past circumstances or actions. This perspective is perhaps the most skeptical about the possibility of prediction and departs most from traditional positivist assumptions. (Although Craik recognized the predictive value of trait and behavior setting concepts.) The Wicker and August (chap. 7) and Craik (chap. 8) models seem to fit most appropriately in this theory of action. Their idiographic, naturalistic emphasis in research style produces rich, qualitative data. Wicker and August and Craik regard behavior settings as social constructions: Sense-making and negotiation processes explain the interaction behaviors of setting occupants as they pursue major life goals. The pursuit of major life goals occurs largely as a sense-making process that extends across time and place.

SYSTEM CONCEPTS IN PERSON–ENVIRONMENT PSYCHOLOGY

A revival of various system concepts can be discerned in the fields of personality psychology (Mayer, 1995), and social psychology (Vallacher & Nowack,

1994), generating recent target articles and extended commentaries in *Psychological Inquiry* (Mayer, 1998). Mayer, for example, has advanced a comprehensive *systems framework* to organize the abundant inventory of concepts within personality psychology, as a means of facilitating communication among researchers, preparing integrative textbooks, and so forth. His framework entails a minimal, yet central, commitment to holistic system formulations, for example that personality can be usefully treated as a system whose parts function together in some way that the understanding of parts and their organization is required, and that personality systems can be studied in relation to other systems (Mayer, 1998, p. 171). Thus, Mayer's efforts are directed toward a generic system conception (e.g., Sanford, 1963) rather than a specific grand system such as that of psychoanalytic theory (Rapaport, 1959). At an earlier time, much promise was seen in linking such personality systems to formulations of social and environmental systems but interest then waned (Craik, 1976; Goulder, 1970; Smelser & Smelser, 1964). However, specific theoretical system models of personality are also now making a reappearance (e.g., McCrae & Costa, 1995; Mischel & Shoda, 1995).

What are the implications of system concepts for person–environment psychology? Recourse to system concepts varies dramatically in the contributions to this volume. For example, Wapner and Demick (chap. 2, Table 2.1) present a specific theoretical system model in the grand manner, with an explicit, holistic commitment to understanding person-in-environment as a dynamic system.

Other contributors clearly did not set out to provide a full account of their conceptual frameworks, but rather applied elements of them to analyze specific issues. Thus, their commitment to system concepts may be initially underestimated. Nevertheless, Hogan and Roberts (chap. 1, Figs. 1.1 and 1. 2) and Little (chap. 4, Fig. 4.1) depict systemic ingredients for a personality model. In the case of Hogan and Roberts, the interplay among identity, reputation, role, agenda, and expectations influence an interactional sequence that then feeds back on identity and reputation. In the case of Little, the dynamic interplay among stable traits, free traits, and personal projects is depicted as having an impact on well-being and adaptation. Components of social system models can be found in the analyses of Stokolos, Clitheroe, & Zmuidzinas (chap. 9, Fig. 9.5) and Wicker and August (see Fig. 6.2 in Wicker, 1992). For Stokols et al., the particular interdependencies among personal, social, and physical factors in an event situation can be altered during the process where a prompt is dealt with, thereby yielding a shift or transformation in the situation. Wicker and August conceptualized a person's environment as a nested array of dynamic normative social systems, ranging from behavior settings to nations.

Analyses of entity-environment fit at both the individual (Timko et al., chap. 6) and organizational level (Schneider et al., chap. 3, Table 3.1) focused on the match between selective attributes of each, although the researchers may draw on more comprehensive system models for other purposes (e.g., Swindle and Moos, 1992, Figure 1.3). Finally, although Craik deals with the domains of the environment (behavior setting concepts, see Wicker and August), personality (goal oriented concepts, see Little) and society (traits as community oriented concepts, see Hogan and Roberts), he examined their interrelations in portraying events in the lived days of individuals, without reference to possible systemic properties. Similarly, Nasar (chap. 5) identified potential determinants of consensual evaluations of places (e.g., common species, shared cultures and environments, similarities in personality) but does not elaborate system idea for these sources.

What are the options, promises, and limitations of the system-oriented framework for person-environment psychology? The options include (a) a field-wide commitment to the formulation of a consensual, generic system model for person-environment psychology, akin to, but broader than, Mayer's framework, (b) the continuing pursuit of specific person-environment models of varying degrees of scope and articulation, and (c) eschewal of system models as premature or carrying excessive scientific limitations.

The promise of a consensual generic system model for person-environment psychology includes its press for field-wide conceptual organization and benefits for scientific communication. The current array of serious specific person-environment models shows much evidence of conceptual overlap, and thus, opportunities for integration (see Walsh, Craik, & Price, 1992; also this volume). However, the response to recent systems initiatives in personality and social psychology (Mayer, 1998; Vallaher & Nowak, 1997) included a concern that specific models that represent the creative cutting edge of theorizing, appear to get lost within an overarching, comprehensive framework.

Within person-environment psychology a middle ground might be entertained, in that specific models typically entail both innovative components and more generic elements. Thus, Stokols et al. (chap. 9) examine three levels of person-environment analysis (i.e., micro-, meso-, and macro-levels) and their implications for understanding change within and among them. In doing so, they draw on the rich conceptual resources contributed by an array of prior theoretical system analyses. Similarly, Little (chap. 4) focuses on the functioning of personal projects within a social-ecological framework, but for some purposes, might draw on a standard Five-Factor model of personality structure for the domain of fixed traits; Wicker and August (chap. 7) highlight the nested interrelation among environmental domains, but might draw on established formulations of the behavior setting domain and nation-state domain. Thus, a consensual generic system model might serve a useful purpose for communicating a coherent presentation of the person–environment field, and at the same time, constitute a conceptual resource for more peripheral components of specific person–environment formulations. Even in the case of a specific grand model, such as that delineated by Wapner and Demick (chap. 2), comparison with a comprehensive generic model might highlight the conceptual choices that have generated its distinguishing approach.

A second promise of a generic system model for person–environment psychology is to counter the rather restrictive formulations of recently advanced generic and specific personality system models. The Mayer's generic system framework for personality, transactional and developmental relations with components representing the situational–interactive environment and the incorporative–social environment are recognized but the environmental components of the model are not delineated. Similarly, the specific McCrae and Costa (1995) model entails a single environmental component (external influences: culture, life events, situation), whereas the specific Mischel and Shoda (1995) model offers a single environmental component: psychological features of situations. The opportunity and requirement for broader person–environment formulations are evident.

Some person–environment psychologists will be concerned that a generic, consensual system model will foreclose the more urgent, still unfinished task of fully delineating the domain of person–environment issues and phenomena. Others may wish to examine closely certain implications of adopting a system model, or carefully differentiate among what assumptions to take on (Craik, 1998). For example, Mayer (1998) opted for what Phillips (1975) deems Holism 1 (e.g., parts are dynamically interdependent) but not Holism 2 (e.g., an emergent whole cannot be explained in terms of its parts), nor does his version of a system approach entail commitment to such dynamic system properties as equipotentiality, multi-determinism, and equifinality (Pervin, 1992). Finally, at least two types of functionalism can be entailed by a system approach. *Traditional functionalism* (Cancian, 1968) that specifies the prerequisites for the viability of a system and examines consequence of its functions for adaptation, seems favored by current personality system formulations (e.g., Mayer, 1995; McCrae & Costa, 1995), whereas formal functionalism (Levy, 1968) that stresses system constraints, feedback loops, and so forth, is attracting the attention of social psychologists (Vallacher & Nowak, 1995). Thus, person–environment psychologists pursuing comprehensive, holistic, dynamic system frameworks will be confronted with many important conceptual decisions along the way.

A FINAL NOTE

This volume presents a variety of theoretical approaches to person–environment psychology representing a range of intellectual perspectives. We presented contemporary models and perspectives that make some sensible predictions concerning the individual and the environment using the person–environment relationship. For example, Nasar (chap. 5) suggested that the perceived visual quality of environments links personality predispositions and physical environments, and facilitates an evaluative image that influences meaning and subsequent behavior. It is the human perception and evaluation of the physical environment that gives it meaning. Timko, Moos, and Finney (chap. 6) formulated an integrative person–environment framework, suggesting that people and environments reciprocally influence each other. The person–environment model suggests that a good match of the client's level of functioning with the treatment program (environmental demands) will facilitate adaptive behavior and a favorable outcome. Schneider, Smith, and Goldstein (chap. 3) suggested that good person–environment fit may result in positive outcomes for the individual over the short term, mainly in terms of adjustment, satisfaction, and commitment. However, these authors further suggest that research indicates that over the long term, this cycle may yield homogeneity in thinking, decision making, and action. Hogan and Roberts (chap. 1) viewed behavior as a function of the person and the situation, although they tend to emphasize the person in this formulation. They believe that what we do at a given time depends on our identities, the part or role we are playing in an interaction, and the agenda for the interaction. Little (chap. 4) suggested that fixed and free traits, and personal contexts facilitate the pursuit of personal projects and a sense of adaptation and well-being. To the extent that people are engaged in personal projects that are meaningful, their well-being is enhanced and the person–environment process is rewarding. Wicker and August (chap. 7) attempted to illustrate the viability of naturalistic inquiry as a means of theorizing about person–environment relationships. Their approach presumes that close scrutiny of a limited domain of human activity can yield important insights that broader surveys might miss. Craik (chap. 8) suggested that understanding individual environment transactions involves the interplay of traits, goals, and behavior settings. Traits, goals, and behavior settings are analyzed in terms of the ongoing person–environment process. Wapner and Demick (chap. 2) conceptualized adaption as a congruent person-in-environment system state consisting of optimal relations between the person and the environment. The assessment of adaptation is carried out through an examination of the structural characteristics of the person-in-environment system as a whole. Thus, as we have seen, each theoretical perspective makes a unique contribution to the field of person–environment psychology by focusing on the study of the conduct of ordinary persons in everyday situations.

Also worthy of a final note, is the centrality of the issue of change in the study of person–environment transactions. Stokols et al. (chap. 9) noted that the transactional perspective assumes that continual changes are inherent in the nature of peoples' relationships with their environments, and that these changes vary considerably in their scope, magnitude, behavioral, and health consequences. These authors noted that although person–environment models tend to emphasize the centrality of change in people's relationships with their surroundings, much research in environmental psychology reflects a nontransformational perspective (one that emphasizes the relative stability of people's relationships with their environments). However, since the mid-1980s, research in environmental psychology has begun to emphasize transformational perspectives on the person and the environment. Stokols et al. noted that in contrast to nontransformational approaches, the transformational perspective assumes that certain forms and phases of people–environment transactions are highly prone to rapid change and instability. These authors are concerned with transformational analyses. Stated differently, they focus on the circumstances surrounding fundamental changes in the structure and subjective qualities of people's relationships with their surroundings. They are concerned with the factors that influence the relative stability or instability of people's relationships with their environments. We find their focuses on modeling and managing transactional change to be of vital importance in the person–environment process.

The new directions of person–environment psychology presented in these chapters take on the important task of offering some general theoretical formulations that will serve the purposes of the diverse approaches to the study of human behavior in the person-environment process. At the same time, psychologists continue to extend their contextual approaches through interdisciplinary research in the fields of anthropology, geography, political science, and sociology. Presumably, the present models of person-environment relationships will facilitate these models of interdisciplinary inquiry as well.

REFERENCES

Altman, I., Brown, B. B., Staples, B., & Werner, C. M. (1992). A transactional approach to close relationships: Courtship, weddings, and placemaking. In W. B. Walsh, K. H. Craik, & R. H. Price (Eds.), *Person-environment psychology: Models and perspectives* (pp. 193-242). Hillsdale, NJ: Lawrence Erlbaum Associates.

Angoff, W. H. (1988). The nature-nurture debate, aptitudes and group differences. *American Psychologist, 43,* 713-720.

Barker, R. G. (1968). *Ecological psychology: Concepts and methods for studying the environment of human behavior.* Stanford, CA: Stanford University Press.

Buss, D. M., & Craik, K. H. (1983). The act frequency approach to personality. *Psychological Review, 90,* 105-123.

Cancian, F. M. (1969). Functional analysis: Varieties of functional analysis. In D. L. Sills (Ed.), *International encyclopedia of the social sciences,* Volume 6 (pp. 29-43). New York: Macmillan and Free Press.

Costa, P. T., & McCrae, R. R. (1992). Neuroticism, Extraversion and Openness to Experience-Personality Inventory-Revised Manual (NEO-PI-R) Manual. Odessa, FL: Psychological Assessment Resources.

Craik, K. H. (1976). The personality paradigm in environmental psychology. In S. Wapner, S. Cohen, & B. Kaplan (Eds.), *Experiencing environments* (pp. 55-79). New York: Plenum.

Craik, K. H. (1998). Personality system concepts and their implications. *Psychological Inquiry, 9,* 145-148.

Eysenck, H. J. (1987). Arousal and personality: The origins of a theory. In J. Stelau & H. J. Eysenck (Eds.), *Personality dimensions and arousal* (pp. 1-13). New York: Plenum.

Goulder, A. N. (1970). *The coming crisis in western sociology.* New York: Basic Books.

John, O. (1990). The Big-Five factor taxonomy: Dimensions of personality in the natural language and in questionnaires. In L. Pervin (Ed.), *Handbook of Personality Theory and Research* (pp. 66-97). New York: Guilford.

Lawton, M. P. (1989). Behavior-relevant ecological factors. In K. W. Schaie & C. Schooler (Eds.), *Social structure and aging: Psychological processes.* Hillsdale, NJ: Lawrence Erlbaum Associates.

Levy, M. J., Jr. (1968). Functional analysis: Structural-Functional analysis. In D. L. Sills (Ed.), *International encyclopedia of the social sciences,* Volume 6 (pp. 21-28). New York: Macmillan and Free Press.

Magnusson, D., & Törestad, B. (1992). The individual as an interactive agent in the environment. In W. B. Walsh, K. H. Craik, & R. H. Price (Eds.), *Person-Environment psychology: Models and perspectives* (pp. 89-126). Hillsdale, NJ: Lawrence Erlbaum Associates.

Mayer, J. P. (1995). A framework for the classification of personality components. *Journal of Personality, 63,* 819-878.

Mayer, J. D. (1998). The systems framework: Reception, improvement, and implementation. *Psychological Inquiry, 9,* 169-179.

McCrae, R. R., & Costa, P. T., Jr. (1995). Trait explanations in personality psychology. *European Journal of Personality, 9,* 231-252.

326 WALSH, CRAIK, PRICE

McKechnie, G. E. (1977). The Environmental Response Inventory in application. *Environment and Behavior, 9*, 255-276.

Mischel, W., & Shoda, Y. (1995). A cognitive-affective system theory of personality: Reconceptualizing situations, dispositions, dynamics, and invariance in personality structure. *Psychological Review, 102*, 246-268.

Moos, R. H. (1997). *Evaluating treatment enrichments: The quality of psychiatric and substance abuse programs*, 2nd ed. New Brunswick, NJ: Transaction.

Myers, I. (1987). *Introduction to type*. Palo Alto, CA: Consulting Psychologist Press.

Myers, I., & McCaulley, M. H. (1985). *Manual: A guide to the development and use of the Myers-Briggs type indicator*. Palo Alto, CA: Consulting Psychologist Press.

Pervin. L. A. (1992). Traversing the individual environment landscape: A personal odyssey. In W. B. Walsh, K. H. Craik, and R. H. Price (Eds.), *Person-environment psychology: Models and perspectives* (pp. 71-88). Hillsdale, NJ: Lawrence Erlbaum Associates.

Peterson, D. R. (1992). Interpersonal relationships as a link between person and environment. In W. B. Walsh, K. H. Craik, & R. H. Price (Eds.), *Person-Environment psychology: Models and perspectives* (pp. 127-156). Hillsdale, NJ: Lawrence Erlbaum Associates.

Phillips, D. C. (1975). *Holistic thought in social science*. Stanford, CA: Stanford University Press.

Rapaport, D. (1959). The structure of psychoanalytic thought: A systemizing attempt. In S. Koch (Ed.), *Psychology: The study of a science, Volume 3*, (pp. 55-183). New York: McGraw-Hill.

Sanford, N. R. (1963). Personality: Its place in psychology. In S. Koch (Ed.), *Psychology: The study of a science, Volume 6*, (pp. 488-592). New York: McGraw-Hill.

Schneider, B. (1987). The people make the place. *Personnel Psychology, 40*, 437-453.

Smelser, N. J., & Smelser, W. T. (1964). Analyzing personality and social systems. In J. J. Smelser & W. T. Smelser (Eds.), *Personality and social systems* (pp. 1-18). New York: Wiley.

Swindle, R. W., & Moos, R. H. (1992). Life domains in stressors, coping, and adjustment. In W. B. Walsh, K. H. Craik, & R. H. Price (Eds.), *Person-environment psychology: Models and perspectives* (pp. 1-34). Hillsdale, NJ: Lawrence Erlbaum Associates.

Vallacher, R. R., & Nowak, V. (1994). *Dynamical systems in social psychology*. New York: Academic Press.

Vallacher, R. R., & Nowak, V. (1997). Dynamical social psychology: The next iteration. *Psychological Inquiry, 8*, 152-175.

Walsh, W. B., Craik, K. H., & Price, R. H. (1992). Person-environment psychology: A summary and commentary. In W. B. Walsh, K. H. Craik, & R. H. Price (Eds.), *Person-environment psychology: Models and perspectives* (pp. 243-270). Hillsdale, NJ: Lawrence Erlbaum Associates.

Walsh, W. B., & Holland, J. L. (1992). A theory of personality types and work environments. In W. B. Walsh, K. H. Craik, & R. H. Price (Eds.), *Person-environment psychology: Models and perspectives* (pp. 35-70). Hillsdale, NJ: Lawrence Erlbaum Associates.

Wicker, A. W. (1992). Making sense of environments. In W. B. Walsh, K. H. Craik, & R. H. Price (Eds.), *Person-environment psychology: Models and perspectives* (pp. 157-192). Hillsdale, NJ: Lawrence Erlbaum Associates.

Author Index

Koffka, K., 35, 57
Kohls, L. R., 218, 230
Kohn, I., 144, 168
Kohn, M. L., 275
Korabik, K., 103
Korpela, K., 146, 161
Krahé, B., 90–91, 96–97, 248, 264
Kramer, J. J., 166
Krantz, D. S., 273
Kraut, R., 286
Kristof, A. L., 65, 70, 75
Kuller, R. A., 119, 163
Kuntz, P., 35, 39, 57

L

Lang, J., 124, 150, 163
Langer, J., 59
Lanius, U., 144, 165
Lansing, J. B., 121, 140, 163
Lanyon, R. I., 143, 162
Lasson, K., 203, 230
Launier, R., 272
Lavine, T., 26, 35, 57
Lawrence, R., 150, 162
Lawton, M. P., 169–170, 178–179,
        182–183, 187–188, 272, 298,
        304
Lazarus, R. S., 124, 145, 162, 272
LeCarre, J., 7
Lecci, L., 91–92, 105
Lee, L., 90, 95
Leff, H. L., 125, 144, 162
Lehman, A., 176–177, 189
Lehmann, S., 179, 192
Lemke, S., 189
Lenntorp, B., 240–241, 264
Lerner, R., 59
Leschied, A. W., 183, 185, 192–193
Leveton, L., 52, 58
Levitt, M. P., 237, 264
Levy, M. J., Jr., 323

Lewin, K., 29, 35, 57, 94, 206, 230, 267
Lewis, M., 62
Lewis, S. A., 176
Lewontin, R., 37, 57
Liebert, R., 42, 57
Lightner, B., 122, 163
Linn, M. W., 170
Litt, M. D., 181
Little, B. R., 30–33, 39–40, 51, 57, 88,
        90–92, 94–96, 98–99, 102–105,
        110, 143, 162, 243–244, 248,
        252, 264, 274, 299–306,
        308–309, 313, 316–318,
        320–321
Lofquist, L. H., 66
Longabaugh, R., 181
Lorenz, K., 128, 162
Losito, B. D., 167
Louis, M., 80
Lowenthal, D., 164, 233, 258, 264–265
Luborsky, L., 190
Lundmark, V., 286
Lynch, K. E., 118, 122, 134, 139, 140,
        143, 153, 162, 280, 288
Lynes, 145, 149, 162

M

MacCorquodale, K., 271
Machler, E., 246, 263
Madsen, R., 111
Magnusson, D., 25, 30–34, 37–38, 41,
        56–57, 62, 272, 289, 300, 304
Malek, R., 140, 167
Maltz, M. D., 126, 162
Mandelker, D. R., 122, 160, 162
Mandler, G., 132, 137, 160, 162
Mandler, J. M., 131–132, 162
Mang, M., 146, 161
Mann, B. J., 186–187
Mansfield, E. D., 109

Subject Index